Entertaining Angels

Entertaining Angels

Reflections on the Sermon to the Hebrews

Michael J. H. Godfrey

WIPF & STOCK · Eugene, Oregon

ENTERTAINING ANGELS
Reflections on the Sermon to the Hebrews

Copyright © 2016 Michael J. H. Godfrey. All rights reserved. Except for brief quotations in critical publications or reviews, no part of this book may be reproduced in any manner without prior written permission from the publisher. Write: Permissions, Wipf and Stock Publishers, 199 W. 8th Ave., Suite 3, Eugene, OR 97401.

Wipf & Stock
An Imprint of Wipf and Stock Publishers
199 W. 8th Ave., Suite 3
Eugene, OR 97401

www.wipfandstock.com

PAPERBACK ISBN: 978-1-4982-9687-8
HARDCOVER ISBN: 978-1-4982-9689-2
EBOOK ISBN: 978-1-4982-9688-5

Manufactured in the U.S.A.

Ki a Leisa

*tērā anō ia te hoa aroha, nui atu i tō te tuahine,
i tō te teina, tōna piri mai*

(*Ngā Whakataukī* 18:24b)

Contents

Preface | ix

1. Introduction | 1
2. Establishing a Preaching Relationship | 19
3. Atonement: Heb 2:17–18 | 43
4. A Priest Like Us and For Us: Heb 3:1–19 | 54
5. Take Care, Brothers and Sisters (Losing Moral Coordinates): Heb 4:1–11 | 67
6. The Power of God's Command: Heb 4:12–13 | 85
7. Cling to One Who Knows What It's Like (Christ Entering the World of Human Coordinates): Heb 4:14–16 | 92
8. High Priest for Us: Heb 5:1–10 | 100
9. You Have Not Persevered, Dullard! Heb 5:11—6:8 | 113
10. God Is Faithful: Heb 6:13–20 | 123
11. Melchizedek . . . the Argument from the Lesser to the Greater: Heb 7:1–28 | 127
12. Priest of a *New* Covenant: Heb 8:1–13 | 137
13. The Shadow and the Reality: Heb 9:1—10:18 | 145
14. Endure! Heb 10:19–39 | 153
15. Faith Is . . . Heb 11:1–40 | 158
16. Other Countries: God-Breathed Histories | 169
17. No Pain, No Gain . . . the End Game: Heb 12:1–17 | 198
18. God: That Than Which Nothing Greater Can Be Conceived! Heb 12:18–24 | 207
19. A Sermon Winds Up: Heb 12:25—13:25 | 211

20. Practical Applications: Love . . . Heb 13:1–16 | 213
21. Pray for Us: Heb 13:18–21 | 225
22. Final Thoughts | 227

Bibliography | 229
Subject Index | 243
Name Index | 249
Ancient Document Index | 255

Preface

As with my previous book, these reflections began as material for a study group in a small New Zealand provincial parish church. When I was Vicar of Whangarei in New Zealand's north, I journeyed with a group of intrepid seekers through the book we know as Hebrews, choosing it because, as one friend (the sister of my dedicatee, as it happens) would later comment on my Facebook page, "you do pick the tricky bits of the Bible." I guess I do, because I do have a fervent love for the strange writings that have come to be known as the Scriptures of our faith (and our faiths, for I love the Hebrew Scriptures too). I believe deeply in "canon" as a work of the Spirit of God, and I believe that in the quirky unfathomable mysteries of God, we were given these flawed yet God-breathed writings to steer us through the vicissitudes of life and faith.

I ventured again into Hebrews when I became Dean of Waiapu, back in New Zealand after a short sojourn in Australia's Northern Territory. A new, equally intrepid, and sometimes equally bewildered group joined me in the Hebrews journey, broke open the Word together, and hopefully drew closer to one another and to God. As we journeyed through 2,000-year-old words, I think we did experience some opening of our eyes and minds and hearts. I did.

The work we call Hebrews spoke to me of many things, but above all it spoke of coordinates. I've never been a yachtsman, but for several years as a cox I guided rowers up and down rivers and lakes. They would get cranky if my efforts on the rudder meant they traversed more water than they needed to in order to get from A to B, yet on the other hand, as the only forward-facing member of the nine-man crew, only I could see the obstacles that sometimes blocked the straightest path. As the years went on, I became better at avoiding unnecessary deviations, but floating logs and near-invisible snags could do irreparable damage to the flimsy shell, and deviations happened. Mind you, I would not want to push the "only forward-facing" metaphor too far. We stumble on together, and the author of Hebrews might point out that the risen Lord, not a blundering coxswain, is the forward-facing one.

When I open the Scriptures of my faith, I do so as a flawed human being. Thank God I have never done otherwise. As I write about coordinates of faith and theology and practice in the book of Hebrews, I do so as someone fully aware of the times I have lost my coordinates. I have often described myself as 95 percent atheist, 5 percent believer, then added that this 5 percent somehow clings to the faith to which I converted in 1979. Mentally, I suspect I was parroting Tennyson's famous

> I stretch lame hands of faith, and grope,
> And gather dust and chaff, and call
> To what I feel is Lord of all,
> And faintly trust the larger hope.[1]

Yet now I wonder if I was fundamentally wrong. God clings to me: perhaps I see and cling to only 5 percent (or infinitely less!) of God's available and tenacious grip, yet through all my mis-steerings and meanderings, those tenacious divine arms cling on, and the largeness of the larger hope remains. This seems consistent with the expectations—even demands—of the author of Hebrews, though that writer might demand a few fewer failings on my part!

The author of the Hebrews sermon (for such it is) wrote in the shadow of persecution and, it was thought, the imminent return of Christ. That author (who, you will find, I bless by using the feminine pronoun) had no time for meanderings. "Lose coordinates: lose salvation" was pretty much her view. In the centuries since then, the people of God have found more grey areas around tenacity in faith, and I think and hope and pray that has been a working of God's Spirit. Sloppy navigation is one thing, and rowers get angry. But deviations, even when sometimes the threat of a boat-piercing log turns out to be only an innocuous shadow, are sometimes forgivable. I write of lost coordinates, never denying that I have often lost my way, but knowing too that there is one who has gone before me who has not done so.

The institutional church has often tragically lost coordinates: cases of sexual and psychological abuse and institutional responses to them (and my superficial excursions into the socio-historical writings of Emmanuel Le Roy Ladurie and Cecilia Hewlett remind us that there is nothing new under the sun) serve as dark reminder that we have, both individually and collectively, too often lost our coordinates. The silence of powerful church bodies as European Jews were persecuted and executed serves as a reminder

---

1. Alfred Tennyson, "In Memoriam," canto 55.

that we have too often lost our coordinates. Institutional obfuscation over tales of sexual exploitation serves as a reminder that we have too often lost our coordinates. I suggest in these pages that the dismantling of a cosmic creator, judge, and redeemer—dismantling to the point where God is no more than a fuzzy feeling—is a serious loss of coordinates with stupendous ramifications for our witness to the gospel. Expenditure on infrastructure and the glamour and trappings of office is a serious loss of coordinates—and who is to judge the fine line between necessity and profligacy?

So if my friend's dry comment, "you do pick the tricky bits of the Bible," has merit (though I suspect that the searing gaze of Scripture is tricky from beginning to end when we really break it open), it is because we need the urgent message of Hebrews today. We need it because it was a message to an increasingly passé, blasé Christ community. It is a community that has reappeared over and again through ecclesiastical history, a blasé community of which too many of us are a willing, acquiescent part (and I am safely assuming that those on the front lines of faith, to whom this does not apply, do not have time to read reflections written from an armchair in the global north). Desmond Tutu's famous and wise observation holds true: "If you are neutral in situations of injustice, you have chosen the side of the oppressor. If an elephant has its foot on the tail of a mouse and you say that you are neutral, the mouse will not appreciate your neutrality."[2] It is true every time the institutional church loses its coordinates of love, compassion, justice, or resurrection hope.

So this is not a work of scholarship. These are reflections fueled, I pray, by the same Spirit who informed the Hebrews author's words centuries ago, but with nothing like the critical erudition of the Hebrews and other scholars to whom I owe a debt of gratitude and on whom my reliance will be obvious. The wonderful critical scholarship of Luke Timothy Johnson has been vital to my every thought on Hebrews, as he breaks open the Word with reverence and wisdom ("dancing with his beloved rather than dissecting a cadaver"[3]—words I have never forgotten when I open a biblical text). He is often my go-to for insight on biblical (and other) texts. But many others have provided the keys by which I have been able to journey: Harold Attridge, the late and lamented Fred Craddock, Paul Ellingworth, Robert Gordon, the late Helmut Koester, Tom Long, and Vic Pfitzner. Each of these scholars has, in their own way, opened my eyes to the *taonga* (treasures) buried in—yes, alright then—a tricky text. Errors of interpretation

---

2. Tutu, "Exhibitions."

3. See Luke Timothy Johnson's interview in Tippet, "Deciphering *The Da Vinci Code*."

are my own, but the kudos for hard work communicating in so many ways the nuances of an ancient and nameless visionary Christ-bearer go to these contemporary scholars.

My study groups apparently found these explorations helpful. I certainly found my part in the exploring process helpful, and so my thoughts have been expanded (near-exponentially!) and are now scattered to the four winds in the hope that they may be helpful. The anonymous author of Hebrews was visionary and sometimes a little convoluted, but the words that eventually became a part of that great gift, Scripture, provide a remarkable and rather stern reminder of the Pauline maxim "all fall short." The words whisper corrective too, and I am reminded of the Ash Wednesday liturgy's solemn incantation, "Turn away from sin, and be faithful to Christ."

As a colonial import to antipodean lands, and as a mark of respect for Indigenous (or other pre-European contact) peoples, I attempt to respect the linguistic conventions of the earliest inhabitants. In the case of Māori, the use of macrons in an attempt to convey the nuances of pronunciation for non-Māori readers is growing, but the science is an evolving one. I have attempted to follow protocol where possible, but there are regional variations, chronological variations, and above all my personal ineptitudes influencing the outcome. I apologize to any who may be offended, and here *mihi* those patient Māori *kaiako* (teachers) who have sought to tutor me.

In writing these words on Hebrews, I am deeply aware of my debt to many who have personally loved and supported me through the journey. Writing this has been an effort that has ensured, as ever, that I have stolen countless hours of time that could have been spent with my sons Julian and Jonty (though I promise I have learned to correct my coordinates and now call that round-ball game "football"!). My farther-off daughters Vanessa, Natasha, Rosalind, Caitlin, Johanna, and Phoebe, and my grandson (*mokopuna*) Zac don't have to suffer the distractedness of a residential parent, but they have been fiercely supportive through some interesting public and private twists and turns in my life with which this small book has become entwined . . . *ngā mihi, whanau*. My thanks beyond words to my wife, colleague, and co-traveler Rev. Dr. Anne van Gend, whose phenomenal commitment to family and work casts a critical light on my lackadaisical Kerouac-esque driftings, and whose extraordinary support has seen words birthed and hard roads traversed: *arohanui, mihi nui*, closest and dearest.

I would like to express my thanks to and admiration for the crew at Wipf & Stock, who have once more given me the nod and brought the gestation of a few ideas to birth in print and pixel; your clarity, attention to detail, and commitment to a polished product speaks well of the heart and soul you place in this unpredictable theological publishing endeavor. I thank you not only for your support of my small works, but also your support of many fine thinkers and writers who have been promoted through your stable. Thanks also to Dr. James Harding of Otago University, whose erudition and critical judgment have saved me many embarrassments, and to Alex Fus of Wipf & Stock, whose attention to detail has likewise redeemed a myriad faults. As with the efforts of my readers addressed below, all faults remain mine, not yours!

So thanks finally to my wonderful critical readers: first to Dr. Gerald Morris, pastor of First Methodist Church in Wausau, Wisconsin, who steered me through more than one incomprehensible convolution and impenetrable fog of verbiage (Thanks for the road trip too, Jerry: not every kiwi's been to Wall Drug!). Thanks too to Rebecca and Grace Morris, Jerry's kith and kin, who have persevered with and entered into this strange transhemispherical friendship.

Likewise, my thanks to Leisa Lance: self-deprecatory MBA with a critical pen and erudite literary bent! While thanking Leisa for her stern pen and great coffee, my thanks also go to her husband and our dear friend Richard Lance, formerly pastor of Dayboro Uniting Church (Queensland, Australia), now chaplain at the Wesley Mission in Brisbane. Together with Leisa, you have sparred, cajoled, and provided endless fruits of God's good earth, liquid and solid, seeing me through a wild journey in print and out of it.

But I dedicate these musings to Leisa Lance, who has stood by this friend in times of darkness and of light. If the dedication is a puzzle, Google will be your friend!

1

Introduction

Tucked away on page 488 of *A New Zealand Prayer Book / He Karakia Mihinare o Aotearoa* is a tiny exchange that I consider to be its greatest contribution to Anglican and indeed Christian self-understanding, not only for New Zealand, but also internationally. It is as if the writers had immersed themselves in the so-called Letter to the Hebrews (neither a letter nor, in any identifiable sense, "to the Hebrews") and emerged with a summary:

> Called to follow Christ, help us to reconcile and unite.
> Called to suffer, give us hope in our calling.

This liturgical prayer captures something of Paul's Letter to the Philippians too, but it is not surprising that themes running through Paul's life and ministry should reappear in this other powerful writing of early Christianity. Whether directly influenced by Paul or not, this anonymous author knows her world and mission well: if we follow Christ, we follow one who is victorious. We *will* however, suffer (Heb 13:12–13). That is the cost of God's eternity. (In the twenty-first century, we might add, "whatever that means," because we are no longer attuned to the expectations of the first century. We can leave the meaning of "eternity" in the hands of God.)

Hebrews has a "high" understanding of Jesus (Christology). He is Lord, he is Savior, he is Son; all this only a few decades after an unimportant Palestinian Jew was executed by Roman soldiers. At the same time it has a "low" Christology. We might almost call this a Jesu-ology. Jesus is thoroughly human, a shepherd, an apostle (Heb 3:1), called as we are called, a builder, a minister, a pioneer, "like his brothers [and sisters] in every way." He is a pretty outstanding, indeed perfect human being, but utterly human nevertheless. His feet are not so heavenly that we cannot reach his footprints: "Oh let me see your footprints, and in them plant my own"[1] is a thoroughly Hebrews prayer.

---

1. From the hymn "O Jesus I Have Promised," written in 1868 by John Ernest Bode.

So Hebrews also has a high expectation of us. In fact that is probably why it was written: it is, according to its own anonymous author, "a word of exhortation," urging the audience to snap out of a period of spiritual sloth and get on with the hard athleticism of following Jesus. It has a very different view of matters to the views of Western civilization's (or the so-called "global north's") twenty-first century. It is perhaps even very different to twenty-first century Christianity's attitudes. For that reason it is very definitely a document for us today.

The Book

I have alluded to Heb 13:22, where the author describes her words as a "brief" written "word of exhortation." This has often been taken to mean that Hebrews was a sermon, and there is no reason to doubt that in a general sense of the word. The same phrase (here in the plural as *tou logou tēs parakléseōs*) is used by Luke in Acts, where Paul and Barnabas are invited to give "exhortation" to the crowd. We should, however, note Andrew McGowan's observation that "we cannot extrapolate from the mere existence of a text like Hebrews to a whole genre of homily or sermon typical of Christian practice, but it demonstrates that there were individuals capable of sustained and sophisticated oratory, and that, by implication, there were real opportunities for composition and communal performance."[2]

The word "exhortation" is notably also used at 1 Tim 4:13, where the recipient is urged to attend to reading Scripture (the public, liturgical reading of Scripture rather than personal devotional reading is implied), to exhorting, and to teaching, and at 1 Pet 5:12, where the reference is to the author's own writing. Luke Timothy Johnson notes, "The noun *paraklēsis*, like the verb *parakalein*, has so many nuances that its precise meaning in each case must be determined by context."[3] The critical point for us at this juncture is that this is a verb applicable to tough spiritual discipline and so does not carry the notion of "to comfort" that it carries at, for example, 2 Cor 1:3. The author of Hebrews far more resembles an athletic coach exhorting athletes to supreme levels of discipline and effort[4] than a benevolent dispenser of cuddles or empty promises. I am reminded of the nuggety and laconic former Rugby World Cup-winning coach Graham Henry, whose "We can't go ahead and win the Tri-Nations unless we do the business tomorrow night"

(1816–1874).

2. McGowan, *Ancient Christian Worship*, 77.

3. Johnson, *First and Second Letters to Timothy*, 252.

4. C.f. 1 Thess 5:14.

showed a similar flair for dry understatement. By contrast, consider a loquacious politician offering a rosy future sketched with empty platitudes, as when American vice president Dan Quayle infamously predicted, "The future will be better tomorrow." Our author was no Dan Quayle.

Whoever this author was, though, they wrote to a group of people they knew and loved, and for whom they felt an abiding and urgent concern. This much should be familiar to any of us who have studied Paul's writings, which reflect the same passionate discipline, or the book of Revelation, which leaves no room for lackadaisical compromise. Our author's avoidance of the empty rhetoric characterized by the Dan Quayle quotation above is deliberate. The Christians were facing tough times, and the temptation to apostasy, or at best spiritual sloth (which approximated the same thing), was considerable. This was a time for hard-hitting exhortation, using all the rhetorical tools available to the writer (the Petrine author faces a similar issue with even less subtlety at 2 Pet 2:17–22).

There is, however, some difference between the Petrine and Pauline writings, for example, and Hebrews. Paul and the author of 2 Peter[5] were writing letters of instruction and correction to be read aloud as the assembly gathered in meeting. The author of Hebrews is also expecting this letter to be read out loud by someone on their behalf, but it has a slightly stronger sense of liturgy—a sense that this reading is a part of an act of worship, a solemn recitation rather than Paul's hasty, if skilled oratory. To some extent, in this respect, it more closely approximates Revelation, a "circular letter"[6] designed to be read in a series of churches known to the author. Here too there is a difference, for Revelation was likely to have been circulated around several small congregations. Our text does not appear to envisage a series of audiences, but rather one particular congregation of Christians who are in danger of lapsing out of the disciplines of exemplary faith (Heb 5:11–14). Our author chooses words and sentence structures with great caution rather than with Paul's hasty rhetorical brilliance or the author of Revelation's flamboyant apocalyptic flourishes. Even in English translation, there is a sense of solemnity to Hebrews—see, for example, the accumulative pattern of chapter 11 and its solemn repetition of the word "faith"; in Greek it is a plosive, sibilant, and therefore solemnly emphatic *pistis*. To have heard this exhortation read aloud might well have been to have heard one of the great oratorical events of history, akin to Winston Churchill's "never before

---

5. Most scholars assess that these letters were written in Peter's name several years after his execution. The editors of the NRSV Annotated Bible make a concise statement of the biblical critical issues surrounding the Petrine letters at the head of the First Letter of Peter, and I refer readers to their statement.

6. Godfrey, *Babylon's Cap*, 12.

in the field of human conflict" or Abraham Lincoln's "in a larger sense, we cannot dedicate—we can not consecrate—we can not hallow, this ground."[7] Hebrews is a solemn exhortation, a solemn liturgical sermon.

This, then, is a sermon. But a sermon is not a form of entertainment, and whoever writes one intends to achieve some end. What does this author want to achieve? What problem is she addressing? There are a few hints that this audience is a faith community whose members, in the absence of ongoing "spectacular" Christianity (the "signs and wonders" with which the faith was first manifested to the audience in Heb 2:4), are losing interest and faith in the Christian Way: "We must pay greater attention to what we have heard, so that we do not drift away from it" (Heb 2:1). Later, the author wants to ensure that "we are not among those who shrink back and so are lost, but among those who have faith and so are saved" (Heb 10:39).

"Signs and wonders" are such an ambivalent element of New Testament experience. Jesus reprimands the crowds seeking for a sign (Matt 12:38-39, 16:1-4; Mark 8:11-12, Luke 11:16, 29-32), yet at John 6 his response is less negative. Some scholars refer to John 1:19—12:50 as "the Book of Signs" (the word "sign" appears some sixteen times in those chapters). Acts 2:19 (a quotation of Joel 3:3) warns that signs will appear, and Luke's book of Acts goes on to narrate signs that have been a proof of the work of the Spirit in and after Jesus (Acts 2:22, 2:43, 4:16, etc.). Similarly, Paul sees "signs and wonders" (Rom 15:19; 2 Cor 12:12) as proof of the integrity of his ministry. But Paul is sometimes more cautious (1 Cor 1:22); the Corinthians have undermined the integrity of the gospel by changing it into a form of entertainment, and the emphasis on the spectacular can distract believers and non-believers alike from the centrality of the one real sign, the cross (meaning the death *and* resurrection) of Jesus.

Many in the Christian community were beneficially touched by the ministry and teachings of John Wimber in the 1980s. Wimber will long be associated with the so-called "signs and wonders" ministries flowing from the Vineyard Fellowship in that period: I write "so-called" because Wimber himself, if I understand the man correctly from accounts of those who knew him personally, was probably uncomfortable with the sensationalism that the title suggests. It was, however, a deliberate echo of the phrase used, as quoted above, by Paul, Luke, and others. For many believers, it released

---

7. See Winston Churchill, "The Few," August 20, 1940, Churchill Centre and Museum, http://www.winstonchurchill.org/resources/speeches/1940-the-finest-hour/113-the-few; and Abraham Lincoln, "Draft of the Gettysburg Address: Nicolay Copy," November 1863, Abraham Lincoln Papers at the Library of Congress (Washington, DC: American Memory Project, 2000–2002), http://memory.loc.gov/ammem/alhtml/alhome.html.

powerful experiences of the risen Lord in a second wave of charismatic experience building on that of the 1960s and 1970s. Perhaps it was appropriate, for a season, as mainstream church denominations emerged from centuries that were often dominated by a kind of "formalist" structure to worship and even mission. Like all these things, such experience can lead to charlatanism, and I fear many began to generate experiences of false faith when this happened.

Sensationalism, even when it is well-intended and avoids lapsing into charlatanism, can from time to time be tragically costly. In February 2014 an American Pentecostal pastor, Jamie Coots, was killed in Kentucky by a cobra in a snake handling accident. He is one of several such pastors who have lost their lives through a literalist reading of the Scriptures (within weeks his son, also a pastor, was handling the same snake that had killed his father[8]). Snake handling, practiced by some forty churches in the US, is easy to dismiss as lunacy and is technically illegal in many states, but its practitioners base the practice on a fundamentalist or literalist reading of Mark 16:18. The scholarly consensus that this longer ending of Mark is not a part of the original Markan writing is of no interest to fundamentalist preaching, and its proponents can in any case cite Acts 28:1–6 as further proof of the appropriate nature of their demonstrative routine (any attempt to bring Deut 6:16 into the conversation is likely to be dismissed!). But it is worth noting that the tiny group of Christian believers who handle snakes do not do so because they believe themselves to be sensationalists, but because they believe that the signs (Mark 16:17) referred to in the Scriptures are eternal and unchanging and that they are laying down a challenge to "the traditional Protestant/Fundamentalist view that God does not presently perform miraculous signs."[9] For them, nothing less than the integrity of God and God's power is at stake, and while an Internet meme proclaiming "textual criticism: it saves lives" may be right in its suggestion that a critical reading of the Markan endings might have saved Pastor Coots' life, it misses the point that the forms of Christianity that engage in the dramatic do so because they believe drama reveals empowerment of and by the Spirit of God.

Paul encountered precisely this belief at Corinth: hence his caution about "signs" there. Following the Toronto Blessing movement, there were many reports of pushed foreheads as over-exuberant ministers confused themselves with God. A potential experience of God's touch was mocked, and many faith lives were damaged or destroyed. For some, the exuberant outpourings of joy have passed in the years since their first charismatic

8. See Kuruvilla, "Snake Handler's Son."
9. Archer, *Pentecostal Hermeneutic*, 69.

experiences, and even for those for whom that enthusiasm has not passed there is always the risk of a kind of dry cerebralism. Worse: for some believers, faith itself has passed. For those of us whose Christian faith eschews dramatics (histrionics, we might cynically suggest), the snake handling setup sounds ludicrous, and the manifestations of Toronto blessing barely less so. But in the first-century context addressed by our author as well as in anti-intellectual (sometimes with good reason) circles in the twenty-first century, a good dose of sensationalism could provide distraction from either the *ennui* (boredom) or the *angst* (terror) of everyday life.

This was the experience of the Hebrews, whoever they may have been. They had experienced magnificent outpourings of exuberant joy in the first throes of faith. There had been signs and wonders and charismatic outpourings of ecstasy. The experience of personal and collective liberation, both emotional and physical, that can come about in conversion and worship is not to be dismissed, though it is too rarely acknowledged in the rites of mainstream churches. On my desk are three volumes, from different but relatively recent eras, addressing the subject of conversion.[10] Only one, Rambo's highly regarded *Understanding Religious Conversion*, makes reference to the ecstasy of a new start, a "new birth" in religious terms: "A religious option can also offer a wide range of emotional gratification, like a sense of belonging or community, relief from guilt, development of new relationships and—something few studies of conversion mention—excitement and stimulation."[11] But Rambo's phenomenological study barely develops the theme beyond that observation, which is a far cry from the ecstasy that appears to have been experienced by the first Christians (however stylized the Acts 2 account may be) and that many of us who have undergone religious conversion may have experienced as well. A fourth volume, Alan Kreider's *Change of Conversion*, provides a historico-theological overview of the early shifts in patterns of conversion experience and explores in greater depth the ways in which conversion underwent reinvention during the first four centuries of Christianity. Kreider is well aware in his analysis that the post-Christendom world has much to learn from the earliest, pre-Constantine experiences of conversion to Christ, especially the emphasis on catechumenal processes and careful preparation.[12] But then or now, ecstasy cannot be maintained: churches that seek to do so by generating states of extreme emotionalism will often experience a high degree of "pass-through" and

---

10. In chronological order they are Nock, *Conversion*; Krailsheimer, *Conversion*; Rambo, *Understanding*.

11. Rambo, *Understanding*, 83.

12. See Kreider, *Change of Conversion*.

burnout amongst their membership. The Hebrews too were losing touch with that experiential dimension.

This experience of a Christian community is probably not limited to any century. In recent years, much has been written about the life cycles of a church. Writing on the subject tends to a Congregationalist understanding of a church, addressing cycles in a faith community that can be traced from germination to expiry, though application for denominations whose communities tap into a long history of some sense of administrative and sacramental "succession" are harder to extrapolate. Nevertheless, there are some simple patterns that are relevant to the Hebrews' experience. In an online article, George Bullard outlines "The Life Cycle and Stages of Congregational Development." His analysis of the life stages, while fascinating, need not detain us here. The more critical issue is the dwindling of the terms of excitement used in his descriptions of the cycle: the word "passion" ("passion to fulfill the strategic spiritual vision"), a reasonable descriptor of energy, appears in his delineation of the "birth," "infancy," and "adolescence" stages of congregational life, but it is gone from the "adulthood," "maturity," "empty nest," "retirement," and "old age" phases.[13] The word appears again only as a vague hope at the "death" stage as a sign of "rescue from death": "a dying congregation relocates into a growing area in the hope that people will join their congregation, but does so out of weakness rather than an intentional, passionate vision."[14] Our author is addressing a congregation that has, in Bullard's terms, slid well beyond adolescence and may indeed be settling into the decays of later life.

Had the Spirit, then, left the Hebrews? Indeed, those heady first days and years of faith seemed to have carried the promise of the imminent second coming of Christ, but as yet the final glorification was not happening (Heb 2:8). Had the Hebrews been lied to? This is the question the author of Hebrews is primarily addressing: Where does faith go when the buzz stops? It is a timeless question that can be addressed not only in terms of life cycle, but also in terms of the wider spread of church history. Theologians today refer to "cessasionism" and "dispensationalism"; these "-isms" are the belief that the spectacular "signs" of the biblical narrative closed at the end of the New Testament narrative. Those of us from a more liberal interpretative school walk a line somewhere between saying that they never happened but are instead stylistic devices of evangelistic and pastoral authors, or that, yes, we reserve the openness to their occasional occurrence but consider such events to be rare and grace-filled intrusions of God into the narratives of

---

13. Bullard, "Life Cycle and Stages," 12.
14. Ibid., 22.

human experience. Can a reading of Hebrews in the twenty-first century take us any closer to answering these questions, navigating us somewhere between snake handling and dry cerebralism?

The Date

When was this happening? Picking the date of biblical writings is a process of detective work that can only provide an educated guess. Obviously, Hebrews was not written before the events of the first Easter, and the tone of the writing, especially at Heb 2:1–4, suggests that some time had lapsed since those events. The word usually translated as "remember" at Heb 13:7 is, in Greek, in a tense that conveys ongoing re-collection, and its application to "leaders" suggests that sufficient time has passed for leadership to emerge and become established. This observation may confirm the sense that the congregation addressed has passed through the "passion" stages of congregational life, as discussed by Bullard, and settled into a "post-passion" stage of belief. The book of Hebrews was known to Clement of Rome, for he cites it in his Letter to the Corinthians, quoting the "skins of sheep and goats" of Heb 11:37, alluding to Heb 3:2, 10:37, 13:2, and other verses.[15]

The dating of Clement of Rome's Letter to the Corinthians is little less elusive than that of Hebrews, but a consensus tends to point to Clement's letter as having been written, at the very latest, during the first decade of the second century. The more common suggestion is that it was written around 96 CE. To quote something as an authority, as Clement does in using Hebrews, requires the source to have been around for a while—maybe a decade? This would push the date at which Hebrews was written back to before around 85 CE, five-and-a-half decades after the first Easter. Luke Timothy Johnson provides convincing arguments that push the date back further: the author appears to know nothing of the sacking of the Jerusalem temple that took place in 70 CE, for, in presenting temple rituals as a key ingredient of the argument, our author does not indicate that the temple rites are, at the time of writing, a thing of nostalgic grief. In Heb 5:1–5, for example, there is no indication that the temple rites are a raw memory of past actions, lamented by the audience of Hebrews or by those with whom they were recently associated.[16] In any case, the author tends to use present tense when describing temple rites (Heb 5:1, 7:5, 8:3, 9:6), so it would appear these events are still occurring at the time of writing.[17] As Ellingworth

---

15. See 1 Clem 36:1–5.
16. Johnson, *Hebrews*, 38.
17. Ellingworth, *Commentary*, 31.

observes, "If Hebrews were written after that news [the destruction of the temple] had reached its author, it is difficult to believe that he would have stated that the old covenant was merely ἐγγὺς ἀφανισμοῦ [*engus aphanismou*, or approaching non-existence] (Heb 8:13), or that he would not have referred to the fall of Jerusalem."[18]

The earliest possible date of writing is harder to establish. Perhaps 55 CE would allow sufficient time for first-phase evangelists such as Paul, Apollos, and others to travel and proclaim the gospel; for the Hebrews, whoever and where ever they were, to accept it; and for them to experience some suffering as a result of their beliefs, perhaps even lapsing into a "post-adolescent church" loss of enthusiasm. There is no suggestion that our author was an eyewitness to the events of Jesus' life, and the "what we have heard" of Heb 2:1 seems to preclude that possibility (contrast John 19:35, although paradoxically that verse may have been written later than Hebrews).

Hebrews has a "high" Christology: Jesus is "Son . . . heir of all things . . . vehicle of creation . . . reflection of God's glory . . . exact imprint of God's very being" (Heb 1:1–4), but Paul is also generating a similarly high Christology just a few decades after the first Easter (Phil 2:6–11), and this simply reflects the awe-inspiring sense of Jesus' post-Easter presence experienced by Christian worshipers in the early decades of Christian outreach. Elsewhere I have noted the rapidity with which the early Christians came to apply "high" titles and terminology to the Carpenter of Nazareth. Of the author of Revelation, I noted,

> John is applying these high expectations to the crucified criminal Jesus within three to six decades after the events of Jesus' life and death. In order not to be considered absolutely insane, these majestic and celestial claims for a recent living figure must resonate with his audience's sense of the awesome presence of the risen Christ in experiences of worship, fellowship, and scriptural study. Anything less than that (for example, if we claimed that Elvis Presley or Che Guevara is alive and well) would be unlikely to inspire believers to risk their lives for their faith.[19]

The high claims made by our author are likely to have been made within two to three decades of Jesus' death.

These tentative dates for the writing of Hebrews parallel those of Paul's communities: 1 Thessalonians, the first of Paul's letters to be written, may have been written at about the same time and addresses similar questions of tenacity amidst the persecution, departure, and absence of the founding

---

18. Ibid., 32.
19. Godfrey, *Babylon's Cap*, 52–53.

evangelists. From its opening salutation, that letter too makes remarkably "high" claims for Jesus' status, ascribing to him the "lordship" normally reserved to Caesar (1 Thess 1:1). For the sake of establishing some date, I will suggest 65 CE as a loose working figure by which to understand the genesis of this document.

The Intended Audience

Who were the Hebrews? To state the obvious, they were a Christian community, for the document is not primarily designed to evangelize but rather to correct the audience's behavior and belief (Heb 2:1: "we must pay greater attention"). The audience members are the author's "holy partners in a heavenly calling" (Heb 3:1) but are showing signs that they are beginning to slip away from "the confidence and the pride that belong to hope" (Heb 3:6, see also Heb 3:12, 6:12), the gospel they have believed. They are familiar with the story of Moses (Heb 3:17), with the book of Psalms (see, e.g., Heb 2:6–8), with the book of Numbers, Deuteronomy, and countless other Hebrew Scriptures. This, however, is unsurprising: the Hebrew Scriptures were *the* Scriptures, albeit primarily in Greek, to the early Christians (this understanding is revealed especially at 2 Tim 3:16). New Testament writers, including Paul, the apostle to the Gentile community, deliberately refer to "Scripture" no fewer than fifty-two times and cite Scripture countless more (see especially Paul's use of the Abraham story in Galatians and Romans, or the story of Moses in Romans and the Corinthian Correspondence). Our author assumes that the audience members are familiar with the rites of Levitical codes, but this does not mean that either author or audience were practitioners of these codes.[20] These believers know their Scriptures, but this indicates only that they have been exposed to sermons for a long time.

The audience members, then, are not new converts. Hebrews 6:1–3 implies, in Greek, a long period of previous belief. They have had time to suffer, as I noted above, for their faith (Heb 10:32–34). The title "to the Hebrews," although attached to the earliest surviving manuscripts, does not headline some earlier references to our document and would appear to be a subsequent title.[21] The addition does not, in any case, identify the audience in any way whatsoever. Were they designated "Hebrews" because they were Jewish Christians or because, as Gentile Christians, they were in some way the new people of God, to whom God has spoken in a new way (Heb 1:2a)? Johnson stresses that Hebrews does not espouse a "supersessionist" doctrine

20. Bruce, *Hebrews*, 5.
21. Ibid., 3.

of salvation—the idea that God has switched allegiance from the genetic tribe of Hebrews to a new "un-genetic" people of God,[22] and Ellingworth notes, "The readers . . . are constantly addressed as standing in continuity with Israel."[23] In the century since the Holocaust, it does no harm to remind ourselves from time to time that there is no theological basis on which to reject the special closeness of the Jewish people to the heart of God.

As with so many biblical scriptural writers, the author doesn't provide us with information by which to identify either the writer or the audience. This is largely because she was not expecting us to read the letter, and because the audience, unsurprisingly, already knew who they were! There are many questions about the Scriptures (both the Hebrew *and* our New Testament Scriptures) that simply cannot be answered. We do not know who this audience was or where they were situated. We can deduce that the audience was, while perhaps not an intellectual elite, nevertheless capable of grasping a detailed theological argument, and members were thoroughly familiar with preaching and teaching that was deeply immersed in the Hebrew Scriptures. This need not define the audience as either Jewish or Gentile Christians, as both ethnic groups within the Christian community would have been exposed to the "breaking open" of Hebrew texts and their application to the event of Jesus.

Ultimately, then, we can say little more than that our audience was made up of Christians who had been around long enough to risk losing their enthusiasm for faith. This was possibly a state exacerbated by experience of some trials (Heb 10:32–33, 12:12–13), and while these trials had not yet led to martyrdom (Heb 12:4), this is not an impossible outcome of fidelity to Christ. The audience appears to have experienced some punitive dispossession of property (Heb 10:34),[24] and perhaps this has led at some stage, not necessarily recently, to a degree of apostasy (Heb 10:39). The author, in a manner reminiscent of Luke, suggests that common sharing of property can be a powerful Christian testimony (Heb 13:16, cf. Acts 4:32–35), a discipline that has generally indicated expectation of a reasonably imminent *eschaton* and that has generally reappeared only in apocalyptic phases of church history. This audience has therefor at some stage exemplified high standards of communal love (Heb 13:1), a trait not unusual amongst the earliest Christians (see Rom 12, especially Rom 12:9, and the Pauline hymn of 1 Cor 13, together with 1 Cor 14:1). That the author re-addresses these traits suggests that there has been a diminution of the exemplary practice

---

22. Johnson, *Hebrews*, 31–32.
23. Ellingworth, *Commentary*, 24.
24. Johnson, *Hebrews*, 35.

in the recent history of the community—perhaps another sign of lapsing from the childhood and adolescent stages of communal existence. The directive to exercise hospitality, "for by doing that some have entertained angels without knowing it" is neither more nor less than a command to be a conspicuous counterculture in a wider Roman community not given to generosity of spirit. It is worth noting at this time that across the Tasman from where I currently live, church leaders are conspicuous amongst the civic leaders making calls for Australia to be generous toward the refugees currently dismissed to subhuman, razor-wire-encircled ghettos on Nauru and Papua New Guinea's Manus Island. Those Australian Christian leaders stand firmly in the tradition of our anonymous author.

We might, in passing for now, note that the author may see the angelic, whom the audience is commissioned to embrace in radical hospitality,[25] as both anointed messengers (for that is all the word *angelos* means) that are human *and* as heavenly messengers. It is probably more accurate to suggest that the writer does not differentiate between the two; there is not necessarily a sense that angels in Hebrews are the translucent winged creatures of popular Western artistic depiction, nor merely the stuff of our sometimes uncanny encounters with passing earthly messengers. For now, I think it is best that we leave the "angels entertained unawares" as both while remembering the stern underlying message of justice: as we turn away the needy from our doors and our national borders (and yes, when living in a church house, I have often done so too) we might be turning away an opportunity to encounter the presence and wisdom and message of God.

The Writer

Who, then, is our author? We can't assume, in the absence of firm evidence, that the writer was male, despite the odds that this was the case.[26] There is simply no self-disclosure: this, the author might say, is not about me (Heb 11:32 is a rare self-reference). The audience knew who the author was, and further explanation was neither necessary nor helpful to the author's aims. By avoiding self-disclosure, the author generates a deliberate artifice in promoting the belief that the "voice" of the sermon is effectively God's or from a source close to God.[27] This author is, however, highly articulate, using more than 150 words not seen elsewhere in the New Testament, plus ten words

---

25. The words are mine rather than Volf's, but they summarize his thesis that "God's reception of hostile humanity into divine communion is a model for how human beings should relate to the other" (Volf, *Exclusion and Embrace*, 100).

26. Gordon argues that the author was clearly male but inexplicably bases this argument on "the natural interpretation of 11.32" (Gordon, *Hebrews*, 10).

27. Ibid., 11.

not seen anywhere else in ancient literature. This author uses long, flowing passages—a style that is evident even in translation (Heb 1:1–4, 2:1–4, 10:19–25)—and a poetic, metaphorical style (Heb 4:12–14, 12:18–24) that draws in particular on metaphors of law (Heb 2:3–4, 6:16, 7:12), kinship, property ownership (Heb 2:14, 3:1, 6:13–18, 7:4–10, 9:16–22, 10:34, 11:1), and agriculture (Heb 6:7–8, 12:11).

The author's subtle changes of rhythm, while most clear in the Greek, are also discernible as translated (in good translations) at Heb 4:12–13, 7:1–3, 12:18–24. At Heb 3:16–18, the author suddenly switches to a staccato interrogation. At other times, this writer engages in prolonged and demanding argument (Heb 4:8–9, 7:11–12, 10:2). Although it is not apparent in translation, this author opens the sermon with a series of powerful repetitions of the consonant *p* (best known to us from "pi r²") that can be transliterated as *polumerōs kai polutropōs palai ho Theos laēsas tois patrasin en tois prophetais* (I have underlined the *p*'s to make this pattern clear). These sounds are carefully chosen for dramatic effect, grabbing the audience's attention with the *p-p-p-* sounds we call "plosives" as the oratory begins. As if to prove this is no accident, the author uses the same technique—alliteration—at Heb 2:1–4, 4:16 and 11:17, though this effect is lost to us in English.

In chapter 11 this author uses a skilled presentation called "anaphora," or the rapid repetition of key words (*pistis*, or "faith," in particular). At other times, we find this author engaging the audience's sensory perceptions, evoking touch, scent, sight, and sound with skill and purpose (Heb 12:18, 20, 6:5, also 2:1, 3:7, 4:7, 5:11, 12:19). This is a master orator using all her skills to convey a critical, life-or-death (in terms of faith) message to an audience that has lost its way. At Heb 12:22–24, even in translation, we cannot fail to notice the skilled piling of phrase upon phrase to make the author's point.

This author, then, is highly articulate, extremely intelligent, and a fine orator. This author may have been the original evangelist who brought the gospel to the Hebrews, though this cannot be definitively stated, and the collective identification of Heb 2:1 makes it doubtful. The message is, however, emphatically *not* about her: there is no self-introduction, and often God is depicted as the speaker (Heb 2:5, 5:11, 6:9, 9:5, 11:32, but see also 2:2, 3:6, 4:13). In reality, the masculine participle visible in the Greek at Heb 11:32 (*diēgoumenon*, "telling of") probably precludes a female author, but in honor of the slender possibility first posited by von Harnack in 1900 that the author was Priscilla[28] and in recognition of the validity of feminist exegetes

---

28. Von Harnack, "Probabilia," 16–41, cited and refuted in Ellingworth, *Commentary*, 623.

and systematicians (Fiorenza,[29] Ruether,[30] and others) assertion that women's voices have been too readily silenced in Christian history, I will use the feminine pronoun in reference to our author. We should note too that some centuries later in liturgical lament, women's choral voices were used in Syrian churches to illuminate biblical narratives "even when not found (but plausibly interpolated) in the biblical text, incorporating into communal prayer an element of women's experience from the wider world."[31]

It is rather moving to realize that the author of this enormously influential document was so emphatically concerned with showing it was not about her that she left no clues as to her identity. Counter to von Harnack's suggestion, there is a tradition, though no firm evidence, that the author may have been Paul's other companion, Apollos. We will never know, at least until all mysteries are revealed in the presence of God!

The Text

Readers with some degree of theological training will have been taught something of the history of the physical transmission of the biblical text. For many of us who entered theological discourse at seminary, theological college, or through formation programs such as Education for Ministry, this

---

29. "A feminist hermeneutical understanding that is oriented not simply towards an actualizing continuation of biblical Tradition or of a particular biblical tradition but toward a critical evaluation of it must uncover and reject *all* biblical traditions that perpetuate, in the name of God, violence, alienation, and patriarchal subordination, and eradicate women from historical-theological consciousness" (Fiorenza, *In Memory*, 32–33).

30. "The fullness of redeemed humanity, as image of God, is something only partially disclosed under the conditions of history. We seek it as a future self and world, still not fully revealed. But we also discover it as our true self and world, the foundation and ground of our being. When we experience glimpses of it, we recognize not an alien self but our own authentic self. We experience such glimpses through encounters with other persons whose own authenticity discloses the meaning of such personhood. By holding the memory of such persons in our hearts and minds, we are able to recognize authenticity in ourselves and others" (Ruether, *Sexism*, 114).

31. McGowan, *Ancient Christian Worship*, 128. Just as—though writing from my own discourse-site of white privilege—I am seeking at least symbolically to incorporate voices from other reading sites, I hope from a perspective of male privilege I am honoring the too-long silenced voices of women's stories, and indeed in the current context of the annihilation of Syria by factional hatred, I am in passing here acknowledging the deep-seated narrative of faith(s) in that ancient land. I also dispute my own use of the phrase "at least symbolically," and its synonym "mere symbol," for as a symbolist reader I hold tenaciously to "the power of symbols in religion and culture," as Dillistone explores throughout his correspondingly titled *Power of Symbols* and his later *Christianity and Symbolism*.

was not a question we had ever previously considered. The form of the Bible was more or less a given, albeit in different translations, and the history of its transmission, at least prior to the Gutenberg Bible in circa 1454, was of little concern to most of us when we entered theological formation. We may not, as it is sometimes satirized, believe that the text arrived in complete form in a parachute drop from heaven, but many of us never really question why we don't believe that. Some of us studied history and were, to some extent, aware of the printing press and its enormous impact on Western civilization but, even so, were reasonably unconcerned about its implications for the transmission of biblical thought.

Indeed, even in teaching and preaching within the wider, non-academic Christian community, too little time and thought is put into relating the story of canonical selection and biblical transmission; punters in the pew are left with an "it just is, that's it" idea of the texts that we break open. A glance at a deeper narrative, without digging deep into canonical theology, may allow just a shaft of light to illuminate a little of our journey into the Hebrews text at this point. I won't, however, revisit the questions I have addressed in my introduction to this book.

Division of the Bible into chapters and verses was a relatively late development. The pattern we follow was mainly introduced by Archbishop of Canterbury Stephen Langdon in the thirteenth century, and it become widely accepted following production of the English Wycliffe translation in 1382. The addition of verse divisions came later still, with Jewish scholars marking up the Hebrew Scriptures by the mid-fifteenth century and the New Testament Scriptures following suit as late as the mid-sixteenth century. Prior to that, our text, for example Heb 4:1–2, looked something like this:

ΦΟΒΗΘΩΜΕΝΟΥΝΜΗΠΟΤΕΚΑΤΑΛΕΙΠΟΜΕΝΗΣΕΠΑΓΓ
ΕΛΙΑΣΕΙΣΕΛΘΕΙΝΕΙΣΤΗΝΚΑΤΑΠΑΥΣΙΝΑΥΤΟΥΔΟΚΗΤΙ
ΣΕΞΘΥΜΩΝΥΣΤΕΡΗΚΕΝΑΙΚΑΙΓΑΡΕΣΜΕΝΕΥΗΓΓΕΛΙΣΜ
ΕΝΟΙΚΑΘΑΠΕΡΚΑΚΕΙΝΟΙΑΛΛΟΥΚΩΦΕΛΗΣΕΝΟΛΟΓΟΣ
ΤΗΣΑΚΟΗΣΕΚΕΙΝΟΥΣΜΗΣΥΓΚΕΚΕΡΑΣΜΕΝΟΥΣΤΗΠΙΣ
ΤΕΙΤΟΙΣΑΚΟΥΣΑΣΙΝ

As we might imagine, it was no easy task to copy such script (there are no guarantees my typed copy of Hebrews above contains no errors!), especially before the advent of fixed forms of printing. Until then, there was not only the unbroken string of letters to contend with, but also handwriting variations between scribes.

Langdon, together with those who further divided the text into chapters and verses following him, did the world of faith a favor. Now, with the exception of the decisions made by those whose difficult task it is to translate the text into our language, we can be sure that we have a close rendition of something like the author's original intent.

These divisions, however, are sometimes a little awkward. Acts 8:1a, for example, probably belongs in a different paragraph than Acts 8:1b, and the editors of my version have made that decision. Division of Gen 1 and 2 would be far more meaningful halfway through Gen 2:4 than at the end of Gen 1:31, and so on. By and large, the divisions are useful, just not one hundred percent of the time. Perhaps Luke 17:10b applies!

The Message of Hebrews

The history of Hebrews is remarkable. As noted above, it was already being cited, along with some of Paul's writings, as bearing scriptural authority by the end of the first century of Christianity. Written possibly within three and certainly no more than five decades from the criminal execution of Jesus, it was already making enormously "high" claims for his significance. Jesus is "higher than the angels" (Heb 1:1–14) and is to be worshiped not only by human beings but by heavenly beings as well. Jesus is there even at creation (Heb 1:2). The claim "Jesus Christ is the same yesterday, today and tomorrow" (Heb 13:8), standing alone and in many ways isolated from the text surrounding it, provides a key to the author's understanding of the subject and institutes a bleak contrast between the eternal nature of Jesus and the mutability of human beings and their institutions. It is a solemn liturgical pronouncement, and its weight underscores the entire sermon-document.

Jesus, though, is no otherworldly figure. Jesus is grounded firmly in human experience, undertaking in his earthly journey the gamut of your experience and mine.[32] Jesus is the journeyer (Heb 2:10, 6:20, 12:2), while we are journeyers. Jesus' life was one of (perfect) right choices, obedient even to the extent of being "the exact imprint of God's very being" (Heb 1:3). We, as subsequent journeyers, must similarly make right life-choices (Heb 2:1, 3:12, 4:11, 6:6, 13:9, 10:25, 12:1), not wrong ones (Heb 4:2, 6, 11). Because Jesus has journeyed our journey, we are encouraged to get our act together and do the right thing (Heb 4:11, 16; 10:22, 13:13).

---

32. Well, not *exactly*—what scholars call the "scandal of particularity," or the need to be incarnate some*where*, some*time*, in some *form*, means of course that there are differences. The biblical Jesus never drove a Ford, experienced marriage, menstruation, or menopause . . . These are part of the wider Holy Spirit interaction between the triune Godhead and humanity and so belong in another study.

Underscoring the author's argument is a worldview no longer popular in postmodern society. To this author, *our* reality is an inferior reality, our world is a lesser version of a "real" world that exists beyond our sight. Our world is transient and corruptible, but that *other* world is not. Paul echoes this view with his famous "now we see as though through a darkened glass, then we shall see face to face" (1 Cor 13:12; a similar view permeates the writings of C. S. Lewis, particularly The Chronicles of Narnia). The author of Hebrews also sees the world this way: the Son, as we perceive him, is but a reflection of God's glory (Heb 1:3) because we could not stand the full revelation of the glory of God (Exod 33:20), even if he is "the exact imprint of God's very being." The old covenant, in particular, provided shadow forms of reality (Heb 9:23), but in Christ a new access to reality is provided (Heb 9:24). The hymn writer William Chatterton Dix has famously captured one idea conveyed by the author of Hebrews: "thou within the veil hast entered / robed in flesh, our great High Priest / thou on earth both priest and victim / in the Eucharistic Feast."[33]

Jesus updates the old rites, becoming a New Way in and through himself (Heb 10:20). I repeat, though, what I have indicated above: Christians do not supplant the place of the genetic Hebrew people in the heart of God. The update implicit in the new covenant does not give permission for Christians to hate their Jewish forebears and the parallel Jewish community. Since the Holocaust, we must always, *always* be sensitive to the wording of supersession or replacement. John Goldingay notes of the story of Cain and Abel that "the story goes on to show that this [election] does not mean Cain is abandoned by God, a principle that runs through subsequent stories in Genesis of God's choice of one person over another."[34] Despite everything, Cain "has the promise that God will protect his life,"[35] but the victim Abel's offering continues even after his death to be pleasing to God, and God's having "regard to" the sacrifice of Abel (Gen 4:4b) continues to reverberate through history.

We cannot yet access that reality in full. That is why some in the Hebrews congregation are reneging on their early faith-enthusiasm (Heb 2:1, 3:12, 6:4–6, 10:29). But by encouraging one another, driving ourselves on, and even being emboldened by the "cloud of witnesses" who have gone before us (Heb 12:1), we can attain the ultimate reality opened for us. We must persevere though (Heb 4:1–11), overcoming any fear of suffering (Heb 2:14–15, 5:7, and Heb 11) or persecution (Heb 10:32–35, 11:23, 27,

---

33. From the hymn "Alleluia, Sing to Jesus," by William Chatterton Dix (1839–1898).
34. Goldingay, *Israel's Gospel*, 150.
35. Barth, *Church Dogmatics*, 2:2:355.

12:13, 13:13–14). The onus is on us to make it to the end, where untold glories await us (Heb 13:14). We persevere without, perhaps, the signs and wonders we once experienced in the first necessary flushes of our faith but aided instead by God's Spirit (Heb 2:1–4) and by the blessing of God (Heb 13:20–21).

Concluding Introductory Thoughts

The complete Trinitarian language of Christianity, together with the language describing the dual human/divine nature of Christ, would take centuries to establish. Yet perhaps as early as 55 but probably by 64 CE, some anonymous, humble author was grasping these concepts and using them to encourage and exhort (Heb 13:22) a faith community—a eucharistic faith community (Heb 13:15). Can we too be encouraged by her words, reading them in a very different but perhaps not *so* different world?

One great contemporary scholar, in a commentary on Hebrews, has this to say:

> Hebrews challenges our imagination to enter a universe that is not defined by quantitative measure but by qualitative difference, to ponder a world in which the unseen is more real, more powerful, and more attractive than that which can be seen and touched and counted.[36]

Can we, *dare* we, enter that universe?

---

36. Johnson, *Hebrews*, 2.

2

Establishing a Preaching Relationship

AN ORATOR OF ANY time or style must use some opening gambits to establish the rules of engagement with the audience. Our author was delivering her words through a proxy, presumably one whose oratorical delivery could be trusted to convey the desired message,[1] but she had to ensure that the words themselves established a relationship of commitment and trust between author and audience. Cicero, following the oratorical "handbooks" of his time, describes an orator's primary tasks as being to "win over" the audience's minds and then to establish the parameters of the case at hand.[2] Cicero is arguing for court oratory, but the case remains the same in our author's process: she must (through her proxy) win over the hearts and minds of the audience and then establish the parameters of her discourse to follow. She does so by grasping her listeners' attention and then establishing a litany of agreed truths using biblical (Hebrew scriptural) texts that have been a part of the faith narrative she and the Hebrews have shared.

While sermon styles have inevitably changed from generation to generation, some fundamentals remain the same. One of those is that a preacher must grab his or her audience's attention from the opening salvo. This author begins without greeting, with a broad flourish that makes quite clear that she is not going to be mealy-mouthed and wimpish! She indicates that the person and work of Jesus Christ is going to be a central theme: from Heb 1:2 onwards, the focus is Christ. Christ's role and purpose together with Christ's achievements are themes that will dwell at the heart of this document.

---

1. "Surely I don't need to add anything about delivery? This must be regulated by the movement of the body, by gesture, by facial expression, and by inflecting and varying the voice," instructs Cicero as he begins to outline the task of oration (Cicero, *De Oratore* 1.18; May and Wisse, 61). As with any ancient document, those outcomes are lost to us!

2. Ibid., 1.142–43; May and Wisse, 89.

This sermon was not going to be delivered by its author. At Heb 13:19, we learn that this author wants to be back with the Hebrews as soon as possible, and she expects to be (Heb 13:23b). This author identifies with the audience strongly; she may have evangelized the Hebrews in the first place or may have been with them from the very beginning of their receipt of the gospel. Hebrews 4:2 suggests the latter, but it may be that this wording is just a tool by which the author identifies more closely with the audience. Does Heb 2:3 indicate that though this author did not know Jesus in the flesh, she, together with the Hebrews, was a beneficiary of the witness of those who had? This audience is just one remove from Jesus of Nazareth, and yet its members are already identifying him as "the reflection of God's glory and the exact imprint of his very being" (Heb 1:3). Other translations will differ slightly, but all bring out the remarkable claim that a humble man living within three decades or so of the time of writing, known and attested to by eyewitnesses only one remove from the author and audience, is "as much superior to the angels as the name he inherited [Lord] is more excellent than theirs" (Heb 1:4).

As suggested in my introduction, the word "Lord" itself is the weightiest word imaginable. How often it rolls so easily from our tongue! Even in a formal liturgy like the "Thanksgiving of the People of God" eucharistic rite in *A New Zealand Prayer Book / He Karakia Mihinare o Aotearoa*, the word appears no fewer than twenty-five times in the prayer book wording alone.[3] Add to that a sermon and readings, and it is likely that the Lordship of Jesus is referred to some thirty or more times in a little over an hour. Many will be familiar with forms of extempore prayer in which the word "Lord" is repeated over and over, often more than once per sentence or even more than once per phrase! Yet how monstrously awe-filled a word this is. To the Hebrews, only YHWH, the Creator, deserved the title. To the Romans, only Caesar, in whose hands lay powers of life and death, deserved the title. Yet, as Heb 1:4 hints and as Heb 2:3 makes clear, this title is now applied to the man of Nazareth, and done so only a few sentences after it has been addressed to the Creator God (Heb 1:10). This "Lordship of Christ" or "Lordship of Jesus" is one of the first central claims of this sermon. But it is not the only one: this man of Nazareth is also, and indeed first, designated "Son"[4] and heir.

All these themes, then, are spiraling around as this (to us) anonymous author launches into her sermon. It has often been said that all the

---

3. *New Zealand Prayer Book / He Karakia Mihinare o Aotearoa*, 404–29.

4. The capital punctuation is an editorial choice that was unavailable to the original author, who had only capitals, or "uncials," at their disposal.

themes that appear in John's Fourth Gospel appear in the first eighteen verses. Similarly, in Hebrews, the themes are largely advertised in the first four verses. In the original Greek, as best we can tell, the first four verses are one sentence, piling theme upon theme and preparing the audience for powerful emotional and intellectual exhortation. The main claim, however, does not seem at first to be that striking: God has spoken to us in the form of a Son. Partly, of course, we are again inured to the radical nature of the word "son" by centuries of use. Ask a Muslim how radical this claim is! Compared to those twenty-five appearances of "Lord" in the New Zealand Anglican "Thanksgiving of the People of God"[5] liturgy, "son" (or "Son") appears only nine times, but there is no doubt it rarely grabs or startles us when we hear it applied to Jesus. It was not new to the Hebrews either, but it was, or had been, startling: "For to which of the angels did God ever say, 'You are my Son?'" The answer, of course, as expected in the light of the sources quoted (Ps 2:4 and 2 Sam 7:14), is "to none." God was not in the habit of having children.

Other themes are aired in the prologue (Heb 1:1–4). Something precious to the ancestors in faith—the word and voice of the prophets—has been surpassed. We again need to be careful that we don't think we are in some way "better than" our Jewish cousins in faith. Our history reveals that to be a lie. Nevertheless, we have been given in Christ, in the Jesus event, a chance they have not had (or taken). A Son has taken over the prophetic role, has revealed the glory of God which is the very being of God, and has made possible unimaginable purification from sin—our sin, as we will read later (though the Hebrews themselves would have no doubt what the preacher meant at this stage!).

It is not particularly helpful, in the twenty-first century, to rattle off lists of scriptural proof texts in order to make a point. The first century, however, had a far less critical and less skeptical attitude toward their predecessors. To cite the authority of the ancients was a recognized oratorical technique, and the author of Hebrews launches into a series[6] of Hebrew scriptural references to make comparison between "son" and "angels." In keeping with the premise "Long ago God *spoke*" (Heb 1:1), this preacher emphasizes the oral authority of God in the past: "God . . . *says*." God is not dependent on written traditions but has instead spoken a "word" into the hearts of men and women.

---

5. One could argue that all eucharistic liturgies are "thanksgiving of the people of God," so I find the title bewildering, but I reproduce it here for clarity.

6. Attridge, *Hebrews*, 49.

Again, ours is a skeptical generation, but to the Hebrews this speaking of God was credible, authoritative, and needed no defense: "God . . . *says.*" God, even from ancient times, has spoken of and even *to* a Son. And now, in the person of Jesus of Nazareth (the preacher never uses this very earthly title, but I use it as shorthand to capture the essence of Jesus "for a time a little lower than the angels" of Heb 2:9), God has spoken anew, spoken finally, and spoken definitively. This speaking has been in and through One who "sustains all things by his powerful word" (Heb 1:3). Once again, the claim is immeasurably vast: The man of Nazareth sustains the universe? It will be some decades before John writes the Fourth Gospel; his "In the beginning was the Word, and the Word was with God, and the Word was God" (John 1:1) reveals a Christology as high as this, while the hymnic Phil 2:5–11 attains the same heights.

To a modern or postmodern reader, many New Testament uses of Old Testament texts seem facile. To us, the citations of Old Testament passages do little to further claims for the "Sonship" of Jesus. Psalms 2:7 and 2 Sam 7:14 (cited in Heb 1:5) are, in context, about the sonship of that other king, David, and would be understood as such by the Jewish community then and now. Hebrews 1:6 is perhaps an allusion to Ps 97:7 or Deut 32:43, but the quotation would not impress a modern examiner for its accuracy (though our author was no doubt quoting from memory)! Allusion to the angels referenced in Ps 104:4 is contrasted against references to a passage about someone who is "most excellent of men" in Ps 45:2.

These references would have been a regular part of our preacher's earlier communications to her audience during their ongoing exchange of ideas. As author and audience shared together in their study of Hebrew Scriptures, these references would have taken on for the original audience a weight and solemnity they barely have for us. They are part of what scholars these days call a "shared narrative" between speaker and listener; if we lived in New Zealand in the 1970s and 1980s, the name "Muldoon" carries for us a significance and a resonance that it might not carry for someone not born in that particular time and place. The eccentricities of that larger-than-life politician carry a weight for those who knew him, if only via the media of the day, that they can never have for those who have access to him only through historical records![7]

---

7. Readers from other countries will have their own larger-than-life figures in their national narratives, though as a result of US global hegemony, readers in the United States may find that America's larger-than-life characters are common to almost all the world: a Nixon or Kennedy is as much a part of antipodean discourse as Muldoon is in New Zealand or, for example, Gough Whitlam is in Australia. Likewise, Margaret Thatcher, together with Ronald Reagan, still generates reverberations across the English-speaking world.

For the audience, then, Heb 1:5–13 bore an argumentative weight that the same references struggle to bear for us. We are not, after all, the audience the author intended. Nevertheless, the implication is clear: the man of Nazareth, through whom the audience members have come to faith, is an incomparably timeless and glorious being, present with the Creator from the beginning of time and before, who will be with God beyond the end of time, now and forever. The author will return to this theme, most succinctly and notably at Heb 13:8: Jesus Christ is the same yesterday, today, and forever.

As a summary of her catena of quotations, the preacher draws a conclusion: is not the task of an angel to point to someone greater than itself (Heb 1:14). The word "angel" simply means "messenger." Our era of New Age spirituality, with its fascination for angels (guardian and otherwise) but disinterest in God (certainly a triune God), might well wonder whose messages these unseen beings bear! But this verse is no mere stylistic flourish. There is a degree of "If it's good enough for them, then surely we . . . ?" about the rhetorical question of Heb 1:14, which might be called in common parlance "a guilt trip." The question is constructed to demand the answer "yes," and the acceptance of that "yes" has ramifications outlined in the next sentence (Heb 2:1).

"[T]herefore we must pay greater attention . . ." (Heb 2:1a) signals this is not going to be the type of sermon that makes us feel warm and gooey inside. The author is concerned about something that is happening in the lives of her audience, and this is her desperate attempt to intervene. While our postmodern and rationalist Western cultures might leave those of us outside New Age circles uneasy with the notion of ministering angels surrounding us as we worship, this decidedly irrational assessment of reality had to resonate with the audience's experience if the author's argument was going to carry any weight. Perhaps, while not embracing the type of angelology suggested above—that translucent-humanoid imagery that appears in so many Facebook memes and well-intended greeting cards illustrated with ethereal figures and luminescent heart-shaped wings—we should acknowledge that the presence of ministering angels gathered with the faithful in "divine service" (*leitourgia . . . diakonia*[8]) was a powerful experience shared by many early Christians. In a post-rationalism church, we need to be cautious in dismissing the idea of either unseen beings or of divinely chosen messengers, and we

---

8. The Greek might clumsily be rendered "are not they [the angels] ministering spirits sent out for service because of those soon to receive salvation."

should listen carefully to the experiences of non-Western cultures for which the unseen world is a powerful presence.[9]

The second sentence makes the issue clear: "so that we do not drift away from it" (Heb 2:1b). As I suggested in the introduction to this book, the single most important issue the author is addressing is that the audience members are growing cold in their faith commitment. The magnificent tour that this author takes through doctrinal issues will primarily address this one question: How to persevere in faith? We will address this issue again and again in these explorations.

This question of perseverance will be undergirded by the belief that God is a God who "speaks" by communicating directly to men and women of God's choice (Heb 1:1). Part of the issue of "backsliding" is that to slip away from faith is to renege on "what we have heard" (Heb 2:1), or the words and experiences of God we have had, which can be so powerful that the author could speak confidently of "ministering angels" as an experience shared by author and audience alike. These experiences are to be had in all facets of our faith lives—in worship, teaching, prayer, and experiences of, in short, "salvation" (Heb 1:14, 2:3). To "hear" is not necessarily to hear an audible voice: although some credible Christians testify to this form of "hearing God," it is not a part of my experience, and I prefer to use the word "hear" in a metaphorical sense, understanding hearing as experiencing God in many different ways. Your experience may of course differ: "God spoke to our ancestors in many and varied ways" (Heb 1:1)! In the context of God's speaking, Tom Long playfully wrestles with the meaning of "spoke," and I will settle with his definition: "The idea of God speaking is but a poetic way to say that God communicates, gets the message across."[10] The test will always be whether the "hearing" leads us closer to the Son (Heb 1:2), closer to the One whose purpose and will are revealed in the Scriptures of our faith, and whether as a result our behavior is about bearing witness to the Christ of the cross or to ourselves. If it is the latter, and we are being brought closer only to ourselves, then we are slipping away, in Hebrews' terms. Our author will be emphatic (Heb 6:4–6) that to fall from faith is the greatest of sins.

There may be a warning here for contemporary Christians, both those for whom the Christian experience is predominately expressed as an overly familiar and emotionally-driven chumminess and for those whose theological and liturgical language tends to speak of God as an externalization of the personal or collective human psyche. A glance at

---

9. One exception is the delightful devotional and scholarly work of Megan McKenna, *Angels Unawares*, which bears a title very close to the present study but has a very different focus. Her bibliography references further scholarly work on this field, which remains rather neglected outside New Age explorations.

10. Long, foreword to Fleer and Bland, *Preaching Hebrews*, xi.

some contemporary worship lyrics highlights, if in extreme form, the risks of the former. This trivialization of the human-divine relationship undergirds our author's thought: after adamantly affirming that he will not suffer[11] or beg and affirming the providence of Jesus, one song's persona affirms over and again that Jesus is his "daddy-o."[12] Apart from some confusion about the identity of the members of the Trinity and despite some biblical allusion to the sentiments of, for example, Phil 4:19, this lyric has reduced either the first or second person of the Trinity to the level of personal convenience and, if one nine-minute rendition accessible on YouTube is anything to go by, to the level of ecstatic entertainment. We might note the sage warning of Ched Myers, "The 'personal Savior' of American Evangelicalism is domesticated, no longer Lord of the world but of our hearts, into which we invite him."[13]

There are myriad examples of this "over-intimate" confusion of God-human relations,[14] but lest the "daddy-o" example be seen as exceptional, another example reveals an intrinsic trivialization of the theological and spiritual complexities that our Hebrews author is addressing: in a song narrating a visit to "the enemy's camp," the narrator, presumably Jesus, tells of his retrieval of that which had been stolen and his placement of Satan "under my feet." The lyrics, by Richard Black of Brownsville Revival, are a solid rendition of biblical imagery, but when sung over and again in a state of ecstasy, they soon begin to generate such identification confusion that the singer may too readily self-identify as the victor of the enemy, developing, we might suspect, an unhealthy Messiah complex![15]

Intrinsic to that song and many like it is a deep-seated confusion as to the identity of the narrator of the song—the "I" figure—and their relationship to the singer. The "I" in "Enemy Camp" is presumably Jesus if the

---

11. One wonders what Daesh execution victim and Christian martyr Kayla Mueller would make of the theology of these words.

12. The lyrics here referenced are by Dobby Dobson, from the 2008 album *Love Songs for Jesus*. Dobson, originally a reggae singer, converted to Christianity in a time of grief and since then has written primarily gospel music. To be fair, "daddy-o" was generic ghetto slang in the 1950s, but it still tended to reference the father figure of a community, and while it remains a useful corrective to subordinationist Christologies, it may fly in the face of John 14:28!

13. Myers, *Binding*, 9.

14. The psalms too generate a range of emotional responses to God from intimate love to abject awe bordering on terror. They do so however with a deep sense of the sacred weight of words.

15. Due to copyright concerns, I will not reproduce the words here, but they can be viewed on the website of the Brownsville Assembly of God Church in Pensacola, Florida, where they form the first part of a medley of contemporary gospel songs. See https://www.youtube.com/watch?v=ezXit3dScWQ. The lyrics are by Richard Black, of Brownsville Revival, 1991.

song is to have any theological or faith integrity, but the six-fold repetition (which can occur twice or many more times in performance) of Satan's placement under the feet of the Jesus-figure (apparently a reference to Rom 16:20, but with what we might call an overly advanced eschatology) risks placing the psyche of the singer at the center of a cosmic drama. This type of confusion may appear to be nit-picky, but our Hebrews author is addressing a group for whom the excitement and ecstasy of Christ-experience, as represented by this modern lyricism, has worn off and for whom tenacity or perseverance in faith is increasingly challenged.

Contemporary liturgical faith expressions can run a similar risk. In one online form of confession and absolution headed "Let us confess our regrets, forgive our own foolishness, and celebrate renewal," there is a distinctive dismantling of any notion that the reconciliation implicit in absolution is enabled by any force or being external to the person voicing the prayer. The prayer ends somewhat narcissistically after a litany of wrongdoing with "We confess, and *forgive ourselves*, and start anew. Come, now: let us wash away regrets, and celebrate renewal."[16] In a manner that is, once the superficial forms are brushed away, surprisingly similar to the confusions of pentecostal worship, these prayers have blurred the "I-Thou" relationship between the worshiper and the distinctively "other" and external first and second persons of the Trinity. The person seeks absolution from within. Psychologically, this can be difficult for a "damaged" person, but this is not the main issue at stake in the context of Hebrews.

The external nature of God in relationship to us may not be a priority for the author or user of the songs or the prayers I have cited, but in the context of Christian worship and experience addressed by our first-century author, these examples serve to highlight something that the Hebrews may have experienced. The ecstasy and joy of encounter with the external risen Christ, who is "at the right hand of the creator" (as our author reminds the audience by reference to Ps 102:25–27 at Heb 1:10 and Ps 110:1 at Heb 1:13), might well remain as an emotional presupposition in these songs and prayers, but the cognitive sense of the otherness of a creating, redeeming God has diminished. When the emotional uplift of this experience of divine otherness diminishes, as it appears to have done for the Hebrews, worshipers' commitment to endurance can likewise diminish (Heb 10:32–39, to which we will return). As we shall see later, the Hebrews have at some stage undergone trials for their belief (Heb 10:33), seemingly in their heady first days of faith. We should perhaps cut them some slack in critiquing their near-apostasy, for there but by the grace of God go we, but our author is in

---

16. The prayers are by New Zealand spiritual and liturgical writer Bronwyn Angela White, and are posted on her website at http://www.spirit-and-faith.com/80312204. Retrieved April 4, 2014. Italics added.

this context *not* prepared to cut them any slack, and it is with the author and her emphases that we must deal here.

Paul likewise addressed issues of perseverance in his writings. Concerned that the Thessalonians are slipping from their faith under duress and persecution, Paul sends Timothy to assess the situation (1 Thess 3:1–3a). Throughout his writings, the apostle demonstrates that faith without suffering and trials (he often uses the word *thlipsis*) is likely to be superficial and ersatz. In opening my introduction, I noted that the *New Zealand Anglican Prayer Book / He Karakia Mihinare o Aotearoa* likewise places trial or tribulation at the heart of Christian experience, so there is some onus on us still to maintain connection with the first-century authors' admonitions.

Paul and our author both knew all this is far easier said than done. With masterful artistry, our author reminds the Hebrews of the first flushes of enthusiasm they had once experienced for faith in Christ, "attested to us by those who heard him." The "us" of this sentence is possibly what is called an "authorial plural," similar to the "royal we" and designating only the author. It may equally be what I call a "collusive plural," engaging author and audience alike in a shared joyful familiarity of having heard the eyewitnesses of Jesus tell of their experiences of him and having collectively shared great ecstasy together in that experience.

It now becomes clear why the author made so great an issue from the beginning of the "lordship" or unparalleled importance of Christ: if the eyewitnesses of Jesus are willing to attest to this humble Palestinian man's divine authority, and if the audience is through those eyewitnesses only one remove from Jesus-in-the-flesh, then it is unreasonable to slip away from such privilege. To be so close to God but to let the experience slip through our fingertips is lunacy, our author implies. The authentication of that initial experience in "signs and wonders . . . miracles . . . and the gifts of the Holy Spirit" (Heb 2:4) is an argument well used by Paul elsewhere (e.g., Gal 1:6) and means that to fall away from the experience and responsibilities of faith is foolishness indeed. There is, though, a rider attached: "according to his will," the will of the Spirit of God. If God should decide that the powerful emotional spiritual experiences of our first flushes of faith are not a permanent arrangement, then so be it! "When I was child I thought like a child," says Paul (1 Cor 13:11). This is true, our author suggests, of our faith-life too: the time of simple experiential faith must pass, and the "milk" of first experiential faith must be replaced with the "solid food" of mature commitment to Christ (Heb 5:11–14).

As a convert to Christianity, albeit nearly four decades ago now, I am privileged to be able to look back on a time when I too experienced the first enthusiastic flushes of faith. In the decades since that time, moments of great ecstasy have recurred, though perhaps their nature, context, and triggers have changed with time. Perhaps the best comparison is with the experience of those who have enjoyed decades of marriage and satisfactory sexual relationship. Of course, with time the sexual union changes its routines, but for many people the depth and breadth of that experience only increases in the years since swinging from the chandeliers in the first enthusiasms of sexual excitement! These people are, of course, those who have worked—who have *both* worked—hard at the negotiations of marital relationship, but they are also people who have exhibited the tenacity, endurance, and perseverance our author is seeking. I write, incidentally, as one who has experienced both the disappointment of failed marriage and the enrichment of a lasting one, and I know my part in both failure and success.

There is another theme already emerging in the sermon. This author is influenced by the philosophy of Plato, who taught that the world we see is only a shadow of the world of forms—a greater, more solid world beyond our sight. Running throughout Hebrews, and indeed many New Testament and early church writings, we find a "like this, but so much more" equation. The author of Hebrews uses this in several ways, not least of which is to outline the distinctive nature of Jesus as prophet, priest, and Son. As noted, the author has used this equation already in the prologue to the sermon: "having become as much superior to angels as the name [Lord] he has inherited is more excellent than theirs" (Heb 1:4). There is *our* reality, but so much more, so very much more is the reality of God.

So the author, having hinted that first flushes were for a bygone day, moves back into one of the doctrinal phases of the sermon. The "this, but so much more" element dominates the next phase of this argument. To some extent the author at Heb 2:5 returns to the themes set aside at Heb 1:14, but our author is too skilled to waste words. Now to the theme of the unparalleled greatness of Christ is added the deep concern that the Hebrews are losing their way *despite* that greatness, despite all that they have heard and experienced, despite the first flushes and even the exhilaration of surviving a wave or even waves of derision and persecution (Heb 10:33). The author turns back to Scripture once more (adopting the spirit of 2 Tim 3:16), using Ps 8:4–6 to bolster the argument.

It can be assumed that all these citations of the Hebrew Scriptures had always been a part of the Hebrews' worship and teaching in the shared discourse between author and audience. Reference back to these familiar teachings serves to reinforce the notion that something once dear to them should continue to hold their attention and obedience. Our author, however, makes slight alteration to Ps 8, as seen in italics below:

PSALM 8	HEBREWS 2
humans ... mindful of them	humans ... mindful of them
mortals ... care for them?	mortals ... care for them?
	for a short while
lower than *elohim* = *gods*	lower than angels[1]
crowned them with glory and honor	crowned them with glory and honor
given them dominion	
subjecting all things under feet	subjecting all things under feet

The addition of time restraints, "for a little while," at Heb 2:7a may operate on a number of levels. It can serve to remind the audience that the human experience of embodiment in a suffering world is temporary only, both for the individual sufferer and indeed for the human race (the idea of the latter as a collective suffering entity is perhaps more a modern than a first-century perspective would allow). But there seems to be a wordplay going on in the author's mind by which the "him," confusingly translated "them" in the NRSV, is paralleled in the "him" who is Lord, who was incarnate "for a season."[18]

The omission of reference to "lordship" is deliberate, as the preacher seeks to avoid confusion between the unparalleled dominion of Christ in relationship and the subjection of humans to Christ. For now, the preacher is using the words of the psalmist to refer not to "this world" but to a "world to come," or technically a world that already is but remains beyond our sight, in which the lordship of Christ (and Christ alone) is absolute, and to which the faithful are invited, provided they persevere in faith.

I have referred to incautious mergers of the external and wholly "other" triune God with internal sources of succor and absolution—that is, to the dangers of finding absolution or redemption within, as suggested by Bronwyn Angela White's liturgy above. There are some whose experiences of oppression, exploitation, and other forms of abuse has made it impossible to accept room for an external, "other" spiritual force. If, for example, a childhood experience of sexual or emotional abuse has made it nearly impossible

---

17. "[L]ower than a god" is variously translatable as "lower than God" or "lower than divine beings"; the difference between Ps 8 and Heb 2 is not as great as translations may suggest in this line. I am grateful to Gerald Morris, who has pointed out in private correspondence "the LXX of Ps 8—which surely was the primary Bible of this very Greek-educated author—renders the *Elohim* of the Hebrew text simply as *angelous*. So the author wasn't changing the text at all; just quoting it."

18. "Humbled for a season / to receive a name / from the lips of sinners / unto whom he came." From the hymn "At the Name of Jesus" by Caroline Maria Noel (1817–1877).

to believe in the inherent goodness of any external force, especially if that "force" is frequently defined along gender stereotypes, then a spiritual journeyer may and perhaps must seek solace, absolution, and inspiration from within. To argue generalities from these exceptions to the rule is, however, dangerous, and we must assume that for most people internal strength is not the final source and provider of solace.

The dominant strand of Judaeo-Christian thought has emphasized that humanity is, on its own, irremediably tainted by "short-falling" or "sin." My observations of news broadcasts day after day, year after year, tend to reinforce the veracity of this belief. Any attempt by human beings to "work out their own salvation"[19] without external help tends to end up in the horrors of genocide, sexual abuse, economic exploitation, and with the subjugation of nature. Consequently, any tendency to dismiss God as an external encumbrance needs to be measured against Job's understandable but ultimately misguided allusion to Ps 8:4 and 144:3 in Job 7:17, where in his suffering the righteous man bursts out:

> What are human beings, that you make so much of them,
> that you set your mind on them,
> visit them every morning,
> test them every moment?
> Will you not look away from me for a while,
> let me alone until I swallow my spittle?

While few of us can claim anything to match the patience of Job, even he, in terms of traditional Judeo-Christian interpretations, falls short of perfection, and his fully understandable but seriously imperfect outburst at this point in his narrative should remind us that we are not really in a position to remonstrate with God as "an oppressive presence."[20]

It is unfashionable, in postmodernity, to repeat the emphasis of Karl Barth on the unlimitable *potestas* ("power" or "faculty") of God as outlined in Jer 18 and re-emphasized by Paul at Rom 9:21. Barth is always difficult to read, but his emphasis on the unquestionability of the Creator is simultaneously an emphasis on the Creator's will always to love and to heal and to redeem. In the context of reconciliation and the absolution of hurting (actively and passively: hurting others and being hurt) human beings, Barth,

---

19. Phil 2:12 is a verse that needs to be read in the context of Paul's overall doubt that humanity can ever *achieve* its own salvation, and it is probably best translated along the lines of "demonstrate the out-workings of your own salvation." As it happens, that too is a call for perseverance in faith-continuance, in the absence of Paul. See O'Brien, *Philippians*, 273–74.

20. Gordon, *Hebrews*, 66.

despite the complexity of his language, delivers an important reminder that God does not need to be removed from the equations of absolution and redemption:

> The love with which He turns to us in this work [Creation, reconciliation and redemption] and in which He has made Himself our God, has not made Him in the least degree poorer or smaller. It has its power and its reality as love for us too in the fact that it continues to be free love, that God has bound and still binds Himself to us as the One who is able thus to bind Himself and whose self-binding is the grace and mercy and patience which helps us, because primarily He is not bound, because He is the Lord, because stooping down to us He does not cease to be the Lord but actually stoops to us from on high where He is always Lord.[21]

What Barth, in all his complexity, tries to convey to us is that the "otherness" of God is, while a thing to be feared (God is not "my daddy-o" in any chummy sense), nevertheless is the only authoritative means by which love can invade and redeem our flawed human state. Psalm 8 together with Heb 2:5–9 in its shadow stand firmly in the same worldview as Jer 18: "What are human beings that you are mindful" and yet . . . "we do see Jesus" (Heb 2:6b, 9).

The subjection of "things of this world," the "all things" of Heb 2:8, is apparent only through the eyes of faith. Things appear to be bleak still (and our preacher didn't even have the questionable advantage of modern media). We cannot yet see the completion of the victory of Jesus (his name is used for the first time at Heb 2:9). But our eyes, as Paul reminded his Corinthian audience, are still dimmed. We can, however, experience Christ in worship (*leitourgia*), fellowship (*koinōnia*), and in Scripture (Heb 10:7), and we can recall the magnificence of those initial experiences of Christ when first we came to faith. The Hebrews were effectively *all* converts: it is unlikely that there were any second-generation Christians of influence yet. For a convert it is always easier, for we are able to point to a moment at which we embraced the gospel, and we can know the changes and contrasts between a life with and a life without Christ. Nevertheless, increasingly powerful experiences of the presence of Christ can be made known to us if we persevere in the subsequent journey.

In the Hebrews author's scheme, we are not yet ready to see the perfection that is in Christ. Following the Hebrew Scriptural belief that no one can look on the face of God and live (because of the infinite contrast between

---

21. Barth, *Church Dogmatics*, 2:1, 527.

our flawed humanness and God's divine perfection), we must look only on Jesus as he was in his incarnational state, "a little lower than the angels" (Heb 2:9b). In telling stories of angelic manifestation, McKenna notes an "awareness of standing in the presence of the Lord and being in jeopardy of one's life is etched deep into the soul of the Jewish people."[22] The angels, McKenna intimates, will step in to protect humans from the vastness of the chasm between them and the divine. Our author is envisaging a hierarchical universe in which the Son has allowed himself to be demoted a few critical rungs of the ladder, below even the angels, to a state in which eyewitnesses saw him with clarity—a clarity even greater than that with which the first-century Gentiles and Jews alike frequently encountered angelic phenomena.

The place of angels was more comprehensible to a first-century audience than to our post-Enlightenment Western audience. Johnson notes, "Those living in technologically sophisticated societies can—apart from the odd glitch and blackout—even pretend that humans are in full control of their destiny, not least because their techniques of manipulation have demystified the world."[23] We do not need to be immersed for too long in non-Western cultures to know that there are peoples for whom spiritual entities are far more real than Westerners can imagine, and we need to be very cautious in taking a paternalistic post-Enlightenment attitude to these experiences. Even those of us living in the techno-dependent global north do not need to be exposed for very long to "glitches" in our technology before we return to unscientific tools and analyses of the world around us.

We can "see" (the word is again used metaphorically; see Heb 2:9a) Jesus in that sub-angelic state as often as we pay attention to "what we have heard" (Heb 2:1). For those of us who were not eyewitnesses to the incarnation—and that is our author and the entire audience—the experience of signs, wonders, and gifts (Heb 2:4) is so powerful that we can speak of "seeing." To those of us who were not eyewitnesses, the experiential dimension was so powerful, as we received and lived out the "message declared through angels/messengers" (Heb 2:2), that we can speak of "seeing." The notion of "attested" (Heb 2:3) reinforces the notion of a tradition handed on, but the veracity of that tradition is reinforced by the experiential dimensions of the signs and wonders and works of the Spirit.

In the charismatic movements of the church, much emphasis has been placed on recreation or reclamation of signs and wonders as theoretically experienced by the early Christians.[24] Writers and teachers such

---

22. McKenna, *Angels Unawares*, 95.
23. Johnson, *Hebrews*, 82.
24. And their Jewish forebears: Exod 7:3, Deut 4:34, 6:22, 7:19, 26:8, 29:3, Neh 9:10,

as the late John Wimber therefore placed a great deal of emphasis on these experiences, as I am indeed suggesting our author is at this point. My interpretation needs to walk a fine line here. I am skeptical of a form of scientific rationalist empiricism that dismisses the inexplicable or unquantifiable as superstition: exposure to the third world or even to the mysticism of Western traditions cautions me against too readily permitting rationality to become the yardstick by which all meaning to life is mediated. When the infrastructure of technology fails, we soon become scared of the dark! On the other hand, sensationalist performances of charismatic experience can be open to manipulation and abuse. What I consider to be the infamous occasions of Wimber yelling from the stage, "More power, Lord!" as he sought to perform healings suggests to me a far greater emphasis on neon-lit dramatics than on a genuine encounter with the Spirit of the Christ of the cross, no matter what subsequently took place in the life of the recipients of his ministry and no matter what personal integrity Wimber may have had.

My own practice is to eschew dramatics: in the understated rhythms of well-structured and well-presented liturgy, the great and all but tangible truths of the Spirit's presence weigh in on me so that I can add my "amen" to our author's experience of signs and wonders. I have experienced no greater miracle, sign, or wonder than that week by week, century by century, believers have reached out to receive simple signs of bread and wine and water, accepting (to various degrees) the attestation that these signs are charged with the meaning of God's salvation and have become "for us the body and blood of Christ." Occasionally, if not always, there are even more tangible moments, as when, for example, an Alzheimer's patient well-accustomed from their pre-illness past suddenly recognizes in the small wafer of communion an in-breaking of God's peace and, just for that moment, is taken back to a more holy and less confused time, adding their amen while consuming their contact with God. (It is of course by no means always the case, and there are no equations by which to guarantee that we, were we in that patient's shoes, would know in that context the touch of God.)

As we hear that message—that Jesus clearly suffered and died and that he suffered and died *for us*—we cannot but know that this was an essential element of the very first preaching the Hebrews received. It was not unique to the Hebrews, of course, but was known also to the congregations addressed by Paul (Rom 5:8b, 1 Cor 1:30, 2 Cor 1:5, Gal 3:13, 1 Thess 5:10) and influenced by Paul (Eph 1:19, 5:2, Titus 2:14). This "for us" was a fundamental teaching from the very first pronouncements of the Christian community. Our author wants the audience members to understand that they can

---

Est 10:9, Ps 135:9.

"see" Jesus, even post-Easter, in that the attestation of the witnesses, together with the experience of the presence of Christ in worship and fellowship, is so powerful that it can be named as "sight."

This, then, gives our author-preacher the opportunity to raise once more the question of suffering (Heb 2:9c). The author uses a different word here—not the *thlipsis* used earlier, but *pathēma*—though not too much significance should be given to the differences. To suffer is to suffer, but to a first-century audience there is now a shocking new dimension to the preacher's argument. Jesus *must* experience the fullness of human suffering and more if the human experience of suffering is to be taken up into the heart of God, if the human state is to be rescued, and if this dreadful experience is to be understood as a sign of the grace of God (Heb 2:9d). There is no magic wand to wave, but there is a gate to be opened (later on, the author will call it a "curtain"; see Heb 6:19, 9:3, 10:20), and that gate can be opened only by "passing through" suffering. The author is not yet quite ready to explore the notion of the perfection and sinlessness of Jesus, but the idea is surfacing, for the word "glory" (Heb 2:9c, 10) is beginning to make its presence felt, and glory (*doxa*) is the domain of God's unsullied perfection. But the main theme as yet is suffering. In Christ, our suffering is now inexplicably taken into the heart of God—an experience shared by Jesus and those who belong to Jesus alike. Jesus "is not ashamed to call them brothers and sisters" (Heb 2:11-13, alluding to Ps 22:22).

God and suffering do not, in the ancient world, belong in the same sentence, yet at Heb 2:10 the author links the two as being "appropriately," or "fittingly" (*prepō*) entwined. It is too easy for us to gloss over the serious and radical nature of this pronouncement. Far less shocking pronouncements might cause us to stumble. Take, for example, "it was fitting that God should be male" or "it was fitting that God should be left-handed." Few of us would allow such statements to pass by, assuming that we believe in the existence of a God at all, without comment or argument. Yet this claim from our author was effectively obscene in the Gentile world in which Hebrews was written. God, according to Plato and Aristotle and those who followed in their footprints, was supposed to be dispassionate, unmoved by feeling or emotion. Like a speed camera, God should be impassive when faced by any aspect of the human plight (and a wise person should aim to be likewise dispassionate). Yet the God of the ancient Israelites has entered into a relational covenant with human beings and opened Godself up to "feelings": "If God has opened his heart in the covenant with his people, he is injured by disobedience and suffers in the people."[25] Our author is not startlingly new

---

25. Moltmann, *Crucified God*, 271-72.

in this approach, for the prophets of the Hebrews had long since posited a feeling God, but our author was nevertheless risking derision—the "folly to the gentiles" of Paul's equation in 1 Cor 1:23—by reminding her audience of this central aspect of their previous experiences and teaching.

The preacher then moves on to explore the essential unity of the life of Jesus and our lives as human beings. We "share flesh and blood" (Heb 2:14)[26] and, therefore, the experiences of mortality. Leaving aside for a moment the question of the devil, the specter of mortality bears further consideration. While Wordsworth rejoiced in "Intimations of Immortality" as he found them in nature and its processes—hints of the hereafter, as it were, "pressing in" through observations of the natural world ("O ye Fountains, Meadows, Hills and Groves, / Forebode not any severing of our loves!")[27]—our author finds humanity weighed down by a "fear of death" (Heb 3:15). From my own experiences of palliative pastoral care, I would not make any generalizations about faith and its impact on our fear of death. I have seen atheists die peacefully and seen Christians die with a Dylan Thomas-like fear and rage against the obscenity and inconvenience of death: "rage against the dying of the light."[28]

Interrogate people and few will, in my experience, own to much fear of dying, even when given medical indications that their life is coming to an end. Christian evangelism, based on the fear of post-existence ("If you died tonight, where would you spend eternity?"), is not only utterly un-Christlike, it is misconceived. Few people care or believe in eternity in my world, a world in which most people "pass" or "pass over" and few "die." Yet we live in a culture whose major malaise is, as Ernest Becker reminded us, "denial of death."[29] This is why we now, at least in my culture, rarely hear the words "death" and "dying" used, as so many prefer to use our various euphemisms—some of which, ironically, are borrowed from spiritualism. "We live today," wrote Alexander Schmemann in the mid-1960s, "in a death-denying culture."[30] While it is hardly unique to the eras of modernity and postmodernity, I suspect the fascination (especially in my own country) with extreme sports stems at least in part from a desire to taunt the role of death in human lives. Byron saw it long before the modern era:

---

26. In the Greek, the order is "blood and flesh."

27. William Wordsworth, "Intimations of Immortality," lines 188–89, in Wordsworth, *Selected Poetry*, 546.

28. Dylan Thomas, "Do not go gentle into that good night," line 3, in Thomas, *Collected Poems*, 116.

29. See Becker, *Denial of Death*.

30. Schmemann, *World as Sacrament*, 118.

> ... there is a fire
> And motion of the soul which will not dwell
> In its own narrow being, but aspire
> Beyond the fitting medium of desire;
> And, but once kindled, quenchless evermore,
> Preys upon high adventure, nor can tire
> Of aught but rest; a fever at the core,
> Fatal to him who bears, to all who ever bore.[31]

Thus, to taunt death is therefore a taunt that must, one way or another, ultimately wither on the lips of the taunter. It is then that our unreadiness to face death's reality becomes even more strident:

> We live today in a death-denying culture. This is clearly seen in the unobtrusive appearance of the ordinary funeral home, in its attempt to look like all other houses. Inside the "funeral director" tries to take care of things in such a way that one will not notice that one is sad; and a parlor ritual is designed to transform a parlor into a semi-pleasant experience. There is a strange conspiracy of silence concerning the blunt fact of death, and the corpse itself is "beautified" so as to disguise its deadness.[32]

When confronted with the realities of death, we become wielders of euphemism, and our ability to face death's stark obscenity stutters into uneasy silence. Usually, the closing of funeral rites, even those that eschew all language of finality, soon segue into an all-too chemically enhanced wake (or indeed, as it often referred to in my circles, an "after-match function"—another euphemism!). If the denial of death is a symptom of post-rationalist culture, it is nevertheless from the malaise of death or indeed of being human that our author believes the work of Christ liberates us. Christ does that by entering into the fullness of our humanity, and our author's understanding of the Christ event had therefore plunged deep into the heart of death itself.

Faith too can be used destructively as a denial of death. Much that bears the name of Christ is simply a form of what Sartre called *mauvaise foi,* or the denial of the brutal but liberating finality of non-existence. Perhaps my faith is no more than this denial? I suggest, however, that there are some litmus tests. At the most insignificant level, such testing is to ascertain whether believers' faith leads them to confront injustice. This may include confronting the injustices of encountering a "neighbor," in Jesus' terms, who is lonely, frightened, bored, or entrapped in any of the other malaises of

---

31. Byron, "Childe Harold's Pilgrimage," canto 3, stanza 42.
32. Schmemann, *World as Sacrament*, 118.

postmodernity. This will include the believer's readiness to touch and transform lives captured in "malaise ways," or inauthentic ways of living. At the infinitely higher level is that which few of us will ever attain, as with the lives and sometimes martyrdoms of a Dietrich Bonhoeffer, a Martin Luther King Jr., a Nelson Mandela, or a Desmond Mpilo Tutu. These lives testify to the ability of Christ-centered existence to rise far above *mauvaise foi,* and the owners of these lives would almost certainly attest to the power of their encounter with Christ to lift them to this level (it might also be suggested that they attained levels of authentic existence far higher than that to which Sartre attained).

I have set aside the question of the devil. Vast screeds of scholarship have been written on this subject. The most exhaustive study of the subject, at least among those known to this author, are the volumes written by Jeffrey Barton Russell, and I refer any reader interested in the subject to Russell's corpus. He writes chronologically of the development of the idea of the devil from antiquity to modernity, and his findings in his comparatively brief treatment of the devil in the New Testament are probably best summarized in his pithy observation that "the figure of Satan in the New Testament is comprehensible only when it is seen as the counterpart, or counterprinciple, of Christ."[33] Our Hebrews author is not presenting a treatise on the origins of evil but is instead addressing the question of living in a context in which evil is varied but palpable. To our author, surrender of faith would be in itself a testimony to the power of evil; our own century would no doubt see this differently! For our author, the work of the devil is simply and unambiguously apparent in any aspect or experience of life that turns the believer away from the central claims of Jesus Christ on his or her life.

The original Hebrew peoples associated the devil with death: "through the devil's envy death entered the world" (Wis 2:24; see also Heb 2:14). The audience of Hebrews has been taught this too, and there is a certain timelessness to the author's observation "to free those who all their lives were held in slavery by the fear of death" (Heb 2:15). Perhaps we do not individually fear death; certainly my work over the years with those who are dying has indicated that "fear" is not the forefront of the emotions of the dying. Nevertheless, aging, dying, and death are not popular notions in our society and, by and large, we lock our elderly and infirm out of the public eye. It might also be added that the fear of living is a greater malaise in contemporary society. Sartre highlighted this malaise in *Nausea*, as Roquentin muses, "I am. I am, I exist, I think, therefore I am; I am because I think, why do I

---

33. Russell, *Devil*, 222. See also ibid., 229: "The function of the Devil in the New Testament is as counterprinciple to Christ."

think? I don't want to think any more, I am because I think that I don't want to be, I think that I ... because ... ugh!"[34] It was a common theme of the existentialists and their successors. Saul Bellow's character Basteshaw acknowledges acerbically, "Boredom is the conviction that you can't change," adding, "It is also the shriek of unused capacities, the doom of serving no great end or design, or contributing to no master force."[35]

Still, the devil is something of a problem. Too much popular Christian discourse of hamartiology (the study of sin) is of "the devil made me do it" genre, depicting the primary opponent of God as a horned beastie lurking on the covers of CDs or books in order to seduce the faithful. The phrase was made infamous by televangelist Jim Bakker following his fall from grace in the 1980s. Regardless of the complexities of Bakker's own life, the phrase is, like many catchcries and clichés, simultaneously superficial and yet reminiscent of a faint residual truth. Bakker's own life story is probably an indication of the truth of Lord Acton's dictum "Power tends to corrupt and absolute power corrupts absolutely," for the power of evangelists and pastors, which is concern enough in its own right, can be vastly magnified in the lives of televangelists (especially those active in the glitzy 1980s, a decade of immeasurable greed).

It is perhaps not wholly a digression to note in passing that Lord Acton, with his insight into the potential of power to corrupt, was both German and English. His original statement was made in a review of a history of the papacy, but it has become a much more widely applied apothegm. On the British side of Acton's bloodline, a left-reformist agenda tended to adopt the "Whiggish assumptions about equality and progress that left God right out of the equation."[36] German reformers of Acton's time were less likely to critique the ethos of social stratification per se, such that a generation later Dietrich Bonhoeffer questioned not social strata but rather the failure of his *Bildungsbürgertum* class to practice the social responsibility and *noblesse oblige* that he felt their privileged position in society demanded of them. Regardless of the contrasts in Germanic and British class-consciousness, the point remains that Bonhoeffer had come to see that the Christian community was lapsing in its responsibility to serve and pay obeisance to the God of Jesus Christ and not to any imposter. Historian John Moses notes:

---

34. Sartre, *Nausea*, 146.

35. Bellow, *Augie March*, 504. Literary and Internet quotations of this observation usually run the two observations together and ignore the detail that Basteshaw is not *necessarily* expressing Bellow's perspective.

36. Moses, "Bonhoeffer's Fiction," 100.

Clearly, for Bonhoeffer, the widespread anti-intellectual, mindlessly nationalistic theological culture in Germany was an insidious evil, somewhat parallel to current fundamentalism, precisely because the pastors who were educated to read the signs of the times and give critical, intellectual leadership prostituted themselves, wittingly or unwittingly, in the service of the false God of nationalism.[37]

Lord Acton saw the potential of religious and social power to corrupt and blind those exercising that power. Lord Acton's balance of Germanic and British perspective enabled him to see that it is not class per se, but rather the neglect of responsibility and abuse of privilege in any culture or class that births corruption. This applies to all possessors of social and psychological (including religious) power from televangelists to church officials under Germany's Nazi Reich and from corrupt bishops to pedophiles—in short, all power that leads to the loss of the same coordinates of justice and compassion that our author feared the Hebrews audience risked losing. Our author simply recognizes that to lose focus on the God whose power is revealed in suffering, in powerlessness, as Bonhoeffer emphasized,[38] is to lose sight of the justice-proclaiming coordinates of faith.

The devil, Satan, Lucifer, Mephistopheles (I use the titles used by Jeffrey Russell) is, if nothing else, a description of the source of all that channels human attention away from the service of God: evil is human acquiescence in that distraction.[39] Russell's treatment of the devil in the New Testament concludes with the observation:

> the Devil is not a principle; the Devil does not limit God's power; the Devil is permitted by God to function; the Devil has some purpose in the cosmos that we cannot grasp; the Devil is God's enemy and our enemy and must be resisted with all our strength. This is true whether the Devil is an ontological entity or the personification of the "demonic" in humanity.[40]

---

37. Ibid., 97.

38. "Only the life of 'participation in the powerlessness of God in the world' will speak a word of renewal" (Bonhoeffer, *Letter and Papers*, 200, cited in Bethge, *Bonhoeffer*, 788–89).

39. "The Devil adapts himself to the times and has even worn the cavalier's sword. This is how the Enlightenment idealized him. The Middle Ages, which talked also of his bad smell, knew him better" (Klaus Bonhoeffer, cited in Bethge, *Bonhoeffer*, 832). One suspects that in the twenty-first century, the devil might wear (possibly Prada, but also . . .) the corporate power to control media.

40. Russell, *Satan*, 230.

"The devil made me do it" may be an ontological observation, but it is never an excuse: that is where Bakker went wrong. But for our author, the main point at this early stage in the Hebrews sermon is that, as we see in the highly symbolic temptation narratives of the Synoptic Gospels, Christ enters in full into the human experience of temptation—the experience of distraction from the main game of service to God[41]—and overcomes by his holiness (or fidelity to the main game of God-focus) those distractions.

As a side note, we might add that the extreme "holiness" of Christ is not some commodity that he possesses to a greater degree than we do, for if it were, then he would not be the "like us" of Heb 4:15. He would just be better off or more honed than we are in possession and use of that commodity; he would be like a Usain Bolt, who owns the same physical equipment as I do but who achieves much better results than I do. But the mechanics of Christ's perfection in the hands of our author are a complex work in progress, and to this point we can only accept that Christ has, in our author's understanding, journeyed pretty much our same path in wrestling with distractions from the main game of God-focus.

Although the complex language of the creeds was centuries away, our author is clearly moving towards this notion of the two natures of the Son, both the human and divine. The One who is Lord shared our flesh and blood: to the ancient world, a genuine absorption of human experience into divine experience is simply not possible, yet our author, within a few decades of the execution of Jesus, is reaching for this explanation. We are engaged with a passage (Heb 2:14–18) that stresses the earthy, like-us nature of the incarnation with a growing emphasis—one stressed in subsequent centuries by the Eastern church—that this being "like us" makes possible a transformation of our being so that we, in turn and in him, can be "like him." The Orthodox call this process "divinization," while Western Christians have preferred to use notions of "sanctification" to describe it. John Wesley in particular was adroit at reintroducing and utilizing the language of sanctification in Christian theology.

For Wesley, the confession of faith in conversion marks the beginning of a life, to borrow his brother Charles' words, "changed from glory unto glory,"[42] so that there is in the believer's life a work of God's Spirit continuing to effect "gradual growth toward perfection."[43] The Wesleys' hymns often set

---

41. I find useful the profound Westminster Confession stricture that the "chief end of human beings is to glorify God." Goldingay notes, however, that "humanity's 'chief and highest end is to work for God in the world." (Goldingay, *Israel's Gospel*, 110).

42. From the hymn "Love Divine, All Loves Excelling."

43. Schmiechen, *Saving Power*, 301. For a brief outline of the Wesleys' position, see ibid., 297–305.

out with an emphasis on the suffering of Christ "for us" ("died he for me, who caused his pain?") and as such are unpopular in some liberal circles of contemporary Christianity. For example, I know at least one Anglican cleric who refuses to sing "And Can It Be?" on the basis of its allegedly barbaric imagery. The death of Christ, through which by whatever mechanism the reconnection of humanity with divinity begins, is an ugly death, and yet as such it is the beginning of hope for the redemption of every ugly human death.

There is, I suspect, no need to stay bogged down in our Hebrews author's reference to atonement by remaining obsessed with any atonement notions of "paying the devil" or "satisfying the Father," but there is in a sentence such as Heb 2:17 a powerful image of Jesus' life invading the horrors of human existence and mortality and transforming these into the hope of something infinitely better. The invasion of human mortality and death by divine love is best responded to not with theological equations and explanations but, as the Wesley brothers saw clearly, with the language of doxology:

> Thee we would be always blessing,
> Serve Thee as thy hosts above,
> Pray, and praise thee, without ceasing,
> Glory in thy perfect love.[44]

I noted in my *Babylon's Cap*, the degree to which New Testament writers break into doxology at times when the mechanics of God's work of salvation "far exceed[s] the power of human telling."[45] Our author has not yet reached this point in this sermon, but the Wesleys' attempts to make sense of a theology of atonement such as that which undergirds this passage leaves them deeply enmeshed in praise.

Our author has referred in passing to the angels once more at Heb 2:16 in order to remind us that there is much that is beyond our ken in God's universe. At this point, the author is suggesting to us that humans (or perhaps more specifically humans of faith, or descendants of Abraham) are less august and perfected than we might like to think we are. Like a masterful composer, the preacher has now introduced a new motif—that of the priesthood of Christ (Heb 2:17)[46]—while plucking the chords of the earlier angelic imagery and returning to the series of contrasts between humanity, angels, and Christ that were interwoven in the prologue. This is a tightly constructed sermon that allows symbols to dance around in our consciousness over and again as we listen and accrue information. So now, suddenly,

---

44. "Love Divine, All Loves Excelling."
45. Godfrey, *Babylon's Cap*, 128–29.
46. This priesthood was, however, hinted at with the phrase "made purification" at Heb 1:3.

we have the notion of Christ as priest set before us. There will be thirty-five references to priesthood in Hebrews: this is no incidental reference but is instead the introduction of a central theme. The critical thing now though is that this priest has suffered, has been tempted, is *like us*. The significance of one who is paradoxically perfect (though only "superiority to the angels," not perfection, has so far been predicated of Christ; see Heb 1:4), yet who is like us and who enters into the holy of holies for us and for all, will now percolate throughout the sermon. The "for us" and the "like us" are now inseparably entwined in our preacher's thought.

3

Atonement: Heb 2:17–18

THE AUTHOR HAS INTRODUCED the idea of siblinghood in Christ in a way that Paul never does: "Therefore, brothers and sisters, holy partners in a heavenly calling" (Heb 3:1). For Paul, the term *adelphoi*, these days generally translated with the inclusive "brothers and sisters" or occasionally (and poorly, despite Luke 12:4 and John 15:13–14) as "friends," is the single most important expression to depict the new network of relationships available to those in Christ; Paul uses it particularly to apply emotional leverage to Philemon in his letter requesting the safe reception of the slave Onesimus.[1] But Paul never explains his use of the term or its theological significance. To our preacher though, it is profoundly theological terminology: Jesus had to be like us in every respect (Heb 2:17), and we are to see that this in some way impacts the way in which he makes atonement for his people. As yet, we are not told how. Hebrews 2:17 is the first full mention of atonement, the first airing of this motif.

That atonement is achieved by a death. This is the death of Jesus, obviously, but before we acknowledge this fact, it is important to know that for the ancient Hebrews atonement is always about covering over (Ps 32:1, 85:2) or purging something amiss. A study of the numerous Hebrew scriptural references to atonement would be gargantuan, though we might note that the sacrifice of blood is not always essential (Exod 30:12–13; even Isa 6:7). In the face of serious sin, however, blood sacrifice was necessary. This was the case even for "unwitting sin" (Lev 4:2), or the accidental sins referred to in some liturgical rites of confession ("we have sinned in ignorance . . ."). By deliberate or unwitting acts, the sanctuary—the place of encounter between God and humanity—is made impure, and God must vacate that place; humankind actually has the power to drive God from God's dwelling

---

1. For more details and development of this theme, see Aasgaard, "Brotherhood," and ibid., *Beloved*.

place.² In order for reparation and reconciliation to be made, the place that has been tainted must be purged and purified.³

Blood is the cleansing agent, and this is the case throughout the range of types of sin from an unwitting or accidental sin by an individual (Lev 4:3–12), through accidental communal sin (Lev 4:13–21), to what Milgrom refers to as "brazen and unrepented violation."⁴ Such brazen violation is purged at Yom Kippur (*kippur* means "purge"), when the high priest enters the sanctuary, where the Ark of the Lord dwells, and makes atonement through a rite that Milgrom equates with the imagery of Oscar Wilde's *Picture of Dorian Gray*. The sanctuary, like Wilde's portrait of Dorian, becomes besmirched with the ugliness of human wrongdoing, and only sacrificial blood cleanses (as with the sacrificial goat of Lev 16:15), transports, and transmits (to the scapegoat) that besmirchment from the holy of holies. The scapegoat is therefore driven from the holy place to an inaccessible wilderness from which it cannot return (Lev 16:20–22).

This interpretation covers the whole range of sin from deliberate to inadvertent sin, or sin that is effectively no more than sin by association. But Milgrom argues that there is no such thing as the latter:

> How would Israel's priests see our world today? Without hesitation they would spot the growing physical pollution of the earth: oil spills, acid rain, strip mining, ozone depletion, nuclear waste. They would be aghast at the unending moral pollution of the earth: the murder of thousands in Bosnia, Somalia, Sudan, East Timor, Armenia, Angola, Rwanda, Chechnya ... the millions dying of hunger or AIDS, while again, the free world, involuntary moral sinners, silently observe the carnage on TV and—flip the channel. How long, the priests would cry out, before God abandons God's earthly sanctuary?⁵

Milgrom was writing in the early 2000s. Only some aspects of this landscape have changed as I write a dozen or so years later. On the day I first wrote these words, my Internet feeds told me of a twenty-six-year-old woman, Meriam Yehya Ibrahim, who, at eight months pregnant, was awaiting execution in northern Sudan for the alleged sin of apostasy. Although she had been born into a Muslim-Christian family, she had been brought up Christian. What's more, Ibrahim was expecting her second child with her

---

2. Milgrom, *Leviticus*, 30–32. In my discussion of purification, I will be heavily indebted to this volume.

3. Ibid., 31.

4. Ibid.

5. Ibid., 33.

Christian husband, a man to whom the Islamic state authorities claimed she could not legally be married, so she was accused of "adultery" as well. She was eventually released in August 2014. The xenophobia, religious bigotry, and persecution of our world is a universal state of sin and concomitant suffering, which I participate in each day as I silently flip the TV channel.

As I first wrote these words, the world continued to wonder how to find and rescue nearly 300 schoolgirls who were snatched from their school in the town of Chibok in Nigeria's Borno State by Boko Haram. Their plight was ignored by the world for some three weeks after the original kidnapping, and it sadly slipped from media attention thereafter. So too, if slightly less quickly, did the viral hashtag #BringBackOurGirls. Despite international efforts, all except one victim[6] remain unaccounted for as I review these words two years after the girls disappeared, and their whereabouts or wellbeing are still unknown.[7] It is worth noting too, while focusing on the plight of the Chibok girls, that Amnesty International's 2015 reports state, "At least 2,000 women and girls have been abducted by Boko Haram since the start of 2014 and many have been forced into sexual slavery and trained to fight."[8] My participation in a world whose media by and large ignore or soon forget the plight of 2,000 Nigerian schoolgirls is sin.

As I first wrote these words, Christians were being murdered for their faith in the regions of Kenya bordering Somalia as well as in northeastern Nigeria (adherents of Indigenous religious practices also risk their lives in this region). As I review my words, the theaters of conflict are only slightly different from those addressed by Milgrom: Somalia, Sudan, Syria, Ukraine, West Papua, Egypt, Iraq, Afghanistan, East Ukraine, Azerbaijan, and Nagorno-Karabakh, to name just a few.

All humanity participates in the breadth and width of the nexus of human sin, giving weight to Paul's *cri de cœur* "all have sinned" and Anselm's "you do not know how great a thing sin is."[9] Those who see individualism writ large in either a doctrine of sin or a doctrine of redemption miss the point of being collectively enmeshed in the human family. Ched Myers

---

6. One girl, Amina Nkek, has been (at time of writing) recently rescued by vigilantes. See Ross, "Chibok Girls."

7. Even as I wrote the final revision of these words, Malala Yousafzai released a statement: "I write this letter with a heavy heart, knowing you have endured another year separated from your daughters," she wrote. "I think of you every day since we first met two years ago—and join millions of people around the world in praying for the safety and swift return of your girls" (O'Connor, "Malala Doesn't Want"). See also Handcock, "Honoring Malala"; and Yousafzai and Lamb, *I Am Malala*.

8. Amnesty International, "Abducted Women."

9. Anselm, *Cur Deus Homo*, bk. 1, ch. 21.

notes, "one of our unconscious etic assumptions is our post-Enlightenment preoccupation with the individual."[10] It is an "etic assumption"[11] we are unlikely fully to set aside, but it is one we must try to overcome in reading the biblical text. At this point, we should probably note that this marks a degree of difference from the evangelical and pentecostal hermeneutic that has so dominated not just North American and especially US Christianity, but also internationally. In particular, pentecostal hermeneutics begin with the assumption that the individual is the primary location and focus of the relationship between God and humanity: "In North America, 'the popular belief was that the individual was the basic religious unit.'"[12]

According to the Code of Leviticus (Lev 4:1—5:13), if the high priest sinned, even unwittingly, the entire community incurred guilt, and expiation had to be made, the damage to the relationship between humans and their God repaired, and the place of God's dwelling purged if God was to continue to dwell there. Even ignorance of sin was no pardon (Lev 4:13): the damage to the relationship between God and God's people must be repaired. According to our Hebrews author though, the High Priest Jesus does not sin, and so the rules for restoring the relationship of humanity to God through cleansing, purging blood, and the expelled scapegoat are all rewritten.

Again though, in the eyes of many New Testament writers, sin summarizes the human state: "all have sinned, and fall short" (Rom 3:23). Perhaps this is another indication of the influence of Paul on our author, or perhaps it became a universal belief amongst the early Christians. Either way, this universality of sin is the bedrock on which the Hebrews preacher bases her understanding of the work of Christ. It is not altogether a popular worldview in the twenty-first century, when personal improvement has become a multibillion dollar industry, a gospel in its own right, and when notions of inescapable culpability for evil are seen as oppressive and destructive to the human psyche.

The person and work of Christ is an entanglement of priest, temple, blood, and sacrificial victims, so that "thou on earth both priest and victim" only begins to hint at the complexity of the work achieved in the Christ event. As an Anglican priest, I have for most of the last thirty years presided at the Eucharist a few times a week and at least twice on most Sundays. As part of that liturgy we include, as do many of the liturgical traditions, a rite of shared or "common" confession, as alluded to above. Words akin to

---

10. Myers, *Binding*, 47.

11. Loosely, a term describing assumptions made on the basis of unquestioned social and cultural conditioning when analyzing a culture from the perspective of an outside observer.

12. Marsden, *Understanding Fundamentalism*, 17.

"we have sinned in weakness, we have sinned in ignorance, we have sinned through our own deliberate fault" are intoned before we hear the presiding priest (the presbyter, not the *hiereus*-priest—that is, a sacramental or ritual priest that Hebrews identifies Christ as) proclaim God's words of forgiveness (pared down to minimal loquacity in one of the New Zealand Anglican versions as "God forgives you. Be at peace"[13]). The theology of this exchange between people and presbyter, or indeed between people and God, is quite different from that of the private "auricular confession" often associated with the Roman Catholic tradition (but present in others too), in which the confessing Christian admits to individual sins and hears personalized absolution and penitential advice. In the collective congregational confession, we acknowledge our corporate sin: "*we* have sinned." I often preside at or attend more than one Eucharist in a day, yet I still participate in this rite. I've barely had time for a passing naughty thought, let alone any deliberate sin between, for example, an 8:00 a.m. and a 10:00 a.m. Eucharist! Yet by being alive, I am participating in the complex web of human sin and am effectively complicit in economic exploitation and environmental destruction. My clothes are made, often, in cheap and exploitative sweat shops in the global south. The car with which I drive to church is polluting God's atmosphere. The electricity pouring through the meters of a cathedral in just two one- or one-and-a-half-hour liturgies could heat a village in the global south for a week. *We* have sinned. Martin Luther King has famously challenged us with the chilling words, "We will have to repent in this generation not merely for the hateful words and actions of the bad people but for the appalling silence of the good people."[14] *We* have sinned. This universalizes sin and guilt, and it is essential to understand this truth if we are to understand Hebrews.

The thought of Jürgen Moltmann can push the meaning of common confession still further. In *God in Creation*, Moltmann reclaims the role of human beings as priests of creation entering the sacred space of God to voice the "praise of all created things before God."[15] This role is explored in the psalms when "thanks are offered for the sun and the light, for the heavens and the fertility of the earth."[16] This notion can be wedded with the Petrine author's[17] famous but more restricted dictum, "you [believers]

---

13. *New Zealand Prayer Book / He Karakia Mihinare o Aotearoa*, 460.
14. King, "Letter from a Birmingham Jail."
15. Moltmann, *God in Creation*, 71.
16. Ibid.
17. I make no claim to knowledge of the identity of the author, though while using the term "Petrine author" I note respectfully I. Howard Marshall's acerbic comments regarding the trends in biblical scholarship of entering authorship debates with presuppositions that the apostles were incapable of writing weighty documents, or "the current

are a chosen race, a royal priesthood, a holy nation, God's own people, in order that you may proclaim the mighty acts of him who called you out of darkness into his marvelous light" (1 Pet 2:9). The Petrine author saw our participation in the priesthood of Christ—the central theme of our Hebrews text—in terms similar to those by which Paul saw his correspondents as "grafted on" (Rom 11:17) to Christ. The author of Colossians, in seeing Christ as "mediator" between God and creation (Col 1:15–20), is saying something along the same lines: Christ participates in the sacred spaces between God and creation, the spaces in which, Paul tells us, the glory of God has subsequently been pushed aside, banished in favor of an animal image (Rom 1:23, Ps 106:20). Our author likewise emphasizes the "supersession" of the role of the previous Hebrew community by the new Hebrew community of Christ-followers, as we have seen (Heb 1:1). We, the new Hebrews, are entering into temple relationship with God through the Christ event, even if, post-Holocaust, we are cautious about supersessionism.

The focus on the active participants in the priestly role narrows from an expectation that all humanity is the priesthood of creation, as seen by Moltmann in his reading of the creation psalms, to a New Testament suggestion that those grafted onto Christ by their participation in the rites of intercession and reconciliation undertake these rites not only on behalf of "dumb" creation, but also the large proportion of humanity who are not willing or able to sing praise or make intercession to God. This is not to imply that these are an elect "saved" (while all others are damned, condemned to a fiery hell), but only that those grafted onto Christ are merely a chosen priesthood (1 Pet 2:9) called to action "on behalf of" humanity and creation.

In the sacramental-liturgical traditions, the presiding priest at the liturgy stands at the communion table or altar not in order to "re-sacrifice" Christ, but to "re-present," in all the nuances of that word, the sacrifice that has been made by Christ. The nuances of "re-presentation" are complex and have been since before the beginning of Christian outreach, as Christians and, to a lesser extent, their Jewish neighbors dealt with a clash of two understandings of time: Hebrew and Greek. To the Hebrew mind, cultic events, such as the Passover rites Jesus undertook with his disciples the night before he died, made past events present once again in the recitations and reconstructions of rites and liturgies. In particular, the Jewish *haggadah*, or the telling of the Exodus events in accordance with Exod 13:8, was a ritual drama that made present once more the historical, contemporary, and future-eschatological aspects of the Hebrews' release from slavery in Egypt. Therefore, for the early Christians, these rites made present all aspects of the

---

tendency to see pseudonymity at work wherever possible"! See Marshall, *1 Peter*, 21.

Jesus event for those who gathered to break bread and share wine in obedience to Jesus' command. Thus, 1 Cor 11:23–26 becomes a new Exod 13:8.

Australian and New Zealand readers will recollect the powerful sense of World War I sacrifices and the "birth" of their respective nations in the Gallipoli remembrances of Anzac Day. British readers will still recall and make present the powerful remembrances of Armistice Day, while US citizens experience a potent sense of history-made-present on the anniversary of September 11, 2001.[18] Each nation has powerful historical determinants. The hidden nations do too: "National Sorry Day" is an increasingly authoritative moment for the Indigenous people of Australia, while the nationally recognized Waitangi Day holds resonances for Māori that are very different and far greater than for non-Māori (pākehā), and I suspect Martin Luther King's birthday has resonances for African American citizens far deeper than for most non-blacks.

In each of these cases, and in the case perhaps of all national days of pride and remembrance, the designated day "re-collects" and "re-presents" and "re-members" events of enormous significance so that the verbs "recollect," "represent," and "remember" fail to do justice to the true significance of making these events present once more. It is at this point that the Greek notion of *anamnesis* became valuable to the early Christians and equally important to our present understanding of temple representation. For Plato and for Socrates before him, *anamnesis* was the imprint on a soul of the shadowy, inchoate memory of the Ideal from which all lives and all time are separated. This falls far short of the Hebrew representation of past events in rite and ritual (my meager understanding of Australian Indigenous lore is that traditional rites and storytelling also make past events dynamically present—a notion colonizers ignored as we trampled over sacred sites and abolished ancient rituals), but the word *anamnesis* provides a useful tool with which to overcome inadequate understandings of the depth and power of Christian ritual.

If we can dwell for a moment longer on the *anamnesis* implicit in the eucharistic rites of Christianity, this points to the vast difference between "low" and "high" attitudes to these rites: if "remembering" is just the acknowledgment of a past event, as I might remember my tenth birthday,

---

18. American friends have suggested to me that the historical bases of Independence Day are lost to many if not most of those who engage in the celebrations and that there are, for example, few if any re-enactments of the signing of the Declaration of Independence on July 4, 1776. Prior to 9/11, it is probable that the remembrance of the bombing of Pearl Harbor was a more poignant memory for US citizens. My thanks go primarily to Dr. Gerald Morris of First United Methodist Church of Wausau, Wisconsin, for these observations.

then no weight need be given to that act of remembrance. If, by contrast, it bears all the weight of making present once more past events, as when Arabs re-member the Crusades or, more trivially but still poignantly, New Zealanders re-member the Welsh try against the All Blacks in the so-called "match of the century"[19] of 1905, all the passion and impact of the earlier event is made present once again. Etymologically, the words I am skirting around attempt to suggest that re-collection, re-membrance, and re-presentation all bear far more weight than mere reminiscence and that the events of the Exodus as well as the life, teaching, suffering, death, resurrection, and future coming (the last a "pre-membrance," if you like) of Jesus are indeed made present in liturgy.

Implicit in that, lest again it appear that we are drifting far from the temples of Judaism, is the knowledge that these buildings likewise made present the events of salvation history and of God's dealings with God's people. The temples were an enactment in stone of the covenant relationships God made possible between God and God's creatures.[20] If the Sinai covenant looms large in Judeo-Christian understanding, it should be remembered that it was not the sole covenant: Gen 6:18 prophesizes the making of the Noahic covenant established at Gen 9:9–17. The Mosaic covenant is provisionally aired at Exod 19:5, though it takes physical form only at Exod 24:7. Deuteronomy 29 narrates the establishment of the Mosaic covenant in an original and updated form (Deut 29:1—30:20), solemnly witnessed (Deut 30:19). Although the word *berît* is not used in 2 Sam 7, God nevertheless clearly establishes a dynastic covenant with David and his descendants[21] that is later summarized at 1 Chron 17:11–14 and 2 Chron 6:16. The author's and redactors' avoidance of a covenantal framework may reflect their desire to parallel Davidic theology with covenant theology.[22]

Hosea writes of a future eschatological covenant (Hos 2:18)[23] but also of the broken covenant represented in his own tortured marriage with the adulterous Gomer (Hos 1:3). At Hos 8:1, the poetic prophet is speaking in generalized terms of a "vulture-like bird" (not necessarily an eagle, though

---

19. So called a little prematurely, given that the century was less than half a decade old!

20. I am grateful to my wife, Anne van Gend, for highlighting this imagery for me and for drawing attention to Milgrom's remarkable analysis. Her PhD dissertation, "Speaking of Mysteries," deals with the issues of atonement in far greater depth than is possible here.

21. This is not, in salvation history terms, the first covenant, which is that made with Noah. See Dell, "Covenant and Creation," 111, cited in van Gend, "Speaking," 198n4.

22. See Birch, "Samuel," 1254.

23. Anderson and Freedman, *Hosea*, 281.

the Hebrew is uncertain) that will hover over "the house of the Lord." This depiction is of the temple, but the temple is in turn representative of the whole land and people of Israel, its God-given rites and practices, and even indeed of creation.[24] This correlation of temple with the wider role and experience of Israel was common usage at the time of Hosea.[25] Isaiah speaks of a broken covenant (Isa 24:5) but universalizes the perpetration of the breakage once more to all humanity[26] (providing no clues as to what apocalyptic events he was initially describing[27]), visualizing a scene like that of Jer 24:4–13 and elsewhere to present an image redolent of Num 35:33–34. This is an image of desecration and desolation for which atonement can be made only by the perpetrator:

> You shall not pollute the land in which you live; for blood pollutes the land, and no expiation can be made for the land, for the blood that is shed in it, except by the blood of the one who shed it. You shall not defile the land in which you live, in which I also dwell; for I the LORD dwell among the Israelites.

In the thought of our author, Christ himself steps into the perpetrator's role and "fully participates in their somatic condition and emotional sensibilities"[28] in terms of Numbers, despite his sinlessness.[29]

To the Hebrew mind, time as a chronological sequence was unimportant: Israel "found the idea of time without a particular event quite inconceivable; all that she knew was time as containing events."[30] In this exploration, we are investigating the meaning of atonement and the temple rites rather than the Last Supper *haggadah* itself, but the two are indivisible, and the understanding of time that shaped Jewish understanding of temple worship after the destruction of the two great temples infiltrates

---

24. "The temple represented creation" (Barker, "Great High Priest," 7). Goldingay is more circumspect: "We may assume that the temple is designed to be beautiful, but also to be symbolic, though we can only guess the symbolism" (Goldingay, *Israel's Gospel*, 567).

25. Wolff, *Hosea*, 137.

26. Wildberger, *Isaiah 13–27*, 451.

27. Ibid., 460–63.

28. Johnson, *Hebrews*, 102.

29. F. F. Bruce nevertheless mistreats the dignity and solemnity of the temple when he writes, "A High Priest who has actually, and not merely in symbolism, removed his people's sins, and therewith the barrier which their sins erected between themselves and God, is a High Priest worth having" (Bruce, *Hebrews*, 88). There is no argument that Christ "is a High Priest worth having," but the insertion of "merely" into the profundity of temple theology misconstrues the power of symbol.

30. von Rad, *Old Testament Theology*, 2:100.

Christian liturgical and theological reflection to an extraordinary degree.[31] Jesus steps timelessly into the "should-be" holiest places of the temple and the creation the temple signifies, and so steps into the "should-be" holiest places of history. Jesus steps into the places that God must otherwise vacate and, by cleansing them with blood, makes creation and history a place God can inhabit once again.

Our author, therefore, at Heb 2:17 reminds us that Jesus entered into the physical temple while himself becoming a spiritual temple where sin is purged and God is given space to dwell with humans once again. She reminds us, as participants in divine liturgy, that we are engaging in the "act of taking part in the solemn corporate worship of God by the 'priestly' society of Christians."[32] This is not a place for enumeration of individual sins, but for the universalization of sin that Isaiah has named at Isa 24:5 and that Paul sternly acknowledges at Rom 3:23 (but also Rom 1:18–32, which points the finger firmly at "us" rather than "them," and even at Rom 7:14–20). Former British Prime Minister Margaret Thatcher is reputed to have declared, "There is no such thing as society" as she sought to shift responsibility for welfare from the state to the individual in an act of ideological Darwinianism writ large. By contrast, I prefer the African proverbial statement *umuntu ngumntu ngabanye abantu*, or "a person is a person through other persons."[33] The biblical authors in general also contradict Thatcher's etic assumptions, tending to suggest there is no such thing as the individual. Certainly, as Milgrom sees clearly, there is no place here for an individualistic reading of "sin." Writing about temple rites concerning genital discharge, Milgrom observes

> [T]he contracted impurity, be it ever so slight at the outset, will grow in force until it has the power to pollute the sanctuary from afar ([Heb] 5:1–11). Let electromagnetism serve as an illustrative analogy. The minus charge of impurity is attracted to the plus charge of the sanctuary, and if the former builds up enough force to spark the gap, then, lightning-like, it will strike the sanctuary.[34]

---

31. Not only Christian liturgical and theological reflection: Rabbi Sacks notes that the practice of hospitality, in Judaism, "compensated for the loss of the temple and its rites" (Sacks, *Fractured World*, 49).

32. Dix, *Shape of the Liturgy*, 1.

33. Sparks and Tutu, *Tutu*, 233. As this is a phonetic rendition of the Zulu, there are variant spellings in publication and on the Internet. An alternative construction is given on ibid., 254, 256.

34. Milgrom, *Leviticus*, 42.

There is no individual culpability implied, simply a universality of the impact of genital and thus a sort of cosmic-electrical arcing discharge.

In his science fiction novel *Cat's Cradle*, Kurt Vonnegut creates a tale of (*inter alia*) a deadly chemical weapon of mass destruction called "ice-nine." This is a form of water whose properties differ from standard water in that it is solid at room temperature and will instantly alter the characteristics and freezing point of any water with which it comes into contact. As water is interconnected across the globe, contact between ice-nine and any of the world's waterways would immediately destroy our planet and all life as we know it. Towards the end of the novel, the chemical is released into earth's waterways: "There was a sound like that of a gentle closing of a portal as big as the sky, the great door of heaven being closed softly. It was a grand AH-WOOM."[35] The world ends, as T. S. Eliot prophesied, not with a bang but a whimper,[36] but it ends with the central religious figure Bokonon writing of making a suicidal ice-statue of himself, "lying on my back, grinning horribly, and thumbing my nose at You Know Who."[37] No matter what Vonnegut's complex intentions may have been (and his critiques of bad religion and bad humanity are deeply insightful), this is a powerful image of humanity expelling divinity from the sanctuary of existence.

Ice-nine could serve as an extreme illustration not only of the futility of nuclear weapons, but also (and not unrelatedly) of the arcing power of uncleanliness and sin as understood by both the Levitical code and also by the author of Hebrews. Perhaps we might also speak of the Christ event as earthing an arc of human-generated sin that destroys our chances for survival in the temple-place where God longs to dwell, transmitting that destructive energy through Christ's selfhood and making it possible for God and humanity to coexist in that temple-place once more. It is this arcing power that the authors of the hymn "Blest Are the Pure in Heart" were striving to capture in their concluding lines: "Give us a pure and lowly heart, / A temple meet for Thee."[38]

---

35. Vonnegut, *Cat's Cradle*, 163.
36. T. S. Eliot, "The Hollow Men," line 98, in Eliot, *Collected Poems*, 82.
37. Vonnegut, *Cat's Cradle*, 179.
38. From the hymn "Blest Are the Pure in Heart," by John Keble (1792–1866).

4

A Priest Like Us and For Us: Heb 3:1–19

JESUS HAS, ACCORDING TO our preacher, entered into our human state of mortality, even of horrendous suffering, and is able to aid his kith and kin—us—through the journey. But this is only identification *with* our experience, and as such, while comforting, is not the whole story of the priesthood of Christ. An incarnation by which our Savior is merely thrown into the quicksand to die alongside us is not altogether helpful, as the Jesus saying at Luke 6:39 suggests: "Can a blind person guide a blind person? Will not both fall into a pit?" In my brief service as a firefighter, we were taught over and again that assessing risk and forming an exit strategy were essential first steps in any rescue or recovery operation. It is of no use for a firefighter to race headlong into a building only to become a liability, because getting injured or killed only adds to the complexities of the rescue operation. The atonement and priesthood aspect of Jesus' death will become more and more central to the Hebrews sermon, not merely as an entrance into the place of destruction (human existence) but also as an exit strategy from that place. At this first mention, there is as yet only the sense that Jesus has gone ahead of us into the dying experience and will help us through the curtain.

The author returns to the technique of "like this, but so much more" in establishing a comparison between Jesus and Moses. This part of the sermon is at first glance almost anticlimactic; after portraying the man Jesus in the company of angels (Heb 1:5–13) and even as an emanation from Godself (Heb 1:1–4), Moses seems something of a retreat from celestial heights of Sonship (Heb 1:3). Yet we need to be careful not to superimpose a contemporary Christian attitude—one that borders on nonchalance towards Moses—onto a first-century audience. It is worth reminding ourselves of the reverence with which Moses is held in the traditions of our Abrahamic cousins, Muslims, to whom Moses is deeply revered as a prophet and forerunner of Mohammed. Despite the ugly scars of global politics and militarism, Christians are, according to Qur'an, "nearest in affection"[1] to Muslim believers, and reverence and respect towards the first and shared great prophet of the three Abrahamic faiths, which might almost be termed a duty of care amongst Christians today, might go at least some way toward opening the ever-necessary dialogue that alone will help us coexist on God's earth.

To our author and to the audience of our sermon, Moses was enormously significant not only as a model of fidelity to his call (Heb 3:2), but also in his "astonishing intimacy with God."[2] The issue of fidelity to a call is of course of paramount importance to this letter, so the reference here serves not only to make a christological point, but also to remind the listeners of the pastoral "parenetic" or exhortative thrust of the sermon: stay faithful (Heb 2:1) as Moses was (mainly: Deut 32:51!) faithful, just as Jesus was *perfectly* faithful. Moses' task was no easy one to emulate. Only a few decades before our author was preaching, Moses is referred to as *logos* and suppliant (intercessor),[3] as high priest,[4] and as "kingly"[5] in the writings of Philo. Above all, in Philo's works Moses even reaches the celestial heights of divinity:

> What more shall I say? Has he not also enjoyed an even greater communion with the Father and Creator of the universe, being thought unworthy of being called by the same appellation? For he also was called the god and king of the whole nation, and he is said to have entered into the darkness where God was; that is to say, into the invisible, and shapeless, and incorporeal world, the essence, which is the model of all existing things, where he beheld things invisible to mortal nature; for, having brought himself and his own life into the middle, as an excellently wrought picture, he established himself as a most beautiful and Godlike work, to be a model for all those who were inclined to imitate him.[6]

---

1. Qur'an 5:82. See also Brown, *Nearest*.

2. Johnson, *Hebrews*, 108.

3. "[S]uppliant to the immortal God on behalf of the mortal race" (Philo, *Heir* 42.205–206). All references to Philo's works are taken from Kirby, "Philo of Alexandria."

4. Philo, *Life of Moses* 1.60.334.

5. "[S]ome persons say, and not without some reason and propriety, that this is the only way by which cities can be expected to advance in improvement, if either the kings cultivate philosophy, or if philosophers exercise the kingly power. But Moses will be seen not only to have displayed all these powers—I mean the genius of the philosopher and of the king—in an extraordinary degree at the same time, but three other powers likewise, one of which is conversant about legislation, the second about the way of discharging the duties of high priest, and the last about the prophetic office" (ibid., 2.1.2).

6. Ibid., 1.28.158.

Moses is a revered figure in the ancient Jewish people's consciousness, and this Hebrews reference to him is no anti-climax after the opening doxological movements of the sermon. Yet our preacher is adamant that in Jesus the new Hebrews participate in a "like Moses, but so much more" equation. All that Moses was, Jesus is, and more.

These "greater than" equations do not help the progress of twenty-first-century interfaith dialogue, hardly a first-century concern, but are equations that should remain within the discourse of, and encourage tenacity in, the daily faith-life of the specifically Christian community. The main theme now established is simply, "like Moses, but immeasurably more so." This incalculable "greater than" is above all based on a reference made by our author in the opening gambit of the sermon: Moses may have conversed with God and looked cautiously on the divine glory (Exod 33:18), but Jesus *is* that glory and is radiance of, exact representation of, and bearer of God's glory and Word (Heb 1:3).[7] Jesus the Christ[8] is inseparable from that Word.[9]

Since Heb 3:2, the author has been playing with the notion of a house. Moses was faithful in "all God's house" (Heb 3:2, see Num 12:7), the builder of a house is more honorable than the house itself (Heb 3:3), God is the builder (Heb 3:4), Moses was a servant in the house (Heb 3:5), and Christ is the son in and ruler over[10] the house (Heb 3:6), but unexpectedly, at Heb 3:6b, *we* are the house (in which Christ is son and God is builder). While there is a sense in which "household"[11] can be extrapolated from the *oikos* that is repeated here,[12] it may be more helpful to picture the community of faith as a human building in which God chooses to dwell in a concept more akin to 1 Cor 6:19. In order to avoid an individualistic reading of the text, we should see the members (Paul's word from 1 Cor 12:12) of the faith community as a network of rooms forming the building built by God—a network in which Christ dwells (Heb 3:3). Having established that, we must then hear that solemn conditional, "*we* are his house if *we* hold firm" (Heb 3:6), and indeed, "we are his house *if* we hold firm."

The image of a house is an image of an edifice with very clear demarcations between that which is "in" and that which is "out," as well as a very clear sense that there is a possibility of transition from "in" to "out," since that "in"

---

7. See Johnson, *Hebrews*, 70.
8. Heb 3:6 is the first naming of Jesus (3:1) as "Christ."
9. Johnson, *Hebrews*, 110.
10. Bruce, *Hebrews*, 93.
11. Cf. Eph 2:19.
12. Ellingworth, *Commentary*, 210.

status "is conditional on fidelity to their calling."[13] My previous mention of Abrahamic faiths was neither random nor unrelated to our text. We live in a different world than that of the "new Hebrews" who were the first audience of the sermon, and while the notion of "global village" is something of a cliché, it does describe some aspects of our differences compared to the first-century Christians' world with a degree of accuracy. While the first-century Christians rubbed shoulders uneasily with Jews and the varied rites of Roman antiquity, they were not as aware as we are of the vast array of human cultures and the almost equally diverse forms of religious experience humanity embraces. Islam, the third great Abrahamic faith, came along several centuries after the new Hebrews heard this sermon. Even so, the relationship between our hearers and their Jewish neighbors was prickly at best, and, as indicated earlier in these reflections, slid slowly downhill until the obscenities of the Third Reich. There was little need or ability to reflect creatively on the coexistence of the Abrahamic religions, let alone people of unrelated faiths. We cannot afford to be insular or supremacist: Goldingay, referring to the Genesis creation narratives, sagely observes, "this account of God's creation of humanity and God's words of blessing remind the chosen people(s) that God's choice of them is subordinate to a commitment to humankind as a whole."[14]

But as our author segues into a new admonition to perseverance, we need to ask what fidelity to our faith means in today's very different culture. To the first-century Christian addressed by the sermon, adherence to Christ meant continued profession of the Lordship of Christ (1 Cor 12:3) and a growing sense of otherness from either the synagogue rites of post-temple Judaism or, most definitely, from the Caesar-worshiping that was from time to time stipulated by Roman authorities. Christians today have to tread the minefield of discerning what these calls to tenacity look like in a global community.

In the Central African Republic, where the labels "Christian" and "Muslim" designate warring militia just as "Catholic" and "Protestant" have designated warring militia in Northern Ireland (and "Sunni" and "Shiite" likewise designate warring wings of Islam); or in the northeastern border regions of Kenya, where the predominately Christian nation rubs uneasy shoulders with Muslim Somalia; or in Egypt and indeed throughout northern Africa and the Middle East, where the great Abrahamic faiths coexist in varying degrees of disharmony, fidelity to a faith may look very different to fidelity to a faith in a Religious Studies seminar at a Western university

13. Johnson, *Hebrews*, 111.
14. Goldingay, *Israel's Gospel*, 101.

campus. In the ivory towers of intellectual dialogue, proponents of the three great conversational stances of "exclusivist," "inclusivist," and "pluralist"[15] Christianity can assess the merits or otherwise of their respective positions in relative comfort as they negotiate key concepts.

Under the threat of either annihilation or simple disintegration, the early Christians had no such luxury. On the other hand, they were not in a position of social power (as Paul famously observes at 1 Cor 1:26). Yet in the Central African Republic or northeast Kenya today, as Muslims and Christians threaten to kill each other, it is unlikely that abstract notions of the generous inclusivity of God[16] will gain traction. Indeed, "exclusivism" of the vilest kind is exercised under the power of a gun, machete, or panga.[17] Each of these weapons represents a shift from the powerlessness of the first-century Christians to at least a limited and immediate, dangerous, and destructive alliance with power. In such a context, "power"—the power Lord Acton warned against—is dangerously demonic. Cycles of this sort of exclusivist evil can only be broken when swords are turned into plowshares (Isa 2:4) and claims to possession of God's authority are set aside. In such a context, interfaith dialogue becomes a crucial element of brokering peace and reconciliation, which is at least one reason why the non-confessional disciplines of Religious Studies should continue to be an important part of the global north's university curricula.

Nevertheless, veiled suggestions such as those made by John Hick, Paul Knitter, or Raimon Panikkar-Alemany[18] that rubbing shoulders between religious traditions should lead to the establishment of an *ur*-religion incorporating the best of all religious perspectives would have appeared to our author as a desertion of the faith her sermon was exhorting hearers to cling to. When members of a religious dialogue lay down their central symbols of faith and ask each other to do likewise—the position presumably envisaged in John Lennon's much-loved but surprisingly vacuous "imagine . . . no religion too"—meaningful dialogue can be lost in the attempt to speak from a position that is not truly confessional. The heart of our author's sermon, "be faithful . . . as Moses . . . as Jesus," is lost when that idea is advanced.

To be honest, my own "inclusivist" position that all humanity, not just "confessing humanity," is redeemed in the Christ event is equally unlikely to be attractive when representatives of any religions are raping[19] and pillaging

---

15. The labels originate with Race, *Religious Pluralism*, 1–105.
16. "Jesus establishes a social practise of inclusivity" (Myers, *Binding*, 117).
17. An African machete.
18. Also known as Raimundo Panikkar.
19. I use the word advisedly, not only with indication to the probable forced

adherents of other religions and cultures. I do, however, see some hints of this position emerging in some more generous New Testament texts—texts that emerge from environments where the swords have been, if not turned into plowshares, at least laid down, and Christ has been acknowledged as Savior of the world rather than of the few.[20] The difference is that I can hold this position while standing in an extant and identifiable confessional place, respecting and learning from the faith-perspectives of those who adhere to other beliefs across the range of edifying human thought. My picture of what it is to "hold firm the confidence and the pride that belong to hope" (Heb 3:6) away from the coal faces of inter-religious warfare will look very different from the view from places where believers are being executed for their faith.

Michael Barnes has expressed the theological conundrum well:

> Pluralist theologians look first at the world of many religions and only then at the position of Christianity. They are less concerned with Christian mission than with asking what Christians have to learn from the other. This, of course, is highly complex, not to say emotive, area. But, in looking at the issues raised by the pluralist model it should be emphasized that there is room for a good deal of nuance, that pluralists have important insights to offer and that, however much they may seem to challenge the traditional version of Christian theology, they cannot be rejected out of hand.[21]

A pluralist position that looks for common ground between religions, believing that all religions in differing ways lead to a single truth, is not the missiological and pastoral worldview of our author. There is immeasurable value in dialogue with, and mutual learning from, other religious practitioners, but any attempt to gloss over profound differences in worldviews is not helpful to that dialogue. Moreover, any attempt to syncretize religious worldviews is far removed from the perspective of our author. In all this, of course, we should remember that our texts focus on a Master and a Teacher whose radical practice, while pointing out hypocrisy and exploitation with outrage (John 2:13–16 and its synoptic parallels), exercised a pattern of compassionate embrace and welcome (Luke 15:20). Thus, we must remember that "holding on" to Jesus will include holding on to his practice of compassionate welcome to both the neighbor and the guest.

---

marriages of the Nigerian kidnapped schoolgirls, but also with reference to the atrocities experienced by Western aid worker Kayla Mueller and others like her.

20. See Godfrey, "Run," 360–95.
21. Barnes, *Christian Identity*, 67.

So, to recapitulate, the solemn pronouncement of a conditional element in our relationship to Jesus at Heb 3:6, "we are his house, if we hold," has brought the author back to the theme of perseverance. Some ancient manuscripts added the words "to the end," borrowed from Heb 3:14. While this was a interpolation made by subsequent scribes reading Heb 3:14 into this text, it emphasizes the degree to which this is an intensely urgent entreaty. Indeed, this is a plea emphasizing the preacher's most desperate purpose in writing her sermon: remain faithful to your collective calling. It is almost safe to say that, in New Testament texts, the word "call" will always have a double meaning: "to name" and "to beckon" (appearing sixty-four times in writings attributed to Paul for a start, especially 1 Cor 1:1 and 1 Cor 1:26). In responding to the beckoning of Christ, we are "named" as Christians as being "in Christ," as kin of Christ, and as caught up into his High Priestly actions as dwellers in his house. By responding to the call, we are renamed: the nicknaming of followers of Jesus acknowledged by Luke at Acts 11:26 was fortuitous, if not providential, and the Christ-following community was given a distinctive identity.[22]

So the preacher returns to a series of Hebrew Scriptural texts (albeit in the Greek) to anchor her case in the authority of the Scriptures of the past. The Holy Spirit is at Heb 3:7 identified as the voice that speaks through the Scriptures (see also Heb 10:15). In the Christian community, we are saying something similar when we speak of Scriptures as the "living Word" and "God-breathed" (2 Tim 3:16). The claim is not unique to our author by any means, and this assertion reflects the thinking of much of the early Christian community. But what does this usage mean? It would not be appropriate to garner the entire range of Hebrew scriptural references to the *ruach* of God here, but while this could not yet be described in fully-fledged Trinitarian terms as the "third person" of a triune God, it is nevertheless an emanation from and an action of God that bears all the weight of God's activity in human and even cosmic history. This is the emanation and empowerment from God that has inflamed the Hebrew Scriptures and the great human voices whose words and actions they narrate. The author of the Fourth Gospel interrelates the command of God, the *logos*, with the incarnate Jesus, and in turn with the coming Paraclete-Comforter. Our author interweaves the voice of the Holy Spirit with the command of God.

Our author's reference is to Ps 95:7–11, and the "today" of the psalmist becomes the "today" of the preacher's writing, the "today" of the audience's

---

22. In two-way radio and more recently in Internet parlance, this is sometimes called a "handle," which is itself a useful metaphor for this two-way relationship of identification and control.

hearing, and even the "today," we might add, of our reading of the text. Thus, the later solemn pronouncement of Heb 13:8 is not a throwaway phrase:

> This "today" should probably above all be understood as the hour of the word and work of Yahweh pressing the hearers hard. Now—in this *hic et nunc*—no one can exempt oneself from the decisiveness of the situation described by the voice of Yahweh. Now—under God's sharp address that compresses all of time—hardening and self-exclusion have immeasurable consequences such as can be indicated only from a distance by means of judgment in the wilderness. True Israel hears and comes to meet its God with thanksgiving and praise.[23]

The psalm makes solemn declaration of the ongoing need for cultic or liturgical recognition of God (Ps 95:6), and an echo of that preceding verse would not have been far from our author's mind as she demanded that the new Hebrews learn from their forebears and not slack off in their relationship of service and devotion to the God who has called them.

Psalm 95 is one of the great festive psalms, recalling and making present in liturgy the memory that God's people have a checkered history of right and wrong relationship with God. In our author's thought, the psalm serves to remind the new Hebrews that they do not stand in cozy or complacent relationship with an acquiescent coconspirator, but rather in awe-filled relationship to a God who draws lines in the behavioral and devotional sand. "Like an ultimatum the prophetic speech warns against the depths of exclusion in hardening" notes Kraus,[24] and while the primary warning is against sclerosis of the human heart caused by a lack of disciplined focus on God in cultic and liturgical observance, it would be hard to read the New Testament message without an awareness that such focus should also be reconstructed in compassionate action towards neighbors and outsiders alike. If we lose that focus, we are surrendering to sclerosis.[25]

The specific section of the psalm cited is an appeal to obedience. There is little doubt that our author believes the same Spirit is speaking through this sermon: "Jesus Christ is the same yesterday, today and tomorrow"! As a twenty-first-century people of God, we would add our own amen while noting that this first-century sermon *did* go on to be canonized as official documentation of faith within the New Testament. So this is a stern call to obedience. The

---

23. Kraus, *Psalms 60–150*, 248–49.
24. Ibid., 248.
25. For "sclerosis," see also Rom 9:18 and Rom 11:25. There may be strong indications of Pauline influence on our author here, though in this context there is less indication that the sclerosis was an act of divine grace.

crescendo of the psalm quotation is unambivalent: "in my anger I swore 'they will not enter my rest'" (Heb 3:11, Ps 95:11). This is no feel-good sermon, and to make this quite clear, the preacher turns once more to the audience: "take care, brothers and sisters, that none of you have an evil unbelieving heart that turns away from the living God" (Heb 3:12). I sense that in the twenty-first century, these words can sound more stern and admonishing than inviting—perhaps it was ever thus. Yet if we rephrase them in the context of Ps 95, they can take on a more attractive hue, for Ps 95 was nothing if not an invitation to a great and wonderful cultic dance, however lamentably we as a church community have often communicated that truth.

Our preacher adds words of encouragement in the form of a command to the audience to encourage one another. The word here, often translated "encourage" or "exhort," is the same word John's gospel account gives as name of the Holy Spirit: Comforter or Counsellor. "Exhort" is as good a translation as any, for it has a weighty tone to it. It is at this point that we might be reminded of the difficulty of living as a Christ-believer without involvement in a faith community and its accompanying relationships of mutual encouragement. In a recent sermon, Pope Francis drew on the thought of his predecessor Pope Paul VI:

> This is why the great Paul VI said that it is an absurd dichotomy to love Christ without the Church, to listen to Christ but not the Church, to be with Christ at the margins of the Church. It's not possible. It is an absurd dichotomy. We receive the Gospel message in the Church and we carry out our holiness in the Church, our path in the Church. The other is a fantasy, or, as he said, an absurd dichotomy.[26]

In extremis of course, such a life is possible, as a figure such as Terry Waite demonstrates—though in noting that during his 1,763 days in chains "past, present and future are carried into the experience of the moment, and the exhortation of Christ to live for the day has assumed a new meaning for me,"[27] Waite is, perhaps not inadvertently, echoing the Hebrews author's Christology. Out of his experience, Waite can conclude his narrative of solitary confinement with the words from a victim of Hitler,

> *I believe in the sun even when it is not shining.*
>
> *I believe in love where feeling is not.*
>
> *I believe in God even if he is silent.*[28]

---

26. Francis, "General Audience." For further details on Pope Francis' address given at Saint Peter's Square on June 25, 2014, see Catholic Online, "Pope Francis."

27. Waite, foreword to *Taken on Trust*, n.p.

28. Ibid., 358. Italics in original.

Waite, even in confinement, was palpably connected to his own disciplined pre-captivity life of liturgical observance and prayer, and during his captivity he was connected to a worldwide community of praying people: "I turned the card over and there was a message from someone whom I didn't know simply saying, 'We remember, we shall not forget, we shall continue to pray for you and to work for all people who are detained around the world.'"[29]

But we cannot argue from the extraordinary exception to the ecclesiastical norm. The Genesis notion that a person should not live alone (Gen 2:18) is usually applied, as in its original context, to the relationship of marriage (or at least sexual partnership), but it is also a fundamental truth of being human in general. Made in the image of the community God, humans too are designed to live in community, and the church of the community God must be community, foreshadowing what Hippolytus called the "cosmic festal gathering" when "the people that were in the depths arise from the dead and announce to all the hosts of heaven: 'The thronging choir from earth is coming home.'"[30] As Jürgen Moltmann points out,

> the well-known Shaker song 'The Lord of the Dance' goes back to these ancient and patristic metaphors about the word as dance, and the Logos as the leader of the dance which moves the world. The eternal perichoresis of the Trinity might also be described as an eternal round danced by the triune God, a dance out of which the rhythms of created beings who interpenetrate one another correspondingly rises like an echo.[31]

Saint Gregory of Nyssa used a similar image of "dancing ranks of the angelic spirits"[32]: it is a little hard to dance effectively in isolation, and if the church is to be a prolepsis of the coming reign of the triune community God, the church too must dance in community. The word "prolepsis" describes a future event as if manifested in the present, and this is the fundamental chronological understanding at the heart of our author's thought. The mutual exhortation that can sound like little more than a stern teacher's command to behave in Heb 3:12 can be re-expressed as an invitation to a wonderful mutually enriching dance. This dance is not trivial or individual-

---

29. Ibid., 360.

30. Hippolytus, *De Pascha Homilia* 6. In fact, this paschal sermon has been attributed to several sources, including Gregory of Nyssa and John Chrysostom.

31. Moltmann, *God in Creation*, 307. My debt to Moltmann in this discussion of "mutual exhortation" will be obvious to anyone familiar with his work; it is his book that brought my attention to Gregory of Nyssa's words. "Perichoresis" is the interpenetration of the persons of the Trinity, central to Moltmann's theology and to the theology of the Orthodox church.

32. Ibid., 307. See Hugo Rahner's chapter entitled "The Mystery of the Cross" in Rahner, *Greek Myths and Christian Mystery*, 67–68.

istic, for it serves a purpose: it is a coming together in the liturgical dance of mutual exhortation and encouragement, and it is a solemn yet not miserable responsibility in Christ that must last "as long as it is called 'today'" (Heb 3:13). Need we add that it still is that "today" today?

The conditionals of the sermon are never far below the surface of this text. At Heb 3:14, the preacher warns, "we have become partners of Christ, *if only* we hold our first confidence to the end." The notion of partners suggests that while the actual imagery of a dance is pushing beyond our author's immediate repertoire, it is not pushing beyond the boundaries of the mutual responsibility that this sermon is seeking to engender. Partners, kin . . . The terminology changes, but the idea of mutuality with and mutual responsibility towards Christ—the idea of mutual connection with the Godhead and with one another—does not change. Neither does the conditionality change: renege on this and there is, according to this preacher, no coming back. This would be a major debate later in Christian history: Could a person who had renounced Christ ever be readmitted to the faith community? Eventually, our Hebrews author was overridden and "apostates," those who had left under duress or otherwise, were readmitted. But not in the first century: this was the stuff of eternal do or die, as far as our author is concerned, reminding us again that our world of vast clashing civilizations and religions was not our author's world.

The sentence from Ps 95:7–8 is repeated at Heb 3:15, where some powerful deterrent extrapolations are made. Roughly, the equation generated in the sermon is "They hardened their hearts in their time of testing . . . You are in a new wilderness being tested . . . Will you harden your hearts and be excluded from the rest" (we might say, "the eternities"[33]) "of God?" This is the stuff of dire warning, an unconcealed and unambiguous threat. Luke Timothy Johnson emphasizes the extent to which the questions of Heb 3:16–19 are governed by the command of Heb 3:12.[34] That is, the extent to which the "see to it" of Heb 3:12 becomes a "see to it that we the audience are not the rebellious, the nonchalant, the grumblers,[35] the hardened and disinterested of the rebellion against God and Moses." The penalty for failure to obey the preacher's command is exclusion: "they were unable to enter." Our preacher echoes the sermon of Moses as Moses recalls his petition to God to "overlook the stubbornness of this people, their wickedness and their sin" (Deut 9:27) and his plea that "they are your people, your inheritance that

---

33. Johnson notes "God said, after all, 'they shall not enter into *my* rest,' rather than 'they shall not enter into *their* rest'" (Johnson, *Hebrews*, 122, italics in original).

34. Ibid., 118.

35. See Deut 1:27, Num 14:29.

you brought out by your great power and your outstretched arm" (Deut 9:29). Underlying these petitions from Moses is a reminder of how God had excluded the journeyers from the promised country and the mocking cries that "Because the Lord was not able to take them into the land he had promised them, and because he hated them, he brought them out to put them to death in the wilderness" (Deut 9:28). This is not the language of inclusion and embrace, but the language of exclusion. The exclusion, however, is wielded not by believers, but by God.

In a footnote to the conclusion of his *Exclusion and Embrace*, Miroslav Volf reserves the right of judgment and exclusion to God. Noting novelist D. H. Lawrence's detestation of the book of Revelation (an irony, given Lawrence's dislike of anemic Christs[36] and his celebration of rites of human sacrifice![37]) Revelation scholar Adela Yarbro Collins rules out violence and exclusion from the arsenal of God's ability.[38] Volf will have none of this, and even without the extremes of Volf's experience, I suspect anyone aware of the horrors that come across my computer screen *via* Al Jazeera or the BBC each day should recognize that the recurring phrase "'judgment is mine' says the Lord" is no empty threat in the biblical narrative.[39] Violence is ugly beyond words, but if I have seen my loved ones raped and killed by hooded militia, I will probably need to know that God has more than gentle acquiescence or nonchalant collusion to offer the perpetrators before I am able to share God's eternity with them (all the while remembering my own potential to be a perpetrator of evil too).

---

36. In a December 3, 1907 letter to his family's Congregational minister, the Reverend Robert Reid, Lawrence wrote, "'It cannot be . . . that a pitiful, *omnipotent* Christ died *nineteen hundred* years ago to save these people from this and yet they are here.' Women, with child—so many are in that condition in the slums—bruised, drunk, with breasts half bare. It is not compatible with the idea of an *Omnipotent*, pitying Divine" (Lawrence, *Letters*, 40, italics in original).

37. Many of Lawrence's mid-period novels and novellas, particularly *The Plumed Serpent* and "The Woman Who Rode Away," are obsessed with ritual sacrifice.

38. Collins, "Persecution and Vengeance," 747, cited in Volf, *Exclusion and Embrace*, 303.

39. My reading of Revelation in *Babylon's Cap* may come perilously close to making the same assumptions as A. Y. Collins, but I hope in my self-reminders in that text that I permit God to be God *in extremis*: "I live a privileged armchair existence, and have never been on the wrong end of the sheer evil of a serial killer in the Belanglo Forest of New South Wales, nor watched in terror the manic rampage of Norwegian serial killer Anders Behring Breivik, nor experienced the depraved atrocities perpetrated by a Charles Manson. But even in such cases, might not God's capacity to redeem extend further than human capacities for evil?" (Godfrey, *Babylon's Cap*, 103). Such evil, though visible and abhorrent to an infinitely holy Creator (whose perspective is, to say the least, far greater than mine!), is within God's realm of forgiveness and redemption.

Judgment remains a central theme of not only our author, but also the entire biblical witness, and it may even be said that a church that surrenders a theology of judgment out of complacent unease with the thought of a stern judge is itself failing to heed the stern words of our author in Heb 3:12–19. Liberal theology's tendency to invite everyone to the eternal dance (if it retains a theology of "eternity"), regardless of the explosive devices hidden in human hearts seemingly irreparably scarred by xenophobia, exploitation, and hatred glosses over the deep horrors of evil. Such theology is the theology of ivory towers and armchairs. Fundamentalist and other exclusivist theologies tend to draw lines in the soteriological sand, condemning "the other" or the "outsider" to eternal flame.[40] Such theologies of blinkered self-satisfaction (even if dressed up in platitudes of "by grace alone") are equally the product of myopia and sclerosis of the human heart.

---

40. When Roman Catholic priest Klaus Klostermaier asked rhetorically, "Will the God of the air conditioned libraries redeem him who dies of heat-stroke in the desert?" he was emphasizing the need to ground theological speculation in the communal realities experienced by religious practitioners. See Klostermaier, *Hindu and Christian*, 48.

5

Take Care, Brothers and Sisters (Losing Moral Coordinates): Heb 4:1–11

The division of text makes it hard to register that Heb 4:1 is very much a continuation of Heb 3:1–19. Again, our author crafts this sermon so tightly that these divisions are all but impossible to introduce effectively. There has been a buildup of the promising insight that Jesus has somehow, in his person and his priesthood, opened up for us a new Way—what the author will call "a new way, a living way"—out of the morass of human existence, particularly human sin (Heb 1:3) and mortality (Heb 2:15). But there is the buildup as well of the warning that we must persevere, hanging on as believers "while the promise of entering his rest is still open." This is one of the verses in Scripture that lends itself to the commonly held belief that at the moment of our death the doors of grace snap shut: confess Christ before you die or burn! I am not convinced that either this or any New Testament author is really meaning to turn death into a bogey man, bigger than grace, in this way. Do our loved ones die and burn because they failed to take notice of this and similar verses? I doubt it. For one thing, such a belief makes a mockery of prayer, and what's more, it belittles God's grace. The message for *us*, not them, is "Take care!"

The author turns back to the Hebrew Scriptures again, drawing parallels from . . . From what? Who are the "they/them" of Heb 4:2? They are the wilderness generation of Heb 3:7–19, but here we need to be cautious. Yet again, we must avoid interpretations that give the impression that the gospel in some way superseded God's covenant with the Hebrew people, turning them into the enemies of the gospel (Heb 4:6). As one scholar puts it, "the contrast is between two generations, not between two peoples, races or religions."[1] Perhaps, at the risk of imposing an existentialist interpretation on the text, the contrast is between two attitudes rather than two generations? While the author may not have intended my last interpreta-

---

1. Ellingworth, *Commentary*, 240.

tion, in a post-Holocaust world we need to say that those two attitudes dwell within each of us: the "them" and the "us" struggle for supremacy in your life and mine.

Hebrews 4:1 is a return to the "hortatory" (appealing to the emotional and intellectual responses of the audience) or exhortative technique we have already noted. The author identifies with the audience in terms of the "us," beseeching them to do the right thing: "let us take care." No claims are really being made in Heb 4:2 about the fate of the Jewish people in the hands of God, but a claim *is* being made—a reminder *is* being made to this audience of the cost of reneging on their previous experience of the risen Lord. This author, like Paul (Rom 10:15), believes the Hebrews did receive the good news but that they failed to allow it to transform them (Heb 4:2). Rather than pointing fingers at our Jewish co-believers, we should ask if we risk the same: Does the gospel transform our lives? If the answer is no, and that "no" is revealed in our attitudes to the "praxis" of faith—the way we demonstrate our encounter with Christ in action as well as in, and far more significantly than, our words—then we are slipping outside the "us" of our author's worldview.

In order to explore the metaphorical world of Heb 4, it may be useful to take a tour through a handful of examples of ways in which we as contemporary follows of Christ might lose *our* way. I have in the past found terminology of a hardened heart, or sclerosis, helpful, and in the context of the Hebrews author's extended metaphor of a wandering people of God,[2] this idea together with the image of lost coordinates may be equally useful (Even if they are not normally related in navigational discourse!). For a moment, I will weave together images of sclerosis, lost coordinates, and from my own tradition "marks of mission," in order to attempt to break open our author's concerns as they might apply to our twenty-first-century world of faith and praxis.

The Anglican Communion to which I belong has since 1990 used the "Five Marks of Mission" as a navigational aid to determine Christians' fidelity to Christ and to Christ's gospel. While not perfect (The last two "marks" increasingly give the impression of policy made on the run as they reform and expand!), the five marks are a reasonable litmus test of our response to the Hebrews author's exhortation. Are we effective in the command to . . .

1. proclaim the good news of the kingdom;
2. teach, baptize, and nurture new believers;
3. respond to human need by loving service;

2. See Käsemann, *Wandering People*.

4. seek to transform unjust structures of society, to challenge violence of every kind, and to pursue peace and reconciliation; and

5. strive to safeguard the integrity of creation and sustain and renew the life of the earth?

If we are not, as is often the case, then we need the renewing energies of God and indeed the forgiving, re-creating energies of God's Sabbath rest to reach us in the wilderness of our inadequate faith and praxis.

Jürgen Moltmann has emphasized the place of Sabbath rest (Heb 4:1–11) in God's purposes as "goal and completion" and as creation's "true future."[3] This day of God's rest reaches through human and cosmic history, breathing, rumoring its presence, and drawing all that God has pronounced "good" (Gen 1) into its final and eternal blessing. This rest is foreshadowed in the rites and observation of Sabbath, sabbatical, and jubilee, often more honored in the breach than the observance, and has a kind of entelechy[4] that draws us and all creation to its as-yet unfulfilled fullness. This is the "promise of entering his rest" that the Hebrews audience is exhorted not to neglect. By "practicing the presence of God,"[5] the Hebrew Christians can ensure that unlike their wilderness-wandering predecessors, they are not alienated from God's blessing or, to express this state more forcefully, trapped in the sclerosis of disobedience.

We must differentiate between rest as a form of stasis and rest as eternal blessing. Too much Christian teaching has opened itself to scorn by giving the impression that its doctrine of eternity is a doctrine of cloud-sitting, harp-playing tedium. Such a state would be akin to an infinite extension of the state of ennui deplored by existentialist philosophers and would hardly exercise any entelechy on the human or cosmic journey. Biblical images of eternal existence are generally active. The beatific vision of Isa 65:21–25, for example, is full of the energy of active verbs, while the great parabolic images used by Jesus are of feasts, and the language of Ps 95, which is about to reassert itself in this sermon, is the language of dance. Johnson notes, "If God ceased 'working' on the seventh day (*tē hebdomē*)—if creation is not an ongoing activity of the living God revealed in his saving acts—then God is

---

3. Moltmann, *God in Creation*, 276.

4. For "entelechy" as God's energy, drawing creation into God's future, see Godfrey, *Babylon's Cap*, 137–38. It is this that Ludwig Köhler has in mind when he writes, "creation in Old Testament theology is an eschatological concept" (Köhler, *Old Testament Theology*, 88).

5. The reference is to a work by seventeenth-century Carmelite monk Brother Lawrence, *The Practice of the Presence of God*, which is available in many print and online editions.

otiose, not truly a living God who continues to 'speak' and 'act,' but a passive retiree."[6] Whatever the "rest" envisaged by our author, it is not passive ennui on a celestial pillow but is instead imbued with the re-creative energy of the Sabbath on which God renewed divine energies (Exod 31:17). It is perhaps best envisaged by comparison with a highly active and energized human vacation of the sort that popularly earns the aphorism "a change is as good as a rest." Certainly this is more akin to the Sabbath understanding of the Johannine Jesus and his solemn proclamation that "My father is still working, and I also am working" (John 5:17).

So the idea of rest here is an echo of the resting of God on the Sabbath Day of creation, but it carries with it the notion of eternal "active rest" that we capture in the phrase "rest in peace." It is the eternal Sabbath Day of God's hereafter. The author expounds upon this dual meaning by turning our attention back to the creation story (Heb 4:4–5) but then delivers a warning that there is a present and future dimension to this Sabbath: "it remains open for some to enter it" (Heb 4:6). The establishment of this present tense leads the author to make another stern warning, reminding the audience of the "today-urgency" of the gospel and the crisis of decision forced in the eternal Now by gospel proclamation. This is the proclamation the audience had already received and responded to at some previous time but towards which they were now growing blasé. As the unplanned audience, we too are invited to feel that urgency, for (we might add "by the grace of God") that today is *our* today too: "Today, if you hear his voice, do not harden your hearts" (Ps 95:7b–8a, Heb 3:7b–8, 4:7). Our author is weaving back and forth through Ps 95, from what was generally assumed to be the time of King David to the time when Hebrews was written—our today, our *sēmeron*. There is a "today" in which the promise of God is available, but it will not last forever; this "not forever" applies as much to us in the twenty-first century as it did to our author in the first.

The "eschatological pressure" of this Now—the sense that we are as audience running the risk of living in the "too late" (the sort of risk we find darkly sensationalized in the glib eschatology of Timothy LaHaye, Hal Lindsay, and others since)—is one ingredient of the author's message. But the author stresses this point to give the audience a behavioral compass by which to ensure they do not lapse out of the gospel-life to which they were called and into which they have already entered (Heb 2:1). What litmus tests might we apply in our own individual and communal lives as followers of Christ and as the putative body of Christ? What yardsticks are there by which to ascertain whether we are remaining in or lapsing out of the "we

---

6. Johnson, *Hebrews*, 128.

who believed"? Indeed, within each of us as individuals, what aspects of our lives are demonstrating our propensity for lapsing?

In Paul's writings, there are several signs of lapsing from fidelity to the gospel that might be summarized as "diverting from the gospel as preached by Paul in any circumstance."[7] Our author is demonstrating another similarity to Paul: any deviation from the original enthusiasm and tenacity of faith that was the audience membership's response to partnership with Christ (Heb 3:14) is a form of boundary crossing, of slippage from "us" to "them," that risks losing access to God's eternal active rest. There is more than one way to lapse from fidelity to the gospel calling, and the "marks of mission," though of course many centuries post-biblical in origin, may serve as useful indicators. Where we do not proclaim, in both action and word, the good news of the Reign of God, we are in slippage. Where we do not teach, baptize, and nurture new believers, we are in slippage.

What is "good news of the Reign of God"? Is it merely political utopia, or the establishment of justice that re-emerges as the focus of the fourth mark of mission? Karl Marx surely did as much, yet his profound vision of social justice has never been realized. A form of Christianity that disengages its message from eschatological coordinates, from a doctrine of judgment, and in that sense from "otherworldliness" may well be engaging in the slippage our author is stridently warning against.

It is this disengagement that is the hallmark of a theology such as that of John Selby Spong, or most famously in my own country, Lloyd Geering. When Spong announces, not perhaps without some hubris, that his theology offers "those in my world, who are willing, a journey that many of my fearful religious brothers and sisters, hanging so desperately to the last vestige of their literal affirmations, are too afraid to take,"[8] it may just be the case that he is slipping into the hope-denying disinterest that the Hebrews audience was beginning to embrace. While he sets about dismantling the narratives of "miracle and magic [which] were assumed by the general population to be both normal and commonplace,"[9] Spong neglects to remind his readers that the flawed narratives by which the first Christians attempted to convey the mystery of the first Easter were so powerful, so unexpected, so challenging, and so worth dying for that they transformed lives beyond measure. The gospel writers, especially Luke in his two-part narrative, attempt to convey the enormity of this transformation by nar-

---

7. For a more detailed analysis of "lapsing" in the Pauline correspondence, see my "Run," 274–315.

8. Spong, *Resurrection*, 21.

9. Ibid., 41.

rating the regeneration of the disciples from cowardly buffoons to martyrs for faith. It is doubtful that when, for example, Dietrich Bonhoeffer risked and then surrendered his life for his convictions, he was what Spong dismisses as a "fearful religious brother" clinging to the last vestige of literal affirmation. Eyewitness accounts of Bonhoeffer's last days seem to indicate that he did not see the need to jettison the traditional narratives of faith tenaciously clung to by so many of the complex and the simple followers of Christ. Without indulging in the naïvely hagiographical, it may be worthwhile to revisit the words of one witness to Bonhoeffer's execution, as narrated in the primary Bonhoeffer biography:

> Through the half-open door in one room of the huts I saw Pastor Bonhoeffer, before taking off his prison garb, kneeling on the floor praying fervently to his God. I was most deeply moved by the way this lovable man prayed, so devout and so certain that God heard his prayer. At the place of execution, he again said a short prayer and then stepped to the gallows, brave and composed.[10]

It is doubtful that Bonhoeffer was a fearful religious brother clinging to the last vestige of literal affirmation, and his last recorded words, "This is the end—for me the beginning of life,"[11] tend to confirm this to be the case. Likewise, when Terry Waite, who in his autobiography refuses to see himself as an exemplary Christian, observes, "In Christ I see the light side of God, which gives me strength and hope"[12] despite not knowing whether he will live or die in his solitary confinement, he is not likely to be considered a fearful religious brother clinging to the last vestige of literal affirmation.

The history of Christian martyrs provides a powerful contra-narrative to the history of Christian recidivism. A few tales will suffice as demonstration. In Christian circles in my home country of Aotearoa, New Zealand, the story is often told of a young Māori girl, Tārore, daughter of Ngākuku, a chief of the Ngāti Hauā people of the Waikato region in the North Island, which is southeast of modern-day Auckland. As the missionary endeavor reached out through Aotearoa, New Zealand, in the early nineteenth century, mission schools were established. Tārore was enrolled in one such school, where she developed a deep love of Christian Scriptures, particularly of Luke's account of the gospel. Her recitations of Luke in her native tongue were so evocative that Tārore was recognized as an evangelist in her own right: she was presented with a copy of the gospel and wore it in a *kete*—a

10. F. Fischer-Hüllstrung, cited in Bethge, *Bonhoeffer*, 830–31.
11. Bethge, *Bonhoeffer*, 830.
12. Waite, *Taken on Trust*, 321.

bag made of woven flax—worn around her neck. In 1836, the decision was made to move Tārore's mission school to the coastal region that is now the city of Tauranga. As the party of some twenty-one children trekked east led by a mission worker and Ngākuku, they camped overnight at Wairere Falls, which plunge down from the rugged Kaimai Ranges to the Hauraki Plains beneath. During the night, the school group was attacked by a raiding party. While Ngākuku and the mission worker escaped with twenty children in the confusion that followed, Tārore was missed and was killed in her sleep by a warrior named Uita. The *kete* and Luke's gospel account were stolen from the dead child's neck.

Traditional Māori practice, like many cultural practices, held to a strict protocol of revenge, or *utu*, and Ngākuku and his iwi[13] would be well within their cultural rights to demand *utu* killings of Uita and his party. At the *tangi* (funeral rites[14]) Ngākuku made a plea for an end to cycles of *utu*. In my book *Babylon's Cap*, I refer to the northern *iwi* Ngāpuhi and their decision to cease cycles of *utu*.[15] Ngākuku's decision was, if anything, all the more remarkable, for it was taken in a context of immeasurable personal grief. The impact of the decision was extraordinary: the killer, Uita, heard that revenge was not being sought, but he was unable to read, so the words of the stolen book remained undecipherable to him or his people. Sometime later, a literate slave's visit to Uita would prove a watershed: the Lukan gospel account was read to Uita, and he was convicted of the need for Ngākuku's forgiveness. At enormous risk and in a scene reminiscent of the Prodigal Son, Uita approached Ngākuku's home and sought and received pardon from Ngākuku for the killing of Tārore.

Ngākuku and Uita together built a church at Ngākuku's base at Wahora, but the ramifications of the story of Tārore's death did not end there. The literate slave Ripahau returned to his base at Otaki on the Kāpiti Coast (nearer to modern-day Wellington at the south end of the North Island). The Lukan gospel was read again, this time to the chief Katu Te Rauparaha, whose warlike father had wreaked retributive havoc along the length of the country. Katu Te Rauparaha (who later changed his name to Tamihana

13. Out of respect for Māori self-identification, I do not use the European word "tribe," which is an inadequate description of the complex subgroupings of Māori society.

14. Technically, the *tangi* is more than just the burial, for it involves a complex web of procedures honouring the deceased, including rituals of cleansing, preparation, and orations.

15. Godfrey, *Babylon's Cap*, 119. The story of Tārore has become known to me since that book was written, but both the sociological factors of Ngāpuhi exhaustion and the brave decisions of Ngākuku and his Ngāti Hauā people serve to demonstrate the way in which Christian doctrines, at their best, can sever cycles of hatred.

Te Rauparaha) was, like Uita, deeply convinced of the integrity of the Lukan message of reconciliation, justice, and peace. He converted and took Tārore's little gospel book to other Māori communities further south in Te Wai Pounamu (the South Island[16]). The Lukan messages and images of reconciliation soon began to infiltrate Māori communities in the Kāpiti and Wellington regions and, subsequently, Te Wai Pounamu. While there would be many subsequent betrayals of Māori by the colonial settlers, Tārore's death would go on to achieve far greater missiological impact than almost any other missionary effort.[17]

A second and less salubrious tale emerges from Japan. From 1587 onwards, the tide of official opinion began to turn against the embryonic Christian faith in that country. Seeded by Portuguese Jesuits and accelerated by Jesuit printing presses, the new faith came to the attention of authorities near the end of the sixteenth century. In 1597, twenty-six Christians were executed in Nagasaki. In 1622, another fifty-five Christians were executed in the same region. By the late 1630s, the new religion was forced underground, while public practitioners of the faith were slaughtered wholesale. The cycle was to be repeated: the Christians emerged from secrecy in the mid-1860s only to be forcibly removed and resettled or, if they resisted, tortured and executed in the two years after they emerged. Yet by the mid-1880s, international pressure had forced Japanese authorities to relent, and the practice of Christian faith had emerged once more from the forests, caves, and ghettos (literal and metaphorical). As has often happened in the history of Abrahamic faith—Jewish, Christian, and Islamic as well—this persecution bred tenacity, and even a final wave of persecution in the period of Japanese expansionism did not silence the Christians' witness.

One thing that came perilously close to silencing Christian witness was syncretism. By 1942, the Japanese leadership recognized that this persistent faith was not succumbing to the pressure of persecution. "The 20th-century revival of Emperor worship renewed Japan's ancient hostility to Christianity. Tokyo's samurai leaders considered Japanese Catholicism an unspeakable wart on the face of the *Kokutai*[18] and Japanese Catholics no less than traitors."[19] In a footnote to the story of Nagasaki, Paul Ham mentions a piece of unsettling and cautionary history that not only serves as subtext

---

16. Also known as *Te Waka a Māui*. We will address the word *waka* below.

17. The story of Tārore is told for children in a book by Joy Cowley, *Tārore and Her Book*. Former Anglican Archbishop of New Zealand David Moxon has also narrated the story on a website celebrating two centuries of CMS mission in New Zealand: Moxon, "Tarore and the Spread of the Gospel."

18. Roughly, "National self-identity."

19. Ham, *Hiroshima Nagasaki*, 40.

to his story of the bombed Japanese communities, but also a useful key to understanding the exhortatory emphasis of the author of Hebrews:

> While believers tried to reconcile their love of Christ with faith in the Emperor, the modern Japanese state found ingenious methods of assisting them. Some Japanese scholars interpreted Christianity as an extension of Confucianism. Others found elements of *Bushido*—the samurai creed, in the Christian willingness to die for his or her beliefs . . . The marriage of Catholicism and Shinto was masterfully demonstrated at a meeting of the Catholic Japanese hierarchy in April 1935. Christians "may show reverence at Shinto shrines," they declared, in answer to a Ministry of Education edict that "such reverence is merely an expression of patriotism and loyalty."[20]

Like European Christians enmeshed in the liberal theology of the nineteenth century, many[21] of the Japanese Christians lost sight (under the influence of skillful state manipulation) of the coordinates of their faith and allowed syncretistic confusion and an elevation of the Emperor to the lordship-place of Christ to pollute their missiology. While we too might succumb to such a temptation and perhaps have done so,[22] it is not the path to which our author and other New Testament authors summon us. Japanese Christians were soon required to insert prayers for Japanese victory into their liturgical observances[23] and were swallowed up in a completely understandable but, certainly to our author, reprehensible slippage from reference to faith in Christ.

Sadly though, it was not even theological syncretism that nearly exterminated the Christian presence in Nagasaki, but a bomb dropped on the primarily Christian sector of the city by a nation that styles itself as one of the most Christian nations on earth. Ironically, even the US Secretary of War

---

20. Ibid.

21. Not, by any means, all: Ham goes on to tell the story of Roman Catholic Christian convert and radiologist Takashi Nagai, whose compassionate ministry and writings after the US bombings led those he inspired to refer to him as the "Saint of Urakami." See ibid., 374–76, 444.

22. Donald Trump has successfully, even more successfully than Ted Cruz, garnered the energies of fundamentalist right-wing Christians to deify something that might be called "once-great America" and to make that deification and the reinstitution of that shibboleth a cornerstone of his gospel—the gospel message "make America great again."

23. Ham, *Hiroshima Nagasaki*, 41.

Henry Stimson paused to wonder if America was "losing its moral compass just as it might be about to claim military supremacy over the world."[24]

The story of the young black Houston woman Keshia Thomas might serve as another example of cycle-breaking heroism. Her actions, which almost certainly saved the life of one of her Ku Klux Klan opponents, have recently been re-publicized in the "A Mighty Girl" series.[25] In June 1996, a rally of the Ku Klux Klan assembled in Ann Arbor, Michigan, along with a counter-rally of protestors. As the tension mounted, the counter-protestors attacked a Klan sympathizer who had become isolated. He fled the blows but fell as he was set upon by the angry crowd. Keshia Thomas threw herself over him to protect him, later saying simply that "someone had to break the cycle of mob mentality."[26] Later, she would expand on the statement: "Someone had to step out of the pack and say, 'this isn't right.' . . . I knew what it was like to be hurt. The many times that that happened, I wish someone would have stood up for me. . . violence is violence—nobody deserves to be hurt, especially not for an idea."[27] By breaking cycles of hatred, motivated in part by her own faith beliefs and in part by her own backstory of suffering, Thomas probably saved a life and certainly impacted a crowd that was losing its own coordinates of humanity, compassion, and no doubt for some, faith.

My passing mention of so-called "natural" or "liberal" theology of the nineteenth century may also serve to fly a flag for the exhortational purposes of our author of Hebrews. Karl Barth, when attempting to address questions of liberal theology's failure to speak out against rampant nationalism, argued that if the Christian community is to speak out against dominant nationalist paradigms by which Caesars usurp the place of God, it must do so out of a fundamentally biblical analysis: "If we are to progress further today [1938], we must at all costs go back to the Scriptures."[28] Our author's sermon, saturated as it is with liturgical references, indicates that she would have added a firm "amen" to Barth's plea. She makes this obvious at Heb 4:12 with "The word of God is sharper than a two edged sword," a challenge to which we will return shortly. Critically at this juncture, this reminds us how we might ensure as a Christ-community that our coordinates remain focused beyond the calls of syncretistic convenience.[29] The words of New

---

24. Ibid., 158.

25. A Mighty Girl's Facebook page, last modified March 4, 2014, https://www.facebook.com/amightygirl/photos/a.360833590619627.72897.316489315054055/647802188989431/?type=3&theater.

26. "Alone Against the Mob." *The Day*. July 11, 1996. Retrieved June 20, 2015.

27. Wynne, "Man with an SS Tatoo."

28. Barth, *Community, State, and Church*, 106.

29. For a fine study of Barth's emphasis on what I am referring to as "theological

Zealand Anglican bishop Richard Randerson seem to this reader to provide a useful set of coordinates: "I want to suggest that the question of faith is not one of intellectual assent to the *existence* of 'God as a Being' but arises out of our *experience* of 'God as Being,' a reality at the heart of life."[30] That experience, I would add, must be deeply anchored in the liturgical life of a faith community, though for many of us that is an increasingly difficult challenge, for ecclesiastical institutions themselves are too often perceived as placing managerial structures and institutional self-preservation ahead of the simple gospel of divine grace revealed in the life of Jesus the Christ.

Yet coordinates were ever being lost, not merely in our author's century and in our own time. It is worth a historical digression to remind ourselves that, as Paul himself tells us, "all have sinned." In the iconic study of the medieval village of Montaillou, Emmanuel Le Roy Ladurie exposes the day-to-day life of an unimportant rural community in his exploration of the records remarkably preserved by the Inquisitor Jacques Fournier (later Pope Benedict XII). The records Fournier took to the Vatican included matter-of-fact recitations of financial and sexual exploitation and violence. "*The priests and the clerks . . . because they are wicked, extort and receive from the people the first-fruits and the tithes . . .*"[31] Sexual opportunism was rife:

> *In the bedroom shared by master and pupils, I slept for a good six weeks in the same bed as Arnaud Auriol . . . On the fourth or fifth night we spent together, when Arnaud thought I was asleep, he began to embrace me and put himself between my thighs . . . and to move about there as if I were a woman.*[32]

In one disturbing account—disturbing not only for its tale of sexual predation, but also for its tangential narration of a devastating disregard for the medical and social outsiders once loved by Jesus—an interviewee reveals far more than he intended:

> *At the time when they were burning the lepers, I was living in Toulouse; one day I 'did it' with a prostitute. And after I had perpetrated this sin my face began to swell. I was terrified and thought I had caught leprosy; I therefore swore that in the future I would never sleep with a woman again; in order to keep this oath, I began to abuse little boys.*[33]

---

coordinates," see Lawson, "State."

30. Randerson, *Slipping*, 203–204.

31. Le Roy Ladurie, *Montaillou*, 21. Italics in original.

32. Ibid., 145. Italics in original.

33. Ibid. Italics in original. Le Roy Ladurie observes, "One thing is certain; Arnaud had not caught leprosy. But in a period of popular hysteria against the lepers, fear of

Our tendency to self-absorption sometimes gives the impression that we dwell in an era more decadent than any other. This impression allows us to think that we practice a faith more strikingly heroic when we don't succumb to dominant paradigms and manage to maintain at least some countercultural behavior. Yet Le Roy Ladurie provides many examples of a culture at least as decadent as our own: "When they were young, the women of Montaillou or Ariège in general were in danger of rape, perhaps in even greater danger than elsewhere and in other ages."[34] Biblical references such as Gen 19 and 34, Judg 19, and 2 Sam 13 reveal that violent sexual exploitation of women and men by powerful individuals and groups is as ancient (and no doubt more ancient) than the biblical narratives.

Le Roy Ladurie's narrative explores some of the manipulative psychology involved with greater depth than it is possible to extract from the biblical texts: "*I love you more than any woman in the world*" the medieval priest Pierre Clergue would assure the women he seduced,[35] utilizing the tools of power imbalance. That destructive power is well documented by Australian pastor and theologian Neil Ormerod and his wife, domestic violence project officer Thea Ormerod. Their analysis of sexual abuse by clergy, *When Ministers Sin*, exposed this manipulative psychology in detail:

> When Christian leaders break the trust which has been given because of their position in the church, they do a great deal of damage to their victims. Positions of power and authority have been used in a way that is against the Christian calling. They have violated the rights of someone who had less power and authority.[36]

This theme of power imbalance occurs over and over again in the Ormerods' study, but neither the imbalance nor the abuse of trust in this woeful loss of coordinates is unique to the postmodern era. Like most unremitting perpetrators, Clergue was able to find justification for himself:

> Fabrisse [Rives],[37] referring to village gossip on the subject, said to Pierre . . . '*You are committing an enormous sin by sleeping with a married woman.*'

---

the disease was caught up with sexual dread" (ibid). Le Roy Ladurie goes on to write of the young man's "conquests," which "included adolescents of between sixteen and eighteen" (ibid).

34. Ibid., 149.
35. Ibid., 156. Italics in original.
36. Ormerod and Ormerod, *When Ministers Sin*, 159.
37. Wife to a tavern keeper of Montaillou.

'Not at all,' said the priest. 'One woman's just like another. The sin is the same, whether she is married or not. Which is as much to say that there is no sin at all.'[38]

Clergue was not alone in justifying himself; the dominant moral narrative of his community was that rape was a relatively minor crime[39] and that sexual infidelity and extra- or pre-marital sex were not sinful if money exchanged hands (as in the case, of course, of a liaison with a prostitute) or if both parties enjoyed the event.[40]

Montaillou was not a unique or even distinctive community. In a study of Renaissance Tuscany, Australian scholar Cecilia Hewlett mentions a chronicle in which "a local woman from the *contado* of Pistoria was condemned for engaging in sodomy with her local priest and was forced to ride through the city on market day on a donkey, wearing a miter as ritual humiliation, [while] her companion in 'crime' was nowhere to be seen."[41] This glimpse of Tuscan intrigue, sexual libertinism, betrayal, power and gender imbalance, set alongside Le Roy Ladurie's exposure of medieval libertinism from the early fourteenth century, not to mention Hebrew Scriptural texts of oppression and exploitation, suggests that our New Testament author's concern at her community's lost coordinates is a timeless and recurring motif in Judeo-Christian history, not merely apposite to the first century, ours, or both.

Underscoring this discussion of lost coordinates is our author's exhortation to her audience not to deviate from their original path, not to lose sight of the "rest" God promises the faithful. Are these coordinates on which Christ-bearers should focus merely the eschatological pie in the sky of a coming "heaven," and is this all that our author is indicating with the stern note of judgment introduced at Heb 4:12–13? Millennial groups have ever proclaimed this celestial pie, yet the horrendous tragedies of a Jonestown or a Waco or the plain expensive silliness of any group that awaits rapture in the desert is far from an effective demonstration of the values proclaimed in the Jesus parables of the Reign of God. As such, it is no less a form of slippage and a loss of coordinates than myriad sorry tales of contemporary sexual abuse. An Internet search for groups awaiting rapture or other manifestations of the second coming will reveal many variations on the theme of misguided faith (without even digging back in history to the sad tale of the Montanists). In 2010, for example, a small group led by Reyna Marisol

---

38. Le Roy Ladurie, *Montaillou*, 157. Italics in original.
39. Ibid., 150.
40. Ibid., 151.
41. Hewlett, *Rural Communities*, 143–44.

Chicas fled into the deserts of Southern California. They were ultimately rescued at considerable financial cost to the state (as were the Montanists centuries earlier). Before casting too many aspersions on Reyna Marisol Chicas, however, there is another dimension to her tale: even superficial analysis of the story should raise questions about the impoverishment and (again) ennui that led this group of El Salvadoran immigrants to seek so desperate and irrational a release from the normalities of life. What cultural oppressions and economic injustices led this group to embrace this degree of foolishness? Whatever the full story of their misguided adventure, the implication is that someone lost the compass of fidelity to the proclamation of the Reign of God as depicted in the New Testament narratives.[42]

Similarly, if we momentarily turn to the fifth mark of mission—loosely "care of creation"—as the lens through which to assess our response to the eschatological warnings "they shall not enter" (Heb 4:3) or "let us make every effort" (Heb 4:11), we may find some cautionary tales. If Heb 4:3 and 4:11 serve as boundary markers between "us" and "them" in our author's scheme, then I find myself facing critical issues in my own small country. New Zealand has long prided itself as a "clean green" nation and markets itself in tourist brochures and other media as such. At the same time, my country is economically reliant on agriculture as its primary industry, and much agricultural practice leads to willful, negligent, or seemingly unavoidable pollution of the nation's waterways. As one scientist dryly observes, "Dairy farming is a very leaky process."[43] Dairy, though only one branch of agricultural industry, is the fastest-growing and perhaps most culpable of this country's industries, primarily because it returns the highest profit margins.[44] While the watchdog National Institute of Water and Atmospheric Research is, despite reduced government funding, attempting to find solutions to a growing problem, the question for a reader of our first-century text is whether the Christian community should be speaking out regarding the matter of clean water.

Clearly, if "striv[ing] to safeguard the integrity of creation and sustain and renew the life of the earth" is a mark of Christ-bearing mission, then the Christian community's voice should be joined with those of other land-care communities, but a question remains: Is caring for land an element of

---

42. See Mail Foreign Service, "Hospitalised."

43. See Profitt, "How Clean?"

44. "There is no doubt that our declining river water quality over the last 20 years is associated with intensification of pastoral farming and the conversion of drystock farmland to dairy farming" (ibid). Farmers groups, in any case, are emphatic that it is urban practices that are damaging the waterways, not rural land management, and they have a point.

the gospel? Even assuming we have decided environmental stewardship is a part of the gospel, it is clearly not the totality of the gospel, and we may need to reflect on why and to what extent it is a part of the gospel mission. To ignore the environmental question of *escherichia coli* populations in my nation's riparian regions may not sound like a "hardening of heart" according to the author of Hebrews, but given the serious nature of the command to "till and nurture" God's earth in Gen 2:15, as well as the many Torah references to care and justice for the land and its species, it may well be that bland acquiescence in the destruction of any small parcel of God's earth is just one more sinful sclerosis of the heart.

Cleaning a nation's waterways is not in itself the good news of Jesus Christ, but it is a demonstration of our desire to follow Jesus. Over the last half-century, Britain's Thames has undergone a renewal from being biologically dead to numbering amongst the cleanest fresh waterways in the world,[45] but no claims are being made for the arrival of the eschatological reign. Yet for the Christian community to lose sight of the divine imperative in its cries on behalf of waterways is a sclerosis of the heart and an invitation to be excluded from the "rest" of God. Care of creation is a fundamentally Hebrew scriptural perspective, for as Margaret Barker argues, "creation care is fundamental to the temple world view and so was fundamental to the original Christian teaching."[46] Adam, as first priest of creation, was placed in the garden to "till it and keep it," but:

> [T]he writer of Genesis chose his words carefully and did not in fact describe Adam as a gardener. Jewish interpreters in the time of Jesus did not think of Adam as a gardener. The Hebrew word translated 'to till' also means 'to serve a liturgy,' and the Hebrew word translated 'to keep' means to preserve the teachings. The ... [[47]] high-priestly role of Adam and of every human being was to lead the worship of creation and to preserve right teachings about how we should live in the world.[48]

Care for God's garden, as I like to refer to it, is a fundamental aspect of participation in Christ, and neglect of this dimension of faith is yet another form of slippage. The temple itself was "the meeting place of heaven and earth, time and eternity. The holy of holies, the place of the throne of the

---

45. Green Diary, "5 Cleanest Rivers in the World."
46. Barker, "Great High Priest," 9.
47. An error in Barker's text has been removed here. The original reads, "The role of high-priestly role of Adam and ... "
48. Barker, "Great High Priest," 9.

Lord, was simultaneously heaven and earth."[49] Rabbi Jonathan Sacks notes the extent to which the author of Exodus utilizes the same terminology as the author of Gen 1: "The key words used in describing the making of the sanctuary are the same as those used in Genesis 1, the creation of the universe."[50] Care of this meeting-site is a non-negotiable element of right relationship to the Creator, and if in Christian understanding this site has once again extended from the now-destroyed temple to the whole hurting world, its nurture is no less a missiological duty of care.

While the five marks of mission provide a useful litmus test for the state of the Christian community's heart, whether sclerotic or healthy, there are differences of degree. In the commitment to the third, fourth, and fifth marks of mission, we outwork our primary commitment to the first mark of mission and demonstrate our own benefit from the second mark of mission. It is worth returning to them again, with our author's exhortation ringing in our ears:

1. proclaim the good news of the kingdom;
2. teach, baptize, and nurture new believers;
3. respond to human need by loving service;
4. seek to transform unjust structures of society, to challenge violence of every kind, and to pursue peace and reconciliation; and
5. strive to safeguard the integrity of creation and sustain and renew the life of the earth.

In the first mark of mission, we are undertaking a specifically Christian task. Our Buddhist, Hindu, Jain, or atheist friends might well proclaim news, and it may be good, but it is not specifically the *euangelion tēs Basileias*, the good news of the Reign of God. In the second mark of mission, the subject of this action is specifically "new believers" (in Christ), or those who have responded to the first mark of mission. While technically anyone can *in extremis* baptize in the triune name, it is most likely that the baptizing agent will be a Christian (while *in extremis* anyone can baptize, in non-extreme circumstances the rite is reserved in my tradition to a priest or bishop).

In our commitment to third, fourth, and fifth marks of mission, we are outworking the first mark of mission and demonstrating our own response

---

49. Ibid., *Great High Priest*, 46 (please note that the essay and the volume of the same title are two different publications). I am grateful to my colleague Dr. James Harding for also drawing my attention to the verbal links between God's walking in the garden (Gen 3:8) and being "present" in the temple (Lev 26:12; Deut 23:14; 2 Sam 7:6–70). See also Beale, *Temple*, 66.

50. Sacks, *Fractured World*, 151.

as beneficiaries (and always ongoing practitioners) of the second. In doing so, we will often participate shoulder to shoulder with humans of many religious outlooks, and the outcome for which we will strive will be identical to theirs. To fail to do so would be to demonstrate a degree of sclerosis, but to fail the first mark of mission would be apostasy and desertion of our faith. It is worth noting, with Luke Timothy Johnson, the inadequacy of "a vision of discipleship that is completely ordered to the transformation of social and political structures."[51] The author of Hebrews is careful to hold in balance the missiological dimensions of Christology so that neither the transcendent dimensions of Christ-worship nor the imminent dimensions of Christ-following dominate the lives of those who follow the High Priest Christ. Perhaps this is what Alexander Schmemann was emphasizing when he wrote, "the 'social activist' has no interest for the personal, and easily sacrifices it to the 'common interest.' Christianity may seem to be, and in some ways actually is, rather skeptical about that abstract 'humanity' but it commits a mortal sin against itself each time it gives up its concern and love for the person."[52]

The five marks of mission I have introduced into this section of the analysis of Hebrews are a useful lens by which to understand our author. We might well measure our commitment to the gospel by the degree to which we speak out about environmental injustice, about sexual exploitation, about degrading sexual libertinism (and the vast complex of arguments surrounding abortion, which in the end is an argument about our love of self and others), about the economic injustice that leaves Bangladeshi women working in sweatshops to produce the running shoes with which the global north works out the body beautiful, about the immeasurable and growing chasm between rich and poor, about the exploitation of women and children in the sex trade, about the marginalization of the elderly, about these and myriad other matters, but in the end our author applies only one yardstick: receive, believe, and therefore proclaim the good news of the Reign of God or be excluded from the energized "rest" of God.

We are trained in the twenty-first century to filter news through lenses of drama and sensationalism. In the examples of "sclerosis" that I have explored here, there are degrees of drama, but in the Pauline worldview by which all humans sin and all sin *is* sin, gradations of dramatic effect are meaningless. The growing toxicity of New Zealand rivers, the growing syncretism of Japanese Christians in the twentieth century (but of other Christians in subsequent decades), and the sexual exploitation by

---

51. Johnson, "Hebrews' Challenge," 27.
52. Schmemann, *Great Lent*, 25–26.

clergy and other beneficiaries of power imbalance in almost every century[53] all serve to remind us that our Hebrews author's concern for the gradual sclerosis of her community's spiritual heart was a timeless matter. If I have stated that the Anglican Consultative Commission's five marks of mission are useful but flawed, it is because any slippage from the first mark of mission is enough to give our author cause for concern: Need there be a yardstick of missional fidelity beyond "proclaim the good news of the kingdom," the Matthean Christ's "Go . . . make disciples," or our author's "make every effort to enter that rest"?

---

53. Certainly this has been true since the conversion of Constantine, and perhaps since the first missionaries set out from Jerusalem with their flawed humanity cheek-by-jowl with the in-dwelling Spirit of God—the Corinthian correspondence suggests a fair degree of corruption within years of the first Easter!

6

The Power of God's Command: Heb 4:12–13

THE WORD OF GOD may be sharper than a two-edged sword, but text wars (my text is bigger than your text) are an unhelpful approach to Christian faith. When our author firmly states, "the word of God is living and active" (Heb 4:12), we are not being encouraged to engage in that kind of meaningless battle (I see your 1 Cor 14:34 and raise you a Gal 3:28) but are being encouraged instead to submit to God. God's Word is action: God sees into the deepest recesses of the human heart and observes those places where we play games, where we hide, where we would rather not be exposed. God, our author suggests, can know our motivations better than we can ourselves.

We should ask what is meant by "word of God." Barth reminds us of something non-negotiable in the Christian witness when he affirms (and he does this in many ways and forms) that "in the vocabulary of trinitarian doctrine God's Son cannot be differentiated from God's Word."[1] When our author was writing, we must re-emphasize, the New Testament Scriptures were not Scripture and were not yet "canon."[2] The "event" (Barth's word, but not only Barth's) of the pre-existence and the conception and the birth and the life and teachings and passion and resurrection and future coming of Jesus-who-is-Word, taken together was the "word of God [which] is living and active, sharper than any two-edge sword." That Word of God, the Second Person of the Trinity (as he came to be known long after our author was preaching), was powerfully known to the Hebrews community in their fellowship and worship and in their "breaking open" of the Hebrew Scriptures as they interpreted them in the light of all they knew of the sayings and actions of Jesus of Nazareth. That process of interpretation—a process in

---

1. Barth, *Church Dogmatics*, 1:1, 137.
2. A brief summary of the formation of canon is to be found in McGowan, *Ancient Christian Worship*, 89–93. More complete studies are von Campenhausen's *Formation* and Metzger's *Canon*.

which our preacher is desperately engaging and to which she is exhorting her lackadaisical audience to return—was not "an" but rather "the" revelation of God and was not a relatively good but rather an exclusive path to the "rest" promised by God.

Chapter 4:12–13 is not a digression or an apothegm designed to stand alone but is instead an essential part of the author's argument building through the sermon. Since Heb 3:1, the author has been pleading that the audience should remain faithful to the call they have received in their encounter with Jesus Christ. Here the author returns the audience to that psychological impetus each of them experienced in their conversion. This is not an address to a second or later generation of Christian believers but an address to those who were the first generation of converts from outside the Way of Jesus to inside that Way. Many and indeed most Christians in the ensuing centuries have grown up in a different environment, in which that narrative of Christianity has been a part of the faith community's long-standing heritage.[3] That sense of cultural Christianity has dwindled in recent decades. I was a convert from adolescent atheism to Christian faith. In my introduction, I mentioned Rambo's work on the psychology of conversion, and it is worth recalling once more that it is this powerful sense of new beginning and radical reversal of life-direction that our author is appealing to here. For those of us in mainstream churches, especially those outside the evangelical tradition, this radical caesura is difficult either to recall or recreate. In *Babylon's Cap*, I refer to radical caesura in the context of Rev 8:1, where history receives a "complete and unexpected break,"[4] but it may serve to describe that decisive break in life's narrative that has been the experience of many through the centuries (not only in terms of conversion to Christianity).

C. S. Lewis has famously described his conversion to Christianity (or, more accurately, to Christ):

> You must picture me alone in that room at Magdalen, night after night, feeling, whenever my mind lifted even for a second from my work, the steady, unrelenting approach of Him whom I so earnestly desired not to meet. That which I greatly feared had at last come upon me. In the Trinity Term of 1929 I gave in, and admitted that God was God, and knelt and prayed: perhaps, that night, the most dejected and reluctant convert in all England.[5]

---

3. I find the Māori word *whakapapa* helpful here. Perhaps best roughly translated as "backstory," it is that sense of all the story that has brought a person to this moment in personal and cultural history.

4. Godfrey, *Babylon's Cap*, 61.

5. Lewis, *Surprised*, 182.

Augustine, centuries earlier, had written of the child's voice summoning him to "take it and read, take it and read" and of his subsequent reading of Matt 19:21 and Rom 13:13–14 followed by his surrender in conversion to Christ: "for in an instant, as I came to the end of the sentence,[6] it was as though the light of confidence flooded into my heart and all the darkness of doubt were dispelled."[7] Dostoevsky's Raskolnikov undergoes a similar conversion at the end of *Crime and Punishment*, describing in the closing words of the novel "the beginning of a new story, the story of the gradual rebirth of a man, the story of his gradual regeneration, of his gradual passing from one world to another, of his acquaintance with a new and hitherto unknown reality."[8] It is to the powerful psychology of this conversion experience that our author is appealing as he reminds the audience of the manner in which "the word of God" that separates, enigmatically, soul from spirit and, more straightforwardly, joints from marrow (Heb 4:12). It is this same reference point that was lost by the Japanese Christians in Nagasaki; the understandable joy of at long last receiving official recognition as a state religion in May 1940 led them to lose sight of the demands of the sharp sword of God's Word of justice and peace, or the sharp invitation to "follow me" rather than to follow the lordship of the Emperor. Thereafter, in conflating Christ and Emperor, they began willingly to insert prayers for Japanese victory into their liturgies of Eucharist.[9] That reference point was perhaps never even on the radar of the medieval village priest of Montaillou, for those who have grown up in a culture in which Christianity (or its Christendom version) is the dominant and often oppressive narrative often have difficulty reconnecting with the coordinates of Christ-following.

This is not, however, to say that our motivations are all in some way inherently evil: overjoyed by their new affirmation, the Japanese Christians in particular wanted simply to be obedient to civil authorities. They had, however, placed civil authorities above the lordship of Christ, and in that disorientation they lost their coordinates. Less dramatically, as a Christian minister and priest, I might want to be better at my job because I enjoy the positive feedback that work provides me. If this were my sole motivation, I would be opening myself up for some disappointments, but that does not mean I should go and drive a taxi in order to *avoid* any praise that does come my way. The question that is a paramount coordinate is that of my *primary* motivation: hopefully, for me it is to serve God and God's reign and,

---

6. Rom 13:14.
7. Augustine, *Confessions* 8:12; Penguin ed., 178.
8. Dostoevsky, *Crime and Punishment*, 559.
9. Ham, *Hiroshima Nagasaki*, 41.

if there are moments of joy and pleasure along the way (and there are), to thank God for that. It does no harm though for those of us who are converts to remember the moment of total surrender and the resultant joy of our first submission to the Way of Jesus Christ. Since then, if my motivation in serving Christ has merely been to put bread on the table or to enjoy adulation or power or wealth, the coordinates of my faith have been badly lost and I stand in dismal solidarity with Father Clergue of Montaillou.

There have been priests and ministers in all denominations who have enjoyed and even entered the job for all the wrong reasons, as the tragic history of abuses of power by "prince bishops" or by sexually opportunistic and predatory clergy sadly attests. Hopefully, these days our selection procedures in the Christian communities are more rigorous, and where they have failed in the past the church is at last learning to exercise retrospective wisdom. Pope Francis' 2014 removal from office of Monsignor Franz-Peter Tebartz-van Elst, who had come to be known as the "bishop of bling" and had allegedly misused church funds to build and decorate a $43 million building complex, is an example of church authorities attempting to re-establish appropriate coordinates and reference points of behavior. It is unlikely that Tebartz-van Elst would find it easy to use biblical coordinates to justify the decisions he made, though we must of course emphasize that we are not privy to all facts in the case and he may well prove this author wrong. Expenditure is not always evil per se, as Jesus reminded Judas (Matt 26:11). The example is in any case just one of countless like it in Christian history: that fact should not detract from the credibility of the coordinates to which our author calls her people to return, and the response of Pope Francis is a useful illustration of the shape such a return might take. The alleged behavior of Tebartz-van Elst is a repeat of that Lord Acton apothegm discussed earlier in the context of televangelist Bakker and also of the insights of Dietrich Bonhoeffer: "only the life of 'participation in the powerlessness of God in the world' will speak a word of renewal."[10]

A doctrine by which the heart and purpose of powerlessness stands at the center of God's dealings with humanity is all but synonymous with the name of Jürgen Moltmann. At the center of Moltmann's theology, there remains a more or less unchanging dynamic:

> When God becomes man in Jesus of Nazareth, he not only enters into the finitude of man, but in his death on the cross also enters into the situation of man's godforsakenness. In Jesus he does not die the natural death of a finite being, but the violent death of the criminal on the cross, the death of complete abandonment by God. The suffering in the passion of Jesus is abandonment, rejection by God, his Father. God does not become a

---

10. Bethge, *Bonhoeffer*, 788–89.

religion, so that man participates in him by corresponding religious thoughts and feelings. God does not become a law, so that man participates in him through obedience to a law. God does not become an ideal, so that man achieves community with him through constant striving. He humbles himself and takes upon himself the eternal death of the godless and the godforsaken, so that all the godless and the godforsaken can experience communion with him.[11]

This was not, however, some novel finding of the twenty-first century but rather a strand that runs throughout theological history. Although made famous by Benjamin Britten and his *Ceremony of Carols*, the song "This Little Babe" is an ancient one, reaching back into the anonymity of the medieval centuries. Its central motif is the powerless conqueror:

> This little babe so few days old
> is come to rifle Satan's fold;
> All hell doth at his presence quake,
> though he himself for cold do shake;
> For in this week unarmed wise
> the gates of hell he will surprise.
>
> With tears he fights and wins the field,
> his naked breast stands for a shield.
> His battering shot are babish cries,
> his arrows looks of weeping eyes.
> His martial ensigns Cold and Need,
> and feeble flesh his warrior's steed.
>
> His camp is pitched in a stall,
> his bulwark but a broken wall;
> The crib his trench, haystalks his stakes,
> of shepherds he his muster makes.
> And thus as sure his foe to wound,
> the angels' trumps alarum sound.
>
> My soul with Christ join thou in fight;
> stick to the tents that he hath pight.
> Within his crib is surest ward;
> this little Babe will by thy guard.
> If thou wilt foil thy foes with joy, then
> flit not from this heavenly boy![12]

---

11. Moltmann, *Crucified God*, 276.
12. Southwell, *Complete Poems*, 111–12. See also Bullett, *Shorter Poems*.

Sadly, this perspective has not always informed Christian practice in the societies in which Christianity has been called to dwell.

The trimmings of power and abuse of position can take many shapes. In *When Ministers Sin*, the Ormerods describe the ecclesiastical bind that both produces and sadly protects sexual predators within the ecclesiastical community: "abusive ministers are camouflaged by a culture which encourages those with power, most often men, to have a sense of entitlement more than to act responsibly."[13] Abuser and institution alike have lost appropriate coordinates and focus on eschatological "rest" and so have slipped from good news to disobedience (Heb 4:6). Most academic papers on sexually predatory personality types will emphasize that perpetrators are often drawn to careers or pastimes that provide opportunity for their propensity to exploit victims. The recent and outstanding response led by Pope Francis to combat a culture of predation within his church, while for many likely to be "too little, too late," is a demonstration that institutions too can hear the voice of God's Spirit calling them to rediscover their powerless place of encounter with divine grace.

While no system is perfect, most of those who simply love the presumed power or the liturgical garments of office in the liturgical churches, or even the sometimes less obvious trimmings of more informal churches' positions of authority, are sooner or later weeded out of the system. Our author's solemn pronouncement that "before him all are naked and laid bare" (Heb 4:13a) draws attention to the eschatological dimension of that exposure, which is beyond even that which Pope Francis can wield. The author leaves hypocrites (and a few will always slip through the system) nowhere to hide: "laid bare to the eyes of the one to whom we must render an account" (Heb 4:13b). It was ever thus, at least since power structures placed the sociological aces into the hands of church leaders.

Paul treats the issue through what he sees as a God-given gift of conscience (*suneidēsis*), explored primarily in Rom 2:13–16. Paul is in harmony

---

13. Ormerod and Ormerod, *When Ministers Sin*, 53. Since the Ormerods' book was published in the early 1990s, many improvements have been made in the protocols and reporting procedures of responsible denominations around the world. Nevertheless, the offences continue, and the church institutions and their membership must never lose sight of the coordinates of not only appropriate sexual behavior, but also of appropriate demands of justice where evil has been perpetrated. Sadly, the Ormerods were able to include several earlier studies and recounts of sexual abuse that had taken place in the churches before the 1990s, and several further accounts have emerged since. See Pais, *Suffer the Children*; Fortune, *Is Nothing Sacred*; Rutter, *Sex in the Forbidden Zone*; and Lebacqz and Barton, *Sex in the Parish*; all of which are referenced by the Ormerods. To that list I would add Sinclair's disturbing self-published *All God's Children* and Mooney's *All the Bishop's Men*.

with his modern kinsman Rabbi Sacks, who emphasizes that "the birth of the moral imperative—command, prohibition, 'Thou shalt not'—occurs at the moment *Homo sapiens* is first capable of understanding that with freedom comes responsibility."[14] But s*uneidēsis* can gradually be cauterized: while I doubt many people enter career structures that offer predatory opportunities primarily *for* those opportunities (though it may be that potentially predatory personality types, especially narcissistic personalities, are particularly drawn to those fields), as unchecked opportunities accumulate, conscience can be anesthetized or cauterized ("The abuser lives in the illusion of his own goodness"[15]) and trails of abuse may begin to form. The sense of a life "laid bare to the eyes of the one to whom we must render an account" is lost, and the narcissistic predator loses all coordinates of credibility. Disobedience has excluded the possibility of God's dynamic rest.

---

14. Sacks, *Fractured World*, 137.
15. Ormerod and Ormerod, *When Ministers Sin*, 69.

7

Cling to One Who Knows What It's Like
(Christ Entering the World of Human Coordinates):
Heb 4:14–16

THE AUTHOR RETURNS TO the theme of tenacity—hold tight (Heb 4:14)—but interweaves this with an emphasis on Christ's entrance into human experience. The priestly role of Jesus was flagged at Heb 2:17–18; now the theme is to be developed further. Tenacity is merged with the earlier question of Jesus' identification with our own experiences of human suffering: "we do not have a High Priest who is unable to sympathize." In English, we should use the stronger word "empathize." If nothing else, the strange and surreal Synoptic Gospel tales of the temptation of Jesus in the wilderness make it clear that Jesus underwent brutal temptation, and while these tales in the form we have them may not have been set to papyrus until after our text was composed, they were likely to have been around in oral form when our author was teaching.[1] This is the first time Jesus has been named since Heb 3:1 or referred to even obliquely since Heb 3:14.[2]

The theme of empathy is not uncommon in leadership narratives. I am no great reader of military biographies, but from those I have read the quality of leadership-empathy emerges as one of the most inspiring motivators of the rank-and-file troops. For example, the Australian military leader John Monash exemplifies this value of compassion in leadership. As he set about the task of demobilizing a fractious, frustrated, homesick, and shell-shocked Australian troop contingent stranded in Britain in the months after World War I, he warned his officers that troops were "to be treated with the greatest consideration, as men who had done their work were entitled to be" and cautioned them to "Be strict from the very start about everything

---

1. "There is no reason to think that Hebrews is dependent on any canonical account, but good reason to conclude that Hebrews ... makes use of an independent tradition" (Johnson, *Hebrews*, 145).

2. Ellingworth, *Commentary*, 267.

that matters, and indulgent about everything else."[3] As Jesus interacted with the entire range of his social milieu, he sorted out the "everything that matters" from the "everything else," affirming the hearts of those who strove for right and castigating the double standards of those whose capacity for justice and compassion was cauterized by self-importance and self-interest. Likewise, during the period of intense frustration and dislocation following the Great War, General Monash remained with his troops and ensured that they learned trades and professional skills to facilitate their demobilization and reintegration into civilian life. Monash was deeply loved by his troops,[4] and as they parted his senior administrative officer Colonel Farmer wrote sadly, "Will you let me say that you inspired those of us who served under you with so great a respect and affection that it was hard to leave your staff and hard now to say Good Bye [sic]."[5] Monash's inspirational leadership was born from empathy with his troops, for "Monash was clearly an empathetic leader and cared deeply about the troops under his command."[6] Jesus, in the hands of our author (and of all who wrote of him in the decades after his life on earth) was clearly deeply empathetic and inspired dedication in those whose lives he transformed.

If, as the Hebrews author tells us, Jesus has "in every respect been tested as we are, yet without sin," we are to some extent entitled to wonder whether he is "in every respect . . . as we are." The author's understanding of "sin," however, is not merely as the universal state of fallibility, but as "deliberate disobedience of God's will."[7] Our fallibility and our willful disobedience might be described as having become entwined in contemporary understanding, but in our author's view they remain separate in the person of Jesus Christ. Most of us are aware of the darkness in our own lives. These are not necessarily, pray God, headline-grabbing darknesses, but we are not exactly perfect either. The synoptic temptation stories, which may in some oral form or other have been known to our author, make it clear that the divinity of the Christ (if we can return to the "dual nature" theme once more, recited faithfully in our creeds as "God from God, Light from Light . . . became fully human") does not protect him from the gamut of human feelings.

The temptation narratives are representative tales that artistically detail the "type" of temptations all humans experience. The Greek word *tupos*

3. Serle, *John Monash*, 408.
4. Ibid., 408–412.
5. Ibid., 421.
6. Rosenfeld, "Nature and Nurture," 4.
7. Johnson, *Hebrews*, 141.

(type) is much more powerful in meaning than the English "sort," for we also get from it the weightier words "typology" and "typological," meaning something like "totally representative." Few of us are ever likely to be in a position where we can embezzle squillions of dollars or slaughter, in Stalinesque fashion, millions of opponents. The tragedy of human history is that most of us would if we could: every cycle of evil news in every generation is, tragically, no more than another story of human beings who resemble you or me losing any sort of moral coordinate and perpetrating evil on their neighbor because they can. To counter the volition to darkness (well, the attendant isn't paying attention, and I'm not waiting forever, and it's only a newspaper after all) we have to consciously apply light (but I *will* pay for the paper, even if I have to go and find the attendant). To do the right thing, we need a little—or a lot—of extra help.

The cycles of evil change their name and personnel, but the big picture remains the same. Like most children growing up, I was blissfully unaware or much of humanity's impulse to inflict evil on itself, though as a very British child I naively consumed stories of the Great War, World War II, and the other great historic wars of British history with concern for little more than romantic tales of goodies, baddies, and derring-do. As a teenager, I was informed as much by Biggles and war comics as by the formal textbooks of history lessons, but my bias remained the same. As I watched the classic Westerns that were my childhood diet, I did so deeply enmeshed in a cultural narrative that made it quite clear that Native Americans (known to me, of course, as "red Indians") represented forces of chaos whose membership deserved all forms of oppression, persecution, and execution. When picking sides for games of "Cowboys and Indians," few players wanted to be nominated "Indian." Suppression of any pro-Indigenous ideologies was a given: the "Indians" need to be repressed.

Even as a young adult, I was so immersed in unsophisticated cowboy-and-Indian readings of history that when, like most literature students, I encountered Joseph Conrad's *Heart of Darkness,* I did so with the conqueror's deep sense that the darkness of Africa indeed had to be vanquished and that Kurtz's absorption into the entrails of darkness, reaching its apotheosis in the cry "The horror! The horror!",[8] was simply the desertion of Europeanized moral coordinates. Near the beginning of *Heart of Darkness,* our ostensible narrator, Marlow, is perched at the foot of the mizzenmast of the *Nellie.* There, floating safe on the Thames, he makes a wry observation: "The conquest of the earth, which mostly means the taking it away from those

---

8. Conrad, *Heart of Darkness,* 149. See also T. S. Eliot's "The Waste Land" in Eliot, *Collected Poems,* 61–86.

who have a different complexion or slightly flatter noses than ourselves, is not a pretty thing when you look into it too much."[9] To this point, Marlow offers insight into the problems of a "Eurocentric" view of the "other," for as Edward Said notes, "[N]either Conrad nor Marlow gives us a full view of what is *outside* the world-conquering attitudes embodied by Kurtz, Marlow, the circle of listeners on the deck of the *Nellie*, and Conrad."[10]

Conrad and his characters never step beyond the expectation that the "darkness" of Africa is something into which the "light" of European sophistication must pierce. When "darkness" becomes synonymous with evil, as indeed it often is in the scriptural tradition, we may lose sight of deeper and more meaningful coordinates. There is for Conrad (who does not, of course, claim to be writing a theological treatise) no understanding that Europeanization took its own deep darkness into what would become the colonized world.[11] Conrad, as even the much-maligned F. R. Leavis notes, piles adjective upon adjective to ensure that his imaginary Congo is symbolic of humanity's most degenerate excesses: "The same vocabulary, the same adjectival insistence upon inexpressible and incomprehensible mystery, is applied to the evocation of human profundities and spiritual horrors; to magnifying a thrilled sense of the unspeakable potentialities of the human soul."[12]

The ostensible or frame narrator,[13] Conrad's Marlow, has to be situated on the Thames, in "a luminous space" (even if surrounded by encroaching darkness),[14] before he can tell the tale. As such, he is far removed from "the two women [who] knitted black wool feverishly,"[15] "guarding the door of Darkness."[16] When the tale ends, the actual notional narrator observes that even the Thames, as the gateway to the colonies, was being absorbed into an

---

9. Conrad, *Heart of Darkness*, 50–51.

10. Said, *Culture and Imperialism*, 24.

11. This is conspicuous in the hymn "From Greenland's Icy Mountains" by Reginald Heber (1783–1826), especially the first verse:
"From Greenland's icy mountains, from India's coral strand;
Where Afric's sunny fountains roll down their golden sand:
From many an ancient river, from many a palmy plain,
They call us to deliver their land from error's chain."

12. Leavis, *Great Tradition*, 204–205.

13. I use the phrase because the reader is in fact two removes from Marlow's story: Marlow is an invention of Conrad's, and Marlow's tale is itself narrated through the voice of another traveler on the *Nellie*—a character who is likewise an invention of Conrad's.

14. Conrad, *Heart of Darkness*, 45.

15. Ibid., 56. The women first appear on the previous page.

16. Ibid., 57.

encroaching "black bank of clouds, and the tranquil waterway leading to the uttermost ends of the earth flowed somber under an overcast sky—seemed to lead into the heart of an immense darkness."[17]

As an undergraduate, I was able to unquestioningly read this view more or less as Conrad intended. The dark heart of Africa that had absorbed Kurtz and that eventually threatened even the mouth of the Thames was the "native" realm that my childhood games had symbolized by "red Indians." If I had thought about it then, I could have seen that there was a degree of injustice in the removal of wealth from colonized lands, but instead it was just the way things were, and the balances of justice were not given much thought by even this earnest undergraduate. I was aware that, as a child in West Africa, I had watched the African children playing and swimming in the stormwater drains of Takoradi (Ghana) while my family drove past them to the chic coastal swimming complex. I was uncomfortably aware of the incongruity, but no more than that. Later, it occurred to me that an appropriate response might have been redemptive aid, but I never considered as an option the empowerment of self-determination—empowerment for the peoples of the lands once conquered and arbitrarily divided at high-level European drawing boards in what Said refers to as "the scramble for Africa"[18] at the Berlin Conference of 1884–1885. My moral and ethical coordinates were set in a different space. I had in any case been born into the denouement of the Mau Mau[19] uprisings of Kenya, and the narratives of my upbringing were not supportive of African or any other colonial empowerment.

This is not a blame-game: the uprising of oppressed peoples is never a one-dimensional narrative, and the individual pain inflicted on those in power is no less intense than the individual pain inflicted on those who eventually resort to revolution. Surely one of the most haunting photographs known to history is that of the daughters of Tsar Nicholas II, their heads shaven and their privileged lives reduced to home imprisonment following Russia's Bolshevik Revolution. Previous photos show a homogenous but relatively carefree group of well-to-do girls in matching dresses and luxurious surroundings. These girls, together with their parents, were executed in a few moments of terror at Yekaterinburg soon after the last photos were taken. No matter how privileged their lives had been, their individual suffering and terror, like that of countless before and after them, must have been immeasurable.

17. Ibid., 162.
18. Said, *Culture and Imperialism*, 59.
19. Or, more correctly, Kenya Land and Freedom Army.

There is, however, a difference between the experience of the powerful and of the powerless when it comes to what I might call the "collective" experience of pain. It would be hard to argue that the pain of, for example, white slave-owners in the American South or of British landowners in Kenya was *collectively* greater than the pain of those they oppressed. Few people experience the degree of privilege the Romanovs, the family of Tsar Nicholas II, enjoyed. Few people in the global south can aspire to the rarified atmosphere and surroundings in which I type these words, or in which, conceivably, you are reading them (though as to your "reading site" I should make no assumptions, for as Franzen has powerfully reminded us, "Reading is an ethnically diverse, socially skeptical activity,"[20] and this is as applicable to a series of theological reflections as to a novel). There is, however, a marked difference in quality of life on either end of the world's socioeconomic spectrum, and those who struggle to survive on the lower end have the least to lose in violent uprising. This is one set of interpretive coordinates through which we must view all international conflict: Who has the least to lose?

My comfortable undergraduate lenses began to crumble as I began to read what were then termed "new literatures," especially the writings of Ngũgĩ wa Thiong'o and Chinua Achebe.[21] In Ngũgĩ's seminal *A Grain of Wheat* (a biblical allusion), which is in part a postcolonial engagement with Joseph Conrad,[22] the British administrative officer John Thompson reveals much about Conrad's[23] moral and ethical coordinates in his musings. Newly living in East Africa, Thompson observes the world around him, remembering some seminal moments in his awakening to African potential:

> And then a casual meeting with two African students crystallized his longings into a concrete conviction. They talked literature, history, and the war; they were all enthusiastic about the British Mission in the World. The two Africans, they came from a family of Chiefs in what was then Gold Coast, showed a

20. Franzen, *Alone*, 89.

21. Māori use the word "mihi" (either as verb or noun) to mean "pay tribute to" (not in a fiscal sense). I here mihi my patient lecturer Peter Alcock of New Zealand's Massey University, who started me on this investigative journey into non-Eurocentric perspectives—a journey that unfortunately has been too often lackadaisical and peripheral to the main games of my work and study in literature and theology.

22. The context overall, despite the immediate reflection on Kipling, is Ngũgĩ's wrestling with Joseph Conrad. See Sewlall, "Periphery." It was Achebe, not Ngũgĩ, who famously called Conrad "a bloody racist" (ibid., 56).

23. Or, more accurately, Kipling's, for the character Thompson is at that moment musing about the author that Orwell called the "prophet of British imperialism." See also "Rudyard Kipling" in Orwell, *Collection*, 118.

real grasp of history and literature. This filled Thompson with wonder and admiration. His mind started working. Here were two Africans who in dress, in speech and in intellectual power were no different from the British. Where was the irrationality, inconsistency and superstition so characteristic of the African and Oriental races? They had been replaced by the three principles basic to the Western mind: i.e. the principle of Reason, of Order, and or Measure.[24]

Ngũgĩ is not even accentuating the paternalism of a Eurocentric worldview. By contrast, Achebe recalls with rightful anger Conrad's *Heart of Darkness* persona's observation that "you know, that was the worst of it—this suspicion of their [Africans'] not being inhuman,"[25] and observes, "a more deadly deployment of a mere sixteen words it would be hard to imagine."[26] I now recall with shame the passionate arguments I presented to my form teacher at age ten as to why Māori children should not, and indeed would not really like to enter the elite fee-paying school where I was receiving my primary education. From where had my ten-year-old self gleaned this paternalistic worldview? To say "from my parents" is a poor reflection of the reality: I had absorbed this attitude from the entire cultural milieu in which I had grown up. I had lived a privileged existence (though nowhere near Romanov standards) and had not yet seen the arrogance of my paternalism. It would be Ngũgĩ, Achebe, Soyinka, and other novelists, followed by postcolonial theorists such as Frantz Fanon, Edward Said, and Linda Tuhiwai Smith, who would begin to force me to critique my worldview.

This is a work still in progress, and indeed in its infancy in my own life's journey. There is an inevitable paternalism to writing of other cultural perspectives and of collective experiences vastly different from my own; I am inescapably limited to my own experience and cannot fully imagine the life stories through which our Hebrews author expects the Christ story to permeate. Chimamanda Ngozi Adichie poignantly captures the attitude of patronizing voyeurism into which it is all too easy to slide:

"Hello, I'm Ifemelu."

"What a beautiful name," Kimberly said. "Does it mean anything? I love multicultural names because they have such wonderful meaning, from wonderful rich cultures." Kimberly was smiling the kindly smile of people who thought "culture" the

---

24. Ngũgĩ, *Grain of Wheat*, 47.
25. Conrad, *Heart of Darkness*, 96.
26. Achebe, *Home and Exile*, 46.

unfamiliar colourful reserve of colourful people, a word that always had to be qualified with "rich." She would not think Norway had a "rich culture."

"I don't know what it means," Ifemelu said, and sensed rather than saw a small amusement on Ginika's face.[27]

As our cultures and experiences diverge across the face of the globe and across human history, our ability to empathize with one another dwindles. This is the story of Babel and its "confusion of tongues," for not only languages were rendered disparate in this biblical fable of tearing down human arrogance. It is into this world of displaced coordinates that many of the biblical authors, including our own, see Jesus stepping. The Pauline *Carmen Christi* of Phil 2:6–7 is one such profound passage that illustrates the scope of this entrance into human suffering and sin.[28] The Johannine prologue (John 1:1–18) is another. Our Heb 4:14–16 is another. Here is a leader who steps out of the safety of perfect coordinates into the murky realms of human degradation. Here is a leader who enters both our own personal dysfunctionality and individual proclivity for sin and the vast corrupt human narrative of exploitation and oppression of others—both of our fellow humans and of other species. The Great High Priest of our author's understanding takes this cosmic step in order to guide humans to some state that is here called "the throne of grace," but which was previously called "rest." That notion pulses through the arteries of this section of our sermon.

According to our author, if we have constantly sought or even sought to seek that help, the grace of the One who has journeyed this way before us (made available to us by the Spirit) is available: "Let us therefore approach the throne of grace . . ." (Heb 4:16). We can do so because there is One like us who has been there, who has made it through our morass, who has overcome his own will by perfect submission to the Father's will, and so can be there for us always. Above all, when called upon to die, this Jesus overcame the human desire for survival and died "for us." It may seem far removed from the terrible narratives of colonial exploitation and oppression, of arbitrary lines on maps that willfully ignore cultural and ethnic differences, of revolutionary struggle and hoped-for reconciliations, but that is precisely the world into which our author sees the Incarnation stepping.

---

27. Adichie, *Americanah*, 146.

28. In private conversation with this author, biblical scholar Paula Gooder made it quite clear that Phil 2:6–7 should not be separated from Phil 2:1–5 and is therefore a teaching on human coordinates, not divine salvation-methodology.

8

High Priest for Us: Heb 5:1–10

OUR AUTHOR SETS OUT a series of likenesses between the High Priest Jesus and the high priest of ancient Hebrew understanding. At the head of these associations is the notion of being chosen. This is not to suggest an Arian Christology, as if Jesus were a reasonably adequate sort of a candidate drawn from first-century Hebrew males who would do for the role. The emphasis on the unique nature of Christ's role in salvation history is not being explored here, but rather the benefits that role holds for us. In Heb 5:1–7, the preacher expounds the historical process of selecting a high priest, being "chosen," and being "from among mortals," and she does so to expand her listeners' concept of the Jesus event. We need to recall that although this particular passage is not, unlike the previous passage, an exhortation, that exhortation is still ringing in the listeners' ears. The tender notion of a high priest "dealing gently" with the wayward (Heb 5:2) has extra emotional weight, following as it does on the heels of such exhortation, much as a revivalist preacher might follow a depiction of human sin with imagery of a weeping, beckoning Jesus before initiating an altar call.

The task of the biblical high priest was to offer sacrifice at the intersection of earth and heaven[1] on behalf of the people, imploring God's mercy and grace (Heb 5:1). The high priest knew well his own sinfulness and therefore "is not in a position to be high-handed or haughty towards those who sin out of ignorance (*agnousin*) or error (*planōmenoi*),"[2] and the offerings he makes are made for his own sins as well as for those who ask his intercessory actions (Heb 5:3, Lev 9:8, Lev 16:6). At this point, we walk a tightrope between the identification of Christ *with us* and his sinless distinctiveness *from us*, but our author does not wish to become bogged down in this christological detail.[3] The author effectively sets out a job description

---

1. Barker, *Great High Priest*, 46. See Jer 17:12.
2. Johnson, *Hebrews*, 143.
3. However see 2 Cor 5:2, 1 Pet 1:18–19, 1 Pet 2:22, 1 John 3:5, John 8:29, perhaps John 19:4.

(Heb 5:1–4) and then demonstrates the unique and indeed the final and definitive way in which Christ fits this role. Unlike the earlier exhortatory passage (Heb 3:12–18), the emphasis is now on Christ's inviting compassion rather than the *orgē*, or anger (Heb 3:11), that dominated the earlier passage. The depiction is of a very human Christ[4] weeping and crying (the nouns "cries and tears" used by the author are simple synonyms used for accumulative rhetorical effect as a parallel to "prayers and supplications") simply underscores the passionate identification that the Christ High Priest makes with the audience. This identification is emphasized still further by the submissive and subordinate "reverent submission" at the end of Heb 5:7. Once more, there is no attempt at a full-blown Christology, so there are no more grounds here for arguments of subordinationist Christology than there are bases for Arian Christology: these are not the issues our author is addressing. What is being addressed is the extent to which intercessory action has reached in Christ, and the extent to which the salvific action of God in Christ involved suffering.

To emphasize the centrality of a suffering High Priest in our author's doctrine of salvation, it is worth noting the careful audial construction of Heb 5:8. Luke Timothy Johnson draws attention to the "rhetorical flourish on a commonplace of Greek moral discourse, based on the wordplay *mathein pathein* ('to learn is to suffer')."[5] The Greek reads, *emathen aph hōn epathen*, words whose rhythms fall on an ear accustomed to aural discourse with an invitingly comforting pattern. The infamous English "no pain, no gain," popularized by Jane Fonda but itself reaching back to the second century,[6] achieves a similar aural emphasis.

In a moving excursus on "Suffering and the Obedience of Faith" emerging particularly from Heb 5:7–8, Luke Timothy Johnson asks whether the process of incarnation in the thought of our author was some sort of educative "formation" by which the Son gains new insight into the Godhead and the universe. While we, at least from my theological perspective, need to be cautious about suggesting some sort of transmutation or change in the essence of God, there is no doubt that the incarnation, at least chronologically speaking, takes some degree of new experience into the being of the triune God, whether it be an experience of internal separation from self or the physical experiences of suffering incarnation and death. The experience of prayer itself (Heb 5:7) is presumably (and again, I stress

---

4. The NRSV "Jesus" at Heb 5:7 is interpolated, replacing the author's pronoun.
5. Johnson, *Hebrews*, 147.
6. From the *Pirkei Avot* or *Ethics of the Fathers*, 5:21. See Chabad-Lubavitch Media Center, "Ethics of the Fathers: Chapter Five."

that we must not see this from a linear, chronological perspective) "new" to Godself. Johnson notes,

> If Hebrews thinks of Jesus as "learning from the things he suffered," then it must have more in mind than the physical sufferings of Jesus' passion, even though the depiction of him pleading with the one "who could save him from death" evokes the Gospel accounts of Jesus' prayer before his arrest. It would be difficult to think how Jesus "learned" from the brutal moments before his death, unless we understood "learned obedience" in the sense of "learned what obedience really involved," or "learned the consequence of obedience." In this case, however, why speak of learning" at all? Why not simply state, with Paul, that Jesus was "obedient, even unto death" (Phil 2:8)? It may well be, then, that the author of Hebrews is thinking of a learning that took place over the course of Jesus' human existence, and a learning that involved the very process of obedient faith.[7]

Johnson, and indeed the author of Hebrews, is pointing to a critical element in God's relationship with humanity. If, as Moltmann stressed, the perichoresis (or interpenetration) of the persons of the Trinity implies a transmission (as it were—words are hopelessly inadequate in Trinitarian language!) of experience or knowledge or purpose between and amongst the persons, then in the incarnation the whole experience of mortal existence, even as far as the experience of brutal pain of separation from the Father, is absorbed into Godself. Our author, again without the benefits of a fully developed Trinitarian language, is striving towards this point, depicting a divine Jesus High Priest who "offered up prayers and supplications, with loud cries and tears, to the one who was able to save him" (Heb 5:7). That which is absorbed into the Trinity is the whole gamut of human experience, from every era, culture, gender, sexuality, and economic state (to name just a few variables).

It is easy to write of suffering from my position in the global north (albeit the cartographical south), seated as I am before my expensive computer, at my comfortable desk, in a church house with awe-inspiring view, in a provincial city whose greatest uprising is the occasional mutterings of a quasi-outlaw bikie gang on noisy Harley-Davidsons. Every time I click on links to meaningful global news on the Internet or TV, I am confronted with images of the horrendous suffering taking place as a world once divided by the arbitrary, ethnicity- and culture-ignoring lines on the Mercator

---

7. Johnson, *Hebrews*, 149.

projection's northern-biased world map sloughs off its colonialist oppressions.[8] Just as the self-serving placement of Greenwich mean time at the center of the globe's chronology served the interests of the British Empire and its self-understanding, the Mercator projection that has dominated mapmaking since the mid-eighteenth century[9] serves a Eurocentric view of culture, economics, and history.

In *Babylon's Cap*, I wrote of the Staines family—Graham, Philip, and Timothy—martyred in India in 1999. When I was first writing this section of thoughts on Hebrews, I was recoiling from the image of James Wright Foley in photographs taken immediately before his brutal execution at the hands of Daesh[10] fighters in Northeast Iraq in 2014. As the months went on, more executions were carried out by Daesh in a propaganda war of terror.[11] Much later in the processes of my writing and revising, I heard of the execution of Bangladeshi professor Rezaul Karim Siddique, who was murdered for the crime of being an alleged atheist (an accusation his daughter denies).[12] Were I to keep on writing and revising, the roll call of what we might call "victims of honor" would grow, as ever it has. As Franzen observed, "The writer who wants to tell a story about society that's true not just in 1996 but in 1997 as well can find herself at a loss for solid cultural referents. What's typically relevant while she's planning the novel will almost certainly be passé by the time it's written, rewritten, published, distributed, and read."[13] Franzen published those words in 1996, and they are still truer as I write now in 2016. Franzen wrote those words about the publication of novels and social commentary two decades ago, yet as I observed above, they may be true of biblical theological reflections as well. The martyrs' roll of honor grows tragically long, yet, *contra* Franzen, the insight of our Hebrews author remains true 2,000 years after she narrated her sermon.[14]

---

8. Geraldine Brooks tells of Winston Churchill's boast that he "created Jordan on a Sunday afternoon with the stroke of a pen" (Brooks, *Nine Parts*, 122).

9. Gerardus Mercator in reality drew the map in 1569, but its use was not widespread until two centuries later. For a useful social history, see Monmonier, *Rhumb Lines*.

10. I use the "official" French nickname for the group, a nickname whose basis in an acronym is shadowy but one that respects the opinion of Islamic representatives who drive a wedge between Islam and the atrocities this group is perpetrating.

11. Tragically, as the weeks went on, Foley's execution was followed by the executions of Steven Sotloff, David Haines, and Alan Hemming, and the world recognized that this was to be a prolonged method in Daesh's version of war by terror.

12. BBC News, "Rezaul Karim Siddique."

13. Franzen, *Alone*, 67.

14. John Allen estimates, as his most conservative allowance, the rate of execution of Christians globally to be "almost one per hour" (Allen, *Global War*, 4). His 2013

I cannot even begin, in my comfortable state, to imagine the mental condition of the Staines family or of James Foley or of Rezaul Karim Siddique as they died, or even the emotional suffering of their loved ones, yet it seems to me that the author of Hebrews is suggesting that even these unimaginable (and historically ubiquitous) experiences of horror are taken up into the heart of God, where every Good Friday suffering gives way to the resurrection triumph of Easter. Pope John Paul II wrote of martyrdom as preserving communion amongst the disconnected Christian communities:

> In a theocentric vision, we Christians already have a common Martyrology. This also includes the martyrs of our own century, more numerous than one might think, and it shows how, at a profound level, God preserves communion among the baptized in the supreme demand of faith, manifested in the sacrifice of life itself.[15]

Martyrdom is the ultimate expression of fidelity to the call of Christ,[16] and of the tenacity the author of Hebrews is demanding.

Luke Timothy Johnson suggests that the whole gamut of human experience of *mathein pathein*—to learn is to suffer—is taken into the heart of God. Any obedience to God enmeshes the follower of Jesus into *mathein pathein*. Our author is no premature Arian and so has been careful to maintain belief in a pre-existent Son (Heb 1:2), but this author, like all the New Testament authors, is also careful to avoid any suggestion that God remains removed, distant, or disconnected from human suffering in all its forms. Our author is equally adamant that to follow Christ is also to suffer, and to suffer for and in the purposes of God is to encounter the glory (*doxa*[17]) of God: "The moment of death, which to outward appearance is the ultimate closure to human possibility, was therefore in the case of Jesus the ultimate

---

publication may be dated already too, though I do not have access to data that may indicate whether that rate is now high, low, or unchanged in its estimation.

15. John Paul II, *Et Unum Sint*, section 84.

16. Indeed, to the cause of all Truth: Daesh continues to shock with the deepest possible offense against human decency. When I revised these notes two years after first penning them, news was breaking of the death of Qassem Abdullah Yekya at Palmyra in Syria, where he was executed for his attempt to defend the priceless artefacts there, and of eighty-two-year-old Khalad al-Asad, who was beheaded some weeks later after weeks of torture. Khalad al-Asad had valiantly refused to reveal the location of the priceless historical items and paid for his defense of truth and decency with his life.

17. Johnson notes that *doxazein*, "to glory," appears in Hebrews only at 5:5 (Johnson, *Hebrews*, 144).

opening to the presence of God, an exaltation to the right hand of the throne of glory."[18]

This is not to suggest that I or any human being will stride to our deaths with the quiet confidence expected from hagiographers. Hagiographical traditions will almost always encourage God's people (or any group) to believe their forebears boldly strode toward death with a benign smile and airy wave. Such traditions will often revel in the contrary image too, almost sneering in the superior belief that those who do not share their beliefs face death in final abject terror. I have a faint memory of a Christian book written in the months following the Tenerife air disaster of March 1977. The author laments the cry of desperation from one of the crew in his last moments of life, dismissing it as a blasphemous outrage separating the speaker from salvation for all eternity. According to transcripts of the tragedy, the pilot of the Pan Am flight exclaimed, "Goddamn that son-of-a-bitch is coming!" ten seconds before the collision. The God of the author of Hebrews would not be defeated by the desperate and all too human cry of a man about to die. I know that when I once experienced a front-tire blowout on a motorcycle travelling at speed on an Australian freeway, I did not have the presence of mind to utter a prayer, and I fear my utterance was far more monosyllabic! That does not mean I did not mumble a shocked prayer of thanksgiving when eventually the bike stopped and I emerged from the "tank-slapper" experience unscathed.

It has been my pastoral privilege to journey with many people as they or their loved ones travel that final and mysterious path, albeit in less condensed circumstances. I have witnessed peaceful deaths and struggling deaths (all these, of course, of natural causes) both by believers and nonbelievers alike. I have no idea if I will march resurrection-confidently into my own death and certainly doubt I would be praying benignly if I were about to be torn asunder by lions or terrorists. That is not ultimately our author's point: the point is that the Great High Priest has rendered terror and death meaningless. The point is that divinity and eternity have entered into not only the throes of my death or yours, but also into the darkest extremes of death at the hands of the most horrific terrorism. This includes victims of Christian terrorists of the kind who lynched Jim Crow blacks or who beat gays or who abuse women, for in that pain God has struck the match of resurrection light (even when we who are religious practitioners do our best to extinguish it).

That is why the gospel narratives tell of the absolute cry of dereliction from Jesus on the cross: "How can one believe in God in the face of such

---

18. Ibid., 151–52.

horrendous suffering as slavery, segregation, and the lynching tree?"[19] That is why resurrection has to be the inseparable outcome of the execution of perfect righteousness and justice, so that for lynched Jim Crow blacks or abused women or bashed gays or the poorest of the poor condemned to an agonizing death at Bhopal, human hatred and its no-better cousin disinterest do not have the final word. That is why dismantling resurrection to a bourgeois metaphor of comfort is fundamentally destructive—a privilege that the global north's first-world white intellectuals might enjoy, but one that is not available to the family of a lynched man hanging from a tree. Even absolute dereliction, as represented in Jesus' (historic or otherwise) cry of the psalms' darkest moment, is caught up and transformed in the experience of the triune God. If "My God, my God, why have you forsaken me?" can be transformed into resurrection light, so too can the oh-so-human "Goddamn that son-of-a-bitch is coming!"

Therefore, when the High Priest of Hebrews is "subject to weakness" (Heb 5:2) it is the entire gamut of desperately normal humanness that he is subject to. While not reliant on the gospels, our author appears to reflect a common tradition that Jesus was not unmoved by the prospect of arrest, torture, and death portrayed in all the passion narratives.[20] Our author did not envisage the terror of colliding jumbo jets, but the whole gamut of human experience is caught up into the authorial vision of a "High Priest for us." Our author did have some limited exposure to varieties of economic and cultural experiences and believed that all were caught up into the Christ event. Your weakness, my weakness, and all the varieties of human weakness undergone in every human life is taken into and transformed by the redeeming, suffering heart of God as Jesus passes through the experience of "reverent submission" to all that humans undergo (Heb 5:7).

Christ's reverent submission to human experience, including suffering, is all the more incomprehensible when the Hebrews author reconnects to the Son's eternal status—the status by which the entire sermon is headlined (Heb 1:1–3). This status is re-emphasized when the preacher returns to stress the "Sonship" of the Christ at 5:8–9 as well as the salvific gateway that is opened in that Sonship. Reiteration of Sonship is, as Johnson notes,[21] a deliberate and heavily emphatic rhetorical ploy that does not reappear at any other point in the sermon.[22] Later, at Heb 12:4–11 the author will extrapolate a call to human obedience from the Son's obedience, but for now

---

19. Cone, *Cross*, 106.
20. Johnson, *Hebrews*, 145.
21. Ibid., 147.
22. Ellingworth, *Commentary*, 293.

christological obedience is the focus. In Graham Kendrick's memorable phrases, the Son's hands, which have "flung stars into space," are "to cruel nails surrendered."[23] That is our preacher's renewed and shocking reminder.

This surrender to the human experience of suffering and terror may represent not only experiences of passive submission to terror, but also submission to enmeshment in the circumstances that generate the opportunity to actively perpetrate terror. This is a passage about the author's soteriology, her understanding of salvation (Heb 5:9). While the emphasis here, as the author prepares to return to the exhortation that has been a dominant theme of the sermon, is on audience obedience, there is an underlying belief that the Son has entered into the deepest depths of human experience. This entails not only the experience of his being on the receiving end of evil, but also his experience of the potential to perpetrate evil. This understanding undergirds the temptation narratives (Matt 4:8–10, Luke 4:5–8) and serves as a reminder that all humanity has the ability to be exploitative. While it may seem impossible to us when confronted by daily news reports of global and domestic evil, the impression given by some New Testament authors is that even the perpetrators of evil—those ultimate expressions of cardiac sclerosis—are simply, if tragically, demonstrating the outcomes of their own surrender to sin and sinfulness. They have opened themselves up to the tyranny of their own propensity to inflict evil on themselves and others. The New Testament authors are adamant that perpetrators too can be included in the transforming, redeeming work of God in Christ. Paul, in the first chapter of Romans, is wrestling with this question as he outlines a series of indications of human imperfection, sin, and of God's "giving up" (Rom 1:24) humanity to the implications and out-workings of our own volitions.

The temptation narratives emphasize that Jesus does not succumb to temptation; at Heb 2:17, our author is clearly reiterating the identification of the Son with human failing, and then, with a significant subclause added, she repeats the idea at Heb 4:15. A contemporary understanding of sin recognizes that we are all entrapped in the webs of deceit that produce corrupt politicians, exploitative giants of commerce and industry, narratives of oppression and exploitation, imbalances of economic opportunity, and inequalities in health and life expectancy. Such an understanding must indicate that even the incarnation experience of the eternal Son has immersed him in humanity's inescapable web of sin, even if Jesus of Nazareth as such remained innocent of deliberate sin. The ritual cleansing of the high priest was, as we have noted, recognition and acknowledgment of his participation

---

23. Kendrick, "The Servant King" (© 1983 Thankyou Music).

in inadvertent sin: the Incarnate Son is endlessly enmeshed in the global evils of his day of incarnation and our days of embodiment in human flesh.

The transforming and redeeming efficacy of Jesus' death does, however, make his death, in one sense, a death unlike ours. Goldingay notes that even creation, long before redemption, was not about a chosen few: "this account of God's creation of humanity and God's words of blessing remind the chosen people(s) that God's choice of them is subordinate to a commitment to humankind as a whole."[24] The action of God is not about selecting an individual or a tribe over and against other individuals and tribes, but about efficacious action for all humanity and creation. Paul wrestles with the question of dying for, or on behalf of, another person at Rom 5:7, but neither Paul nor our author will allow the death of Jesus to have "merely" the efficacy of self-sacrifice (though that might be all that is deduced from the public recitations of John 15:13 at war memorial services).

Wilfred Owen is wrestling with the ineffectualness of mere self-sacrifice as he writes his tragic lines "O Love, your eyes lose lure / When I behold eyes blinded in my stead!"[25] Most of us in the third millennium have moved beyond that ideological nonchalance directed in the 1960s and 1970s towards those caught up in the Great Wars—a nonchalance that drove much cynical rhetoric of the post-Beatles era and, outside of the United States, led the majority of military remembrance events to dwindle to a hardy few participants. Now, even in my left-leaning, anti-military nation, the crowds that gather for our near-sacred ANZAC observances are growing exponentially. Yet even as we recognize the desperate magnificence of those who risked and sacrificed their lives (and recognize that the loved ones of the dead and injured lived emotionally maimed lives too), we would not elevate the sacrifice they made to divine status. Along with Wilfred Owen, we might well recognize that the dead and maimed were simply the by-product—George W. Bush's tragically expressed "collateral damage"—of malignant forces that chose to slay "half the seed of Europe, one by one"[26] as Western civilization joined together in its bloody "march from progress."[27]

Death, even in a noble cause, is not altogether good news if all that remains is the perpetration of continued evil: such perpetration would appear to be the story of human history as cycles of hatred endlessly continue. We might even recognize today that those saved by the sacrifice of others can be so damaged by survivor's guilt and posttraumatic stress disorder that

---

24. Goldingay, *Israel's Gospel*, 101.
25. "Greater Love" in Owen, *Collected Poems*, 41.
26. "The Parable of the Old Man and the Young" in ibid., 42.
27. "Strange Meeting" in ibid., 35.

they cease to function within the acceptable boundaries of normality and are pushed to social fringes despite the sacrifices made on their behalf. None of these syndromes equate with our author's claim for the individual man Jesus that "having been made perfect, he became the source of eternal salvation for all who obey him" (Heb 5:9). That claim in turn would not resonate with author or audience if it were not in accordance with the experience of liberation and redemption that author and audience shared. Nevertheless, human flesh (Heb 5:7) is tainted flesh, even after the complex after-the-fact narratives of virgin birth and (later) immaculate conception are included in the narrative of Christ's life.[28] In Jesus Christ, God had entered the human story and human experience in a unique and Godhead-changing way.

To develop this theme, our author turns to the somewhat shadowy figure of Melchizedek. Melchizedek's first appearance in the canon of Scripture is at Gen 14:17–24, where he ministers effectively, appropriately, and honorably, to Abram and becomes the first biblical character to refer to God as *ēl*.[29] Melchizedek's origin is as a priest and a king, and his actions of "bringing out" bread and wine to nourish Abram as the latter returns from an exhausting expedition to rescue his nephew Lot serve as a model of both sacred and civic leadership. Abram responds with a generous donation, a tithe of his belongings, to the warm-spirited and holy outsider priest (Westermann notes that this narrative could have emerged only when Israel and the Canaanites coexisted peacefully[30]). In Ps 110:4, the David priest-king (David and his successors) become bearers of the symbolism of "permanence, finality, immutability"[31] such that, while the chronological details of Melchizedek's life elude us, the symbolism carries all the weight of eternal significance.

Outside the canon of Scripture, there are further references to Melchizedek, and the Melchizedek text of Qumran elevates this figure to almost-Messiah-status, arguably beyond the "prototypical city-king."[32] The bringer of bread and wine of Gen 14:18 becomes in the Qumran documents one who "will make the final sacrifice at the end of the tenth Jubilee."[33] While Barker appears to suggest cross-fertilization between the Melchizedek of Qumran documents and Hebrews, I suggest that we need

---

28. Though this refers to an event or state at the beginning of Mary's life, it is a doctrine effectively "protecting" the purity of Jesus' bloodline.

29. Goldingay, *Israel's Gospel*, 242.

30. Westermann, *Genesis 12–36*, 207.

31. E. Jenni, "Das Wort *'ōlām* im Alten Testament," *ZAW* 64 (1952) 237, cited in Kraus, *Psalms 60–150*, 351.

32. Kraus, *Psalms 60–150*, 351.

33. Barker, *Great High Priest*, 71.

only propose that our author and the authors of Qumran documents were reaching deep into a common pool of symbols in an attempt to express the beyond-words significance of their respective priestly figures. Our author is not entirely interested in the "outsider dimensions" of Melchizedek in the Genesis text, but it might be significant to a twenty-first-century reader that this figure in the Abram saga can represent not only a "righteous Gentile" in Jewish terminology, but also a holy figure, Rahner's "anonymous Christian,"[34] even in a conservative understanding of a Christian doctrine of salvation. This is a faith-outsider whose praxis is exemplary, and we should not downplay our author's admiration for him. This, I repeat, is the first character of the biblical text to name the Hebrews' God as *ēl*. If for this reason alone, that as an outsider this Canaanite Melchizedek recognizes the Hebrews' God as "strength, might and power" (the underlying meanings of *ēl*), then we should not downplay our author's admiration for him. In a list of Christian martyrs above, I paid my respects to Bangladeshi professor Rezaul Karim Siddique, who as an alleged atheist, refused to bow to the brutal God of religious extremists, and died for his purported non-faith. The martyred outsider, even the martyred outsider who denies the existence of God, is closer to the Melchizidek narratives than those who promulgate hate in the name of faith.

Melchizedek, this outsider who is paradoxically the archetypal first temple priest, becomes a fulcrum between the sinful fallibility of the people of God and the restoring forgiveness of the redeeming God enacted in the temple rites. Barker, extending her identification of heaven and earth as revealed, symbolized, or enacted at the temple, moves beyond language such as my "fulcrum" so that the identification of heaven and earth and the identification of priest and YHWH become absolute: "the heavenly High Priest was the Lord who came from his holy place on the Day of Atonement in order to save his people from the power of the fallen angels, to punish their enemies, and to *kpr* the land."[35] Priests in the footsteps of Melchizedek, or "Melchizedek priests,"[36] became dispensers of the reconciliatory rites available through temple worship and upholders of righteousness.[37] The first temple, long destroyed, had represented all of creation both visible and

---

34. See, for example, Rahner, "Christianity and the Non-Christian Religions," 115–34.

35. Barker, *Great High Priest*, 51. Barker is referring to Ps 82:1, Isa 52:7, Dan 9:25, and Isa 61:2–3. She adds, "I suggest, in the light of this, that *kpr* has to mean restore, recreate, or heal" (ibid.).

36. This terminology is also Barker's. See Barker, "Great High Priest," 2.

37. Ibid.

invisible,[38] and there the priests had overseen and administered symbols and symbolic actions that represented the relationship between God and God's earth.

Following the sacking of the first temple and the building of the less grand, less complete second temple, many of those items were not restored, and the shadowy story of a Melchizedek priesthood, along with rites of anointing, were relegated into abeyance: "Voices in the final chapters of Isaiah complained that the restored temple was a mockery."[39] Longing for the reinstitution of that priesthood became a hallmark of Judaism into the second temple period, and this longing resurfaces in the early Christians' use of Ps 110 as a key christological proof text. There, the dialogue of "The Lord" with "my Lord" (Ps 110:1) and the fulfilment of God's promise of the Melchizedek priesthood's endlessness (Ps 110:4) combine in the belief that Jesus of Nazareth reinstituted and incarnated that priesthood eternally. Barker notes that the attribution of the title "Christ," or "Anointed One," to Jesus was inseparably linked to the Melchizedek-longing: the oils of anointing and the Melchizedek priesthood had together been omitted from second temple rites and practices, and that deliberate absence crystalized in longing for a figure to pick up the Melchizedek mantle. Jesus is "depicted as the great High Priest throughout his ministry, taking away sins and making the broken whole."[40]

If an early date for Hebrews is accepted, then the second temple was still standing when the sermon was preached. If a later date is accepted, then it was gone. Either way, Christians were disconnecting the experience of temple from locality and associating it instead with the believer (1 Cor 6:19). Christians had quickly utilized Jesus' sayings to demonstrate that the gathered people were themselves temple priests (1 Pet 2:9) ministering within the temple Jesus, the Christ released through space and time by the ascension and made present through space and time by the coming of the Spirit. In baptism, the symbolism was unambivalent:

> The name 'Christians', first used in Antioch[41] meant more than just 'followers of the Christ, the anointed one.' Since Christians were also anointed at their baptism, the name means something like 'little anointed ones', and so we are all little Melchizedeks,

---

38. Ibid., 4. She notes also that it was "a larger, permanent version of the tabernacle" (ibid., 5).
39. Barker, *Great High Priest*, 151.
40. Ibid.
41. Acts 11:26.

little royal High Priests. This is what St Peter said to those Christians in Asia Minor: 'You are a royal priesthood.'[42]

Our Hebrews author has traversed into a theological lesson of universal Melchizedek priesthood, or "Melchizedekism," a theological understanding from which, after flagging its importance, the author withdraws: these things, the author indicates, are probably too hard for us to understand. This mild insult is a rhetorical trick devised to rattle us in our complacency. But, as the author returns to a tone of exhortation last used at Heb 4:14–16, the point has been made: as little Melchizedeks, we are called to be a blessing, not curse, to those around us.

---

42. Barker, "Great High Priest," 4.

9

You Have Not Persevered, Dullard!
Heb 5:11—6:8

THE PREACHER RECOGNIZES THAT the time is right for a change in tone: "Like effective communicators today, ancient rhetoricians knew how to alter the rhythm and pace of their discourses."[1] Another cyclical theme has been building through the author's sermon: persevere. It is a theme well-grounded in the Judeo-Christian witness (e.g., Sir 2:10b, 12–14, Mark 13:13b, and indeed all the apocalyptic vision of Mark 13). The preacher returns to that theme, generating a not altogether flattering contrast between the perfect obedience of the suffering Son and the audience's below-par faith performance: "by this time you ought to be teachers: you need someone to teach you again the basics" (Heb 5:12, my translation).

This is not a contemporary sermon from a gentle preacher of my denomination! Still, with a faintly ironic and self-deprecatory twist, the author begins a reprimand with a reference to the length of the sermon in which both preacher and audience are engaged. It appears that audiences of first-century sermons were little less complaining about loquacious sermon delivery than a twenty-first-century audience, and it may be that tales such as the infamous "autodefenestration" of the young man of Troas in Acts 20:9 or the faintly ironic observation of 2 Pet 3:16 reflect the little-remarked-upon self-mocking humor of the earliest saints. It is worth noting though that in first-century contexts, the 4950 or so words of the text of Hebrews did not constitute a long oration, so the claim that the "word of exhortation" is "brief" (Heb 13:22) is less ironic than it might sound to contemporary Christians from some denominations. The author is generating a sarcastic warning: the audience's potential failure to maintain concentration during this sermon contrasts poorly with the exemplary obedience even in suffering of the Son.

1. Johnson, *Hebrews*, 154.

While in the evangelical and pentecostal traditions of our era a sermon of some forty-five to fifty minutes, as I estimate the book of Hebrews to be when orated in Greek, is not unusual, in my more sacramental and liturgical tradition anything more than fifteen minutes is considered to be beyond the pale. In either case, the orator must use changes in pace, style, and other aural devices to maintain the audience's interest. The author therefore breaks the didactic theological reflection on Melchizedek and Melchizedek priesthood with a fleeting glimpse of derogatory humor, delicately crossing the line to deliver a rebuke to the audience for its collective obtuseness. Few preachers or homilists today would risk the direct admonition of "About this we have much to say that is hard to explain, because you have become dull in understanding" (*nōthroi tais akoais*; see Heb 5:11).

In the Greek, there is an awkward but revealing key to the life-or-death purpose that underlies the author's rhetoric at this point. Scholars note the disempowering effect of the English construction "we have much to say" at Heb 5:11. The author's use of the awkward English phrase "we have much wordage" (my translation) contains the biblically weighty word *logos*, that word beloved of John in the opening of the Fourth Gospel. At one level, our author's construction should not be given the full weight of, for example, John's usage, for phrases similar to *polus hēmin ho logos* are a procedural description of a long speech:[2] "We have much to say" captures this idea. But Craddock is right to draw attention to an inevitably deeper implication to the word *logos*.[3] When George W. Bush, arguably inadvertently, used the word "crusade" to describe his forthcoming military response to the events of 9/11,[4] he used a word that was mere descriptive language in non-Muslim usage but one that was pregnant with meaning to a Muslim world. Our author was operating in a context where *logos* had far deeper meaning than mere "talk." The use of *logos* at Heb 6:1, as well as the echo of the word in the use of *logion* (oracles[5]) at Heb 5:12 suggests, if only at a subconscious level, that this construction is carrying at the very least the weight of "discourse," that word of postmodern literary and sociological analysis that means so much more than mere conversation or speech.[6] In Māori, the word used to translate *logos*

---

2. Ellingworth, *Commentary*, 299.

3. Craddock, "Hebrews," 67.

4. "This crusade, this war on terrorism is going to take a while" (George W. Bush, "Remarks by the President Upon Arrival," Press Conference on the White House South Lawn, September 16, 2001, https://georgewbush-whitehouse.archives.gov/news/releases/2001/09/20010916-2.html).

5. Note especially the usage at Num 24:16.

6. I have used the word several times already in this study and will several times more. Also note Johnson's careful use of the word in this context (Johnson, *Hebrews*,

is *kōrero* (pronounced as three syllables);[7] if my understanding of Māori is correct, this too bears all the weight of deeper discourse.

So, even if there is a faint touch of humor in the portrayal of the audience as obtuse, it also holds a deadly purpose: this first-century preacher has no time to indulge in pleasantries. This preacher is reaching a stage of critical desperation exacerbated by a firm belief that it is not possible, once a person has lapsed from faith, to return to it. The preacher draws a delicate contrast between Jesus' readiness to exercise obedience to God (Heb 5:8-10) and the audience's nonchalance. Ellingworth's observation that "the author's hesitation to embark on the difficult teaching about Christ's High Priesthood is not a rhetorical device"[8] is not entirely correct, as in fact Ellingworth goes on to acknowledge. At the very least, it bookends a phase in which the preacher turns to stern exhortation that reappears at Heb 6:20. But it is more than just a bookend; it is a skilled rhetorical device engineered to sting the audience into concentrated attention and response. Offense is a risk the author is prepared to take, because the audience members' conversion and post-conversion experience has provided such a powerful contrast to their previous lives without Christ that they will not, once they have been reminded of the stakes, renege (Heb 6:9).

The author is not about to pull any punches, and so builds on the sarcasm regarding the audience's inability to endure a difficult sermon with the even more acerbic observation that "you need milk, not solid food"—an observation that reverberates through the rebuke of 5:12-14. The echo of 1 Cor 3:2 suggests, at the very least, that this author is drawing on a rhetorical pool similar to Paul's.[9] Sarcasm, popularized as the "lowest form of wit," was not unheard of in the arsenal of biblical writers, as Paul's loaded tones in 2 Cor 10:7 or 2 Cor 12:11 remind us. If this author was influenced by Paul, then she has learned the master's rhetorical skills well.

Beneath the rhetorical irony, the sentences of Heb 5:11-14 do not prevaricate: if you lapse from the disciplines of faith, then your brain and indeed your life become ill-disciplined and ultimately useless. The author is returning to an earlier motif but allowing the return to appear almost tangential. This theme was first introduced at Heb 2:3-4, emphasizing that the experiences of the past, the first flushes of faith, and the signs and wonders were reserved for "back then." Experiential dimensions were mushy infant

---

158).

7. *He maha nei ā mātou kōrero mō tēnei.*

8. Ellingworth, *Commentary,* 298.

9. For use of the "milk/meat" metaphor outside biblical sources, see Attridge, *Hebrews,* 159n59.

food, not the solid matter needed to sustain mature faith in troubled times. Our preacher is suggesting that if we want to loiter, wishing things were the way they once were, then our brains will atrophy. To fall back is, we will later be told, "destruction" (Heb 10:39).

So the audience, in seemingly slightly gentler phrasing now, is urged to "go on towards perfection" (Heb 6:1). Perfection is here a shorthand term to embrace all that might be meant by "eternity" or by "heaven"—both of which dwell beyond our ability to comprehend—together with the fulfilment of human potential implicit in that state of perfected and immortalized existence. The alternative translation, "maturity," might be preferable. Craddock again expresses the notion well: "[T]he term is used to describe the moral, ethical, intellectual, and spiritual goal of the believer's life—a goal achieved by learning, practice, and teaching others, a goal expected of all who submit themselves to the resources for Christian growth."[10]

But the author is once more using a rhetorical ploy by stating, point by point, the matters she is professing not to be about to reconsider. It is a benevolent form of apophasis,[11] or ostensibly pretending to set aside common and agreed ground between author or orator and audience, in order simultaneously to reiterate it. It is also an oratorical ploy consistent with the immediately previous use of sarcasm: our author is utilizing every ploy to make the audience recognize their obtuseness, their unreadiness for the "perfection" that is presumably extolled as their life-target. The items listed are representative of the audience's early catechesis, reaching back to the time in which faith was an ecstatic and vibrant experience. It is worth noting, in the context of a contemporary reading of Hebrews, just what those representative "constituents"[12] were: repentance, baptism, some rite of healing or perhaps transmission indicated as the "laying on of hands," resurrection, and judgment. Robert Gordon and others have noted that there is nothing specifically christological in this list, and they draw contrasts with 1 Tim 3:16 and its more developed christology.[13]

The audience is called to leave behind the solipsistic, self-centered first flushes of faith—the "it's all about me" phase of childish and perhaps even, we might say today, fundamentalist faith—but they are *not* to leave behind the teaching and knowledge of Christ that was their first formation in faith (Heb 6:1–2). Again, it is worth remembering the self-obsession of much

---

10. Craddock, "Hebrews," 68.

11. Apophasis is an oratorical form of saying one thing and doing another. The oft-cited example is the parliamentary ploy of announcing, "I will not mention the Member's propensity for drunkenness."

12. Craddock, "Hebrews," 71.

13. Gordon, *Hebrews*, 91. C.f. Lane, *Hebrews 1–8*, 140.

contemporary Christian lyricism, which is constantly returning to self-centered experience: "I went to the enemy's camp and I took back what he stole from me"! It is to be hoped that as we go on in faith, our knowledge of the teachings of Christ and of faith in Christ will grow deeper. This depends on the grace of God, of course: "we will do this, if God permits" (Heb 6:3).

There is a hint here that life may not always be so easy. We are challenged to accept the years and the circumstances that God gives us, not, thank God, knowing what lies around the corner. Karl Barth, with his strong sense of the unquestionable authority of God, may not be the most popular theologian in the twenty-first century, but he offers an insight that is fundamentally akin to that of our preacher when he recognizes the importance of Jeremiah's perspective: "Can I not do with you, O house of Israel, just as this potter has done?" (Jer 18:5).[14] Barth links Jer 18:6 and Rom 9:20 with Matt 20:15, "Am I not allowed to do what I choose with what belongs to me?"[15] While there are certain legal circumstances in which the answer to the rhetorical question of the Matthean Jesus' landowner is "No, you are not," the general implication remains the same: "You may do as you chose. God may do as God chooses." The God of the author of Hebrews remains free to take us on the path God chooses for us.

The author's understanding is that we are not in this alone. The archetypal Melchizedek priest is there on the journey with us and for us. The notion of "perfection" that has undergirded Heb 6:1 is about our maturity in faith, as Craddock has emphasized, but it is also about the perfection of Christ. Perhaps the author is trying to load too much into the Greek word *teleiotēs*, this perfection or maturity, and what Craddock refers to as "the eschatological flavor of the word."[16] The word *teleiotēs*, from *teleos*, is the same word from which we derive "teleology," or the study of endings and last things. That completion is the driving force of process theology visions like that of Teilhard de Chardin or even the atheistic philosophy of Thomas Nagel. Nagel, while not departing from his philosophical atheism, suggests that the philosopher should at the very least allow the possibility that "principles of a different kind are also at work in the history of nature, principles of the growth of order that are in their logical form teleological rather than mechanistic."[17]

Therefore, deeply imbedded in this word *teleiotēs* is the author's dual sense that if we, the audience, persevere, then the perseverance of the One

---

14. Barth, *Church Dogmatics*, 3:1, 36.
15. Ibid., 2:1, 526. See also Isa 29:16, 46:9, 64:8.
16. Craddock, "Hebrews," 70.
17. Nagel, *Mind and Cosmos*, 7.

who has already persevered will lead us into the fullness of completion: there is no word that can bear the full weight of these intertwined ideas. Teilhard is strangely helpful at this point (though atheistic Nagel should not be discounted as an aid to our comprehension of our Hebrews author). Teilhard's notion is that all creation is striving forward under the energies of God to a completion, a universal Omega Point. Our author might demur at the cosmic dimensions of Teilhard's vision, for our author is addressing only a potentially lapsing community of faith without interest in cosmic visions. But the direction of the divine energies is the same. That is why there can be no looking back (Heb 6:1, cf. Luke 9:62), in thought or behavior, from this point: God's energies are striving forward, and for our author, unlike Teilhard, the audience runs the risk of stepping outside the direction of those energies.

We are taken back to an earlier theme: there is no return for those who fail (Heb 6:4–8). Perhaps at Heb 6:8 we hear an echo of the Jesus parable of the Sower? The New Testament writers rarely seem to quote Jesus sayings exactly (they weren't written down until perhaps a few years after our document, if an early date is proposed for Hebrews), but they appear to know them well enough to use them as part of the common pool of shared ideas in their discourse. Images of destruction by fire are a vivid metaphor for the fate of those who incur the wrath of God in judgment. They have long been a part of the arsenal of weaponry in Christian preaching and, dare I say it, propaganda.[18] These images have been used as leverage to persuade outsiders or lapsing believers to adopt or continue in Christian belief, motivated by fear of eternal torment.[19] Our author's motivation was to deter members of a vulnerable and socially marginalized faith community from lapsing, but I am not convinced such language works in a contemporary context. The plethora of websites, essays, and monographs dedicated to the needs of those "recovering" from faith or religion[20] suggest that contexts in which

---

18. Dr. James Harding has reminded me that the word comes from modern Latin *congregatio de propaganda fide* "congregation for propagation of the faith."

19. Paul Bayly, quoting Livingstone's letters, writes with respectful amusement of the hellfire preaching of David Livingstone and his confreres: "The church services were an interesting spectacle; over three hundred natives normally attended services. But it was not always a happy occasion; in response to warnings about the promise of eternal damnation for those that chose not to follow God's path, the congregation would shrink away in terror; some of the Bechuanas would hide their faces under their karosses while others would fall to the floor and creep around under the pews. More distracting would be those that actually ran out of the church and disappeared into the distance, fleeing with all their might'" (Bayly, *David Livingstone*, 36).

20. In particular, I draw attention to the Richard Dawkins Foundation website, https://richarddawkins.net/recoveringfromreligion, and the website of the Skeptical

Christian belief (as well as other belief systems) have done great damage are legion, and the lack of respect Christian representatives, particularly in the global north, have shown to practitioners of other faiths and of no faith is a blight on our history. I do not recommend a bowdlerized Bible in which texts that no longer suit our communal taste are excised, but we must always remember that our post-Constantine (and post-Holocaust) world is a very different one from the world in which our author put pen to papyrus to deter her struggling faith community from apostasy.

Consequently, I will not dwell greatly on a passage that once cast me, then a fresh convert, into paroxysms of fear. Would I be able to hold to the faith I had just embraced and to continue in it until what I assumed would be the imminent second coming, expected long before my natural death?[21] Was I likely to be guilty of the attempt to "re-crucify" Christ,[22] slipping under duress or perhaps ennui (though I felt little of that at nineteen!) from faith only to find no way to return? Hebrews 6:4–8 was a passage designed to urge potential lapsers back to the fold of faith—a passage written in the shadow of imminent judgment and without the long corporate history of Christianity's and Christians' myriad lapses from integrity and authentic witness. Today, while wanting to encourage those around us to return to the Christ-encounter in which we rejoice, we might simply ensure the credibility and integrity of our own witness so that others are not dissuaded from the warm embrace of the Christ event. We might, and should, stress that a narrative of individual apostasy rates somewhat lower on the Richter scale of pastoral or prophetic concern than the apostate moral evil that re-crucified Christ over and again in the lynching fields of the Deep South and in the many other theaters of evils perpetrated against blacks, gays, women, and other persecuted groups in Christian history.[23]

Poets Society, http://skepticalpoet.blogspot.co.nz/p/coming-out-godless.html. See also Sentilles, *Breaking Up*; and DeWitt, *Hope after Faith*.

21. See my comments on the imminent and misguided apocalypticism of the 1970s in Godfrey, *Babylon's Cap*, 23–24.

22. I had not at that time encountered Kazantzakis's powerful novel *Christ Recrucified*.

23. I would not encounter James Cone's powerful narrative "The Re-crucified Christ in Black Literary Imagination" (chapter 4 of his *The Cross and the Lynching Tree*) until many years after coming to my faith. That is surely a far more important tragic narrative than the individual apostasy I feared in the late 1970s. I did, however, encounter Cone's *Black Theology and Black Power* as part of the reading list of a paper entitled "Critical Issues in Modern Religion" in the Religious Studies Department of Massey University in that era. I remain forever grateful to the Department's Brian Colless, Peter Donovan, and the late Enid Bennett for their navigation of the thorny issues raised in that and other papers I studied under their guidance. The Department was later axed in the name of progress and outcomes-based fiscal policy in the tertiary sector.

The implication of Heb 5:11–14 may have been that the author fears her audience members are too indolent in their faith to take the allusion to the challenging solid food of Jesus's teachings on board at all. Nevertheless, the preacher proceeds in faith, believing in the power of oratory and the infusion of the oratorical venture by God's Spirit. Thomas Long observes:

> Like all preachers before and since, the author of Hebrews knows that his only resource, his only weapon, his only scalpel, his only lifeline is the spoken word. If the gospel is to be preached and believed, it will not be because of skits, stained glass, PowerPoint™, or praise bands. If faith is to be born, it will come because some preacher climbs into a pulpit somewhere with nothing but the frail vessels of human words, prays like mad that they will be filled with the cargo of the Spirit, and launches them across the wide sea of human hearing, hopeful that they will find safe harbor in receptive ears.[24]

The tone therefore becomes more conciliatory after Heb 5:14, recognizing that there had been, in the recent past, good and productive effort on the part of the Hebrews, even if this effort had now faded (Heb 6:10). This may have been the mutual support—incorporating not only support in prayer but also economic support—that appears to have been a hallmark of the early Christians. This can be seen, for example, in the correspondence of 1 Thessalonians (see 1 Thess 4:11–12) and the narrative account in Acts 2:44–45 and Acts 4:32. The term of endearment "beloved" (Heb 10:9), much loved by Paul in his writings, is used for the first and only time in this context in Hebrews as if to add weight to the author's appeals. Under the weight of apocalyptic urgency,[25] a corrective stick has been wielded in an attempt to bring this congregation of faith back into the succession of those who stand faithful to God's promises (Heb 6:12), but that stick is now withdrawn, and a seed of hope is introduced. The congregation members' energies are waning, but God's energies are not, and it is God's energies that may, ultimately and if God is willing, re-energize and re-focus the Hebrews.

So, using the authorial plural to add emphasis, the author pronounces "we are confident of better things in your case." This change of tone is designed to maintain the listeners' interest in restoring relations after the reprimands of previous statements. At Heb 6:10, the audience of believers is encouraged by the affirmation that God has noted their past achievements—achievements presumably made during times of or closer to those

---

24. Long, foreword to *Preaching Hebrews*, xii.
25. See Johnson, *Hebrews*, 164.

first flushes of faith. Their track record is not "thorns and thistles."[26] A contemporary Christian might be reminded of his or her individual achievements in the past, while the Christian community *en masse* might today be reminded of the great philanthropic achievements made in the name of its faith, including contributions (much forgotten today) to science and scientific investigation, to medicine, to social welfare, to the humanities—all these could be attributed to Christianity, and the Christian community could own to them with joy. This is the technique to which our author momentarily turns: a bouquet is offered after the brick-bats. Obviously, atheists and agnostics, Muslims and Jews, Buddhists and Hindus and Jains and Confucians could all line up their pantheons of saints and contributors to human wellbeing. My point is not that Christianity is unique in having made beneficial contributions to human wellbeing. My point is that the author wants the audience to know that there *is* room to take pleasure in runs on the metaphorical board and take joy in our achievements. There is not, however, room for complacency or nonchalance, and it is into that syndrome that this audience is sliding.

Caught up in that for which the Hebrews can be praised is their demonstration of mutual love. The great early observation "see how they love one another" is an outflowing of an imperative running through the exhortative passages of the New Testament and early Christian texts. Paul again and again challenged his audiences to the responsibilities of mutual love; the second half of Rom 12 is effectively a panegyric to the challenges and outcomes of love to community members and to those beyond alike, while Rom 15 returns to the themes once more. The great "Hymn to Love" of 1 Cor 13 is a celebration of the potentials and challenges of exemplary love. Even in the cool disciplinary tone of Galatians, Paul takes time to emphasize the responsibilities of mutual love (Gal 6:2). Sentence after sentence of the Johannine epistles is devoted to the call to mutually supportive and enriching love (1 John 4:7), and even the strained tone of 3 John is lightened by reference to the beloved Christians' achievements of love (3 John 6).

In turning to this theme and offering qualified praise, the author is laying a foundation for a link back to an earlier salvo in the sermon. The slipping Hebrews are being called to imitate their earlier selves; this would be a contradiction of the idea that they are not to hanker after the "milk" and hyped ecstasy of their first flushes of faith, but they are not being called to dwell on their passive but rather their active earlier selves. "Diligence" (Heb 6:11; the verb has previously appeared at Heb 4:11) is a word of applied action (Rom 12:8) that reminds the audience there is nothing haphazard

---

26. Ibid., 165.

about attainment of the badges of honor (Heb 12:1).[27] Audience members are to train as diligently now as in any time during their early enthusiasm and in fact more so, for now the hype has passed and the going is tougher. Most athletes will note that towards the end of their career, the application of discipline and that attribute known in Australia as "hard yakka" is the only way of ensuring continuance in their sport. Of course, the metaphor breaks down: the athletes in reality go on, usually, to other phases of their life until life ends. The faith-endurance our author is seeking goes on until life closes. It does not, at least in my own experience, grow easier, and the application of discipline becomes a greater and greater imperative.[28]

The author now reproduces some earlier illustrations. The fidelity of Jesus to his vocation has been a subtext since Heb 2:18 and 5:7–10; the author returns to hints of the patriarchs' fidelity to their cause by reminding her audience of the tenacity of Moses (Heb 3) and Joshua (Heb 4:8). Hebrews 6:9–12 is best summarized as the coach's more conciliatory tone: you have shown what you can do, now keep doing it!

---

27. Metaphors of athleticism are used also by Paul and his school: see 1 Cor 9:24–26, Phil 2:16, Gal 2:2 and 5:5, and 2 Tim 2:5, 4:7. They are a commonplace in an era still rejoicing in the Olympic tradition, as for example in the work of Epictetus (*Dissertations* 4.4.11–13) and Seneca (*De Otio* 6.2, 94.45).

28. Serious mention should be made of the pastoral dimension of dementia. I have encountered many times those whose faith appears to be distorted or lost in the "sinuous rills" (Samuel Taylor Coleridge, "Kubla Khan," line 8.) and muddles of this state. I have known pious people whose vocabulary has been swallowed up by four-lettered expletives in their manifestations of copralalia, sometimes associated with Tourette's syndrome, and other complex and distressing manifestations of what is ultimately no more than a chemically malfunctioning organ, the brain. These are in no way manifestations of the person's departure from the embrace of a loving God!

10

God Is Faithful: Heb 6:13–20

To support this new tone of encouragement, the author shifts her argument from exhortation to exposition once again and moves to a particularly dense and difficult phase of the sermon. The question of God's promise was originally flagged at Heb 2:16, when Abraham was introduced into the sermon as a prototype of faith and patient endurance. Abraham, as Paul emphasizes in his writings (Rom 4:13–25, Gal 3:6–29), was the recipient of a promise, and he held tenaciously to that promise against all odds. Can the Hebrews do the same, knowing, as they have been reminded, that God will keep to the divine side of the equation? Like Paul, and perhaps learned from Paul, this author wants her listeners to seize that promise offered to Abraham and make it their own, thereby becoming the "descendants of Abraham" referred to at Heb 2:16 both in belief and in practice. Abraham, in offering his son Isaac for sacrifice (despite the promise that he would receive offspring by him), demonstrates such tenacity in faith that he becomes the archetype (*tupos*) of right faith, right perseverance, and persistence against all odds. At the time of the Isaac's near-death, an angel repeats the promise that has been made earlier to Abraham (Gen 22:15–18), but Abraham does not in any mortal sense live to see fulfilment of that promise, despite our author's summary statement "Abraham, having patiently endured, obtained the promise" (Heb 6:15). Given the time scheme of the expounded promise (Gen 15:5), fulfillment of the promise in the recipient's lifetime is not possible, but the majestic sweep of the promise is unambivalent. Comparing Gen 15:5 with the Old Testament's other command to stargaze (Isa 40:26), Westermann notes "in both cases looking at the stars is looking into the broad expanse of the activity of the creator which transports man's gaze from the narrow horizon of human events."[1] The hint of course here is that no matter how tenacious the Hebrews are, they may not see fulfilment of the promise they are challenged to hold to tenaciously (Heb 11:13), but that

---

1. Westermann, *Genesis 13–36*, 221–22.

is simply a fact of the human journey. Most of the designers and builders of the great cathedrals of Europe never saw completion of their labor either.

Despite the remarkable philosophical depth of Kierkegaard's exploration of the Isaac saga in *Fear and Trembling*, it probably does not serve the ancient narrative well to engage in too deep a reconstruction of the tale according to post-Enlightenment interests in the human psyche. For Kierkegaard, the Isaac sacrifice scene is a test of human obedience to absolute divine will, just as it is in the hands of our author. But the deeper questions of the damage done to the psyche of the almost-victim Isaac by Abraham's fanatical adherence to perceptions of divine will are not addressed in the broad symbolic narrative the original authors and narrators used to paint the Abram saga.[2] The aim of the ancient authors is similar to ours: Abraham was tested, Abraham obeyed, Abraham triumphed. The mental health wards of modern society are full of those whose fanatical adherence to an obsession has led them to commit or attempt murder.

International military campaigns are being waged against Daesh, the Taliban, and other forms of maniacal religious extremism that are committed to the firm belief that some form or other of divinity condones slaughter. In the week in which this paragraph was first composed, Taliban extremists shot more than 130 children and ten adults dead in Peshawar, Pakistan, in the name of Allah. Meanwhile, a "lone wolf" and clearly mentally disturbed individual, Man Haron Monis,[3] seized hostages in a Sydney café, citing allegiance to militant Daesh and its pretensions to Islamic supremacy before he and two others[4] were killed in a hail of bullets. Neither Monis nor the Taliban represented the heart of Islam, and the Islamic Council of Australia and Islamic leadership throughout the world condemned these actions.

Terrorism is not a product of religion, and the chain of events leading to the uprisings of the Taliban, Daesh, or the maniacal actions of a mentally ill Iraqi refugee in Sydney cannot be laid at the feet of religious traditions. Those traditions, as represented by our text, may when appropriately interpreted even provide answers. Liberation theologian James Cone notes:

> I wrestle with questions of black dignity in a world of white supremacy because I believe that the cultural and religious resources in the black experience could help all Americans cope with the legacy of white supremacy and also deal more

---

2. Once more, this must be said with due deference to survivors of sexual and other forms of abuse by authority figures in the Christian community.

3. An assumed name—the man's real name was Manteghi Bourjerdi.

4. Café manager Tori Johnson, aged thirty-four, was killed when he attempted to overcome the hostage-taker. Customer Katrina Dawson died shortly after as a result of her injuries as the police ended the siege with gunfire after Bourjedi killed Johnson.

effectively with what is called "the war on terror." If white Americans could look at the terror they inflicted on their own black population—slavery, segregation, lynching—then they might be able to understand what is coming at them from others. Black people know something about terror because we have been dealing with legal and extralegal white terror for centuries. Nothing was more terrifying than the lynching tree.[5]

Can the Hebrews hold to the promise our author believes to be at the heart of their faith? The argument from the Isaac saga is complex and obscure: God swore to Abraham but could swear on no higher authority than God's own self. There is much swearing of oaths in the Hebrew Scriptures (e.g., Jer 22:5) and the author of our text appears to know nothing of Jesus' injunction against oath-taking (Matt 5:34–37). Other authors do: James, who shared a close relationship and ministry with Matthew, opposes this kind of contract (Jas 5:12). In the Hebrew Scriptures, God is often self-binding, meaning that ultimately the choice of whether a follower of Christ should or should not take an oath is probably between that person and God. It is not altogether the issue here in any case. The issue here is that God is, as Saint Anselm put it, "that than which nothing greater can be conceived," or an authority beyond which there is no authority, the greatest authority and the author of authority (the words are, of course, related).

This solemn promise of God then is not about God's integrity (if God had no integrity, God would be less than perfect and therefore less than Anselm's "that than which no greater"). The promise is a reassurance to God's people. It is a reminder that God is not an abstract being at the outer edge of a friendless universe, but is instead a being who understands human doubts and fears. It isn't easy, but God knows that, and by remembering the power of that divine promise to Abraham, we might be "strongly encouraged" to continue our faith journey, seizing "the hope that is set before us" (Heb 6:18). This hope is to be for us (the author again includes herself with the audience) a sure and steadfast anchor of the soul (Heb 6:19).

This may seem abstract to us. We live in a world in which there are no anchors: choose your truth. Authority is unpopular. Can an old story about a Hebrew patriarch really encourage us, especially when faced with the dark ambiguities of twenty-first-century medieval executions paraded on postmodern social media? Yet it is doubtful that it is harder for us to believe than it was for the Hebrews. Our greatest postmodern enemies are flaccidity and marginalization: Christians are becoming nonchalant in faith (like the Hebrews) and being pushed to the comic sidelines of society (where the

---

5. Cone, *Cross*, xviii–xix.

Hebrews were). Yet we have a hope in a promise. Indeed, it is the best we have, but we could do far worse. At the very least, this belief in a promise trumps, it seems at least to this twenty-first-century believer, belief in imagined combinations of stars (i.e., astrology) or the endless pull-yourself-up-by-your-bootstraps self-help programs that fill our retail bookshelves. It beats hugging crystals, reading tarot cards and tea leaves, or polishing auras. It trumps these popular alternatives, I suggest, because an essential dynamic of the promise narrative of Judeo-Christian storytelling is its willingness to permit God-in-Christ to enter the very depths of human experience of sin and suffering, even that perpetrated by terrorists. That theological emphasis has underpinned the narrative since Heb 2:17–18.

For the Hebrews and for us, for all the faults of our shared faith, there is nevertheless the offer of ancient narratives of lives transformed by belief and trust in a Creator God. We cannot know exactly what Abraham and Isaac experienced (I am presupposing some degree of factual, historical basis to the Abram saga), and we certainly don't want to join them in that experience, but we can see that it formed the consciousness of a nation-people that followed after them. We can't even know exactly what Jesus experienced that first Easter morning, but we can see that it transformed his followers from fear-filled blunderers to martyrs for a faith. From a purely objective perspective, were such a thing possible, we are engaged here in a circular argument. I am not keen on the type of Christian evangelism that proclaims the proof of some sort of attestation of faith to be the mere fact that the Bible cites it as true; this was the sort of circular argument in which Josh McDowell engaged in his *Evidence that Demands a Verdict*. In the terms our author uses, Jesus passed through a curtain and invites his followers to do likewise in his footsteps. At the very least, we might suggest the benefits of believing outweigh the disadvantages, no matter what our society thinks should be the dominant narrative of our time.

11

Melchizedek . . . the Argument from the Lesser to the Greater: Heb 7:1–28

THE TRADITION OF WESTERN scholarship in which you likely and I certainly stand (whether we are janitors' assistants, as once I was, or astrophysicists or anything in between) is very scientific rationalism. We like proof, which authenticates the experience of encountering a pudding, as it were. Many Christian fundamentalists are critical of "scientific rationalism" (as they are of "humanism" and indeed of many other "-isms"). I am not. My vehicle generally stays on the road because scientific rationalists have put it together and maintain it. The cathedral at which I was based when writing these thoughts stays standing and open to the public because the scientific method, the outcome of scientific rationalism, was applied to its design and construction. Scientific rationalism, or the application of intellectual and deductive reason to material problems, is critical to a postindustrial world. The problem, as I indicated in my introduction to these studies, is when scientific rationalism is applied where it has no place being. Robbie Burns' love was not like a *Rosaceae Rosa*, red or otherwise, and we know it. But we know what he meant too.

Rabbinical scholars had a wonderful means by which to interpret and elucidate Scripture. A section of Hebrew text would, to most of us, look bewildering:

בְּרֵאשִׁית בָּרָא אֱלֹהִים אֵת הַשָּׁמַיִם וְאֵת הָאָרֶץ:

To the rabbinical scholar, the shape of every letter was sacred: "When Rabbi Meir came to Rabbi Ishmael and gave his profession as a scribe [of the Torah] the latter required of him the utmost care, 'for if you leave out a single letter or write a single letter too much, you will be found as one who destroys the whole world.'"[1] The Matthean Jesus plays with this notion when

---

1. From the Babylonian Talmud, *Erub.* 13a, quoted in Handelman, *Slayers*, 27.

he declares, here in the beautifully evocative King James, "Till heaven and earth pass, one jot or one tittle shall in no wise pass from the law" (Matt 5:18). The spaces between the letters, which look like << >>, are equally sacred. To these rabbinic scholars, particularly when using the playful interpretative tools of Aggadah,[2] this space within and between the letters is where interpretation and application—your role and mine—begin: "For the Rabbis, the oral Torah is precisely what lies between the lines."[3]

If we look at the first letter in the text above, the one on the right, ב (*beth*) we might notice that it closes off everything to its right—that is to say (since Hebrew is read from right to left), everything *before* it. This is not insignificant, because this text reads, "In the beginning God created the heavens and the earth . . ." or, perhaps, since the Hebrew is ambiguous, "When God created . . ." or "When God set about to create . . ." or "In creating . . ." (Gen 1:1). The Hebrew, which includes no vowels,[4] provides no clue as to whether this sentence begins with the time reference "In the beginning" or the dependent clause "When . . ."[5]

The space to the left of that first ב (*beth*), which embraces you and me and all that has happened since God created, is "open only forwards."[6] In a midrash on the opening of Genesis, a rabbinical writer notes, "It is forbidden to inquire what existed before creation, as Moses distinctly tells us."[7] In more philosophical terms, within the opening words of Genesis there dwells "a supreme challenge to the entire classical tradition of Western metaphysics. To assert that matter was not eternal, that the world had a temporal origin, that substance came into being through divine fiat, indeed through divine *speech* ('and God said, "Let there be. . ."') threatened the foundation of Greek ontology,"[8] and, we might add, post-Enlightenment ontology.[9] Thus, the scope of inquiry is limited to the time since the creation, and the time

---

2. Aggadah is an interpretative style developed between 100 and 550 BCE.

3. Handelman, *Slayers*, 40.

4. The Hebrew above does contain vowels or "pointing," which are a subsequent development.

5. Ibid., 53–56.

6. Goldingay, *Israel's Gospel*, 43.

7. The biblical reference is to Deut 4:32, while the Talmudic reference is to *Talmud Yerushalmi, Chagigah* 2:1. See the opening verse of the midrash in Horne, "*Bereshith Rabba*," 44. Goldingay notes, "the traditional less polite response to the question, 'What was God doing before creating the world?' is, 'Devising Hell for people who ask impertinent questions like that'" (Goldingay, *Israel's Gospel*, 43). See also Givens, *When Souls*, 130.

8. Handelman, *Slayers*, 27. Italics in original.

9. "Ontology" is the study or theory of "being."

prior to creation remains the business of God alone. We should note that Jesus at Heb 1:1–2 is placed into this impenetrable realm before, positioned to the right of the first stroke of the initial *beth* of the biblical story. Everything to the left of the initial *beth* of the creation story—that is to say, everything after the first "stroke" of creation—is open for discussion.

This everything includes Melchizedek. That is why I am telling you this. If we accept a rabbinical worldview that sees no aspect of the text as an accident, we might say that you and I and Melchizedek are in the space in the middle of that first *beth*, embraced by the arms of the One who created. In Heb 1, Jesus is placed outside history's *beth*. Jesus would surely understand the significance of the scripted letter: Was this what he was doing at John 8:6 and 8:8? It is just possible that our Hebrews author too was playing seriously but poetically, even midrashically, with the ancient texts in skirting around the symbolism of Melchizedek. Harold Attridge refers to our author's "playful exegesis"[10] and we, as postmodern readers, should not be afraid of sacred interpretive play.

We don't know much about Melchizedek. He was, as one scholar puts it, "shadowy and mysterious."[11] Consequently, the author of Hebrews can begin to play in the space between the letters of our knowledge. This author was no fundamentalist, for fundamentalists are ironically so corrupted by scientific rationalism, by literalism, that they no longer permit an interpretive space between the words of Scripture (or perhaps even of Robbie Burns). Rules later developed—open to interpretation, as rules are, but rules nevertheless—to rabbinic interpretation. My love could not become a blue, blue lavender. Resurrection, which dwells at the heart of New Testament writing, was not able to become a resolution of a committee meeting, as it appears to be in some contemporary teaching and preaching, without undue violence to the text. This is the problem with the position of a thinker such as John Shelby Spong, who is able to assert that he is able to travel "through my faith tradition to its center, its core and its depth, and only then move beyond it."[12]

Excursus: A Cloud of Witnesses

The biblical authors would be surprised to discover that dismantling their hard-won wordage for the "unwordable," the resurrection narratives (even Mark's pithy open-ended hints of resurrection), was "to move beyond," was

10. Attridge, *Hebrews*, 197.
11. Craddock, "Hebrews," 85.
12. Spong, *Eternal Life*, 173.

some sort of improvement on naïve Christian faith. The Christian martyrs of any century (and again, as I first wrote these words, the story of the twenty-one Egyptian Coptic martyrs[13] executed in Libya was reverberating around the world) would be surprised to hear that their trust in God while experiencing the brutal depths of humans' inhumanity fell short of Spong's discovery that "Resurrection was an event of inner history at the levels of consciousness where fundamental shifts occur."[14]

I call to mind not only famous figures such as Maximilian Kolbe and Dietrich Bonhoeffer, but also Papua New Guinea's Anglican martyrs. I want to pause with them for a moment. In a sermon preached at the Parish Church of Saint Peter, Melbourne (more familiarly known as Saint Peter's, Eastern Hill), Archbishop Sir Philip Strong spoke out of his personal and intimate knowledge of almost all[15] those Anglican Christians who died at the hands of the Japanese. Strong tells of the teacher Mavis Parkinson, who, along with May Hayman, was executed by the Japanese at Ururu Plantation, having being handed over to the Japanese after several months of hiding in the Papuan jungle. Several months before her death, Strong suggested "that she should be moved to an inland station which I thought might perhaps be safer, though it proved later that it would not have been so—how she implored me with tears in her eyes not to do so, saying, 'what will the children do if I go?'"[16] Her co-martyr, May Hayman, who had become engaged to the Anglican priest Father Vivien Redlich, had also pleaded, "What will the sick do if I am not here?"[17]

---

13. The Egyptian Copts were: Milad Makeen Zaky, Abanub Ayad Atiya, Maged Solaiman Shehata, Yusuf Shukry Yunan, Kirollos Shokry Fawzy, Bishoy Astafanus Kamel, Somaily Astafanus Kamel, Malak Ibrahim Sinweet, Tawadros Yusuf Tawadros, Girgis Milad Sinweet, Mina Fayez Aziz, Hany Abdelmesih Salib, Bishoy Adel Khalaf, Samuel Alham Wilson, Ezat Bishri Naseef, Loqa Nagaty, Gaber Munir Adly, Esam Badir Samir, Malak Farag Abram, Sameh Salah Faruq; the twenty-first martyr was Mathew Ayairga, variously described as from Chad or Ghana, who was not a Christian believer until he saw the courage of those alongside him. He then professed, "their God is my God," and died with them. See Bos, "African Man Turns to Christ"; and ibid., "21 Egypt Christians." The online source from which these facts are gleaned, *BosNewsLife*, is a website dedicated to telling the story of contemporary suffering of Jews and Christians.

14. Spong, *Eternal Life*, 183.

15 The two Anglican martyrs Strong did not know personally, Fathers John Barge and Bernard Moore, were beheaded by the Japanese at New Britain in the Bismarck Archipelago. Strong mentions only Barge. Along with Anglicans, a total of 272 Christians died during the Second World War in Papua New Guinea: 189 Roman Catholics, twenty Lutherans, twenty-six Methodists, two Seventh Day Adventists, and twenty-three members of the Salvation Army. See Booth, *Saints*, 602; and Hodge, *Seed*.

16. Strong, *Good Shepherd*, 3–4.

17. Ibid., 4.

Strong tells too of the Adelaide-based teacher Lilla Lashmar, who wrote home to her mother shortly before the Japanese invasion, reflecting, "I only want to be a good disciple of Jesus Christ."[18] Lashmar worked at the Sangara mission station with nurse Margery Brenchley, who was originally from Britain. They declined an offer to be evacuated to Port Moresby and, after hiding in the Papuan jungle at Isivita, died together on Buna Beach; they were beheaded with John Duffill and Father Henry Holland. Lucian Tapiedi, whose statue stands with nine other statues of twentieth-century martyrs at the entrance to Westminster Abbey, was a Papuan local. A teacher, musician, and evangelist, Tapiedi was one of a small group bringing food and supplies to Lashmar and Brenchley at their hideout; when it was deemed no longer safe, he elected to stay with them and guide them to Buna. He was separated from the group en route to the coast and was executed by a local near Kurumbo village. His assassin later converted to Christianity, taking the name Hivijapa Lucian, and built a church dedicated to the memory of his victim at Embi.[19]

John Duffill, a carpenter, former chorister, server, and scoutmaster from Wooloongabba in Queensland, had been appointed by Archbishop Strong to be master of the coastal supply boat *Maclaren King*. He had been due to take leave but "had refused to go on furlough but didn't go because of the pressure of his work. Had he done so he would not have been with us in those critical days and would not today be numbered among the martyrs."[20]

English-born priest Father Vivien Redlich, engaged to May Hayman, was originally ordained in England. He had served as a Bush Brother[21] in the Diocese of Rockhampton, which covered a large slice of outback Queensland, before voluntarily moving to Papua New Guinea. On a coastal trip he observed the Japanese ships offshore from Buna, but rather than returning to Dogura opted to slip through Japanese lines and join the missionaries at Sangara.[22] He refused to refrain from celebrating Mass with those on the shore, and though the exact manner of his death is unknown, he was executed after his whereabouts and plan were relayed to the Japanese by a villager.[23]

---

18. Ibid.
19. Chandler, *Christian Martyrs*, 7, cited in Bride, *I Wait*, 12.
20. Strong, *Good Shepherd*, 9.
21. For histories of this remarkable organization and its role in Australian Anglicanism, see Webb, *Brothers*; and Hollingworth and Comben, *Memories*.
22. Hodge, *Seed*, 17.
23. Bride, *I Wait*, 16.

Redlich's priestly colleague Henry Holland had been in Papua since 1910. He was ordained in 1938 and had been instrumental in establishing the secret hideaways for Lashmar and Brenchley, for he knew the jungle pathways and river crossings intimately. He was leading two wounded Australian airmen to safety when he was captured and taken to his execution at Buna. Bernard Moore and John Barge, both ordained, died in a different region, New Britain. After fighting in the First World War, Barge had trained at Saint Francis College in Brisbane, served in Brisbane Diocese, and then set out as a medical missionary priest in Papua. He was captured and shot by the Japanese after they lured him away from the Papuan village where he was serving. The circumstances of Moore's disappearance and death remain mysterious, but he was added to the list of New Guinea martyrs in 1992[24] in recognition that rather than accepting offers to leave the region, he had elected to stay with the Papuans in the direct line of the Japanese advance. It is not known whether he died of malaria or was captured and executed, and his body has never been found.

In 2003, seven Melanesians were executed by rebel leader Harold Keke in the Solomon Islands, near Guadalcanal. They were Solomon Islanders Nathaniel Sado, Francis Tofi, Tony Sirihi, Alfred Hill, Patteson Gatu, Ini Paratabatu, and the Papuan Brother Robin Lindsay.

The question remains: Did this modern cloud of witnesses in Libya, Papua New Guinea, and the Solomon Islands, to name just a few, surrender their lives in some sort of misguided idealism and a false hope that the doctrines of resurrection and justice were not a naïve fairy tale? While I concur with Spong that the resurrection narratives demonstrate the authors' struggles to convey a truth beyond "rational credibility,"[25] I maintain that relegation of the meaning of the texts to mere "expansion of consciousness"[26] does brutal violence to the biblical authors' intention and the Christian martyrs' experience. This violence represents exactly the kind of desertion the author of Hebrews was combating. The resurrection event and the absence of restriction on the person and work of the risen Christ as experienced in the Spirit by the earliest and subsequent believers was not limited to the strictures and the straight-jacket myopia of human understanding.

---

24. He was recognized as a martyr much earlier by the Melanesian church: "There can be no doubt that his decision to remain at his mission and with his people after the Japanese occupation led to his death" (ibid., 17).

25. Spong, *Eternal Life*, 174.

26. Ibid., 183.

Melchizedek Continued

Neither we nor our author's first readers knew much about Melchizedek, so our author was able to use him as a demonstration of the argument. At the outset of this argument are the affirmations that Melchizedek is etymologically "King of Righteousness" and "King of Salem" (an aural pun on *shālōm*, or "peace"), but his priestly actions are more important than his kingly role: he blesses. Psalm 110, so important to our author (Heb 7:17) as a descriptor of Christ's role, fuses priesthood and kingship (or "lordship" as at Ps 110:1, 4). At this point though, our author makes argument from silence: the absence of any textual references to Melchizedek's origins or to the end of his life allows our author to see Melchizedek in terms of eternal existence as a "priest forever." Up to this point, our author has played only with Melchizedek and not with Jesus the Christ. Jesus will re-enter the narrative at Heb 7:22, but our author takes a circuitous route to that point.

There may seem to be cause for rising panic when you realize that after many pages I have barely addressed more than one word ("Melchizedek") of the Heb 7:1–28 passage! The sense of overwhelming heaviness that this passage can instill may, to some extent, be alleviated by putting our author's argument simply thus (using "<" in the mathematical sense of "is less than"): you and I<Abraham<Melchizedek<Jesus. Or, expanded in bullet form:

- You and I are less than Abraham (*He* was a patriarch [Heb 7:4]; we are not. He was greater even than Levi, who as his descendent was "in his loins" [Heb 7:10]; we, as descendants of his faith, are in his "faith-loins" [Heb 2:16, 6:15, 17]).

- Abraham was less than Melchizedek (because Abraham tithed to him [Heb 7:4] and was blessed by him [Heb 7:7]), and the descendants of Abraham (Levi and the Levites [Heb 7:11]; Aaron was a Levitical priest), though greater than you and me (Num 18:21–32), were lesser still than Abraham.

- Melchizedek was and is less than "our Lord" (Heb 7:14), for Melchizedek did not conquer death (Heb 7:16) or achieve perfection (Heb 7:19).

In a scientific rationalist age, we might question the final logic: In what way did Jesus conquer death? In what way did he achieve perfection? In the transaction of ideas between our author and the audience, that understanding of Jesus as having achieved perfection has already been agreed upon (Heb 2:10; see also Heb 12:2). Such a claim wasn't scientific rationalist: it was a part of the "gap," or that space between the words our author has played with. In the experience of preaching and worship—an experience unquantifiable by scientific rationalism even if the latter had been invented in the first century—the audience and author alike have encountered the risen, death-conquering Jesus to such an extent that they knew him as Lord (Heb 1:4b) and as co-eternal with God (Heb 1:2). If we add our "amen" to that, it will always only be by faith, not by scientific rationalism, that we have done so. We are dwelling here in the space between the letters.

The circuitous route of Hebrews includes cursory acknowledgment of the affirmation that the Levitical priesthood did not achieve "perfection" (Heb 7:11, 18). This affirmation bookends a brief exploration of the transmission of priesthood and the apparent disassociation of Jesus of Nazareth from any genealogical transmission of it (Heb 7:11), just as the priesthood of Melchizedek had no genealogical connection to the Aaronic priesthood. Nevertheless, the radical introduction of a new priesthood in the person of Melchizedek does at least represent a precedent for new beginnings, for "change of the priesthood," and for "change of the law" (Heb 7:12). But there is no genealogical decent through either line: Jesus of Nazareth is of the tribe of Judah, and this is a newer new beginning (Heb 7:14–5). Interestingly, our author makes no christological conclusions from the Davidic line of Jesus' genealogy.

This is a re-introduction of the idea that the Christ event "perfects" believers, in this case achieving what previous priesthoods have not achieved—a theme that will dominate later passages of the sermon. The perfection of the Savior was aired at Heb 2:10, as was his readiness to perfect others at Heb 5:9 and 6:1. Now though, the author is emphasizing that it is the *priestly* role of Christ that achieves what earlier, lesser, and therefore bygone priests have not achieved: the perfecting of believers. Given the history of Christianity in the centuries since our author wrote, we must acknowledge once more the eschatological dimension, the yet-to-come or, as Oscar Cullmann would say, the "not yet" dimension of this perfection.

We should acknowledge, not quite parenthetically, that this argument opens the door for conversation regarding post-biblical and post-Christian orders of prophetic and priestly ministry. This conversation is germane even if Christians have not technically claimed there to be any continuation of the narrative of priesthood since the priesthood of Christ.[27] While this absence of any claim to be a continuation of priesthood may be true, episcopal-ordaining churches in particular have muddied the waters of conversation by celebrating ordination to the presbyterate with declarations

---

27. As Jean Tillard muses, "Should one see in this the result of an hostility or a contempt for the traditional priesthood, or, on the contrary, a sign of the respect with which the first community would have retained for it, because it still considered itself a part of the People of Israel?" (Tillard, *What Priesthood*, 9).

that the ordinand is, as Ps 110:4 declares, "a priest forever after the order of Melchizedek"! I am not often in agreement with my friends in the Anglican Diocese of Sydney, and I eschew the word "minister" to describe ordained vocation, but am personally in some sympathy with Sydney Anglicans' aversion to the word "priest" in the ordinal as well as with their theoretical preference for using the word "presbyter."[28]

Such arguments were once at the heart of disputes between the Roman Catholic and subsequent splinter churches, including my own Anglican tradition.[29] What kudos should Christians give to the prophetic roles of, for example, Islam, or the Latter Day Saints, to "cargo cults," to the Rastafari movement, or in my country to the prophetic movements of Ratana founded by Tahupōtiki Wiremu Rātana[30] in the early twentieth century and to the Ringatū movement founded by Te Kooti Arikirangi Te Turuki[31] in the mid-nineteenth century? As a rule of thumb, I look to the centrality of Jesus of Nazareth in the narratives of the movement as a litmus test to establish whether resultant conversations are inter-faith or ecumenical.

The claim our author makes for the priesthood of Jesus is of an "indestructible life" (Heb 7:15). This naturally returns us to the language of "by faith" rather than empirical data, but the author will explore that dimension in depth in chapter 10. For now, it must be simply accepted as resonant with the audience members' liturgical and communal experience and as an accepted part of the sermon discourse. The audience is called on mentally to contrast this experiential dimension of Christ-belief with their sense that old dispensation of Torah have not achieved the same liberation experience. This is a completely subjective assessment, though it appears to have been a key part of early Christian experience, conversation, and teaching and is therefore not an unexpected proof of this author's argument. It is probable that the oppressive behavior of some first-century Jewish leaders, caricatured broadly and perhaps unfairly in the gospels as "scribes and Pharisees," as well as the less disputed oppressive behavior of the Sadducees, added weight to the author's argument at this point, at least for those members of

---

28. Here I stand in unity, albeit with slightly different reasoning, with the Anglican divine Richard Hooker, who wrote, "I rather term the one sort Presbyters than Priests, because in a matter of so small moment I would nor willingly offend their ears to whom the name of Priesthood is odious" (*Of the Laws of Ecclesiastical Polity*, cited in Tillard, *What Priesthood*, 6). See also Küng, *Why Priests?* 28–30.

29. See Pope Paul VI's the encyclical *Presbyterorum Ordinis* of December 1965 and Pope Leo XIII's *Apostolicae Curae* of 1896.

30. For a comprehensive history, see Henderson, *Ratana*; and Newman, *Ratana Revisited*.

31. See Binney, *Redemption Songs*.

the audience who had suffered under their oppressive leadership. The argument is essentially "once you experienced . . . but now . . ." (Heb 7:18–19).

Our author ends the Melchizedek reflection—this form of preaching that plays in the gaps between the letters—with a celebration of the unique nature of this new and eternal High Priest, "a Son who has been made perfect forever" (Heb 7:28). *Made* perfect? Wasn't he already perfect? It is difficult to convey the nuances of our author here, as she attempts to summarize in one sentence the argument so far by loading the words (and the spaces between) with all possible meaning. Perhaps we could render Heb 7:28 as "who in the suffering and obedience outlined in chapters 2 through to 5 has been revealed to us as perfect forever," but our author was more succinct than the present writer! The Hebrews audience's own experience of liberation means they can add their experiential and heartfelt reminiscences of an "amen" to the affirmation that "Jesus has become a guarantee of a better covenant" (Heb 7:22).

With that established, the author moves to engage with an eternal future dimension to the intercessory role of Jesus' priesthood (Heb 7:23–25), using the verb "remains"[32] that was used in reference to the lesser and supplanted priest Melchizedek at Heb 7:3.

---

32. Unfortunately, NIV, NRSV, and others adopt the translation "always," losing the contrasting comparison with Melchizedek, whose "remains" came to an end.

12

Priest of a *New* Covenant: Heb 8:1–13

LIKE ANY GOOD PREACHER, ours goes on to recapitulate what has just been established: "the main point in what we are saying is this." In fact, the section is more than recapitulation and "serves as a major transition within the composition."[1] Christ, "seated at the right hand of the Majesty in the heavens" (Heb 8:1), is what Plato might call the *real* Priest, of which the Hebrew priests of the temple were only a shadow form. Earlier in this study, I mentioned that this preacher was heavily influenced by the thought of Plato: the world of shadows, the world we see, is only a reflection of a greater, more solid world beyond our sight. Because the world we see is a copy of the real, the two are intrinsically but unevenly linked: "the imitation depends on the ideal type, so there is a real connection, but it is always derivative and secondary."[2] If a real Lamborghini did not exist, then a toy Lamborghini, though no doubt pleasant enough, would lose something of its meaning. This understanding becomes important now, as the author contrasts the priesthood of Judaism with the Priesthood of Christ.

The point has already been made that Jesus of Nazareth would not qualify for priesthood under ancient Jewish law.[3] For our author, there is a strong Hebrew Testamental strand that does, however, provide a basis for interpretation of Jesus as a priest: "the lips of a priest should guard knowledge, and people should seek instruction from his mouth, for he is the messenger of the Lord of hosts" (Mal 2:7). Malachi's acerbic vision castigates the priests for failing in this role (Mal 2:8–9). In the view of our author, the residual role of the high priests, standing in the Aaronic tradition and

---

1. Johnson, *Hebrews*, 196.
2. Ibid., 202.
3. Küng notes that the New Testament "never uses the word 'priest' in the historical sense of sacrifice ('*hiereus*', '*sacerdos*'), and avoids every cultic and sacred term. This certainly has much to do with the fact that Jesus (himself a layman) introduces the figure of the priest only once in all his parables, and then only to reject the particular example chosen (Luke 10:31)" (Küng, *Why Priests*, 28).

associated by Jesus' time with the Sadducees, was irreversibly corrupted by expedient coziness with Roman authorities. This was a compromise unacceptable to the biblical Jesus and to his Christian followers, including our author. Following the fall of the second temple, the high priestly role collapsed altogether, though in some circles its reinstatement remained as a future-eschatological expectation. In the New Testament and Qumran documents, the coming together of interpretative and personal integrity becomes an embodiment of priesthood.[4] The author of the Fourth Gospel, incidentally, expresses this in a different way, as he portrays a Jesus in whom word and action are indivisible ("In the beginning was the Word and the Word was with God, and the Word was God" [John 1:1]) and whose command becomes reality in each of the "signs." That author is at pains too to emphasize that the source of the eyewitness account is also striving to unite word and truth (John 19:35). Our Hebrews preacher approximates the same equation at Heb 1:3, where the Son "sustains all things by his powerful word." As it happens, John works hard in his narrative to ensure that the lifting up of Jesus coincides with the time of the sacrifice of the lambs in Jewish rites, while our present author, as we have seen, echoes many of the temple rites.

In our Internet era, we find plenty of memes in circulation that remind us that the places where so many religious practitioners expect to find Jesus—or where they, and perhaps most of us, attempt to limit and restrain Jesus—are not the sorts of places the Priest of God chooses to turn up. Is Jesus to be found in a gay bar? An animal rights protest? Does Jesus restrict his presence to the political gatherings of the right wing or the left wing? One such meme, which is probably traceable to a witty comment by John Fugelsang, reads, "Obama is not a foreign born, brown-skinned, anti-war socialist who gives away healthcare. You're thinking of Jesus."[5] The author of Hebrews hints at Heb 8:4's reminder that the Christ of God is not to be found, or certainly not to be restricted to, the places where would-be followers of God are found.

In Judaism, the role of the priest all but disappeared after the destruction of the second temple in 70 CE. Following the destruction of the first

---

4. See Christiansen, *Covenant*, 112–13. The Qumran document "Manual of Discipline" (1QS) speaks of rules "in which men of holy integrity shall walk with one another" (1QS 8:19). The episcopate and presbyterate that grew out of that ideal might well have been considered a compromise to our author, or at best a shadow form of the real. This, I suggest, is precisely the way we should see these ecclesiastical orders today, demanding of their membership exactly the same marriage of practice and theory!

5. See John Fugelsang, Twitter post, March 28, 2010, 7:39 p.m., https://twitter.com/JohnFugelsang/status/11227135976.

temple, the priesthood lost much of its symbiotic relationship with the monarchy. Walter Brueggemann notes that in the first temple era,

> There were visible, legitimated, acceptable, stable, well financed religious structures with recognized, funded leadership. That is, the temple and its priesthood played a legitimated role in the ordering of civil imagination. The role of the stable temple for this model of church can hardly be overaccented.[6]

Following the destruction of the first temple, a replacement was built, but as we have noted, it was a less elaborate affair and "it never came to exercise a dominant place in the community, nor to capture the imagination of subsequent interpreters."[7] Many of its rites, as Barker has noted, were mere shadow forms of the already-shadow form of first temple rites and roles (Isa 66:1).[8]

Brueggemann notes that during the continuance of the second temple, an era dawned in which "temptations to cultural syncretism and the disappearance of a distinct identity were acute, particularly in the Hellenistic period."[9] In a stern form of boundary maintenance, our author is specifically emphasizing the risk of syncretism and resultant loss of faith-cultural identity, and this drives both the depiction of Christ's priesthood as the real and the stern challenge to faith tenacity in the audience. In the era after the second temple's destruction, the Jewish priesthood disappeared altogether, though some Jewish sects expect it to be re-instated in full when the Messiah comes.

The temple to this Hebrews audience was a shadowy form of the temple-that-is-heaven. The covenant that once existed and was administered ("enacted"; see Heb 8:6) by the priests is now perfected in Christ, the only *hiereus*-priest (Heb 8:6–7). This perfect priest offers not an interim symbol to atone for the sins of the people, but his own perfected self (Heb 8:7). The writer's logic is at this point reasonably straightforward and sequential, though of course the negotiations between author and audience are in the realm of the spiritual and unverifiable and are not designed to convince a skeptical outsider audience. They will no more do so in our twenty-first century than in our author's first century.

Again, we must be cautious in how we express this: perhaps we could say that practicing Jew and practicing Christian alike see only through a

---

6. Brueggemann, "Church Models," 130.
7. Ibid., 133.
8. Barker, *Great High Priest*, 151.
9. Brueggemann, "Church Models," 134.

darkened glass? Perhaps we might say that our liturgies of faith as we await the second coming and the very different corporate prayer rites of our cousins in faith as they await the coming of the Messiah are equally shadowed forms of the eternal relationship between God and God's people. Our author would not have agreed with me in the first century, but times do change, and we must cautiously modify peripheral aspects of our understanding of the Christ-event, discerning always—and always humbly—the peripheries from the core. Should Christians who believe and then fall away be readmitted to the community of faith? Most of us agree they should, but our author doesn't, and many Christians of Christianity's first centuries didn't. Should women remain silent in church? Most of us think they shouldn't, but Paul in particular disagrees (though our author may not have!). There are also some curlier questions of interpretation to which I will return at the end of this study. God is at work in history. Or maybe God is at work despite history! God is not a fossil, and nor is the living, Spirit-breathed Word of God.

Hebrews returns to proof texts. At Heb 8:8, the preacher cites the prophet Jeremiah as evidence for the case. A favorite proof text of the early church, Jer 31:31 looks towards a new covenant, and our author applies a variation of the adage "If it isn't broken, don't fix it" to that text: "If it were not broken in the first place, it wouldn't have needed fixing." Jeremiah had seen that this covenant relationship was broken, so these new covenant times have the authentic voice of faith history and an ancient prophet on their side, and thus our author can echo the ancient pronouncement. In the Hebrew, Jeremiah reads, "a covenant that they broke, though I was their husband," but as Attridge notes, "our author is not particularly interested in the original context of what he cites"[10] and reproduces the Septuagint's "they did not continue in my covenant so I had no concern for them." Nor, though, is our author interested in a slavish reproduction of the Septuagint version of the Jeremiah text. Textual divergence from the Jeremiah prophesy may simply reflect our author's hasty quotation from memory, but in Jer 31, the verb used to describe God's action in establishing a new covenant may be translated as "to cut" (or, loosely, "to make"), while in the Greek translation from which our author was working, it reads "to complete" a new covenant and so bears the weight of fulfilment inherent in the events of Jesus' priestly role.[11] Ultimately, the subtleties of verb changes between

---

10. Attridge, *Hebrews*, 227.

11. The Septuagint Greek verb "to speak" is also altered from *phēsin* to *legei* and the Septuagint *diathemēn* to *epoiēsa*, but these alterations appear to carry only the weight of stylistic preference. As it happens, the original Abrahamic covenant was made when the light from God passed through the *cut* portions of Abram's offering (Gen 15:7–11, 17). Though the verb used at Gen 15:9 is unique to that verse, the noun form reappears at Jer

Hebrew and Greek and between Jeremiah and Hebrews probably do not need to weigh too heavily on interpreters today: the point is that humans have betrayed God and God is making a new start.

The brutal imagery of a broken marriage devised by Jeremiah, "They did not continue in my covenant and so I had no concern for them," emphasizes the "infidelity" of the people of Israel. They have brutally destroyed a spiritual marriage between God and God's people. The NRSV maintains the pain of this lament: "a covenant that they broke, though I was their husband" (Jer 31:32b). This sense of pain-filled lament allows our author to generate a contrast, already present in Jeremiah's image, between ritual action and internal belief. Now there will be something new: a spiritual covenant of mind and heart (Heb 8:10) that will not peter out because, in Christ, it has been made perfect (compare this with John 19:30, where "it is finished" captures the same idea). Later, the author will address the implications of this changed relationship for the people of God, but for now the christological implications of the change are the primary focus.

The Petrine author will develop the idea into a doctrine of the priesthood of all believers (1 Pet 2:5), but this author at this stage simply wants to emphasize the priesthood of Christ, and only later to remind the audience of their mutual responsibility to maintain access to and interest and participation in that priesthood by mutual encouragement (Heb 10:24).[12] The immediate concern is that now no intermediary *hiereus*-priest is necessary (Heb 8:11) because that access to the Father is made directly through the Son. Hymn writers of the Protestant tradition have often captured this imagery well "Intercessor, friend of sinners, earth's redeemer, plead for me," as Anglican hymn writer William Chatterton Dix famously wrote in his "Alleluia, Come to Jesus."[13] "Oh come to the Father though Jesus the Son," wrote American Baptist hymn writer Fanny J. Crosby (1820–1915) in her celebrated "To God Be the Glory." If the Reformation and its subsequent echoes got one thing powerfully right, it was to dismantle the ambiguities about the role of a *hiereus*-priest.

34:18, where Jeremiah depicts the breaking of the covenant. This Jeremiah usage could well have aided our author's use of the broken covenant imagery as well as the implied contrast between that and an unbroken covenant. This is completed in the Great High Priest, but the connection is not made in the sermon.

12. Ellingworth, *Commentary*, 314.

13. Douglas Farrow notes the extent to which this famous hymn "slides over the controversy about transubstantiation with 'faith believes, nor questions how'" but notes too that the final stanza of the hymn is "sometimes omitted by Protestants for want of a Mass, or by Catholics wanting to leave Mass!" (Farrow, *Ascension Theology*, 71).

As an aside, it is my liturgical practice to occasionally adopt the old and very sacramental Catholic liturgical position of standing with my back to the people at the Eucharist. I do this only when celebrating Holy Communion from the *Book of Common Prayer*, and I do so because the language of the liturgy has hints of the place of the clergy as standing with their people "facing" God. Similarly, I almost never preside at the Eucharist in any form (except outdoors in, for example, a forest or a beach) without wearing a chasuble, a garment similar to what Jesus wore and removed at the Last Supper, which holds symbolic echoes of his presidency over the community gathered at the table. I observe these patterns despite my assertions that the person presiding at a Eucharist, even in the episcopal-liturgical churches, is in no way a sacramental or ritual priest, a *hiereus*. I maintain, however, that though I am in my tradition a *presbyteros* (elder) and not a *hiereus*, it is not a bad thing to carry out actions in this sacred drama that may remind us of the priestly and presidential actions of Christ.[14] In the same way, our *diakanos* (deacons) wear a stole sideways to remind us of the towel associated with the foot-washing servant role of Christ, and our *episcopus* (bishop) carries a shepherd's crook to remind us of the shepherd role of Christ (or, as Margaret Barker suggests, the "snake-rod" of the priestly Aaron[15]). But in undertaking these roles, the bearers do not replace Christ, they signify him. The three-fold order of ministry in episcopal traditions can, at its best, call to mind the aspects of Christ after which it is modeled and which its modelers—its ordained ministers—are called to represent in life and ministry. At its worst, as we have noted, the orders of ministry can be tragically abused to establish self-serving power structures that are too often used to oppress vulnerable victims. There is no doubt that abusers of this form have, no matter what covenant they pretend to uphold, deserted the responsibilities of relationship to the Creator and stepped outside our author's understanding of the people of God.

The critical point for our author is to reemphasize the recurrent message that the first covenant is obsolete and passing away, for it is no longer needed now that faithful believers dwell in the light of a new one (Heb 9:13). We cannot so easily pass by the issues presented to a

---

14. The segueing of the *presbyteroi* into a pastoral and liturgical extension of the *episkopoi* is to some extent lost in time, but it was probably necessitated by the rapid expansion of Christianity through the Roman Empire. To remind *presbyteroi* in my Anglican denomination that they are "mere" extensions of our bishop's pastoral presence, it is imperative that the bishop's chair remains present in all diocesan sanctuaries. Other less symbolized denominations could do worse than to find alternative "signs" of the authentication of ministry, though such a suggestion may well set the Reformation back 450 years!

15. Barker, *Great High Priest*, 136.

twenty-first-century reader of Hebrews. Once more, we must sit still in the presence of that dreadful question: Where we who are claimant to the second or new covenant have so often abysmally deserted its demands, do we just blithely claim that our religion is the final word on God's dealings with humanity and with us as individuals? I have alluded to one option before: Should we see the new religious movements Christianity has spawned as a third, fourth, or fifth covenant? Are the new revelations to Joseph Smith, or the equally non-Trinitarian beliefs of the Jehovah's Witnesses, or the cargo cults of many colonized nations to be seen as a further covenant? Are the teachings of the Prophet Mohammed (and I am willing to add the salutation "Peace be upon him") a covenantal recognition of our failures as Christendom? I want to draw some doctrinal boundaries, including the Trinitarian boundary that is post-biblical and post-canonical. But I see them as sociological boundaries rather than as soteriological boundaries. While there may be defining boundaries of belonging to the Christian community—and Trinitarian orthodoxy is one such boundary in my assessment—I believe there is a further sign of covenantal orthodoxy and belonging: integrity. Where I see practitioners of deep human compassion, justice, and integrity in any faith or non-faith tradition, or where I see the husbanding (in Jeremiah's terms) of God at work, I would never for a moment believe that such a practitioner of good would be excluded from the welcoming embrace of the God of Jesus Christ. For those who are Christ-bearers yet who perpetrate great evils or who promulgate the hatreds put forth by groups such as the infamous Westboro Baptists, the road of redemption is a little rockier than a cozy complacency suggests. The concern that our author had for the stagnation and bored potential apostasy of the first Christians spreads down through history.

With customary sensitivity, Luke Timothy Johnson addresses these matters another way that is worth quoting at length, though his primary focus is the impact of Christian supersessionism on relations with Judaism:

> It is not only the sense of moral revulsion created by Christians' awareness of their role in the suppression and murder of Jews, and the sense of theological revulsion generated by Christian awareness of how distorting such supercessionist views are of Christianity itself, but equally the way in which the historical events have forced Christians to reexamine the premise that they are history's darlings, that lead contemporary interpreters to a chastened attitude when dealing with language about old and new covenants. Recent history has not been particularly kind to Christian pretentions: Christianity has been politically disestablished and intellectually marginalized within

modernity. Christian theologians are called to recover grounds for Christianity's truth more significant than its simply not being Judaism. Christian exegetes are therefore correctly cautious when they tread warily among language that their predecessors took for granted.[16]

Johnson notes that "Hebrews does not . . . speak as representative of a Gentile Christianity that claims to have superseded Judaism."[17] Tillard notes, "the Epistle to the Hebrews itself does not say that Jesus inaugurates a *new* priesthood. It sees the priesthood of Christ much rather as a fulfilment, the *teleiosis*, the goal to which the old institution was moving."[18] It does not show disrespect for or rejection of the validity of God's historic dealings with the Hebrew people in earlier covenantal relationships. In a post-Christendom world, we must cultivate generosity of divine Spirit towards those beyond and those yet to come within the porous boundaries of faith. Johnson's concerns may be applied equally to our attitude towards parallel belief systems that are not of the Abrahamic stable. It is worthwhile to note the words of Rabbi Sacks: "'You are', said God through the prophet Isaiah, 'My witnesses' (Isa 43:10)—not by seeking to convert those of another faith, but simply by reaching out to embrace the image of God in another human being, by seeing the divine Other in the human other, because that is how God reveals himself."[19] There is no permission for supersessionism in Hebrews. Neither is there a command in Hebrews to destroy the faith or even the "unfaith" of those who live out by any means their experience of the *imago dei*—of being compassionate and just humans made in the image of God.

---

16. Johnson, *Hebrews*, 210–11.
17. Ibid., 212,
18. Tillard, *What Priesthood*, 9. Italics in original.
19. Sacks, *Fractured World*, 47.

13

The Shadow and the Reality: Heb 9:1—10:18

In Heb 8:4–6, our writer draws a contrast between an earthly sanctuary and an as yet unseen "true tent" beyond our sight. The methodology is of course influenced by platonic contrasts between shadow and reality. Now the preacher has an opportunity, having considered the shadowy echoes of heavenly realms reflected in temple practice, to add secondary matters to the argument. In Heb 8:4–6, the shadowy rites of worship were introduced but not expounded. Now these are developed further. But this author's interest is not in dictating the shape of Christian liturgy, which was largely based then, as now, on a stylized combination of domestic Jewish prayer rites and the agape rites of the Upper Room's Last Supper. The interest here is in extrapolating some meaning and implication to glean some understanding of the workings of the Jesus event and the salvation it has wrought.

We should pause momentarily to address yet again the question of the meaning of "salvation." Ellingworth notes that our writer "generally speaks of 'salvation' as something already present and available through the Christian message first announced by Jesus (Heb 2:3)."[1] Our preacher is careful to maintain a future dimension to the language of salvation (Heb 6:9–12), or an "already *and* not yet" dimension to the believer's experience as well as to God's outworking of this bequest (Heb 1:14). In this way, Hebrews ensures that no artificial wedge is constructed between the grace emphasized, for example, in Paul's Letter to the Galatians and the works-responsibility emphasized in James. There can be no such wedge if Christianity is to be true to its heritage, and only if Paul's writings are brutally stolen from their proper context can Paul be made to suit a one-sided approach to the question. For James, the equation is simple: "Someone will say, 'You have faith and I have works.' Show me your faith apart from your works, and I by my works will show you my faith" (Jas 2:18). For our author, it is no less so:

---

1. Ellingworth, *Commentary*, 73.

"Let us consider how to provoke one another to love and good deeds" (Heb 10:24). This provocation will ensure endurance (Heb 10:36), and endurance alone ensures participation in the fullness of the "not yet" of salvation. But to expound on this narrative of incentive, the preacher returns to explore the role of Christ as priest that was originally developed at Heb 8:4–6. The pattern here, as at the earlier mention, is that of shadow and real: we see a shadow; Christ dwells in the reality. This is no scientific rationalism but rather a fundamental and deeply platonic belief that our eyesight is limited and our perspective flawed.

Above all, the author wants to contrast the "again and again" nature of temple rites with the "once and for all" nature of the Jesus event. She picks up a hint made back at Heb 2:14, where the common expression "flesh and blood" is now revealed to have held a deeper meaning, foreshadowing the blood of Christ that will now be discussed as having been shed to redeem our flesh (Heb 9:13). Unfortunately, the author presupposes that the audience is familiar with one single old covenant rite of purification, whereas in reality there are significant shades of difference between the sources of Exodus, Leviticus, and Numbers. It is easier for us, as twenty-first-century readers, not to dig too deeply into the specifics of lampstands and tables and breads: let it suffice to say that in the Hebrews author's understanding, the blood rites of the old covenant serve, albeit imperfectly, to carry away the sins of the people (interestingly, no mention is made of the scapegoat rites of Lev 16:20–28). But this has only been a temporary arrangement, and those rites of the Hebrews had to be repeated year after year. Not so the rite of Christ.

These levels of symbolism are overwhelming to a casual reader, as most of us are. In his commentary, Johnson masterfully cuts through the complexities by identifying a spatial and a temporal dimension ("axis") to the argument.[2] The priests entered a space of tents, veils, and inner and outer sanctuaries (but only the high priest entered the inner sanctuary), and they did so either frequently (priests entering the outer sanctuary) or annually (the high priest entering the inner sanctuary). There is another temporal dimension operating: the old *versus* the new. As Johnson says (and he makes many further distinctions), "It is small wonder, given these two kinds of difficulties, that Hebrews sometimes grows obscure, and readers sometimes get confused."[3]

At this point, we can keep the matter simple: the vast and complex systems of the old covenant have been circumvented, even short-circuited, by

---

2. Johnson, *Hebrews*, 218.
3. Ibid.

the new covenant made available by continuation in Christ (though our author does not use Paul's recurring construction "in Christ" as a description of the relationship of believer to salvation). The new High Priest, as both priest and victim ("thou on earth both priest and victim / in the Eucharistic feast," as Dix put it) has opened for us a new access to the Father. The inner veil of the old temple rites is passed through by the One who is sinless and those who remain in him, as they too (as *we* too) pass through death, may enter the presence of God (Heb 9:15, 27). The blood had to be shed, our author maintains (Heb 9:16, 20, 22, 25), but it has been shed, and so the need for it is done, dusted, and sorted. The inner sanctuary into which Christ has entered is no shadow (Heb 9:24) but the real beyond the shadows.

The sermon's underlying emphasis on endurance is never far away as the writer keeps in mind the slow, languid apostasy of the audience. The work of Christ has been done to save "those who are eagerly waiting for him" (Heb 9:28), and that eager expectation must be maintained. There is a two-dimensional aspect to this demand of endurance from our preacher. There is the command to endure, but implicit in it is the command to expect. Whatever we might make of the troublesome Christian doctrine of eschatological judgment, this author stresses that they are not to be jettisoned, collapsed into some finite limitation of the gospel to the present, or turned into a comfortable present-hour aesthetic.

The eschatological expectations of suffering believers are a poignant warning to those of us who live out our faith in comfortable surroundings. As James Cone emphasizes over and again, reduction of Christianity to the here and now may be a luxury in which the complacent can wallow, but it is not an option for those who face execution for either their race or their faith.

Apostasy, then, may include the sin of "backsliding," much feared in some evangelical circles, but it surely includes the much more dreadful sin of corporate Christian nonchalance towards suffering and the persecuted groups (human and otherwise) with which we share our planet. The future dimension of "eagerly waiting for him" is at the heart of the New Testament. Language of the cross must always imply language of resurrection and future completion, but in what Moltmann calls over and again its "cruciform" shape, it can speak a word of hope even in its immeasurable suffering. Cone notes, "The cross places God in the midst of crucified people, in the midst of people who are shot, burned and tortured."[4] Our author uses different imagery, but the completion and our appropriation of the work done by Jesus always carries with it the proviso to "endure" (Heb 6:15). The cross stands in opposition to exploitation and oppression. The cross is God's entry into

---

4. Cone, *Cross*, 26.

every lynching of the Deep South (often perpetrated by Christians), God's entry into colonial persecution of Indigenous peoples everywhere, God's entry into the deaths of the victims of Boko Haram in East and North Africa and of Daesh in the Levant, and God's entry into the suffering and deaths of victims of Indonesian government genocide in West Papua and all victims of the silence of the world's response. But full appropriation of the work of the cross continues to have a future dimension, and the Hebrews author's word "endure" points always to that dimension (Heb 9:24–25) of judgment for the oppressor and hope for the sufferer.

Margaret Barker has pointed out that the architectural layout of our churches, together with the often-abstruse clothing worn by *presbyteros* (priests) in the liturgical traditions, can serve as reminders of the ancient arguments put forth by our author. Barker observes, "Christian customs, then, perpetuated practices which had very ancient roots but had not been current in the second temple,"[5] and adds, "We are not looking for continuity with the actual temple practices of the first century CE, but with a remembered, perhaps idealized, system that was much older."[6] As long ago as 1980, Anthony Boylan was noting, "To support and nourish the Christian faith through symbols that are more easily understood and have a more vital impact will be one of our foremost tasks in the liturgical renewal movement."[7] He also observed, "As we do all we can to increase the power of the words we use [in liturgy] so we should do all we can to increase the value and authenticity of the symbols we use."[8] Boylan notes that the Roman Catholic tradition pre-Vatican II tended to freeze gestures and symbols in an ancient form as "the shriveled symbols of the past"[9] and that Protestant traditions tended to eschew them in favor of a word-intensive approach to liturgy. Anglicans split the difference, as is their wont, between the two alternatives. Nevertheless, enter a traditional Anglican or Roman Catholic church, and you will find that some of the old resonances are still there. A sanctuary reminds us of the future holiest sanctuary of all. A communion table is in the sanctuary—we should not be afraid to call it an altar, for it reminds us of the cost and bloodied, cruciform shape of God's entrance into human hopelessness.

In his commentary on Hebrews, F. F. Bruce edges towards eschewal of liturgical drama, emphasizing instead that "the 'boldness' which believers in

---

5. Barker, *Great High Priest*, 78.
6. Ibid.
7. Boylan, "Symbolism," 4.
8. Ibid., 14.
9. Ibid., 15.

Christ have to enter the heavenly sanctuary through him is set in contrast with the restrictions which hedged about the privilege of symbolic entry into the presence of God in Israel's earthly sanctuary."[10] Bruce also reads the words "through the curtain (that is through his own flesh)" (Heb 10:20) as being in contradistinction to any "material symbol of his throne."[11] While Bruce doesn't enlarge on the liturgical implications of this emphasis, similar statements are often used to extrapolate a renunciation of ceremony and symbolism from the text, as if they in themselves weakened the once-for-all event of the cross. Though we don't "re-sacrifice Christ," as some misinformed or deliberately polemical interpreters of Eucharistic actions suggest, we do carry out actions at the altar that *re*-present and *re*-member the sacrifice Christ has made. This does not compromise the "once for all time" of Heb 10:12 and 10:14, nor does it suggest that the activation of the sacrifice of Christ is reliant on priest or church.

Rowan Williams has tiptoed delicately through the minefields of "activation language" in order to neither freeze Calvary to a Christ "immobilized" in the past and "remembered" with an as-absent-as-possible interpretation of that verb, nor make his presence in the present dependent on "a strongly hierarchical understanding of the relation of ministers and laity" by which the presiding priest at the Eucharist is "custodian of holy things, equipped with supernatural power and privileged access to the resources of the invisible world."[12] My Anglican tradition has attempted to downplay the centrality of the presider by emphasizing that at least one other person must be present when the Eucharist is celebrated. In my liturgical practice, I have often interpreted the "amen" of the people as ratifying the presiding priest's recitation of the Words of Institution as a *sine qua non* of the rite,[13] though this, I admit, still leaves us appearing to "need" the presence of the congregation to ratify God's Calvary action. We start measuring angels on the point of a needle if we attempt too closely to define the mysteries that dwell at the heart of our Hebrews author's considerations of rite and symbol and narrative. Hebrews commands the faithful not to neglect to meet together (Heb 10:25). One reason for this command is that whenever *anamnesis* (memory that makes present) of Calvary and the cross occurs, "the effect

---

10. Bruce, *Hebrews*, 249.
11. Ibid., 250.
12. Williams, *Eucharistic Sacrifice*, 3–5.
13. "Brethren, your Amen is your subscription, your consent, your agreement" (Saint Augustine, Sermon Fragment 1:3, cited in Wainwright, *Doxology*, 228).

of Christ's offering is to make us capable of offering, to count us worthy to stand and serve as priests."[14]

To explore the ecclesiastic and liturgical symbolism further, however, we encounter communion at the sanctuary rail not because the "important people" want to keep the *hoi polloi* out, but because we can be reminded that although we have had a foretaste or "earnest" of the eternal kingdom that is yet to come, it is still yet to come, and we are not there yet. Barker notes other echoes of the first temple in Christian liturgy. There is, in liturgical traditions, a moment in liturgy known as the *epiclesis*, or calling the Spirit down on bread and wine in the Eucharistic prayer. In my "high" liturgical tradition, the worshiper will often make the sign of the cross at this point to remind him- or herself that the outpouring of the Spirit on life and worship is made possible only through the sacrifice of Christ.[15]

As it happens, the sign of the cross itself, according to Barker,[16] echoes the diagonal cross of the Hebrew letter *tau* or *tav* (ת in the Aramaic square script adopted after the exile, but in the old Hebrew script, the letter was a diagonal cross, or X) with which, according to Ezek 9:4, the foreheads of the faithful (and according to *b. Horayoth*,[17] the priests) were marked to show their enduring fidelity. The sign of the cross has long played a part in non- and pre-Protestant Christian liturgy, marking points of special christocentric (or "cruciform," we might say) significance. The sign is used at the pronouncement of absolution to remind the worshiper that such absolution is made possible only in the cruciform shape of Christ. It is often used at the conclusion of the recitation of Gloria and Credo (each a "visible punctuation mark" for those who could not understand Latin, but later reinterpreted as a sign that either glorifying God or believing the triune mysteries of God is made possible only in Christ). Finally and more frequently the sign is used at the pronouncement of triune blessing by which believers' lives are enriched as they are sent out into God's world. Similarly, the east-west axis of church buildings was effectively a sermon too, by which the proximity of the sanctuary to the east and to the rising sun—allowing that part of the building to represent "heaven"—was also an echo of first temple symbolism.[18] Each of these otherwise obscure symbols can serve as a reminder of the call to fidelity that undergirds Hebrews.

---

14. Williams, *Eucharistic Sacrifice*, 30. See also Radcliffe, *Why Go to Church?*
15. Barker, *Great High Priest*, 79.
16. Ibid., 78.
17. Folio 12a.
18. Barker, *Great High Priest*, 77.

Lest it seems this discussion of liturgical symbolism has drifted too far from the Hebrews author's intentions, we should pause to remind ourselves that Hebrews was a fundamentally liturgical text. It was a sermon preached in some form of congregational liturgical gathering, though the shape of that liturgical gathering eludes us now. Liturgy and proclamation alike rely on the transmission of images: "the Bible is a great wellspring from which pour forth a flood of images, some specific, others universal."[19] Our author is drawing on a vast tradition of images that were familiar discourse between author and audience, and it is imperative that we should draw our understanding from the same pool of images that inspired this text even as we reflect on how the images that add comprehensive depth to our own faith flow from it.

It may also be useful to emphasize that our author spent *so* much time engaging in arguments that seem obscure to us not for the purposes of long-winded entertainment, but because she had important truths to remind her audience of. At the heart of the theme is the nature of Christ and all that Christ has achieved. It is imperative, therefore, that the nature of Christ as Son (Heb 5:5), as King (Heb 1:3), and as Priest (Heb 2:17, 3:1, 4:14, 5:5, 5:10, 6:20, 7:26–28) are firmly established, perhaps in ways that seem to us laborious, if the case is to stand on solid ground.

The author continues the reflection on Jer 31:31–34. Details about the minutiae of Jewish ritual continue to underscore the theme; for us, the important matter is the relationship between the lesser reality that is remembered, known, and seen in human experience—in this case, of worship—and the higher, unseen reality that is the work of God in Christ. At Heb 10:1, the language of shadow and reality is explicit: "the law has only a shadow of the good things to come and not the true form of these realities."

This is yet again a recapitulation of ground already established for the sake of emphasis; we must again remember that this sermon was written to be heard, not read. Hebrews 10:1 revisits ground prepared at Heb 7:11, at Heb 7:19, and at Heb 7:28. Yet repetition in this author's hands is never "vain" (Matt 6:7), and she now applies a new spin. The shadow/real terminology is now explicitly in the open for the first time, but if we return momentarily to Johnson's "temporal" and "spatial" axes, we are now being led along a "temporal" path: what we see now is a shadow of what is to come. *Spatially*, the trimmings and actions of Jewish worship are shadows of the heavenly structures. *Temporally*, the argument is that our experience foreshadows future, "heavenly" realities (Heb 10:13).

---

19. Platten, "Bible," 4.

The point is labored, but the issue is now that we have yet to experience the achievement of Christ on the cross in full, just as the rites experienced and offered by the ancient Hebrew people were no more than a foreshadowing of a future reality. The famous verse Heb 11:1 will memorably reiterate the futuristic dimension, but at the moment the author is simply building a theme: past, present, and future contain a consistent and unswerving narrative that includes and presents over and again the experience of forgiveness of sin (Heb 10:18). That experience was the basis of the "confidence" (Heb 3:14, 10:19[20]) the audience once enjoyed, that experience was ratified by the signs and wonders the audience once witnessed (Heb 2:4), that experience the author will shortly refer to as "hearts sprinkled clean from an evil conscience" (Heb 10:22b) was deeply liberating, and that experience will be lost if the audience does not endure in faith. The author now turns once more to the subject of endurance.

---

20. The use at Heb 6:9 is referencing the author's confidence and therefore, though related, is not quite the same as the audience's experience.

14

Endure! Heb 10:19–39

BECAUSE THERE IS A future dimension to faith, there is a present imperative (that theme again) for those who have fallen or are potentially about to fall away: "Let us hold fast to the confession of our hope without wavering" (Heb 10:23). More than that, "let us consider how to provoke one another to love and good deeds" (Heb 10:24). Let us meet together, because faith lived in isolation is (except in rare cases of the Terry Waite sort) faith likely to grow cold (Heb 10:25). Centuries later, Saint John of the Cross would observe that "a soul without a director is like a kindled coal, which, if taken from the fire, cools instead of burning."[1] This is the difficulty with the great postmodern mantra "spiritual, not religious": it allows the spiritual person to recreate spirituality in his or her own shape rather than in the justice-seeking, love-proclaiming, resurrection-announcing cruciform shape of the Spirit of Christ of the cross.[2] To some extent, we all do this: Westboro Baptists remind us, if nothing else, that it is possible for a corporate body to recreate the witness of Christ in the shape of bigotry, especially when separated from wider networks of faith, to merely become a bigger coal separated from the fire. Generally speaking, it is harder for the broad and small-c catholic church of Christ to ignore the cruciform shape of its founder than it is for a "spiritual, not religious" lone wolf to do so.

There is urgency for our author: "all the more as you see the Day approaching" (Heb 11:25). This "Day"—the *Dies Irae* or day of judgment—approaches, and, as Jesus made clear in his many parables, it is not altogether wise to be napping when it comes. So the author has returned to exhortation: hang in there, endure! We have a great High Priest, and we have already been reminded that he has suffered all we have suffered and more (Heb 4:15), so we can persevere knowing we are not on our own treading untrodden paths. Now that our preacher has expounded upon the sanctuary image, it

---

1. John of the Cross, *Living Flame*, 215, maxim 177.
2. See Radcliffe, *Why Go to Church?*

becomes clear that this eschatological dimension of this sermon was never anything but central: there was no way we could "enter the sanctuary" (Heb 10:19) without the prior and once for all entrance of Christ the Priest. Now though, the future dimension of the sermon is becoming stronger. We can enter the sanctuary, or at least a foretaste and shadow of it, in our gathering together (Heb 10:25), and if we persevere, then we will enter into it utterly and completely, and enter too its final perfection, on the day of judgment.

But we must sort out our lives. The ancient high priests offered sacrifice for "unconscious" or "un-deliberate sin" once a year, and that is now covered once for all by the sacrifice of the new and eternal High Priest; there is, however, no basis on which to test or stretch the mercy of God. "If we willfully persist in sin, after having received the knowledge of the truth, there no longer remains a sacrifice for sins but a fearful prospect of judgment" (Heb 10:26–27a). For our writer, as we have seen, there is no way back, no way by which Christ should or even can be crucified again. The Anglican Prayer Book's general confession, which was largely generated from the fifteenth to seventeenth centuries, is less equivocal: "We have sinned by our own deliberate fault . . . Father forgive us." Though the fifteenth to seventeenth centuries were turbulent, those times were less threatened by apostasy and faith-abandonment. For our author in the first century, this was a matter of life and death: "they are crucifying again the Son of God and are holding him up to contempt" (Heb 6:6). In the cyclical methodology typical of this sermon, we have been brought back to the issues aired at Heb 6:4–8. The author, however, now cites Torah to aid the argument (Heb 10:28, citing Deut 17:2–6) and uses the platonic "like this but so much more" argument in a negative "like this but so much worse" form (Heb 10:29). There is no room in the theology of this sermon for a chummy relationship with God: "It is a fearful thing to fall into the hands of the living God" (Heb 10:31). Aslan is not a tame lion, C. S. Lewis warns the children in *The Lion, The Witch and the Wardrobe*. This too should warn the author's unintended twenty-first-century audience of the spuriousness of "Jesus is my daddy-o" and the many songs that reduce divinity to the feel-good lover of popular schmaltz.

The audience members are challenged to call to mind their own backstory. They were once doing well (Heb 10:32–39) and must not allow amnesia to rob them of that truth. The argument provides examples of their past success: they should return to these good attitudes and good works to demonstrate the life touched and transformed by Christ the Son, Lord, King, and Priest. They, and therefore we who are accidental readers, should overcome trials (Heb 10:32), withstand persecution (Heb 10:33), exercise compassion (Heb 10:34a), know that our greater possessions are beyond sight (Heb 10:34b; see also Acts 2:44), remain confident

(Heb 10:35), and above all endure (Heb 10:36). It is a list that recapitulates memory-treasures already narrated. It is a list that is timeless in its implications for the body of Christ.

It is worth taking a moment for our own recapitulation at this point. As the author took us on a journey that highlighted the worth of "meeting together," presumably in the context of liturgy and teaching (of some sort), we might well ask whether our own gatherings for liturgy and teaching either recapitulate the mysteries of ancient rites—which, while superseded, may still bear the weight of great truth—or foreshadow the immeasurable dimensions of timeless adoration in what the author of the New Testament Apocalypse calls "the New Heavens and New Earth." In my tradition, I see so much that speaks of absent joy, empty mechanicalism (whether "high" or "low"), and turgid banality. In the realms of hymnody, since we have returned again to "Jesus is my daddy-o," we need to recall that a hymn (I prefer this word to "song," for the latter already flags disinterest in weighty form or historical value) is a prayer prayed twice.[3] It is said that we become what we meditate, and we may even suggest that the potential of a hymn to transport us beyond the everyday is one basic form of meditation.

As a cathedral dean, my bias was towards the great hymnody of past centuries. I have to admit that there is much that is really romantic dross (not least that which was a product of the Romantic era). Much needs translation or even exegesis if it is to be meaningful today, though this should not necessarily deter us from tapping into its ancient wisdom. Directors of music and pastors or priests of faith communities should take the trouble to ensure that profound lyrics, like the words of Scripture, are "broken open" to enhance the faith of the gathered worshipers. Kudos should be given to editors of hymn books who provide explanation, for example, of the "mystic rose" imagery of "Crown Him with Many Crowns."[4] By offering explanation and even exegesis, they are ensuring that the potential of such images is not lost and is instead intertwined with the same hymn's "Crown him the Lord of years / the Potentate of time / Creator of the rolling spheres / ineffably sublime" (though those words too could benefit from exegesis!). Kudos should be given to church worship leaders who ensure that so profound a

---

3. The full saying by Saint Augustine was "For he that singeth praise, not only praiseth, but only praiseth with gladness: he that singeth praise, not only singeth, but also loveth him of whom he singeth. In praise, there is the speaking forth of one confessing; in singing, the affection of one loving." See Augustine, *Exposition*, Ps 68.

4. The editors of *Common Praise*, although it is not my favorite hymn book, are to be commended for their footnote to this hymn, in which they explain, "The expression 'mystic rose' in v. 2, l. 5, is a mediæval title for the Blessed Virgin, and is combined here with a reference to Isaiah 11.1." See *Common Praise*, 357, hymn 166.

prayer as Charles Wesley's "O Thou Who Camest from Above" is not lost to the people of God:

> O Thou who camest from above,
> the pure celestial fire to impart
> kindle a flame of sacred love
> upon the mean altar of my heart.
>
> There let it for thy glory burn
> with inextinguishable blaze,
> and trembling to its source return,
> in humble prayer and fervent praise.[5]

Credit should be given to those who are ensuring that new worlds of depth are being tapped in ways that are both culturally appropriate and theologically profound. There is an increasing readiness to allow Indigenous languages to convey truths that are lost to English, utilizing these new-old insights in the life of the Christ community, though paternalism needs to be avoided. In the Arnhemland communities where for a short time I was privileged to work, the words of some of the local Aboriginal languages were used to produce the hymn "Garry Jesu Marrkapmirr," in which the word "marrkapmirr," as one hymn collection editor notes for her users, "is a term of endearment, meaning 'altogether lovely and worthy of affection.'"[6] The hymn has since grown a degree of popularity in non-Indigenous communities far removed from Arnhemland. Similarly, in my present country hymn writers such as my colleague and friend Bill Bennett are beginning to explore the depths of Māori language and imagery in hymnody, tapping a source that is rich and rewarding and ensuring that the gospel proclaimed is not a gospel of Europeanism anymore.[7]

Lyrics are not the only issue. I have to confess that when I visit many churches in my Anglican tradition, I am often underwhelmed by the liturgies I encounter. I find much bland trivialization and clunky, meaning-denuded liturgy that has been given a quick attempt at modernization (frequently referred to as "relevance") by throwing in a hymn or two from recent decades, but often with little consideration to the depth of their lyrics and music. "Clunky liturgy" is when bits are pre-announced, back-announced, or performed in ways that have no logical explanation. Liturgy is sacred drama . . . I suspect if the Royal Shakespeare Company announced each act and scene of *Macbeth* and invited the "congregation" to join in the great soliloquys,

---

5. "O Thou Who Camest from Above" by Charles Wesley (1707–1788).
6. See Russell and Cohn, *Together in Song*, hymn 253.
7. See especially Bennett's *Gradual Praise: Ngā Waiata Whakapono*.

their ticket sales might suffer. But the analogy breaks down: liturgy cannot be passive, so therein too we find a tightrope to balance.

So we might at this point in a journey through Hebrews ponder whether in fact our worship does foreshadow the Reign of God yet to come, or whether our worship is aiding and abetting the loss of faith that the author of Hebrews abhors. There have been moments in liturgical and so-called non-liturgical worship alike when I have experienced what might be termed a "beatific vision" when time has stood still and all suffering, all meaninglessness, all sorrow, and all that is bad has slipped away. These moments can, to some small extent, be manipulated—or, to use a kinder word, choreographed—but they are often greater than the plans orchestrated by liturgical planners, craft-persons, and presenters. The experience of singing in tongues, or glossolalic song, is carefully choreographed, but no less uplifting for this choreography, so that Donald Hustad's oft-quoted words will frequently ring true: "It is as if the strings of a huge Aeolian harp have been set in motion by the wind of the Holy Spirit. The strangely-beautiful sound rises in volume, lasts for a longer or shorter period, and then gradually dies away."[8] In *Babylon's Cap*, I refer to Lucy Winkett's singing of evensong at Saint Paul's Cathedral in London when my wife, Anne van Gend, and I and were visiting in 1999.[9] Most of us will have experienced powerful moments of prayer or song or even silence when time has stood still and the Reign of God has seemed immediate and all-pervasive. Christianity runs the risk of losing credibility in worship no less than in every other facet or mark of its mission, and when our worship habitually fails to present those foretastes of the coming Reign of God, it is aiding and abetting the slippage that our author abhors.

---

8. Hustad, "Historical Roots," 7. Theological musicologist Donald Hustad's original quotation has been lifted into texts such as Wayne, *Whose House*, 191, presumably because it has been immortalized in the e-pages of Wikipedia. See also Riss, "Singing in the Spirit."

9. Godfrey, *Babylon's Cap*, 120.

15

Faith Is . . . Heb 11:1–40

As we enter into our author's roll call of exemplars of faith, I will again cast a glance sideways into narratives of faith and faithlessness from our own era. It is my hope that a glance at parallels and contrasts will help illustrate something of what the author of Hebrews was looking for in her own era, what she drew upon from narrative histories available to her, and what she might, if we could translate her to the present, observe, applaud, and abhor in contemporary postmodern (and post-postmodern!) faith journeys.

There are a number of passages in the Scriptures that it should be an offence to read silently! Hebrews 11:1—13:8 (roughly) in particular, along with 1 Cor 13 and John 1:1–18 (or 16) are foremost amongst those passages. While best heard in the original languages (and some of the aural nuances may well be captured by those of us who remain linguistically challenged, unable to translate the rich vocabulary of the original writers), good translations will capture at least some of the depth of the auditory impact. This is probably a useful moment to remember that there are strengths and weaknesses in all translations and that it is sometimes valuable, if we are not fluent in Greek or Hebrew, to have at our fingertips both the accessible, the scholarly, and the more sensitively poetic translations. Many passages should be read aloud. Hebrews 11:1—13:8 takes about 10–12 minutes to read aloud, and the exercise is a valuable one in any language.

Hebrews 11:1—13:8 was meant to be heard, and even translation from Greek to English does not altogether damage the soaring, emphatic, accumulative majesty of these words. In Greek though, the cadences are of immeasurable finesse. In chapter 11, the repeated "by faith" is "*pistei . . . pistei . . . pistei*," a word that explodes each time it is spoken (technically, *p* is called a "plosive" consonant, which is why it explodes or "pops" annoyingly in an ill-equipped microphone). The opening, which we have as "Now faith is the assurance of things hoped for," is transliterated in Greek as *Estin de pistis elpidzomenōn hupostasis* (the *ō* is a long *o*, as in the English "loan"). The *p*'s and *t*'s pop again and again, adding emphasis to the speaker's message.

Slowly, the speaker (we can forget the writer for now) builds up the rhetorical case, accumulating phrases and stories to underscore that first, basic, resounding premise: faith is the assurance of things hoped for.

The orator, not being interested in a post-Enlightenment obsession with biblical history, takes us on a biblical historical tour: "By faith . . . Abel" (Heb 11:4), "By faith . . . Enoch" (Heb 11:5–6), "By faith . . . Noah" (Heb 11:7), "By faith . . . Abraham" (Heb 11:8–12). We take a breath, and the sermon introduces a new emphasis in its theme of "faith as assurance of things hoped for." The platonic notion that all this (and Melchizedek) is just a shadow of the reality that lies beyond our sight is reintroduced with a vengeance: the faithful died without seeing their hope fulfilled (Heb 11:13), just as the great designers, benefactors, and builders of the great cathedrals of Europe died without seeing the completion of their majestic works. This is perhaps the opposite of the infamous Ozymandias of Percy Bysshe Shelley's acerbic poem. Ozymandias' vision was of a monument that would render him eternal: "look on my works ye mighty, and despair." But, as Shelley sourly observes, "Nothing beside remains."[1] For Abel, for Enoch, for Noah, for Abraham, and for the cathedral builders whose task was to magnify the eternal God, the knowledge was that their constructions would long outlive their mortality, serving not to glorify the manufacturer but the subject of the building: the eternal God. In ecclesiastical architecture even more than in classic hymnody, the time span reaches infinitely beyond the ephemeral, and while realistically not eternal, such monuments reach as far towards the eternities as the original constructors could imagine.

Should transience reign, as postmodernity tends to advocate, as the final word on human existence? At the very least, this seems to contradict that strange sense of the numinous, or awareness of the sacred, that has tended to surface in human beings since we emerged from the primeval swamp. I'm not sure we should dismiss, disregard, or denigrate what Otto called the "idea of the holy" quite so readily. It is worthwhile, however, to listen to voices that explore the implications of transience more fully.

My erstwhile broadcasting colleague Lyn Gallacher refers in a blog to Chris Mann, who once produced a collection of ephemera consisting of "a drinking glass, a paper napkin, a matchbook and a play money note all in a small cardboard box."[2] Why? Gallacher refers to the collection, entitled "Da Dum," as a "socially beneficial information processor."[3] It was Mann's thesis,

---

1. Percy Bysshe Shelley, "Ozymandias," lines 11–12.
2. Gallacher, "Pissy."
3. Meehan, "Rare Books." Another version referred to in the ether does not contain the play money note.

or perhaps Gallacher's interpretation of Mann's thesis, that meaning undergoes a sort of shattering deconstruction in the gap between utterance and reception. Neither glass, nor matchbook, nor paper napkin, nor the words of poetry written on some or all of the items was ever "used" for its designed purpose, so the meaning of the piece is effectively forever captured, frozen in the moment between writing and reading (or, more probably, *seeing*), and thus is not socially beneficial. Gallacher muses, "It's as if the language wants to be more socially beneficial than it actually is, and its very presence renders the other objects useless by turning them into art. No one has ever drunk out of this glass or used this napkin."[4]

Mann, or perhaps Gallacher, or perhaps both, have captured a central ingredient of postmodernity: the vast gap between the utterance of a communication and its reception by an audience, whether intended or otherwise. Gallacher cites Mann again: "There is no scientific explanation of language. There may be one for data. Statements. But propositions, arguments? No way. That you turned right ten seconds after I said turn right is not explainable scientifically."[5] In the ten-second gap between utterance and reception, postmodernity (or Mann, or Gallacher!) argues, certainty is lost. In the much longer gap between the time Ozymandias commissioned his statue and the time the "traveller from an antique land" encountered it, all purpose and intention was lost, and the opposite of Ozymandias' aim was achieved.[6]

In musical terms, the philosophy of indeterminacy, which originated with Charles Ives but has perhaps been best explored in the work of John Cage, exemplifies this outlook. Because every moment is fleeting and every life is made of ephemeral indeterminate moments, all existence is indeterminate and all directions, such as Chris Mann's directive to turn right or Ozymandias' commissioning of a statue, are meaningless. Perhaps the ultimate indication of this in musicological terms was the total eschewal of musical notation in favor of broad-based instructions, as exemplified in Penderecki's *Threnody to the Victims of Hiroshima*. Like Picasso's tortured images of Guernica, the impact of Penderecki's piece is fragmented, cacophonous, and anti-aesthetic. There is little that is aesthetic about war, particularly war in the decades since the Trinity bomb was detonated above the New Mexico desert and the decision was made to detonate an atomic bomb above the heads of thousands of civilians at Hiroshima.

---

4. Gallacher, "Pissy."
5. Mann, "Rationales," cited in Gallacher, "Pissy."
6. Shelley, "Ozymandias," line 1.

I am effectively a post-deconstructionist or "*post*-postmodernist," so it is probably unsurprising that I find that the far more aesthetically accessible, but I suspect the no less chilling tones of Henryk Mikołaj Górecki's *Symphony of Sorrowful Songs* are able to convey far more of the torture of the human heart revealed at Auschwitz and Hiroshima. Perhaps that is because I am living and writing in a comfortable room with a magnificent view, far from the harsh realities of Auschwitz, Hiroshima, the hellholes of Syria, or the rejected death-boats full of Rohingya Muslim refugees. As I was first writing this, between 6,000 and 8,000 Rohingya were circling the Andaman Sea, rejected by Thailand, Indonesia, Malaysia, and much of the global north. Their story was soon matched by that of Syrian Yezidis fleeing execution in Syria, and that story was in turn matched by the death of seventy-one refugees in a refrigerated truck near Nickelsdorf in the Austrian state of Burgenland. Briefly, this international narrative of neglect began to change as German Chancellor Angela Merkel and her Austrian counterpart, Werner Faymann, began to demonstrate counter-narratives of inclusion and embrace, even as Icelandic activist Bryndís Björgvinsdóttir dared to challenge the sclerosis of her small country's leadership by inspiring a movement of 10,000 or more Icelanders to offer their homes to refugees. Nevertheless, as the world reeled at the tragic and iconic image of the lifeless body of three-year-old Aylan Kurdi in the arms of a Turkish official, the complexities of the international refugee crises became unmanageable. Days after Austria opened its borders to Syrian refugees and witnessed the arrival of 18,000 in one weekend, it became clear that no one nation could solve what was quickly becoming the worst human refugee crisis since World War II. Is the logical outcome of this bewildering tragedy simply to renew old narratives of razor wire and sclerotic hearts, so that the eerie grief of Górecki's Polish soprano has the final say?

Australian novelist Robyn Cadwallader writes of a new anchoress, freshly sealed away from the world in her prayerful captivity, rebuffing the desperate plea for food by a leper. In her new ascetic spirituality, she has in her cell a cake that she refuses to eat: "I looked down at my desk to the cake Anna had brought me. I would not eat it, but I would not pass it to his tainted hands."[7] Every afternoon, most of the cafés in my town and towns like it all around the global north throw out their leftover cakes and pastries and sandwiches, either because food safety regulations or because economic interests dictate that they must. Every night in my town and towns like it all around the world, men and women are hungry on the streets and in the doss houses. Humankind, as T. S. Eliot famously said before postmodernism ar-

---

7. Cadwallader, *Anchoress*, 33.

rived, cannot stand very much reality. . . . God in Auschwitz and Auschwitz in the crucified God—that is the basis for real hope that both embraces and overcomes the world.[8] Perhaps I am too human to deal with the realities of human hells?

Jürgen Moltmann has over and again reminded us in his theology that faith must find a voice in the shadow of Hiroshima and the Holocaust. Penderecki and Picasso, each in their different disciplines, find one possible philosophical mode in which the scream of hopeless audial or visual discord has the final say. Perhaps grunge rocker Kurt Cobain exemplified this too, becoming so entrapped in meaninglessness that his suicide became the final passage in an artistic scream against the universe. Cobain famously left his driver's license next to where he shot himself; in doing so, he was juxtaposing, it seems, the institutionalized but whole self in the photo with the shattered reality of a life ended with a self-inflicted shotgun blast: "Suicide, especially one as violent as Cobain's, is the loudest possible invocation of silence; it's a perfectly clear way of turning your life into a mystery. His commitment to contradiction got him in the end, but even as he cut himself off forever, he was trying to make himself speak."[9] Cobain was only one and not the last example of the tragic "27 Club," but perhaps his death can represent a narrative that begins and ends with the ephemeral and meaningless.

There was for a while even a school of liturgical music that ensured all the great passages of a Mass setting remained more or less discordant until the final "amen" brought a harmonious foretaste of heaven. It was philosophically profound, but it could be deeply discomforting to sit through in a liturgical context—it did not belong there. It was meant to be awkward: we are not yet a part of the completed and suffering-free hereafter. Leonard Bernstein, who wrote his magnificent *Mass* in response to the death of John F. Kennedy and the subsequent dark vicissitudes of the 1960s, grasped that Cold War discomfort very clearly and used that understanding to influence *avant garde* liturgical music. But Bernstein was not writing functioning liturgical music. Did the angst he explored belong in the context of liturgy? Liturgical music, while not existing purely for the sake of an aesthetic pleasure, nevertheless exists to rumor more than one miniscule glimpse of eschatological perfection. Bernstein's esoteric but profound *Mass* was always designed as a theater piece with a complex cast of characters, and it was created with the assistance of *Godspell* author Stephen Schwartz and singer-songwriter Paul Simon, amongst others.[10]

---

8. Moltmann, *Crucified God*, 1.

9. Powers, "Nevermore," 102.

10. Subtitled "A Theatre Piece for Singers, Players, and Dancers," BBC Proms

Bernstein's *Mass* is a deeply profound and remarkable synthesis of high Tridentine Catholicism, Judaism, pop, rock, music-hall, and the angst of the late Vietnam era with the hope of final eschatological harmony. After hurling listeners into torment and tumult, it concludes with an injection of an eschatological note of hope. Our biblical author of Hebrews may well have understood that feeling, but in her roll call of exemplars of faith she does not dwell on the difficulties that the faithful overcame.

Mann, Penderecki, Picasso, Cobain . . . Bernstein brings to us a different perspective, one far closer to the note our author is generating in the great roll call of the exemplars of faith. I am no philosopher, but it seems to this philosophical Philistine that an outlook that places the fleeting nothingness of my own experience at the center of the universe may prove to be nothing more than narcissistic, winding back by centuries Copernicus's discovery that planet Earth is not the center of the universe. Ironically, it may be that it is not the highly intellectual philosophy of the musicologists of indeterminacy or of the poststructuralist philosophers that has the final word on meaninglessness, but the narcissistic obsession with selfies, Snapchat, and the (often naked) self-obsessed ephemera of a pixelated universe.

Gallacher's conundrum—and the tortured ephemerality of Mann, Penderecki, Picasso or Cobain—is very different from the world of our author of Hebrews. For Gallacher's Chris Mann, meaning is and needs must be frozen and inactive. It is our author's intention that in the "ten seconds" between speech and reception, interpretation, and resultant action there will be a common purpose. To our author, that common purpose will turn into human action the intentions and will of the God who has instilled faith in the human heart in first place. This may not be a popular postmodern notion, but to the biblical authors, by and large, it was a way of narrating human participation in the will and the purpose of the God whose word and action are inseparable. In the opening of Genesis, God's word and resultant outcome are one and the same: "God spoke . . . and it was." Our preacher uses the construction "by faith" with a series of verbs attached to a series of biblical characters whose lives were opened to the possibility of God's presence in this connection between their hearing, believing (or "faith-ing"), and doing. The frozen moment of Chris Mann's napkin is removed, and hope can find an opening in human existence.

If the focus of belief is the existence of a "better country"—the promise of Heb 10:36, which reverberates through chapter 11's great celebration of

---

presenter Petroc Trelawney described it as "a musical about a Mass" (1:30), as seen in a 2012 performance conducted by Kristjan Järv available online at "Bernstein, Mass. BBC Proms 2012," YouTube video, 1:56:15, posted by "El Jardín de Epicuro," March 18, 2014, https://www.youtube.com/watch?v=9tjsKzhpSwE.

faith—then we are posed a question: *Is* there a better country, a real country, as our author might put it, beyond our sight? "Scholars who criticize blacks for their 'otherwordly' religion should look a little deeper into the ways blacks resisted the demonic in their midst,"[11] notes Cone, astringently. Is this mere pie in the sky, and we should stay frozen in the interstices between spoken word and resultant action, in Penderecki's and Picasso's and Cobain's hellholes of meaninglessness? Perhaps Mann's choice of frozenness or Penderecki's and Picasso's and Cobain's hellholes are right, yet historically there have always been people of faith (Christian and otherwise) who are willing to die for their hope of another country (Heb 11:16). R. S. Thomas refers to a God who "keeps the interstices / In our knowledge, the darkness / Between stars."[12] In Thomas's *via negativa* (which provides the name of the poem), this is not a static, frozen space between word and action but a space recently vacated by a "fast God" whose energies draw us forward into eternities.[13] This interpretation leaves space for the inspiration of those who have lived their lives—and even those who have died the death of martyrdom—by faith. On the balance of outcomes, I suggest that the choice of those who have celebrated a hope beyond apparent darkness can outweigh the choice of those who dwell frozen and trapped in the eternal angst of the present moment.

Sometimes, of course, such martyrdom is merely for the "another country" of political vision. In her outstanding and deeply disturbing historical novel *Half of a Yellow Sun*, Chimamanda Ngozi Adichie portrays the hope-filled and self-sacrificial dreams of those who willingly forfeited their lives in the hope of a triumphant and independent Igbo Biafra in the 1960s. Like many freedom fighters, revolutionaries, and strugglers for national (or tribal) identity and independence, their dream was demonically ill-fated. Was this the extent of the dreams our Hebrews author held dear and wished to re-instill in the hearts of her audience?

Some freedom struggles are more successful than the ill-fated political dream of an independent Biafra. Providentially, as I originally typed the previous paragraph, a South African song played on my shuffle. The song "Another Country" was written in 1993, when apartheid was being dismantled, when red blood (never black or white or colored blood) was brutally spilled, and when fear ran rife. In June and September of 1992, two massacres had accelerated the increasing international pressure on the national government of South Africa. No evidence of South Africa's ruling National

---

11. Cone, *Cross*, 140.
12. "Via Negativa" in Thomas, *H'm*, 16; ibid., *Later Poems*, 23.
13. "Pilgrimages," in ibid., *Frequencies*, 51. See also ibid., *Later Poems*, 125.

Party's involvement in the massacres was forthcoming, but the African National Congress was able to demonstrate that the government had failed in its duty to protect those who had died.

"Another Country" was a signature tune of the multiracial group Mango Groove and celebrated another, future country beyond the recriminations of blame and the shedding of blood and tears. The stirring song gave voice to the dream of a new South Africa in which blood would not be spilled in the interests of political supremacy. "Let's begin to look within, to where the future lies / and find the strength to live beneath another country's skies."[14] The imagery might well have been taken from Adichie's novel of Biafra, except that Adichie was writing a decade later. Nevertheless, songs frequently serve the same place in the hearts of the ill-fated Igbo revolutionaries in Adichie's novel. Spirituals had kept alive the hopes of another segregated people in another nation:

> If you get there before I do,
> Coming for to carry me home
> Tell all my friends I'm coming too
> Coming for to carry me home.[15]

Mango Groove used methodology akin to that of the Negro spirituals[16] Cone has poignantly re-explored in his recent writings: "The spirituals enabled blacks to retain a measure of African identity while living in the midst of American slavery, providing both the substance and the rhythm to cope with human servitude."[17]

Another well-known song identified with the international emergence of South African voices was the earlier song coauthored and popularized by Paul Simon on his oft-maligned but ground-breaking *Graceland* album. Recorded in the mid-1980s, *Graceland* generated the ire of critics because Simon was breaking the anti-apartheid boycotts of the period. There is merit in those arguments, yet at the same time *Graceland* had a major impact on popular culture. The album highlighted the voices and perspectives of the

---

14. Mango Groove, "Another Country," on *Another Country*, WOND120 Tusk Music, 1993, compact disc, http://www.mangogroove.co.za/music.html.

15. From "Swing Low, Sweet Chariot." For notes on the song, see "Historical Background of 'Swing Low, Sweet Chariot'" at http://www.swinglowsweetchariot.org. The lyrics are in the public domain and are widely available, but Eric Clapton's recording on his 1975 *There's One in Every Crowd* album provides a traditional form.

16. Barack Obama, in his 2004 Democratic National Convention speech, described faith as "the hope of slaves sitting around a fire singing freedom songs" (Obama, "Transcript"). He returns to the theme of faith as hope often in public addresses, not least in his 2009 Nobel Peace Prize acceptance speech.

17. Cone, *Spirituals*, 30.

South African townships, and as one critic wrote at the time, "Although the notion that popular music should have a global consciousness has been in the air since at least the late 1970s, *Graceland* pursues that ideal with a passion and an intellectual seriousness unprecedented among contemporary Western pop stars."[18] The chorus of the song "Homeless" returns to the image of sleeping, homeless, beside or "on" a lake.[19] The simple imagery and phonetics of the song does not evoke a romantic idyll, even if the lake is moonlit: Paul Simon and his coauthor Joseph Shabalala (from a capella band Ladysmith Black Mambazo) fused the lyrics and images of two worlds, two cultures, and two very different writing spaces into a metaphor of homelessness that not only bears the weight of a harsh political reality, but also of estrangement from meaning, equality, and socioeconomic justice. Shabalala observes, "We're far away from home and we're sleeping. Our fists are our pillows."[20] The Judeo-Christian narrative of Hebrews suggests that the home from which the lyricist is estranged is not only the sociopolitical Rainbow Nation longed for by contemporary collaborators such as Mango Groove and the Paul Simon / Ladysmith Black Mambazo combinations (though the implementation of that dream was important), but also that eschatological longing that remains unfulfilled as a home beyond our sight.[21] It is more comfortable for a listener in the privileged global north to hear only the words of a romantic idyll rather than the challenge of implementing justice.

Oppressors are always happy for the oppressed to dream dreams of another, better country—dreams such as those which our author was espousing. Silly Christians: let them dream all they like of another country while we exploit, oppress, and kill them! To some extent, pie in the sky is a dangerous "assurance of things hoped for" that can keep uppity underclasses in their place (as the early history of Anglicanism shamefully records: silly Presbyterians, silly Puritans ... We'll send them to another "other country"). "Without concrete signs of divine presence in the lives of the poor, the gospel becomes simply an opiate; rather than liberating the

---

18. Holden, "Paul Simon," 1. Paul Simon is quoted as saying, "I later learned that the black musicians' union took a vote as to whether they wanted me to come. They decided that my coming would benefit them, because I could help to give South African music a place in the international musical community similar to that of reggae" (ibid.).

19. From Paul Simon's album *Graceland*. In my opinion, the song is best heard on the album *Ladysmith Black Mambazo and Friends*, which features Ladysmith Black Mambazo singing with Canadian folksinger Sara McLachlan.

20. One source for this oft-repeated claim is Wiser, "Homeless by Paul Simon."

21. Paul Bayly, describing explorer David Livingstone's permanent state, observes "he was a man with a country, but not a home" (Bayly, *David Livingstone*, 185). Livingstone's faults were legion (though so too were his qualities), but there is no doubt that he shared our author's sense of a platonic Home.

powerless from humiliation and suffering, the gospel becomes a drug that helps them adjust to this world by looking for 'pie in the sky.'"[22] But human history, let alone divine history, seems to gain the final laugh. When Mango Groove's Claire Johnston sings wistfully of "another country" embedded in her eyes and of another state of grace in which she will enter that country with a beloved—or perhaps even *the* Beloved—walking alongside her, it is a poignant image, rich with both eschatological and erotic longing.[23] Paul Tillich would approve.[24]

Did South Africa change as a result of the political action of singer-songwriters and others? There will always be a yes-no (*ja-nee*, a very South African expression!) to such a question. The gospel must have a political implication: this is the truth that Christian oppressors, including the Anglican Church of the seventeenth and eighteenth centuries, like to suppress. But it can never *only* be political. As former Director of the Evangelical Alliance Sir Frederick Catherwood once (before inclusive language was widely accepted, itself a revolution) wisely wrote of revolution:

> Because it requires men to change their actions without changing their minds, everything has to be imposed by force. In the absence of self-regulation, the revolutionaries are driven to resort to terror. In the course of the terror, the hard men come out on top and if the idealists protest, they are liquidated. Then as the saying goes, "the revolution devours its own."[25]

The South African revolution against apartheid was in the end, if not velvet, then certainly less bloody than the French or Russian Revolutions. Blood flowed, but less of it. Equivalents are impossible, but Pieter Willem (P. W.) Botha, the last hard man of apartheid South Africa's white leadership, bred no Napoleon or Hitler, and the Rainbow Nation emerged from its tragic past, aided in no small part by the Truth and Reconciliation Commission chaired by Desmond Tutu.

Power vacuums breed new evil. The scenes of Matt 12:45, paralleled in Luke 11:24–26, suggests this concept was not unknown to Jesus. Christ-bearers such as Mandela and Tutu, together with F. W. de Klerk, did their best to ensure that the "another country" into which South Africa would transform would be, like the dream of our first-century author, a "better

---

22. Cone, *Cross*, 155.

23. "Mango Groove-Another Country," YouTube video with animation by William Kentridge, 4:19, posted by "Neil Gill," March 3, 2007. https://www.youtube.com/watch?v=mMmUtvYL4B8.

24. See Irwin, *Eros*.

25. Catherwood, "Reform or Revolution?" 40.

country." Only history will confirm the relationship of South Africa's Jacob Zuma to the dreams of those who longed for a fair and equitable nation and ultimately determine whether he is in fact leader of "another country, another state of grace." At the time of this book's writing, racial tensions in Durban are disturbing, but now the anger is the anger of South African blacks directed at Malawian blacks who are perceived as taking jobs from the locals.

What is apparent in the history of relationship between gospel narrative and oppressed peoples is that for many, the great narratives that grew out of the Exodus experience of the Hebrew people provided both political inspiration and emotional succor. Cone writes:

> The violent crosses of the Ku Klux Klan were a familiar reality, and white racists preached a dehumanizing segregated gospel in the name of Jesus' cross every Sunday. And yet in rural black churches I heard a different message, as preachers proclaimed the message of the suffering Jesus and the salvation accomplished by his death on the cross. I noticed how the passion and energy of the preacher increased whenever he talked about the cross, and the congregation responded with outbursts of "Amen" and "Hallelujah" that equaled the intensity of the sermon oration. People shouted, clapped their hands, and stomped their feet, as if a powerful, living reality of God's Spirit had transformed them from nobodies in white society to somebodies in the black church.[26]

Our author is encouraging her first-century audience to reconnect with outbursts of "amen" and "hallelujah" and to rekindle the ecstasy of their earlier Christ-enthusiasm.

---

26. Cone, *Cross*, xv.

16

Other Countries: God-Breathed Histories

THE HISTORICAL DIGRESSION THROUGH arts and politics does not lead us away from the world of Hebrews. The "living word" of our author's text is an interactive one, vivified by God's Spirit and thus engaging with her world and ours. Although she never expected to write for us, she is, in the mysteries of God's purpose, challenging us to engage in what some writers like to call an "intertextual reading" that weaves between the story of the Hebrew people of God the story of her "new Hebrew" Christian people of God, between these biblical peoples and their worlds, and between their experiences and ours.

Can any human nation be the "better country" of our author's sermon? *Ja-nee*! Our life on earth is a shadow form of the better country or "heavenly city" (Heb 11:16)—a form rumored by our lives and life choices as a rehearsal and foretaste of the better country that waits beyond the Red Sea (Heb 11:29) of our life journeys. Our author returns to the history lesson: the Abraham comparison of Heb 11:8–12 is interrupted by the longing for another country shared by author, subject (the narrative character Abraham), and audience alike (Heb 11:13–16) before resuming once more (Heb 11:17–19). The faith narratives momentarily become a "begat-narrative," as the faith of Abraham "begets" the faith of Isaac, Jacob (but beware the fate of Esau mentioned in the same breath at Heb 11:20), Joseph, and his sons (Heb 11:17–22). Then more: "by faith . . ." Moses (Heb 11:23–28) and his people (Heb 11:29), "by faith . . ." the fall of Jericho (see Josh 6:14–26, though our author never names Joshua himself), and "by faith . . ." the holy intervention of the prostitute Rahab (Heb 11:29–31).

At that point, our author changes gears into a series of emphatic but more representative and less expounded historical figures, which she rattles off for dramatic effect without detail (Heb 11:32–38) before finally pausing to make her first extrapolation. This extrapolation could, were we hearing it for the first time, surprise us: Could we not expect that this long list of faith-heroes are now ahead of us, gathered in the future eternal city to enjoy their reward? The author suddenly, unexpectedly, changes tack: all these figures—for they were all commended for their faith—did not receive what was promised (Heb 11:39). Suddenly, we are back on the time axis that the author used in the Melchizedek argument: these paragons of faith did not enter the holy of holies, because Christ had still not yet come to open the gateway through his own self-sacrificial priesthood.

It is too easy to read our author's illustrations of faith as if the humans named were some sort of crystal ball-gazing soothsayers, confident of each promise that was set before them. I find such a reading unconvincing, perhaps because I am not a visionary or a prophet. Graham Greene's iconic whiskey priest of *The Power and the Glory* wakes up at the dawn of his execution day "with a huge feeling of hope which suddenly and completely left him at the first sight of the prison yard."[1] He muses for a while on the failings of his life and the infinite emptiness that awaits him. "Soon he wouldn't even be a memory," he reflects. Soon that emptiness is confirmed: he is executed and becomes "something unimportant which had to be cleared away."[2] Moments later, "everything had been tidied away . . . there was no grave."[3] The whiskey priest is never given a name. Yet his story is told, like the story told by the women of Mark 16:8, despite that fear. In the final sentence of Greene's powerful novel, another unnamed priest arrives in the nation where priesthood is illegal and, though Greene's Catholicism was something of an agnostic Catholicism, readers are left with a prevailing sense that in this strange apostolic succession there is something greater happening than a mere empty sequence.

If the camera of my narrative were to shift at this point, it would shift to a Maximilian Kolbe or an Oscar Romero. Kolbe was executed in Auschwitz in place of a stranger, not knowing whether his act of self-sacrifice would ultimately save the man whose place he was taking, Franciszek Gajowniczek. Romero was shot in El Salvador because he spoke out ceaselessly against the Salvadoran government's oppression and violation of basic human rights. Both men, despite the Roman Catholic tradition's tendency to overlook faults in the process of canonization, were deeply flawed human beings much like Graham Greene's whiskey priest. Kolbe had, to a certain extent, harbored or at least failed to denounce some degree of anti-Semitism. Romero had championed the oppressive voice of Opus Dei, whose opposition to liberal Catholic voices has not always displayed conciliatory

---

1. Greene, *Power*, 210.
2. Ibid., 216.
3. Ibid., 217.

tones. Yet the narratives of faith in both the real and the fictional lives addressed here speak louder than the faults of the practitioners.

Perhaps because I am a deeply flawed human being, I would prefer to look at our author's icons of faith not as calmly clairvoyant readers of the future, but as flawed human beings in whom the sparks of God's "another city" somehow refuse to be smothered. "Faith is the assurance of things hoped for," but assurance is not quite the same as concrete certainty.

"By faith, Abel . . ." Abel is a parallel player in the Cain genealogy. As a foil to the Genesis story, Abel belongs "to the narrative, not the genealogy"[4] and serves only to elucidate the transmission of human violence in history: "The power of the story of Cain lies in its candid acknowledgment, at the dawn of human time, of the connection between religion and violence."[5] As Sacks notes, Cain externalizes and acts out on Abel his own frustrations, then refuses to accept any participation in collective responsibility: "Am I my brother's keeper?" Our author bravely transcends the death of Abel, hears his blood as if it were crying from the ground, and uses the defeated dead man—the Kolbe, Romero, or whiskey priest—as the conveyor of the promise of God.

"By faith, Enoch . . ." Enoch (not Cain's son of Gen 4, though in fact the same name is simply used in two tellings of theological history) barely deserves a place in our author's narrative, for his role is little more than to believe and to be removed. Basically, Enoch pleased God by believing (Gen 5:22), which may at this point serve to remind us of little more than the courage of all who have believed, against all odds, that a narrative of God and God's eternity can reach into either the ennui or the angst of human existence. Almost every day, I encounter the simple, unpretentious adherence to faith of some or another person, whether highly intellectual or highly unsophisticated, who simply believes *because*. Almost every day, I encounter the aggressive disbelief, sometimes with good reason, of those who simply can't, don't, or do so no longer. We see good and bad in each—faith or faithless—and try not to judge.

"By faith, Noah . . ." I was recently in the congregation of an African house church. On that day, at a service ostensibly for children and young families, I heard a sermon in which Noah was held up as a reminder of the crisis of decision with which every human being must stand before God before they die. "Choose this day whom you will serve," was the message of the sermon, with a reminder that failure to choose Jesus and the righteousness available only in Jesus would precipitate an eternity spent in hell. The

---

4. Westermann, *Genesis 1–11*, 292.
5. Sacks, *Fractured World*, 139.

speaker declared that because this was a children's service, she would retreat from narratives of the horrors of hell, though she did conclude with an explication of the artwork of Francis Danby, which shows desperate parents reaching out to their children as they are swept away from hope and life in the rising tide of God's destruction while only the distant, receding ark remains serene amidst the horror.

The analysis in that Zambian church was very selective. If Noah is to be held up as an image of righteousness, it is worth remembering that weeks later, he lies drunk and naked beside the receding floodwaters. Once again, Jonathan Sacks provides a more meaningful analysis of a Hebrew story: "Noah's failure is that, righteous in himself, he has no impact on his contemporaries. He does not engage with them, rebuke them or urge them to mend their ways. Nor does he pray for them, questioning the justice of the Flood, as Abraham was later to do for the people of the cities of the plain."[6] Like the Zambian preacher, our author probably did not want to dwell on the drunkenness of Noah, but I suspect that in today's climate of searing and perhaps septic skepticism, we need to be a little more honest about the complexities of God's chosen prophets. Like Kolbe, Romero, and the whiskey priest, all were flawed examples of humanity who served as outstanding vehicles of the grace of God. Noah was a whiskey priest. If the bloodline of humanity descends from flawed Adam, or whichever parental gathering of DNA that slithered out of the primeval swamp, it is likely to be flawed.

If Noah is a flawed member of our author's checklist, Abraham is a feistier character. Sacks notes[7] that whereas Noah walked with God (Gen 6:9), Abraham walks *ahead* of God (Gen 17:1), and certainly the Abraham narrative is one of energy and motion, with no time for drunken stupors on a beach. Again, I can't visualize the shape of the patriarch's encounter with God or the way such a conversation with God might take place. I doubt he could have conceived the implications of the "multitude of nations" God was calling into being through him. Even as Abraham gained understanding of the covenantal relationship into which God was calling him and his descendants, he would never have dreamed of the vast array of descendants (biological and spiritual) that were to be the continuation of the relationship God was engineering. That an undiscernible number of centuries later, three great religions would trace their heritage back to this son of Terah from the unidentifiable region of Ur would be beyond mortal grasp.

In saying this, I am not ignoring arguments that Abraham was no more likely to have been a historical figure than Noah or Adam was. The

---

6. Ibid., 141.
7. Ibid.

point of Abraham's story for our interpretation of Hebrews is that he represented an encounter with God that our Hebrews author could draw on as an exemplar of faith. Closer to home are those who many of us have met who, in far smaller ways, represent the "by faith" of our author's worldview. I mention the great cathedral builders of previous eras, but there are others closer to our time. While Desmond Tutu, for example, does not recall any one moment in which a vocation to priesthood crystallized in his awareness[8] ("It seems it just grew on him as he immersed himself in his faith after beginning his theological studies"[9]), throughout the world we can be deeply thankful for those who saw in this feisty young African teacher the seeds of priesthood and, "by faith," invested time and effort in his formation.

Tutu is a dramatic example from our own time, but were I to expand the "by faith" into the narratives of my own experience, I would think of those who saw, against all odds in a Eurocentric and deeply postcolonial church, the value of Indigenous clergy and pastors in Australia. David Unaipon (1872–1967) was a South Australian Ngarrindjeri man, a preacher, an inventor, a writer, and the first Aboriginal man to publish in English, having been commissioned by the University of Adelaide to set down on paper some of his people's stories.[10] He is now celebrated on the Australian fifty-dollar note, and the Australian and wider communities can only be thankful for those who saw in him remarkable tenacity and encouraged him in his scientific, musical, literary, and pastoral strengths. While he never benefitted financially from his gifts, Unaipon allowed his gifts to percolate through Australian society. Ironically, Unaipon died before Indigenous Australians were permitted to vote in national or state elections.

David Unaipon's father, James Unaipon (an Anglicization of the family name Ngunaitponi), was also a remarkable example of Christian sainthood and of the "by faith" of our Hebrews author. James Unaipon lived from ca. 1835–1907 and served as the first Indigenous person to be ordained a deacon in any Australian Christian denomination (he served under the auspices of the Aborigines' Friends' Association, a loose and ecumenical affiliation of Christians concerned for Indigenous welfare and mission in South Australia and the Northern Territory). The "by faith" dimension was not only that of the Unaipon father and son, but also the visionary Christian missionaries who saw remarkable value in nurturing and training Indigenous believers in a context in which Indigenous people were widely considered to be of

8. Rowan Williams speaks of a "sense of near inevitability, that obscurely authoritative impulse that crystallizes for some as 'a vocation, the sense that being myself will demand of me a certain kind of commitment" (Williams, "Your Calling Is You").

9. Sparks and Tutu, *Tutu*, 19.

10. Gale, *Dhanum Djorra'wuy Dhawu*.

scarcely more worth than native animals. Congregationalist missionary George Taplin was foremost amongst those who saw the elder Unaipon's value, and though Taplin's diaries reveal that he was sometimes myopic in his dealings with Indigenous Australians, confusing, as many did, Europeanization with Christian proclamation, there can be little doubt that his attitudes were far more advanced than many of his contemporaries among European settlers.

The breadth of both Unaipons' vision—their own "by faith"—was revealed in their readiness to believe, in contradistinction to the dominant Indigenous and European narratives of their time, that there was much to treasure and adopt in rites[11] and narratives of Christianity and Aboriginal spiritualities alike. "Confident of both his Christian faith and his Aboriginality, James Unaipon could confidently embrace what was good and worthy in his people's past."[12] In this, the elder Unaipon contrasted with his mentor Taplin, though allowances must be made for Taplin too, for he was a product of his time. Taplin's belief was that the Australian Indigenous cultures were irreparably damaged.[13] They were all the more damaged by the dangerous narrative of the same era, which upheld the sinister belief that Aboriginal people provided nothing more than cheap and disposable labor and that the inevitable loss of Indigenous people to European diseases or to hunting parties was no more than an inconvenience of supply.

While the missions were continuing in the difficult sociological and geological terrain of Central Australia, similar experiences were unfolding in Aotearoa, New Zealand. New Zealand missionaries were also encountering distrust amongst local communities that was only exacerbated by the wild and often exploitative or destructive antics of contemporary settlers, in particularly the whalers of Aotearoa. Nevertheless, as the Tārore story has already indicated, Māori individuals and groups were converting to Christianity and making their own decisions about that which could be maintained and that which had to be jettisoned from their own culture. Keith Newman notes, "Gradually, less acceptable customs and beliefs were set aside, including infanticide, polygamy, burning crops to starve out enemy survivors, requiring the wife of a chief to commit suicide on his death and his slaves to be killed, and hahunga rites—scraping the flesh off exhumed bodies

---

11. By which I am not implying full-blown liturgies. Taplin tells a delightful anecdote of an impromptu liturgy conducted by his wife Martha. "The natives said afterwards, 'My word, Missis, you very good minister.' I don't suppose my wife seriously infringed any law of the New Testament by acting thus in such very exceptional circumstances" (Taplin, cited in Harris, *One Blood*, 355).

12. Harris, *One Blood*, 363.

13. Ibid., 354.

before reburial."[14] As Māori were empowered to make and communicate their own decisions about the propriety of ancient behaviors, and indeed as Māori were entrusted with proclamation of the Christian message to their own people, there was a new and greater wave of evangelical outreach. A myriad of "by faith" exemplars are available from this wave of Māori self-evangelism, but in each case the European missionaries' "by faith" vision and entrusting of gospel to Māori, together with the "by faith" self-belief of the new believers who, like Saint Paul nearly two millennia before, decided to take the risk of proclamation, is an echo of the perspective our author was demanding of her people.

There was some division even in the 1800s within my Anglican denomination along the high/low boundaries that continue to exist today. The early evangelism of New Zealand had largely been the work of the Church Missionary Society (CMS) and, outside Roman Catholic circles, other less sacramental Protestant bodies. The arrival of George Selwyn in 1842 startled some CMS missionaries, but while his "high church" proclivities disturbed them and his commitment to excellence in theological formation—including training in Greek and Hebrew—stymied some plans for expanding missionary numbers, his commitment to nurture Māori language and empower Māori missionaries placed him on a reasonable footing with some significant Māori leaders. Selwyn did not necessarily adhere to internal Māori hierarchies, but he kept an eye open for potential leadership that could grasp the demands of the Hebrew-Greek Christian heritage while maintaining strong cultural respect for Māori ways. He was grasping what the Unaipons had seen across the Tasman: effective outreach demands a foot in more than one cultural tradition.

One person to catch Selwyn's eye was a young Māori named (or renamed) Rota Waitoa. After being baptized as a young man in 1841, Waitoa worked with Selwyn as a translator (Selwyn's Māori was adequate but not sophisticated) before being sent to the Native Boys' School at the newly-founded theological college in Auckland. By 1853, Selwyn was convinced that the Anglican Church could not keep ignoring the need to ordain Māori believers, and though he was not immediately convinced that Waitoa was the right choice, he accepted the advice of those around him and ordained the young Māori translator to the diaconate on Trinity Sunday, May 22, 1853.[15] While Selwyn was not initially Waitoa's primary advocate, there is no doubt that Selwyn and his advisors collectively exercised a radical "by faith" by

14. Newman, *Bible and Treaty*, 115.

15. It was not entirely coincidental that I was writing these paragraphs on the anniversary of Rota Waitoa's ordination on May 22, the day on which he is commemorated in the liturgical calendar of New Zealand Anglicans.

eventually making him the first Māori ever to be ordained. In the decades that followed his ordination, Waitoa wrestled with the many betrayals and setbacks his Māori kinspeople experienced at the hands of European settlers as well as considerable suspicion by some Māori leaders. "By faith," as our author of Hebrews would put it, he worked tirelessly to advocate for the ordination of Māori and the advancement of Christian teaching in Māori communities (including by putting himself through continued studies in New Testament Greek). Waitoa was ordained a priest in 1860 in the newly-formed Diocese of Waiapu, but he tragically died of injuries he received in a fall from a horse six years later.[16]

History, at least until the birth of postcolonial analyses, has normally been written by its victors. Even biblical history is no exception, and it is hard to read large slices of Hebrew Scripture that speak of bloody conquests over surrounding tribes or internal enemies (2 Sam 18 is a powerful narrative of the complexity of conflict) without a deep-seated sense of horror. Strangely, the Moses narrative our Hebrews author touches on, which is a formative narrative of liberation for the Israelites, has no counterpart in the narrative history of the people it depicts as the defeated army. This would be unsurprising if it were only a case of history's narrative emerging from the victors, but for centuries the Hebrews continued to be a far less significant people in both military and political terms than the Egyptians, whose "horse and rider were thrown into the sea" (Exod 15:21). Archeological evidence or narrative record of the events told from the Egyptians' perspective does not exist. If the event occurred, it was either too embarrassing or too minor for Egyptian records to contain it.

The exodus of Moses, then, is a highly theologized account, and the historical events with which it began are lost to us. Moses stands in our Hebrews narrative as a hero and exemplar of faith, though the slaughter of Egypt's horses and riders in the Red Sea is not altogether edifying to modern ears. But his position in the narrative may serve to remind us of the power of story too. Whatever events occurred surrounding the Hebrew people's enslavement in Egypt and subsequent liberation from tyranny, their telling and re-telling of the story established their identity as a chosen people. Their shared story became a reminder that the God they worshiped was a god of liberation who could overthrow fearsome enemies against all human odds. Moses's fidelity to his call became a trumpet call to all who accepted the tutelage of the Hebrews' God, and it is in that way that our author adopts the story to her cause and to her clarion call to faith.

---

16. For more details of Rota Waitoa's story, see Booth, *Saints*, 184–88.

There are risks in hagiography and in upholding significant events or persons as paradigms of excellence. The stories can become distorted as the context in which they are uttered and heard alters. The narrative character Moses was an inspirational leader of an oppressed people. That people, the Hebrews, went on to experience other moments of remarkable liberation from enemies and oppressors, and other stories were told. Accounts that remain can be still more disturbing than the account of the destruction of the Egyptian army, and the victors' tale of an oppressed people needs some healing once it become the victors' tale of a dominant culture. These stories need redemption. The brutal retaliative slaughter of the men of Benjamin in Judg 20–21 (see especially Judg 20:35–36) makes for unedifying reading, even if the survivors are presented with wives (as if they were livestock) from Shiloh. The wanton slaughter of the men of Jabesh-Gilead to preserve the virgins for the Benjamin remnant is even less edifying. Whatever the historical origins of such a narrative, it can likely be redeemed only by a highly interpreted and applied approach, such as that of Phylis Trible.[17] She observes,

> Violence and vengeance are not just characteristics of a distant, pre-Christian past; they infect the community of the elect to this day. Woman as object is still captured, betrayed, raped, tortured, murdered, dismembered, and scattered. To take to heart this ancient story, then, is to confess its present reality. The story is alive, and all is not well. Beyond confession we must take counsel to say, "Never again." Yet this counsel is itself ineffectual unless we direct our hearts to that most uncompromising of all biblical commands, speaking the word not to others but to ourselves: Repent. Repent.[18]

Biblical narratives sometimes need redemption. So too do other historical narratives, and neither that of Moses nor my more recent example of Waitoa is without need of attention, reorientation, and reapplication in a postcolonial context.

Rota Waitoa's journey was not smooth sailing. He was forced to take refuge during a conflict with a militant cargo cult—the Pai Marire or Hau Hau group—from the other side of New Zealand's North Island, Te Ika-a-Maui. Pai Marire was led by Māori prophet Te Ua Haumene, whose Hau Hau uprisings carried out reprisals against European Christians and their Māori supporters. Te Ua Haumene considered his message to be one of

---

17. Trible, *Texts of Terror*, 65–87.
18. Ibid., 87.

"Christianity purified of missionary error"[19]—a theological perspective that today's postcolonial attitudes might be more sympathetic towards but that Waitoa and orthodox Christian converts of the time saw as subverting Christianity. With the hindsight of history, Te Ua might be seen as a hero of faith[20] too, for perspective is everything, though it might be said that the apocalyptic undertones of his special revelation should generate some caution in approaching his writings, and the taking of enemy heads as trophies following an ambush on British troops was not likely to generate wholesome dialogue or a kindly historical remembrance.

In my own journey, it is a nice coincidence that the nineteenth-century Māori Hau Hau uprising and the twentieth-century East African Mau Mau uprising bear such similar if unrelated names. When eventually I learned to read the history of the Mau Mau uprisings of Africa not through the lens of my European forerunners, but rather through the fresh perspectives brought to me by writers such as Ngũgĩ wa Thiong'o, I was challenged to attempt to read the past of Aotearoa through new lenses too. I do so imperfectly, confronted by the reminder that as a *Pākehā* Anglican in Aotearoa, my speaking must always begin by listening to the voices of my parallel partners, the Māori, whose *waka*[21] is tied inseparably to mine by God's Spirit. In the formative work with which I began these reflections, *A New Zealand Prayer Book / He Karakia Mihinare o Aotearoa*, there is another tiny exchange that is rendered in English as "We shall all be one in Christ." In Māori, it is rendered *Ko te Karaiti to pou herenga waka*, or "Christ is the mooring where all canoes can tie up."[22] I prefer the latter reading.

I am aware too of the possibility of embodying in that preference a kind of paternalistic romanticism. Earlier in these reflections, I cited Chimamanda Ngozi Adichie's most recent novel, *Americanah*. Adichie's exposés of collective hypocrisies—not least of which are my own liberal hypocrisies—are caustic, and if we are even to begin to hear authentic postcolonial voices, we need to sit with the pain of caustic glares. Adichie's central character, Ifemelu, cuts through comfortable liberal dinner party chat with an assessment of race relations in twenty-first-century America, referring to her own pain at constantly being watched as a black Nigerian woman dating a flamboyant golden-haired white man: "We don't say any of this stuff. We let it pile up in our heads and when we come to nice liberal dinners like this,

---

19. Head, "Te Ua Haumene."

20. For a reasoned and sympathetic analysis of his place in New Zealand history, see Clark, *Hau Hau*.

21. *Waka* in "pure" translation is a canoe, but in Māori it is any vehicle, including the grammatical sense of a vehicle of a metaphor.

22. Bluck, *Wai Karekare*, 18.

we say that race doesn't matter because that's what we're supposed to say, to keep our nice liberal friends comfortable."[23] Ifemelu's observations regarding women's magazines and the absence of black-skinned models are even more devastating: "so three black women in maybe two thousand pages of women's magazines, and all of them are biracial or racially ambiguous, so they could also be Indian or Puerto Rican or something. Not one of them is dark."[24] As I tie up my *waka*, I need to recognize that my experience of Scripture, liturgy, of all life is vastly different from those who paddle the *waka* tied up alongside. My life expectancy, my health, my financial resources, and even, were I to use them, my access to beauty products forms a vastly different narrative to that experienced by the paddlers of the *waka* alongside me, and all the more so to those from Nigeria or Tuvalu or a myriad other oceans of experience.

Therefore, despite the enmity that lay between Te Ua and more traditionalist believers such as Waitoa, and despite the traditionalists being on the side, as it were, of history, both served a vision of a gospel, even a Trinitarian gospel. Te Ua's version, although arguably unorthodox in its approach to the nature and person of Jesus, was swallowed up in politics and military action. His movement and eventually his spirit was crushed. Waitoa's story and faith was recognized as orthodox, and it is this story that I have acknowledged in these pages as an exemplar of "by faith." Yet there was a "by faith" in the struggle of Te Ua Haumene too; his was a struggle against colonialist oppression that was deeply embedded in his interpretations of Christian teachings and dogma. As with many figures of history, we may need to step outside traditional narratives to offer redemption to Te Ua Haumene, for it is the winners of struggles who define orthodoxy, and while Te Ua's religio-political uprising was destroyed by forces loyal to the Queen of England, Waitoa's version of faith carried the day.

Obviously, being an antipodean, I am limited in my knowledge of those who underwent similar stories of "by faith" empowerment in the service of the gospel in other parts of the world. Others could tell, for example, the story of John Johnson Enmegahbowh (1820–1902), who was ordained a deacon in the Episcopal Church in the United States in 1859 and was subsequently made a priest in 1867. He too underwent the delicate journey of living and working in two worlds, earning wrath and praise from Europeans and Native Americans alike. Enmegahbowh went on to be cofounder of

---

23. Adichie, *Americanah*, 291.
24. Ibid., 295.

the White Earth (Gaa-waabaabiganikaag) Mission, which is still extant in northern Minnesota today.[25]

Similarly, being Anglican, I have not explored the narratives of pioneer exemplars of "by faith" in other Christian denominations. Each Christian subculture has its heroes of faith, whether they are formerly canonized as saints or not. These subcultures do not even need to be restricted to denominational subcultures and so may reflect gender or sexuality as well as ethnicity. For example, by faith, Bishop Ronald Hall ordained Li Tim-Oi to the priesthood in Hong Kong in 1944. She was the first woman to be ordained a priest in the Anglican tradition. By faith, the diocese of New Hampshire elected Gene Robinson as a coadjutor bishop in 2003 and then as bishop of his diocese a year later, despite being in an openly gay relationship.[26] Opposition to this controversial step in the ecclesiology of my own denomination, like the earlier opposition to the consecration of Barbara Harris, Penny Jamieson, and other women to the episcopacy, was predictably loud and long-lived, but it is worth remembering that the affirmation of James and David Unaipon, of Rota Waitoa, or of John Johnson Enmegahbowh was no less considerable a step in their respective times and cultures. By faith . . .

If I may pay tribute to one further pair of exemplars as practitioners of the "by faith" of the Hebrews sermon, the story of Robert and Mary Moffat is a remarkable one.[27] One hagiography of Scottish Congregationalist missionary Robert Moffat (1795–1883) narrates his experience standing before African tribespeople in what is now Botswana, the former Bechuanaland, daring them to make a martyr of him. He stood, "erect and fearless, threw open his waistcoat, and cried, 'Now, if you will, strike your spears into my heart.'"[28] The scene is likely to have been embellished in the religious

---

25. See the tribute to Enmegahbowh in the June 2002 issue of the Episcopal Diocese of Minnesota newspaper, *Soundings*, including the sermon by M. Lucie Thomas. Unlike Waitoa, Enmegahbowh was given episcopal dispensation to avoid Greek and Hebrew lessons: "Enmegahbowh had long refused to learn Greek and Hebrew, stating that he was being sent to work among the living, not among the dead!" (Thomas, "Enmegahbowh," 12).

26. As I am limiting my scope to my own spheres of influence and information, I am paying even less attention to non-Christian representatives of adventurous faith. It is worth mentioning, however, Imam Daayiee Abdullah from Washington, DC, who is the first openly gay Imam in the United States. I am aware of two other openly gay Muslim clerics who exercise public ministry: Muhsin Hendricks in South Africa and Ludovic Mohamed-Zahed of France. For further information, see Lucas, "Meet America's First Gay Black Imam"; and Kreider, "Openly Gay Imams." A still more remarkable case is recorded by the BBC's Hamedani and Brown, "Gay Mullah Flees Iran."

27. Two of my children are descendants of the Moffats, albeit on their maternal side, so I am not unbiased in my admiration for them!

28. Hodder, *Heroes*, 64.

language of Victorian-era devotion, but the story of Robert Moffat and the less acknowledged story of his wife, Mary, is one more reminder that the pantheon of saints in the Hebrews author's mind has not been limited by place or time. Mary Moffat (who died in 1870, long before her husband) deserves more recognition: while Robert conducted missionary and exploratory journeys from Griekwastad in Central South Africa to regions in what is now Zambia and northern Zimbabwe, Mary stayed faithfully behind at Kuruman, where she underwent ten pregnancies and bore Robert six live children. Perhaps more significant than the romance of Robert Moffat's missionary journeys and his remarkable re-energizing of the London Missionary Society station at Kuruman was his faithful translation of both the Bible and Bunyan's *Pilgrim's Progress* into Setswana. Indeed, Moffat produced the first complete translation of the Bible into an African language since the invention of the printing press (the edition was printed at the Kuruman press). By faith, as our Hebrews author might say, Mary devotedly supported her husband in his missionary journeys in an unknown and, to a European, unpredictably dangerous continent. By faith, he translated. By faith, they printed.

I have suggested that the 1898 narration of Moffat's life from which I quoted was hagiographical and embellished. Such writing is scorned as foreign-sounding in the post-Victorian era, yet beneath its plethora of adjectives it conveyed in the conventions of its own time a framework of meaning for its era, however distasteful that era may be to postcolonial eyes. It was all but *de rigueur* to see the state and church, including missions, as twin handmaids of the one God: "The State is sacred."[29] Sometimes this twinning was deeply deleterious. As Archbishop Justin Welby sagely notes, "the church's sporadic record of compelling obedience to its teachings through violence and coercion is a cause for humility and shame."[30] On the other hand, the Moffat's son-in-law David Livingstone, whose faults were myriad, nevertheless worked tirelessly to erode the influence of the slave trade on the regions he explored.

Given the inflated language of political narratives in our own era, it could be suggested we have not altogether escaped, if not hagiographical, then certainly self-congratulatory embellishment techniques in the era since Queen Victoria. It is easy to mock hagiography, and it is perhaps indicative of that form that the title of the book I have cited, *Heroes of Britain in Peace and War*, confuses Britishness with heroism. To that extent, the

---

29. W. J. H. Campion in Gore, *Lux Mundi*, 444, cited in Nicholls, *Deity and Dominion*, 23.

30. Welby, "Religious Freedom."

hagiographical writers often engaged in the coordinate slippage our Hebrews author warns against. This is often the case when church communities slide too cozily into associations between church and state, and Rom 13:1–7 or 1 Tim 2:1–4 become not a prayer for peace and justice but a re-jigging of the civic state as gospel in itself. But this should not detract from the credibility of the best of those missionaries, who sought to convey the gospel of Christ on the back of the colonial expansion of their era. Humanity needs stories, and humanity needs its stories to be told in style appropriate to each era—a style that enables both listeners and recipients of the narrative to belong to and hold on to the central foundations of their community while challenging them to check their own faith coordinates. Such storytelling is, for example, the great hallmark of brilliance of the author of the gospel we know as Mark, whose original ending invites listeners to imagine themselves in the place of the frightened women hearing of the resurrection for the first time. Our sermon author adopts another technique: Where do we as an audience stand in the narrative of "by faith"?

It remains to return to the exemplars our author provided in the first place. What do Abel, Enoch, Noah, Abraham, Isaac, Joseph, Jacob, the nameless Jochebed[31] (Exod 2:1–2), Moses, the Israelites in general, Rahab, Gideon, Barak, Sampson, Jephthah, David, Samuel, the prophets, the numerous and collective unnamed women, and the countless others cited in "the roll call of the heroes of faith"[32] of Heb 11 have to tell us about the faith to which the author was challenging her audience to return? Underscoring all those named in the roll call is the final and definitive example, which is shortly to be introduced in a crescendo: Jesus himself (Heb 12:2).

Remembering that Hebrews is a sermon designed to be heard, it should be borne in mind that the author transitions from quite discursive exampling of faith-practitioners to a staccato delivery of the later faithful Hebrews, "dipping here and there into the story of salvation history."[33] The impact of this, aurally speaking, is an emphatic snowballing of faith's effect on the lives of those surrounding and subsequent to the faithful as the ripples of faith reach outward and onward through history (though para-

---

31. Jochebed is finally named at Exod 6:20. It is worth bearing in mind Fiorenza's observation that "Although the canon preserves only remnants of the nonpatriarchal early Christian ethos, these remnants still allow us to recognize that the patriarchalization process is not inherent in Christian revelation and community but progressed slowly and with difficulty" (Florenza, *In Memory*, 35). In this case, of course, Moses's father also remains no more than "a man from the house of Levi," a reminder that many of the exemplars of faith are lost in the amnesia of passing time.

32. Johnson, *Hebrews*, 274.

33. Craddock, "Hebrews," 143.

doxically, and *contra* to laws of thermodynamics, growing in energy and impact). Buchanan sees poetic construction in this passage,[34] but it is more likely to be the aural instincts of a fine preacher using cadences and rhythms to full effect. All these faith-exemplars have seized and held on to faith (Heb 3:6) and have diligently—and, we might add, with great discipline—persevered in faith (Heb 6:11, Heb 10:23). These are demonstrations of what might be called, in grammatical terms, the "active voice" of faith: actively, determinedly maintaining faith against all odds.

As Johnson has noted, the oft-quoted notion that "faith is the assurance of things hoped for" is not entirely self-explicatory, and the author's elucidation of the statement with "the conviction of things not seen" adds little to our understanding. The Greek provides difficulties of translation and of original meaning; *hupostasis* (NRSV: "assurance") could be rendered awkwardly as "concretization," meaning that the thing concretized is able to be grasped and clung to, but *elenchos* (NRSV: "conviction") in the elucidation tends to water this down. Johnson offers "substance . . . proof."[35] Perhaps "concretization . . . embodiment" will do, but the onus remains on the audience to take each of the exemplars named and find in them (taking the biblical narratives, of course, as fact) inescapable evidence of the worth of the hope they faithfully clung to. For those of us with a more skeptical view of biblical history, this may be more difficult, though treating the characters as symbolic exemplars should not weaken the author's point, provided we don't add the derogatory adjective "mere"!

What, then, do our author's exemplars represent? She begins with the dual treatment of the ancients' tenacity ("received approval"; see Heb 11:2), which she is about to expound, but she then draws the audience in by encouraging them to recall what I might anachronistically call "the Kierkegaardian leap of faith," or the decision to adopt faith in a Creator. Perhaps this was easier in the first century than in our own? The Internet will bombard us daily, hourly perhaps, with reminders that many of those around us champion the conviction that "there's nothing out there." Johnson notes that this claim "distinguishes believers and atheists."[36] We must simply sit with this differentiation—not as a value judgment, but as a phenomenological division. I can and often do cite great atheists and humanists and other people who do not believe in the deity our author believed in. They can exemplify human magnificence and even faith, but not faith in my God, the God of the Hebrews. My favorite remains eye surgeon Fred Hollows, who

---

34. Buchanan, *Hebrews*, 201.
35. Johnson, *Hebrews*, 276.
36. Ibid., 280.

in his autobiography cites words often attributed to Ralph Waldo Emerson with warm approval: "To know even one life has breathed easier / Because you lived, / This is to have succeeded."[37]

> I regard that as a pretty good summary of what life is all about. I am a humanist. I don't believe in any higher power than the best expressions of the human spirit, and those are to be found in personal and social relationships. Evaluating my own life in those terms, I've had some mixed results. I've hurt some people and disappointed others but I hope that, on balance, I've given more than I've taken. I believe that my view of what a 'redeemed social condition' is has been consistent—equity between people—and I've tried always to work to that end.[38]

Hollows places hope and, without naming it, judgment at the center of his self-evaluation. Despite Rahner's acknowledgment of "anonymous Christians," it might be insulting in the twenty-first century to pretend that Hollows was in some way an honorary Christian; he exemplifies something of hope, if not quite our author's "assurance of things hoped for." Hollows can remind us of tenacity and of the deep-seated belief that the human spirit can transcend ordinariness. In my own theology, I believe he has a special place in the heart of the God he did not feel able to believe in. To say this is not, as I was once accused of when applauding Hollows, to uphold a doctrine of "salvation by works" but to adhere to a doctrine of salvation by Christ—by the faith *of* Christ primarily, long before faith *in* Christ takes effect.[39] Hollows can exemplify the potential magnificence of the human spirit and can even exemplify faith in a better future, but he cannot be made to exemplify faith in the God believed in against all odds by our author's exemplars.

---

37. Hollows and Corris, *Fred Hollows*, 259.

38. Ibid.

39. I am alluding here to the infamous debate amongst Pauline scholars—originating with Johannes Haussleiter in 1891 but subsequently spearheaded by Richard Hays—regarding the faith *in* or *of* Jesus Christ primarily at Gal 3:22. See Hays, *Faith*, 142–62. Within day-to-day discourse in church circles, the hermeneutic seems to divide along a theological spectrum, with those from a more traditional evangelical persuasion championing "faith in" (objective genitive) and those like myself of a more liberal persuasion championing the "faith of" (subjective genitive) construction. I recall with some mild horror sitting down to a clergy breakfast when, before I had even had my first cup of coffee, my neighbor—a stranger to me—turned and flung the question "So do you subscribe to the subjective or objective genitive school?" Now a bishop, my unknown neighbor was a graduate of Moore College in Sydney; it appeared to me that such matters could be dealt with *after* passing the toast!

Exemplars of the leap of faith may well be lesser human beings than, for example, Hollows. But even in our author's time, these exemplars represent the sometimes risky choice of believing in the Creator God of the Hebrew people: "The first requirement of faith is to believe that God exists."[40] I don't claim ever to find this easy! Abel, in the biblical narrative, moves beyond this requirement by offering the sacrifice of the firstborn and therefore most prized animal, one that has at least symbolically[41] been nurtured and husbanded through the life cycles of the herd. In doing so, he undertakes a greater sacrifice than his brother. Like Maximilian Kolbe, Abel had no idea whether his sacrifice would achieve its objective (Kolbe's objective was, as we have seen, to save Gajowniczek; Abel's was to please God), but he carried out his plan in faith. Johnson notes that the continued telling of the Abel story is in itself "attestation" (NRSV: "commendation") of his leap of faith.[42]

Enoch is a minor player in the biblical Genesis narratives and perhaps stretches post-Enlightenment credulity more than most. We should not focus on the factuality of being "taken up" (loosely based on Gen 5:24), but even in our era we can be impressed by a life lived with such faith and integrity that it transcends or, in the literal narrative, avoids death. While I have considerable difficulty with the devotional belief that the bodies of some great saints are incorruptible, I can understand the powerful symbolism of this belief: a vessel that has embodied vast holiness transcends corruption. In a more rationalist society, we will sometimes cling, if not to the immortality of certain figures,[43] at least to the immortal impact of their legacy, even if in some cases it is doubtful that the events happened in the first place. In my two adopted countries, the ANZAC tradition honors John Kirkpatrick Simpson and his donkey, who together supposedly carried some 300 wounded (at the improbable rate of twenty-four per day) through the field of battle over twenty-five days during the Gallipoli stalemate of World War I. The story is both a conflation of at least two medical rescue campaigns (the other rescuer was New Zealander Richard Alexander "Dick" Henderson, who, unlike Simpson, died many years after the war) and a hagiographical embellishment designed to raise flagging wartime nationalistic

---

40. Johnson, *Hebrews*, 283. Enoch receives wide consideration in 1 and 2 Enoch and the book of Jubilees.

41. In real terms, the firstborn of, for example, a lambing or calving season may not be harder to come by than any other, especially as the herd, if Abel's narrative is taken literally, is the inaugural herd. In symbolic terms though, the firstborn brings special joy and is a herald or vanguard of all that is to come.

42. Johnson, *Hebrews*, 281.

43. This theme undergirds the first chapter of Fyodor Dostoevsky's *The Brothers Karamazov*.

spirits.[44] Yet Simpson is for Australians akin to Paul Revere in the American pantheon of saints, and it is probable that any group identity is dependent on the tales of its heroes for self-belief. Enoch's life story was probably a part of the formative preaching discourse common to our author and audience and so receives little exegesis in the Hebrews sermon. Johnson notes that the traditions of Wis 4:10, Sir 44:16, and Philo are, while respectful, less hagiographical than our author in their treatments of Enoch.[45]

With a degree of deconstruction, the story of Noah can be made more accessible to a contemporary audience. I am not interested in the historicity of flood narratives as such, despite some degree of repetition in various ancient narratives. The more important aspect of the Noah saga is his fidelity to God despite the jeering of his contemporaries. In this respect, he becomes a prophetic figure. Noah, however, for all his foibles (Gen 9:21), stands as a symbol of all who have spoken out against dominant discourse, standing in his case for "blamelessness" (Gen 6:9) in the face of a hedonistic and self-indulgent (Gen 6:5) culture. This not an easy stance to take in any self-obsessed culture; Bishop George Bell, who stood out against the nationalistic and anti-Semitic jingoism of the interwar period (but who paradoxically refused to embrace pacifism) might serve as a more modern example of a principled stand against popular and collective self-interest. The church, he wrote, "should set its face against any war of extermination or enslavement, and any measures directly aimed at destroying the morale of a population."[46] Robert Runcie, who faced up to the nationalistic and anti-Argentinian rhetoric of Margaret Thatcher during the Falklands conflict, might stand as an even more recent example. It is of course all but impossible to ascertain the identity of current prophetic voices, though I am conservative enough to suggest, while not pretending the issues are black and white, that some of those who are standing up to dominant narratives regarding abortion,[47] euthanasia,[48] and the premature sexualization[49] of children may have something of the prophet about them. At the time when Donald Trump's "white America" rhetoric and the "border protection" rhetoric of Australia's Tony Abbott are on the rise, we might note the courage of the many who are

---

44. Buley, *Glorious Deeds*.

45. Johnson, *Hebrews*, 283.

46. Cited in Slack, *George Bell*, 84. Sadly, there have more recently been accusations naming Bell as a sexual abuser. He is long dead and unable to defend himself. See Sherwood, "Church of England Bishop."

47. See, for example, Tankard Reist, *Giving Sorrow Words*.

48. See, for example, Keown, *Euthanasia Examined*.

49. See, for example, Tankard Reist, *Getting Real*.

speaking out against them to insist that human worth is not based on color and that human beings have a right to seek refuge from oppression.

Abraham and Sarah make an ambivalent pair of human beings, and we might dig a little deeper into the substructure of their story. At the end of Gen 11, the story of God's dealings with humanity undergoes a remarkable shift that Brueggemann refers to as "perhaps the most important structural break in the Old Testament, and certainly in Genesis."[50] Claus Westermann breaks his magnificent three-volume commentary after Gen 11:26, such that after brief genealogical preamble (Gen 11:27–29) the new section begins at Gen 11:30 with the resounding cry, "Sarah was barren; she had no child." This is the transition, in Westermann's terms, from the "primeval" to the "patriarchal" story: "The primeval story speaks about the basic elements of the world and of humanity, the patriarchal story of the basic elements of human community."[51] This is the beginning of the human encounter with God and God's dealings both with a specific people and, however stylized, specific individuals within that people.

In other words, however we interpret Genesis, we are until near the end of Gen 11 reading of God's dealing with *all* creation, including all humanity. Tales of the creation of the heavens and the earth and of all the species of the earth, together with tales of the creation and the fall of humankind and of the results of that fall fill Gen 1–11. At that point though, the narration changes, and we move into salvation history rather than creation history. In most of the previous verses, the focus was on begetting—with generation after generation of begats—to tell the story of humanity's expansion. The sole interruption is the strategic and tragic tale of the Tower of Babel, humankind's attempt to build its own path to the heavens. But as the Genesis storyteller's camera zooms in on individual lives, the story of begetting reaches a dead end: Sarah is barren. The narrative point is now that only the intervention of God can save the story, and the narrator, long before our Hebrews author, demands faith in that intervention.

Humankind can go no further. The history of humanity has encountered desperation and hopelessness. Sarah is barren. This, the Genesis author wants us to realize, is the place where the encounter with God begins. The Genesis author is suggesting, and our Hebrews author is concurring, that it is only when we encounter barrenness and hopelessness and the realization that in ourselves we can be or do nothing that the encounter with God begins, for it begins by faith. It is no accident that barrenness as the place of salvation is a recurring theme in the Hebrew Scriptures: Rebekah

---

50. Brueggemann, *Genesis*, 116.
51. See Westermann, *Genesis 12–36*, 23.

(Gen 25:21), Rachel (Gen 29:31), and Hannah (1 Sam 1:2), as well as Israel itself (Isa 54:1) must all encounter their own barrenness before they become the person or nation God calls them to be.

Into this context, God speaks the divine Word that is action. Not for the first time, the book of Genesis emphasizes the same message that lies at the heart of the prologue to John's gospel account: when God speaks, it is done. God's speech, God's Word, is action. In the beginning God said, "Let there be light, and there was light" (Gen 1:3). John puts it another way: "All things came into being through him, and without him not one thing came into being" (John 1:1). Our author's preaching task is in part to remind her audience of this absolute fusion between Word and action in God's hands and to remind the audience that God's Word is action (Heb 4:12). In Gen 12, God speaks a word of hope into Sarah and Abraham's world of hopelessness.

This citation of the Abraham and Sarah saga by our author is a technique similar to Paul's method of citation in Rom 4:13–25, where he too cites Genesis, saying that the God of Abraham "calls into existence things that are not." At a literal level, God "calls into existence" the child that was not available to Abraham and Sarah through the processes of nature. God speak-acts, for want of a better word, when the begetting that is no more than the process of history and of biology has become hopeless and when there is nothing left but a desperate need for God's compassionate and intervening response.[52] God speaks into Abraham and Sarah's lives, and therefore into the lives of the people Israel, and therefore into the life of all humanity, by speaking a word of salvation. The call to Abraham is a call to move into God's future. In the midst of brokenness and barrenness, Abraham and Sarah are commanded not to stay petrified or fossilized, but to go out from their comfort zone instead. There is an all too human temptation to stay in the state or the place we know, even if it is a place of hopelessness and, in the case of the Hebrews, comfortable ennui.

When there was no human way to go on in a place where meaning for existence was removed from them, Sarah and Abraham cry out. They then hear a word of promise from God, but that promise remains unfulfilled for several chapters of the Genesis narrative. In Gen 18, however, the story develops. Abraham and Sarah had left their country in accordance with the command of God, but they remained childless. They became accustomed to their barrenness, and it became a place of comfort: they had lost the expectant coordinates of faith. Abraham and Sarah all too humanly failed to maintain their belief in the promise. They elected for the easy and undivine option, and so Abraham has had a child by Hagar. The couple stayed within

---

52. See Goldingay, *Israel's Gospel*, 251–61.

the limitations of human insight rather than raising their eyes to the heavens to take our author's "by faith" perspective.[53]

The Abraham story, however, enters a new phase in Gen 18. Abraham is the key character in the first part of that chapter, and he is a person in a hurry. He runs from the tent to meet the stranger (who is also a plurality of stranger*s*), then he hastens back to Sarah and demands that she likewise hasten in her preparation of the bread. He runs to choose a beast from the herd, orders his slaves hastily to prepare it, and only then slows down to stand with the strangers who are his guests. But the story slows down in the second half of Gen 18 as the narrator shifts to focus on the "three men" who visit. One of these three (Christianity has always found significance in the fact that the narrative mentions both three stranger*s* and one) recounts the promise made by God in Gen 12—the promise of offspring. But this repetition of the promise is met only with the Sarah's bitter laughter.

In that laughter, we are confronted and challenged by a cry of dereliction—not of Christ on the Cross, but of Sarah's emotional pain. Hers is the laughter of disbelief and of the all too human failure to hold on to the divine promise of impossibility. Like the Hebrews audience, she has lost her coordinates, opting to slide instead into the comfortable ennui of the status quo. The apparent hopelessness she and Abraham have grown accustomed to is now their normality, and the call of faith is to them nonsensical. Theirs is a very twenty-first-century existence, but it was not dissimilar to the world of slipping faith our author's audience has slipped into. Yet into this world, the Genesis stranger(s) speak again the promise of God. Mockingly, bitterly, Sarah cries out, "Shall I have pleasure?" (Gen 18:12). In the Genesis narrative the answer of God is, in playful Hebrew fashion, a question: "Is anything too hard for the Lord?" (Gen 18:14). This, for our Hebrews author, is the crux of the matter.

If the Hebrews' answer or Abraham's answer or, by extension, our answer to this not-so-rhetorical question is "Yes," then the Lord is simply not Lord, for we have placed nature and its processes into a standing greater than God's promise.[54] The author of Genesis does not want the people of God of any century to answer "Yes" to God's question. The Hebrews audience members, as their preacher jogs their memory of the Abraham and Sarah narrative, are expected to let God be God, answering, "No. There is

---

53. It should not ever be forgotten that the Jewish Scriptures reveal a God who is compassionate and promise-making also in his dealings with Hagar. Her son Ishmael, who would father the nomadic peoples of the east, is given a wild life, but it too is one breathed into being by God. That fact alone should be the basis for constructive conversation between Christians, Jews, and Muslims, cousins as we are in faith.

54. The nature miracles of the gospel narratives work in the same way.

not and cannot be anything greater than God." We may have good reason to believe that our barrenness or ennui or any demon of our time and experience (Global warming? Economic and ecological collapse? Loss of our careers or health?) is the final and therefore tragic word, but we are asked by faith to see through the eyes of God.[55]

So Sarah laughs. It is the laugh of science at the possibility of a Creator God, or at the possibility of resurrection, at the possibility of life beyond death, or at the possibility of the new heaven and new earth envisioned by the seer of the book of Revelation. It is the laugh of a society that will always mock the God the Hebrews audience had previously come to love and worship. It is the laugh of those outside the community of faith, whose laughter was perhaps increasingly comprehensible to the Hebrews as they saw their neighbors effectively dancing on their new but fading sacred beliefs or even as the Hebrews themselves became too busy in the service of money and security to pause before the resurrected Christ they had believed in. It is the laugh of Michal as she witnessed the dance of David, a mad and manic dance in honor of God (2 Sam 6:5). That dance earns Michal's cynicism, but her subsequent barrenness represents a narrative reversal of Sarah's unexpected fertility (2 Sam 6:20–23).

But as our author realizes, Sarah's laughter does not have the final word. God's promise is not dependent on her response or on Abraham's response. God has spoken, and it will be done, which in Italian is called a *fiat*. God's word is action, and though Sarah has taken a poor option in the past and laughs in the narrative present, the will of God—the promise of God—will be done. Only the promise of God is a definite; human yearning and desire is not a definite. The ultimate promise in the back of our author's mind is that darkness and death are not the final word, but rather resurrection and light. It is to that promise that she calls her audience to return. By faith in "things not seen," they attained what God asked of and promised for them.

The Abraham narrative has many dimensions beyond the story he shares with Sarah, the story of the procreation of generations. Our author, in fact, begins with the traveler's faith that drives Abraham from Ur to Canaan (Gen 11:31—13:18) and contains within its own terms many demonstrations of Abraham's faith in God. But in our author's hands, the faith Abraham shows in undertaking the journey to Canaan simply preempts the journey to which she is calling her audience to the Unseen City that the author of Revelation calls the new heaven and new earth. There are many

---

55. Bearing in mind the sage warning that "God's covenant [with Noah] does not guarantee that humanity cannot destroy the earth, but it promises that God will not, and it invites humanity to associate itself with God's commitment" (Goldingay, *Israel's Gospel*, 183).

parallels between Abraham and Sarah's journey towards a city prepared for them (Heb 11:16) and the eschatological journey our preacher is emphasizing. It is critical to the author's purpose, however, that the "unseen" dimension of an eschatological city must not be lost. If it is lost, or if the Abram saga is reduced to little more than the legendary children of the Oregon Trail in the eponymous children's novel about a family seeking a better political and economic existence,[56] then the sermon of Hebrews is hollow. The tale of the Oregon Trail is inspirational in either its fictional or autobiographical form, but it is not the eschatological inspiration our author is referring to. This brings to mind more questions of what might be termed the skeptical Christianity represented earlier by Spong and Geering: Are we true to the coordinates of the Hebrews author if we denude this sermon of its eschatological and post-palliative references, leaving us with no more than the knowledge "that our own life and those of others will be accepted by God as having contributed to his purpose for the world"[57] (and leaving aside any question of the nature of the God to whom Geering refers)?[58]

There are shadowed aspects to a contemporary reading of the Abram saga. Erich Fromm finds in the dark story of Abraham's near-sacrifice of Isaac a seminal narrative that, while arguably seeking to render obsolete ancient Near Eastern rites of child sacrifice, nevertheless depicts the actions of a man whose love of his faith is stronger than responsible parental love. Abraham is displaying what Fromm calls "conformist aggression."[59] Fromm was writing in the shadow of two world wars; we will never lose those shadows, much less lose our human propensity to turn religious allegiance into evil. Much evil has been perpetrated in the name of Christianity, let alone other faiths, and there is some truth to suggestions that a psychological genetic trail might trace itself from Gen 22:1–19 (or, as Fromm emphasizes, from Neolithic Babylonian Marduk mythology[60]) through the Mount Moriah narrative into Christianity's doctrines of penal substitutionary atonement

---

56. See van der Loeff, *Oregon Trail*. The novel is loosely based on the experiences of the Sager orphans, who crossed into Oregon from Mississippi in 1844. Catherine Sager-Pringle's nonfictional account, *Across the Plains in 1844*, was first published around 1860.

57. Geering, *Resurrection*, 65.

58. For a helpful analysis of the problems presented by Geering, not to mention Richard Dawkins, see Richard Randerson's autobiographical reflections of in Randerson, *Slipping*, 197–217. Randerson's emphasis on God as mystery does not represent a loss of coordinates, in the terms of the Hebrews author.

59. Fromm, *Anatomy*, 178, 207.

60. Ibid., 164.

and downwards to the domestic and institutional violence perpetrated in the name of Christ through history.

It is a sad reflection on the history of the Christian communities that I need to emphasize that this homiletic reflection by our first-century author does not authenticate the types of victimization and abuse that have been carried out in the name of Christian authority and discipline, some of which I have outlined previously in this study and elsewhere. In *All God's Children*, New Zealand abuse survivor Rob Sinclair tells of the unhappy confluence of brutal discipline and predatory sexuality imposed on inmates at the Hokio Beach Boys' Home. Although it was run by the state, the Hokio Beach Boys' Home was frequented by both secular and religious predators in the 1960s. The story is a shocking reminder of the depravity that can accrue when coordinates of common human decency, let alone faith-propriety, are dismantled. Sinclair concludes his narrative with the observation that "no one should stand by and accept abuse, particularly the abuse of children, who will carry it with them for the rest of their lives, as I do today."[61] As a scarred survivor who is understandably without a stated religious allegiance, it can only be suggested that Sinclair is far closer to those coordinates of decency that our author advocates, and *ipso facto* closer to the heart of the exemplars of "by faith," than any perpetrators of psychological, physical, and sexual abuse.

Any suggestion that a narrative such as the near-sacrifice of Isaac justifies brutality in the name of faith-obedience or discipline has violently misread a story intended (however inadequately) to exemplify God's mercy. As a corrective to the tragic and tarnished reputation generated by Christian institutions, Neil and Thea Ormerod observe, "Jesus turned to the poor, the sick and the powerless and through them brought hope to the world. Today God is offering the churches a painful journey of renewal, one that can begin when the prophetic voices of survivors are heard."[62] Earlier in their reflections on sexual and physical abuse in the churches, the Ormerods note that "Abraham is wrong to undertake to kill his son"[63] and

> What we are seeing in Abraham's behavior is not an act of religious faith but an act of compulsive religious fanaticism. If we believe that God can command us to do a morally evil act then really we can justify anything. The outcome of such a position is not religious faith but religious fanaticism. "It is the will of

---

61. Sinclair, *All God's Children*, 210.
62. Ormerod and Ormerod, *When Ministers Sin*, 175.
63. Ibid., 95.

God/Allah/Vishnu/Yahweh" is the constant cry of the religious fanatic down through the ages.[64]

The Ormerods, like Fromm, emphasize that the original narrative, which was subsequently displaced as Israelite culture was displaced, was about the cessation of child sacrifice. Nancy Jay notes, "The only action that is as serious as giving birth, which can act as a counterbalance to it, is killing," and adds, "Unlike childbirth, sacrificial killing is deliberate, purposeful, "rational" action, under perfect control."[65] Our coordinates of decency are faulty until we restore that original perspective.

The knife Abraham wields over his son in Gen 22:10 can be seen as a symbol of blind and irresponsible obedience, but this, as the Ormerods suggest, is a misreading of the narrative. The shift of focus should be, as Westermann emphasizes, on the action of God in intervening to stay the downward blow[66] and eradicate the fanatically abusive patterns, as rightly highlighted by Knust, Jay, and others. In that intervention, a more complete understanding of the right relationship between God and the founders of Israel is born. Abraham's earlier obedience to God's instructions to ascend Mount Moriah should always be read in the context of a "test" (Gen 22:1) and the promise of Gen 21:12: "through Isaac offspring shall be named for you."

We can acknowledge at this point the contemporary political compass graphs that plot quadrants of religious adherence on a liberal-conservative, egalitarian-authoritarian grid[67]—graphs that certainly add weight to Fromm's analysis of human destructiveness. Oppression or damage of others in the name of any religion is not mandated by the suffering Christ-Priest of Hebrews that our author is drawing her audience back to, and her citations of Abraham and Isaac do not point to this masculinist distortion. But destructive behavior can be mandated by misreadings of ancient texts. Youth suicide rates in, for example, the United States' authoritarian religious bodies are obscene. Although some such deaths may have been triggered by brutal patriarchal authoritarianism, they are not supported by any intelligent reading of Gen 22 and the actions of Abraham towards his son. Suicide rates in patriarchal religious cultures of the United States and presumably elsewhere do not indicate deep immersion in the narratives of

---

64. Ibid., 96.
65. Jay, "Sacrifice as Remedy," cited in Knust, *Unprotected Texts*, 221.
66. Westermann, *Genesis 12–36*, 364–65.
67. For a useful analysis of power imbalance structures, see the Duluth Model power and equality wheels outlined by the Domestic Abuse Intervention Programs, "Wheels."

Genesis or our sermon to the Hebrews. One researcher notes, on evaluating data comparing suicide and religious belief, "There was no correlation between suicide and the importance young people attached to God in their lives, but strong, positive correlations with several different measures of individualism, including young people's sense of freedom of choice and control over their lives."[68] Our author, like any biblical author, does not invite her audience to considerations of rigorous individualism and its expression in patriarchal dominance. A form of individualism that allows people to find their own place in society may be empowering,[69] but individualism that reinforces isolation and disconnects personal experience from enforced standards (particularly in areas of sexuality) is ultimately disempowering and can lead to negative wellbeing, including suicide. The latter has no legitimate imprimatur in a reading of Abraham and Isaac's experiences on Mount Moriah.

This, then, is not the pastoral mandate of the Christ-Priest of Hebrews. In the *mathein pathein* Christologies we have previously noted, the hermeneutical and pastoral imperatives are to identify with and empower those who suffer, not to oppress and disempower. God stays Abraham's knife for Isaac's sake and, indeed, for humanity's sake. Victims of sexual abuse within authoritarian churches and families in particular have experienced the worst distortion of our pastoral imperative as Christ-followers. Fundamentalisms crystallize authoritarianism (both textual and personal): "Religions can be made so rigid and sclerotic by inertia, bureaucracy, politics and corruption that they become self-serving institutions lacking any higher purpose; worse they can become potent ideologies of oppression and abuse."[70] Such religious practices have lost their christological coordinates and stand condemned, not empowered, by the terms of the Hebrews sermon.

Erich Fromm was writing a socio-psychological text, not biblical exegesis. Yet he rightly notes that a purpose of the Mount Moriah passage was to eradicate child sacrifice.[71] There is too much source confusion if we separate Isaac's near-sacrifice from its main narrative purpose: symbolic

---

68. Eckersley, "Culture," S55.

69. This is the opposite of the medieval model, by which the individual was repressed by a God-ordained hierarchy, silently obeying the ruler, who dwelt within "the halo of divinity" and presumably divine appointment. As Walter Ullmann observes, "if the Ruler is a superior and the individual an inferior who is merely a recipient of the law given to him, it is hard to understand how an evolution of the individual from a mere subject to a citizen could come about" (Ullmann, *Individual*, 103). This hierarchical gradation collapsed under its own weight, however, and the individual as citizen was effectively reborn in the Reformation. See ibid., 101–108.

70. Eckersley, "Culture," S55.

71. Fromm, *Anatomy*, 178.

representation of God's compassion and the exclusion of fatal absolute obedience and conformist aggression. Fromm notes the tenderness of the Mount Moriah narrative's depiction of Abraham's love for Isaac, but this should not be a tangential reference. Our author, together with Paul, may well recognize in the Mount Moriah event a precursor of the sacrifice of Christ, but even then the focus is not on the brutality of the Father but on the tender suffering—what I have outlined as the *mathein pathein*—that is absorbed into Godself.

We also do the injustice of source and genre confusions to the Genesis and Hebrews texts if we turn them into a psychoanalysis of the characters Abraham or Isaac. Kierkegaard's suggestion that Abraham should have "plunged the knife into his own breast," while consistent with the moody Dane's temperament, is not an altogether helpful piece of interpretation. He reverses the Genesis author's intentions:

> Yet Abraham believed and did not doubt, he believed the preposterous. If Abraham had doubted—then he would have done something else, something glorious; for how could Abraham do anything but what is great and glorious! He would have marched up Mount Moriah, he would have cleft the firewood, lit the pyre, drawn the knife—he would have cried out to God, "Despise not this sacrifice, it is not the best thing that I possess, that I know well, for what is an old man in comparison with the child of promise; but it is the best I am able to give Thee. Let Isaac never come to know this, that he may console himself with his youth." He would have then plunged the knife into his own breast. He would have been admired in the world, and his name would not have been forgotten; but it is one thing to be admired, and another to be the guiding star which saves the anguished.[72]

Kierkegaard's inference is that the incident left the central characters with the fierce existential faith that "begins precisely where thinking leaves off."[73] Canadian literary scholar Robert Lane, who places Abraham's actions back in the entire Abram saga rather than in the contexts of modern and postmodern psychology, provides helpful additions to Kierkegaard's panegyric on existential crises of faith:

> [T]his story of Abraham is a part of a larger narrative, a narrative which has shown important events that have already occurred in the earlier relationship with God. For example, in an earlier scene God has said to Abraham, "I will maintain my

---

72. Kierkegaard, *Fear and Trembling*, 35.
73. Ibid., 64.

covenant with him [Isaac] as an everlasting covenant for his offspring to come." (Gen 17:19). Thus, Abraham has reasons to believe that God will not kill Isaac—in fact he has the word of God. Instead of a set piece on blind obedience the story is a report of rational action.[74]

The character Abraham does indeed exemplify the trust and ultimately the "by faith" that our author attributes to him. Misreading of this text needs to be consciously avoided[75] if we are to benefit from Abraham's example and find a "by faith" narrative that is still helpful after two world wars and amidst rising sea levels and growing fundamentalist aggressions in the Middle East and around the world.

I am reminded, if another personal tale may be allowed, of my then-preschool-aged daughter's response when I read Aesop's *Fables* to her in my attempt to be a mind-broadening father. I began with one of the many animal-based fables, perhaps "The Salt Merchant and the Donkey." At the end of the brief fable, she was close to tears over the cruel treatment of the animal, and I did not read Aesop to her again![76] At the age of four-and-a-half, she might be excused a degree of source, genre, and even authorial-intent confusion, but as adult readers of biblical texts, we need to exercise more caution. In reading Isaac's Mount Moriah story, we could do worse than to call to mind Speiser's evaluation of the scene: "The short and simple sentence, 'And the two of them walked on together' [Gen 22:8], covers what is perhaps the most poignant and eloquent silence in all literature."[77] To return to our author's worldview, the *mathein pathein* of God in Christ is such that divinity has entered into all human contexts of suffering in order to transform them into a pathway to the Unseen City. Our author's suggestion that the restoration of Isaac to his father, unharmed, was a precursor of the resurrection (Heb 11:19) is in a sense rather tenuous,[78] but if we step outside psychological analyses of the text and simply accept the relief of a

---

74. Lane, *Reading*, 94.

75. Nuechterlein offers a helpful tool for analysis: "A shift from the usual psychologizing of this text is alone of great importance. Modern folks try to put themselves into the psyche of Abraham—'How could a person actually consider sacrificing his son on an altar?—and this is a huge mistake. Because the cultural anthropologies are worlds apart" (Nuechterlein, "Girardian Reflections").

76. Sadly, the story of Jesus and the Gadarene swine had a similar effect, and she does not share my enthusiasm for biblical analysis! Now in her thirties, she has, however, made a career out of animal-care, even reintroducing a human dimension by specializing in training guide dogs for the blind.

77. Speiser, *Genesis*, 165.

78. Ellingworth suggests it was a part of the traditional preaching of the early church (Ellingworth, *Commentary*, 602).

parent at the knowledge of a child's life restored, we can see once more the joy experienced in a "by faith" relationship to God.

Isaac himself receives very little attention from our author, and his somewhat counterproductive blessing of his sons—which Jacob gains by scurrilous plotting with Rebekah, Isaac's wife—attracts our author's notice only insofar as it serves to further the story of Abraham's descendants and their blessing. Esau's reception of this blessing is a mixed bag, to say the least, though our author entwines it briefly in her narrative: Esau's merciless dismissal to live by the sword (Gen 27:40a) is hard to associate with blessing at all, however much the second half of that verse (Gen 27:40b) offers some sort of panacea. Esau will in fact be seen in a negative light in Heb 12:16–17, perhaps a reminder to the reader nearly twenty-one centuries later that even a first-century sermon was not without internal ambiguities and possible inconsistencies.

Jacob too is treated little more than parenthetically; he becomes important to the sermon narrative only in his bestowal (as Israel) of blessing on Joseph's sons, Ephraim and Manasseh (Gen 48:14–22). Strangely, our author distorts the original rendition of Gen 47:31 ("Israel bowed himself on the head of his bed") so it becomes an act not of fatigue but of devotion (Heb 11:21b). Then the baton of our author's narrative passes equally briefly to Joseph, the last of the patriarchs. Joseph's place in the Hebrews narrative is, at first glance, even more tenuous: "by faith," Joseph, at the end of his life, made mention of the exodus and gave instruction about his burial (Heb 11:22). It seems to have little importance, but it is noteworthy that the author is adopting an almost *Dr. Who*-like approach to linear time, for it is implied that Joseph is "pre-membering"[79] an event that, at the time of his death, has yet to occur. This to say that Joseph appears here to be, by faith, prefiguring the Exodus (Gen 50:25). The fulfilment of the promise that Joseph's bones will be buried in the promised land is narrated at Josh 24:32.

---

79. NRSV "made mention." The Greek is *mnēmoneuein*, and Johnson convincingly argues for translation as "remembers." The sense is of "prememory," or certainty of that which is yet to come, which dwells precisely at the heart of the Hebrews author's thought. See Johnson, *Hebrews*, 296.

17

No Pain, No Gain . . . the End Game: Heb 12:1–17

THERE WAS MUCH PAIN in the experience of many of the "by faith" characters of the Hebrews narration, and equally in the experience of the characters in my diversions into post-canonical narratives of faith. But there is another dimension to our author's interpretation of God's hand on the history of God's dealings with the world. The saints are not mere exemplars, as I have so far described them, for they enter another dimension. They remain with us, supporting, inspiring, and encouraging us in our journey of fidelity to the gospel. Our author has first engaged in an inspirational outline of the faith of past heroes, and she now switches to encouragement of those engaged in faith-struggles in the present. The idea of Jesus as pioneer and perfecter of our faith (Heb 12:2) was originally flagged at Heb 2:10. The theme of future hope from chapter 11—hope that is drawing the faithful into its heavenly embrace—is now applied to Jesus, who not only suffered for us but, like us, also needed the inspiration of hope to keep him traveling through the shame and pain of death. In this journey, Jesus has traveled ahead of us as our vanguard and so is able to beckon and encourage us from the standpoint of arrival and completion.

This pastoral insight speaks to *all* human experience of death and dying. Crucifixion was a brutal and, according to Paul (Gal 3:13), theologically significant manner of dying. But no death is completely without sorrow, and few are without suffering (Heb 2:9). The pioneer of our faith has, however, traveled this road already and will guide his people through the valley. Jesus is the enabler, in the sense that he made the human journey into the holy of holies possible; he is also an inspiration (Heb 12:3–4), especially since, as our author pointedly emphasizes, to the waning believers of the Hebrews audience have not yet suffered much at all for their faith.

The author is not depicting Jesus as the sole entity exercising finish-line entelechy[1] or magnetism on the runners alone, but rather as the ultimate model to emulate, surrounded as he is by lesser models who have followed his lead. This author sees an immeasurable crowd (Heb 12:1) egging on those who have not yet completed their endurance event. Those who have competed in endurance events will often attest to the inspiration "ordinary" participants draw from super-athletes as these less spectacular participants struggle on towards a finish line that, while never easy even for a champion, is for such super-athletes a more familiar outcome. To first-time participants or to those who participate despite additional physical or psychological hurdles, the encouragement of the crowd of supporters adds inestimable strength to their unimaginably weary knees. There is, however, no doubt that it is the figure of Jesus positioned at the finish line that most inspires those who endure (Heb 12:2).

That thought takes the Hebrews sermon back to the recurring question of perseverance: endure (Heb 12:5–13). Here, the central theme of the call to suffering—the theme with which I opened these reflections—re-emerges. The theme was aired, *apropos* of Jesus, at Heb 2:9 and Heb 2:18, but it now reaches a crescendo. It will appear again at Heb 13:12. Masterfully, the author turns suffering into an absolute corollary of faith: "if you do not have that discipline . . . then you are illegitimate" (Heb 12:8). The road to which the author beckons is to be "painful rather than pleasant," as Johnson laconically puts it.[2] This is one reason why disciplines such as Lenten observance are important in our comfortable Western faith-world. We are not yet persecuted for our faith, and so we run the risk of spiritual flab. Endure discipline (Heb 12:10–11), for the discipline itself, the author is suggesting, is a work of God.

To a sports medicine doctor in the twenty-first century, Heb 12:12–13 may seem a little tortuous. Generally, in my adopted country's dominant narrative of athleticism, an All Blacks rugby player is rested when he tears a muscle. The Hebrews author's idea of drooping hands and weak knees (Heb 12:12) is more applicable to the emotional and muscular tiredness felt by an All Black late in the second half of a test match, perhaps especially one played in the challenging environment of Ellis Park in Johannesburg, where hostile rugby-breathing crowds and high altitudes turn the match into an extreme exploration of human resilience. Or perhaps our author has in mind a context like the "wall" marathon runners must

---

1. Godfrey, *Babylon's Cap*, 137.
2. Johnson, "Hebrews' Challenge," 23.

pass through both physically and psychologically if they are to achieve their goal of completing a race, let alone winning one.

So Heb 12:13 can cloud the issue for those of us who are beneficiaries of modern medicine, for we know that running on despite a torn muscle or broken bone is not terribly helpful in pursuing an athletic career. The exception is, though, if this is our last tilt at a goal that we may never have a repeat chance at and the pursuit of which can be enhanced by passing through the pain of physical damage. All Blacks captain Richie McCaw exemplified remarkable tenacity in completing the final match to win the 2011 Rugby World Cup despite a broken foot. He did so because it was clear to him that his worth as a psychological support to his team and as a masterful player was greater than the pain he had to play through—his metaphorical drooping knee. Generally though, the author's notion of perseverance at this juncture is not applicable to a long-term career in sports, but rather to a one-off or perhaps final event, "specifically a race."[3] But the idea remains valid: pass on through the wall and endure to the end. The metaphor was a familiar one to the early Christians, for it was used by Paul (1 Cor 9:24–26, Gal 2:22 and 5:7, Phil 5:16) and was a common image in an ancient world that was (for men) as sports-mad as our own. Indeed, citizenship of the *polis* was gained only through demonstration of outstanding physical and moral fortitude: no pain, no gain.[4]

Likewise, the audience of this letter will be transformed into full citizens of the heavenly city only through discipline and perseverance. In modern imagery, Christ takes on another role in the lives of his faithful: he becomes the former player who has now turned to coaching but who has himself done what in the antipodes are referred to as "the hard yards"[5] (Heb 12:5–6, citing Prov 3:11–12). Yet the author's image is slightly different, coming as it does from an era long before that of the highly skilled and well paid

---

3. Johnson, "Hebrews' Challenge," 23.

4. Cited in ibid., 20. One possible origin of the saying is from the Mishnaic *Pirkei Avot*, where Rabbi Ben Hei says, "According to the pain is the gain" (*Pirkei Avot* 5:21). It was made famous by, *inter alia*, Jane Fonda, who was applying it, presumably, to physical extension rather than muscular deterioration or damage. See also McKay, *No Pain, No Gain*. It was a mantra of dogged Australian cricketer Dean Jones, whose match-saving 210 in the famous tied test between Australia and India—played in oppressive conditions at Chennai in 1986 while fighting dehydration, vomiting, and cramps—must equal Richie McCaw's demonstration of tenacity in the 2011 Rugby World Cup.

5. Interestingly, while the origins of this Australian/New Zealand vernacular phrase are disputed, one possible origin is derived from rugby, in which other players may do "hard yards" to make up ground in the opposition's half in order for a player to score. It is, however, also a possible reference to the sun-baked process of clearing farmland yard by yard.

former-player coach. This Jesus-coach has completed the race ahead of the Hebrews, has done the hard yards, and has embraced and passed through the suffering (Heb 5:7). He has even passed through the hard yards of death[6] over and beyond the "mere" hostility of Heb 12:3. From that perspective, he urges and exercises his magnetic entelechy on the Hebrews who, the author caustically notes, have begin to surrender to ennui before having even lost blood for their faith (Heb 12:4). For those of us twenty-first-century Western Christians who are tempted to resile from the demands of our faith because of small doses of mockery in the media, there is a stern warning here, especially when sisters and brothers in less comfortable arenas of faith are being executed for Christ.

The author makes three specific exhortations as she emerges from the athletics metaphor. The Hebrews are to "pursue peace with everyone" (Heb 12:14). This pursuit is enacted symbolically in liturgical rites in which the peace is included. In the early church, shortly after the time the last New Testament books were written, the *Pax* took on so great a significance that only those who had been thoroughly prepared and grounded in the faith were permitted to hear the words. Sometimes such preparation took as much as three years, though more often it was several months. These liturgical words were not a general greeting, but rather a liturgical enactment of the faith-reality "God's peace be with you." The liturgical words are words that say, "In Christ hope has come into human experience: let us journey in that hope."[7] They are not "Good morning," but rather "Christ-peace beyond all understanding be with you." It is this notion that our author is encapsulating as she demands that her audience pursue peace. Words about peace are, in our author's usage as well as in the theoretical liturgical usage, words that take the speaker and hearer deep into a narrative of reconciliation. As we have seen, the South African notion of *ubuntu*, or becoming a person through interaction with another person, provides a useful key to understanding this emphasis. Unresolved enmity, betrayal, and all forms of disconnection impede the pursuit of peace between neighbors in or ostensibly outside[8] of Christ. The presence of injustice, as Martin Luther King Jr. saw so clearly, drowns out the language of peace. Our author might well "amen" Desmond Tutu when Tutu cites his mother's Sotho-Tswana language by saying, *motho*

---

6. The death of Jesus was not referenced at Heb 5:7–10, though the hint of it resonates from Heb 5:3.

7. Cyprian, *Epistle* 6.4, cited in Phillips, *Ritual Kiss*, 23.

8. The author emphasized "peace with everyone," not just with those of the community of faith. Whether there is an "outside Christ" is another matter. "There is no reason to think that this pursuit of peace should include only members of the community" (Johnson, *Hebrews*, 323).

ke motho ka batho, or "a person is a person through other persons."⁹ Forgiveness and reconciliation are inseparable ingredients of peace. Peace cannot be pursued without them.

The author likewise warns against allowing a "root of bitterness" within the community and presumably within the community's individual members. The warning is a loose allusion to Deut 29:17, a passage that has underlain much of the preacher's thought and one that warned the original Hebrews to shun idolatry. In the comfort zones of my Anglican Christianity situated in the global north, I am constantly bombarded with experiences of bitterness ranging on the Richter scale from negligible to structurally damaging. The infamous battles within a faith community that are sparked by the threat to move a piece of liturgical furniture—be it an altar rail, a lectern, or a pew—or even change a hymn book seem to all but irreparably harm the witness and integrity of the community. Unless I am a priest with a particularly bad track record, these appear to be an ever-present shadow-side of ministry in an ennui culture. "Defilement," observes Johnson, "stands over and against the holiness that is to characterize the community."[10] One suspects the conflicts of Anglican Christianity in the global north fade into insignificance when Daesh begin ransacking Christian (and other) sites, when machete- or panga-wielding Hutu sweep through Tutsi and moderate Hutu territories, or even when nature turns "red in tooth and claw" and sweeps a tsunami across the oceans and onto low-lying lands in its path.

It is in this context that the third warning, that of not becoming "like Esau" (Heb 12:14) is issued. Esau, who I mentioned as being worth avoiding (see above on Heb 11:20), is suddenly portrayed as "an immoral and godless person" (Heb 12:16), with potential like the "leaven" of 1 Cor 5:6 or Gal 5:9 (the latter also incorporated into an extended metaphor of athletic pursuit) to pollute the entire faith community. Esau, hungry for a morsel, sells his birthright (Gen 25:32), and by doing so becomes a useful image of the sort of ill-disciplined, dissolute existence the author believes can weaken the community resolve. Esau represents the opposite of the much-ridiculed "pie in the sky," for Esau's sin is the very human and certainly postmodern sin of instant gratification: to snatch at his immediate "pie," or gratification, is the ultimate failure in what psychologists since Daniel Goleman have referred to as emotional intelligence,[11] and is the opposite of the athlete's long-term vision.[12]

---

9. Sparks and Tutu, *Tutu*, 254. Note the alternative *umuntu ngumntu ngabanye abantu* (ibid., 233), as cited earlier in this work.

10. Johnson, *Hebrews*, 324.

11. See Daniel Goleman's influential and popular *Working with Emotional Intelligence*.

12. I am here ignoring disturbing and oft-referred-to findings that many athletes

Paul Ellingworth draws a disturbingly long bow when, based on the Greek words *pornos* and *bebelos*,[13] he associates our author's Esau illustration with homosexuality.[14] Attridge is more circumspect, noting that *bebelos* is a cultic term (see Lev 10:10, Ezek 4:14[15]) and should be read "as a term of moral opprobrium."[16] It would be wiser, in a culture in which we are learning to hear more sympathetically the voices of those previously denied sexual companionship, to see the preacher's plea to avoid Esau-esque behavior as imploring the Hebrews community to avoid all exploitative and destructive gratification (though this debate too can rate very high on the Richter scale of intra-church conflict). While the Genesis texts regarding Esau provide little to base such abhorrence of him upon, it was not unique to our author, and we probably don't need to defend the biblical character at this stage. Nevertheless, our author's bow, and that drawn by others in her era from Esau to sexual gratification, would be long enough without limiting it to a specifically same-sex form of sexual expression.

However, once the church's fixation on damning loving and durable adult relationships of any form is dealt with, we should still hear the stern note our author generates. Confronted by the sexual predation of the sort outlined by the Ormerods or Rob Sinclair in their books, it might be that we should take seriously a call to excommunication of those found guilty of destroying the lives of the vulnerable. The Ormerods note, "Church leaders will begin to respond theologically to abusive ministers when they ask whether their sexually abusive actions do not so violate the nature of ministry as to require their dismissal."[17] The Ormerods do not call for excommunication, but for defrocking of church professionals who have become abusers: "anything less than this minimizes the nature of the offence and hence makes of forgiveness an empty charade."[18] Given the sexual and psychological violence perpetrated by some clergy on their victims, and given the inflexible nature of the synoptic Jesus' own admonitions at Luke 17:2 and Matt 18:6, defrocking is the very least that might be done in response

---

would give up a long-term life-future for the medium-term goal of fame and fortune. Responsible national and international sports bodies now implement exit strategies for those athletes who have reached the zenith or end of their athletic careers.

13. See also Eph 5:5, 1 Tim 1:10, Rev 21:8 and 22:15.

14. Ellingworth, *Commentary*, 665.

15. Acts 10:14 captures a similar sentiment but uses the adjectives *koinos* and *akathartos*.

16. Attridge, *Hebrews*, 368.

17. Ormerod and Ormerod, *When Ministers Sin*, 75.

18. Ibid.

to a track record of serial predation, and it is consistent with the "he was rejected" that our author notes of Esau (Heb 12:17).

To return to Esau's instant gratification, contemporary mores in the global north, particularly sexual mores, rate delayed gratification fairly low on the scale of human priorities. As long ago as the late 1940s, Paul Tillich was noting that a focus on the material and transient led to "existential disappointment,"[19] and that such a mismanaged focus lessened any sense of meaning and value to life.[20] At the very least, this suggests that a loss of life-coordinates disfigures quality of life on the long term. Our author, however, is not interested in the merely psychological benefits of long-term focus (the concept would probably be a puzzle to her), but a series of benefits that reaches beyond present existence. Emmons is closer to our preacher's perspective when he observes, "Each of these three goal types [intimacy, generativity, and spirituality] reflects an active engagement with the world, a sense of connectedness to others, to the future, to the transcendent, and thus contains a glimpse of eternity."[21] It was ever thus: the Hebrews were tempted by immediate concerns, immediate gratifications and satisfactions, and were risking loss of their new birthright-in-Christ.

Perhaps the post-palliative dimension of a birthright-in-Christ is one of the most laughable aspects of Christianity in a postmodern world. Delayed gratification in the emotional IQ, or "EQ" tests was about setting aside the immediate desire for candy on the basis of a hope for more and better candy later. Christianity, like all great religions, has traditionally suggested that the immediate gratification is less meritorious than discipline and the hope of life and gratification after death. In a scientific rationalist world, death is *it*. There's little point in delaying the longing for that glorious gratification until after death because there is no after-death: "there's probably no God, so stop worrying," atheist Richard Dawkins's bus advertisements famously declared in London. This is an alternative shade of meaning to that of the hypothetical athlete who will give up all long-term future in the pursuit of Andy Warhol's "fifteen minutes of fame."[22] But to our author, the existence of the God that Dawkins believes "probably isn't" is cause not for worry, but for joy (Heb 12:1–2). Esau's emotional quotient was low, at least in our author's portrayal of him,[23] and the emotional quotient of predators

---

19. Tillich, *Dynamics*, 13.

20. See Emmons, "Personal Goals," 113.

21. Ibid., 113.

22. The late world motorcycling champion and commentator Barry Sheehan used to refer to "legends in their own lunch hour."

23. "How far these vices attached to Esau is a question which cannot be answered from the OT" (Ellingworth, *Commentary*, 666).

is even lower. The implication of our author is that our EQ is low too when we set our sights only on that which can be seen and measured and not on the unseen and immeasurable beyond. Our author's response to Dawkins might well be "there probably is a God, so persevere with joy." But desertion of that call to delayed gratification and perseverance has, for her, eternally punitive implications (Heb 12:17).

There is, then, a shadow side to our author's optimism: "after apostasy there is no possibility of repentance."[24] I have dealt elsewhere[25] with the question of *apokatastasis*, or the restoration of all living beings, but as was the case with Paul's writings, this is not a concept that our author is going to permit in the cut and thrust of her exhortative sermon. I have observed elsewhere[26] too that for Paul, who is fighting for all that he sees to be the heart and soul of the kerygma entrusted to him by his risen Lord, his theological reflections sometimes drive him to a point where the possibilities of a universal salvation and "restoration of all things"—*apokatastasis*—do creep into his language. Our author is no different, and this may well be another stylistic and rhetorical point at which her common ground with the apostle is apparent. As it happens, this question of apostasy and reconciliation lay at the heart of the bitter debates following the persecutions of the early church.

The Christian response to various waves of persecution had ranged from surrender to the demands of obeisance to the emperor or Roman gods on the one hand and to stubborn martyrdom in preference to compromise on the other. The Edict of Tolerance issued by Galerius in 311 CE brought such martyrdom to an end, at least in the form it had taken under Roman emperors culminating in Diocletian (although as Frend has noted with some irony, "The Church was never to know harmony again"[27]). There were major issues of scale for the Christian leaders to deal with, as well as regional differences in response to degrees of apostasy.[28] But indications are that the community addressed by Hebrews was not experiencing anything like the trials its successors would face under such persecutions as those instigated by Nero or Diocletian or modern-day Daesh. As noted near the opening of these reflections, their malaise was related instead to questions of perseverance in the face of boredom and the fading of the first flushes of post-conversion enthusiasm which means their malaise was extraordinarily

---

24. Ibid., 667.
25. Godfrey, *Babylon's Cap*, 138–39.
26. Godfrey, "Run," 256.
27. Frend, *Martyrdom and Persecution*, 537.
28. See ibid., 536–48.

pertinent to the challenges facing twenty-first-century Christianity in the global north.

In her study of "Staying in and Falling Away" in Paul's writings,[29] Judith Gundry Volf argues that "staying in" is an non-negotiable prerequisite to salvation, thus subscribing to the Reformed Protestant doctrine of perseverance as outlined in, amongst other works, the *Canons of Dort* of 1618–1619. These canons are a hard-edged defense of a doctrine of election based on "God's good pleasure,"[30] and affirming that apostasy is impossible: "Just as God is most wise, unchangeable, all-knowing, and almighty, so the election made by him can neither be suspended nor altered, revoked, or annulled; neither can God's chosen ones be cast off, nor their number reduced."[31] It is not germane to my task here to engage with Gundry Volf's soteriological analysis of the Pauline writings,[32] nor to cross swords with the authors of the *Canons of Dort* in terms of their seventeenth-century Dutch context. It is, however, important to repudiate any sense that our Hebrews author did not take seriously the threat of apostasy, as predicated on the disingenuous basis that if someone commits (or slides into) apostasy, then they were never "saved" in the first place. As is the case with Paul, our author is deadly serious about the possibility and the implications of apostasy, and she uses the caricatured image of Esau—with all the evil connotations that figure had accrued by the time of our author's first-century hermeneutics—to deter her community members from lapsing from their faith. The matter at hand is, to our author, a matter of eternal life and death, not least because her concept of the benefits of an encounter with God gained by perseverance in following Christ is so immeasurably powerful.

---

29. Gundry Volf, *Paul and Perseverance*.

30. Westminster Seminary California, *Canons of Dort*, First Head: Article 10.

31. Ibid., First Head: Article 11.

32. That engagement forms a major theme of my doctoral thesis, "Run That You May Win It."

18

God: That Than Which Nothing Greater Can Be Conceived! Heb 12:18–24

THE GOD OUR PREACHER proclaims is not small enough to be tangible, even as a blazing fire, and darkness and gloom and a tempest, and the sound of a trumpet, and a persistent voice (Heb 12:18)—all the signs of terror accompanying God on Sinai. This sudden argument based on the nature of God is to a degree a new step, but the methodology is not. It is the argument *a minore ad maius*,[1] or, as I prefer, "like this but so much more"[2] that the preacher has used throughout the sermon. The list is a reference to the phenomena that accompanied the giving of the Law on Sinai as recounted at Exod 19:9–25 and Deut 9:19 (with hints of Deut 4:11 and 5:22). So terrifying was the encounter with God at Sinai that the wandering people of God pleaded not to hear God's terrifying voice (Exod 20:19, Deut 5:25). This holiest yet most awe- and terror-inspiring of historical Hebrew moments is, we are told, only a shadow of the relationship to God we have in Christ.

The sacred Sinai epiphany (Heb 12:18–21) is paralleled with descriptions of the new relationship with God made available in Christ (Heb 12:22–24). The experience of Moses, even in the Hebrew Scriptures, is depicted as no trivial event, one for which my word "epiphany" is inadequate.[3] The self-manifestation of God to Moses is a matter of dread, especially as it is retold by Moses (Deut 9:19), and our author attempts to convey this with what scholars call a *"hapax legomenon"*—the description given to a word that is used on only one occasion in the New Testament. That Greek word, *phantazomenon* (Heb 12:21), bears little resemblance to its nearest English equivalent, "phantasm," except insofar as phantasms are likely to instill

---

1. Johnson, *Hebrews*, 326.
2. Godfrey, *Babylon's Cap*, 63.
3. Johnson uses the word "kratophany" to describe a "manifestation of power" or, more familiar to me, a "hierophany" (Johnson, *Hebrews*, 329). See also Bowker, "Kratophany."

fear in the psyches of those who behold them. In the Hebrew Scriptures, *phantazomenon* appears at Sir 34:5 in regards to hallucinations or terrors induced by birth-labor.[4] The *phantazomenon* of the encounter with God on Sinai is re-emphasized by the fear that overcomes Moses following the encounter.[5] In Greek literature, the word is used to describe terrifying manifestations of power; Pseudo-Aristotle's narrative of divine marvels[6] uses the word to describe Athene's self-manifestation to the craftsman Epeius. That moment was of such petrifying clarity that Epeius immediately set about building, at Athene's behest, the Trojan Horse by which the Trojans were defeated. Our author's opinion is likely to have been that the Sinai experience was more terrifying than that of Epeius (and the goddess Athene was no pussycat!). The preacher's implication is that the Hebrews' encounter with the race-winning Jesus, whose benevolent entelechy can inspire saints and believers to complete the race of faith-life, has the potential to be still more devastating. Should the audience continue to display nonchalant indifference to the gospel demands of Jesus, she warns, he may be left to reveal his judgmental side.

The preacher contrasts the new relationship won in Christ-blood with the old humanity in which (as Bruce Springsteen put it) "Adam raised a Cain."[7] A series of items are listed in a cyclic crescendo that underscores the solemnity of the encounter with the "city of the living God" (Heb 12:22) that was previously aired as the future of the faithful at Heb 11:16. The series of "like . . . but more" pairs provides a climax: Mount Zion / Heavenly City; angels / assembly of the firstborn;[8] Abel's blood / Christ's blood. Amidst these pairs, the author inserts "God the judge of all" and "Jesus the mediator of a new covenant." These are not a hierarchical pair in contrast with one another but rather the peak of the crescendo, unparalleled in earthly experience and unparalleled even in the heavenly realms. The solemnity and terror of the encounter with God is underscored by the reintroduction of the divine role of judge (see Heb 10:30, and again at Heb 13:4). This is not a trivial encounter, but this encounter with the judge is balanced with the mediating role of Jesus the Priest, which is here presented in another

---

4. Less dramatically at Wis 6:16.

5. The word is borrowed in fact from a slightly different moment in Moses' life; see Deut 9:19 (Attridge, *Hebrews*, 374).

6. Aristotle, *De Mirabilibus Auscultationibus* 108.

7. The title of the second song on Springsteen's fourth album, *Darkness on the Edge of Town*.

8. An elusive phrase that may have been part of the discourse between our preacher and her faith community, but one that is probably shorthand for those who are the saints, reborn, and absorbed into Christ's status as firstborn.

light with his finish-line entelechy as the unparalleled source of unequalled sacrificial, cleansing blood (Heb 12:24).

Though I am not an economist, it is worth noting at this point that the primary Esau-esque sin of the global north's Christianity—greater even (if sin can be measured) than years of indifference to sexual exploitation and abuse—is the sin of accumulative greed. The implications of greed reach tendrils into many aspects of the mission of the church, including the studied nonchalance most of the global north's Christianity has developed in the face of impending ecological near-Armageddon, as well as the exploding cleavage between not only rich and poor nations, but also between the rich and poor within nations. Pope Francis struck an appropriate note as he, as an example, apologized to the descendants of pre-contact peoples in the Americas by acknowledging the deep sins committed against native peoples in the name of economic greed and capitalist opportunism. "I say this to you with regret: Many grave sins were committed against the native peoples of America in the name of God," the Pope said. "Like Saint John Paul II, I ask that the Church 'kneel before God and implore forgiveness for the past and present sins of her sons and daughters.'"[9] It is Pope Francis too who is creating the most effective ripples with regards to rising ocean levels—another result of the nonchalance that is a by-product of the greed of powerful market forces (not only of the capitalist nations): "A rise in the sea level . . . can create extremely serious situations, if we consider that a quarter of the world's population lives on the coast or nearby, and that the majority of our megacities are situated in coastal areas."[10] While our author may never have envisaged or understood ecological destruction on a global scale (the flood aside), we cannot afford to ignore the missiological dimensions of nonchalance and greed if we, as a Christian community, are to be true to our vocation to "seek to transform unjust structures of society, to challenge violence of every kind and to pursue peace and reconciliation [and to] strive to safeguard the integrity of creation and sustain and renew the life of the earth."[11]

---

9. Pope Francis, speaking during the second World Meeting of Popular Movements in Santa Cruz, Bolivia, on July 9, 2015. See San Martin, "Pope Francis Apologizes."

10. Francis, *Laudato Si*, section 24.

11. We might also take time to hear in yet another context the voices of indigenous peoples: "We, Indigenous Peoples, are the redline. We have drawn that line with our bodies against the privatisation of nature, to dirty fossil fuels and to climate change. We are the defenders of the world's most biologically and culturally diverse regions. We will protect our sacred lands. Our knowledge has much of the solutions to climate change that humanity seeks. It's only when they listen to our message that ecosystems of the world will be renewed" (Tom Goldtooth, Executive Director of the Indigenous Environmental Network, cited in Foran, "Paris Agreement").

The sermon is beginning to wind up. The Hebrews audience is reminded of what they have *not* reached in their faith journey: "you have *not* come to something that can be touched." They are then reminded of the point that they *have* reached in their faith journey: "you have come to Mount Zion." But even this hypothesized arrival at longed-for Zion is in itself a lesser destination than that with which the preacher pairs it: "city of the living God . . . heavenly Jerusalem" (Heb 12:22). This, in our preacher's hands, is greater even than the longed-for Zion of the first Hebrews.

19

A Sermon Winds Up: Heb 12:25—13:25

THE CRESCENDO, WHICH MIGHT be called a crescendo of destination, is followed by a moment of dire warning: "watch that you do not . . ." (Heb 12:25). The Greek word here translated "watch" is another plosive, *Blepete mē!* (echoing Heb 3:12[1]): "Watch/see/ensure that you do not . . ." Watch that you do not ignore the one who is speaking. This has a dual meaning: do not ignore the human voice that is producing this sermon, but even more so, do not ignore the God of the previous sentence, the judge of all, who is speaking in and through the sermon. The God who has instilled such terror in the hearts of the Hebrew people at Sinai is not to be toyed with. God is instead "a consuming fire" (Heb 12:29). "Don't mess with God!" is the author's reasonably unambivalent conclusion to the crescendo, for the God of judgment is even more terrifying than the God of Sinai.

Aslan is not a tame lion! We are reminded again of the opprobrium with which our author would hold a Christianity that merrily chants, "Jesus is my daddy-o," or dances and prances and holds Jesus in all the reverence that an adoring crowd affords a Justin Bieber or a Miley Cyrus. I am reminded of a service I once attended for an Anglican priest who was being commissioned to a new "cure of souls" (the quaint but quite meaningful archaic term for oversight of a parish). At some point in the service, the congregation formed a conga line and danced around and around the church yelling tunelessly not "Jesus is my daddy-o" but "Days of Elijah." The words, on the whole, operate on a slightly more edifying plane than those of "Jesus is my daddy-o,"[2] but that conga line performance

---

1. Johnson, *Hebrews*, 333.

2. "These are the days of your servant, David / Rebuilding a temple of praise" is, however, an interesting play with time: Is David building the eschatological temple? Is David building a symbolic temple wherever praise is offered? The previous lines, "These are the days of Ezekiel / The dry bones becoming as flesh," suggest more of a "Latter Rain" theology, by which the present is the time of eschatological fulfilment and of final pneumatological outpouring. For a helpful analysis of pentecostal spirituality, including "Latter Day Rain," see Land, *Pentecostal Spirituality*, 49–116.

(and several of the versions visible on YouTube) do tend to give more of an impression of entertainment for Christians risking eventual post-ecstasy descent into ennui than of a challenge to be renewed in the service of the God of Sinai and of judgment. This conga line Christianity spoke more of indulgent entertainment—or, at best, the very first flushes of new faith—than of the holy bravery of the Egyptian Coptic martyrs of Libya or the sacred self-sacrifice of Dietrich Bonhoeffer. In this sense, it shared remarkable similarities with some aspects of the Hebrews community addressed by our preacher. Conga line entertainment shows very little cognizance of the God who, in the words of Heb 12:26–29 (claimed tenaciously by Paul Tillich for a volume of his sermons), has shaken, is shaking, and will shake the very foundations of existence.

The irony of the crescendo of Heb 12 is that verse 25 is not directed to outsiders who are in some way condemned to eternal torment for not believing, but rather to nonchalant insiders who are a part of a bored and listless faith community whose early exuberance in the salvation experience has degenerated into entertainment fixation or even lapsed altogether. This aspect of the Hebrews sermon may well speak as much to representatives of languid non-Pentecostal faith communities as stridently as I am suggesting it can speak to entertainment-based faith communities. "See that you do not refuse the one who is speaking." Underlying this challenge and the author's allusions to Moses' terrifying encounter with God at Mount Sinai, underlying the preacher's reminder that the original Hebrews even begged that the divine voice be silenced (Heb 12:19; see also Exod 20:19), and underlying the author's insistence that the Sinai encounter is only a shadow of the forthcoming eschatological encounter with God is a reminder that the original bored Hebrews had all too easily lost their coordinates of faith, their exodus experience of salvation, and descended into the worship of entertainment in the form of a golden calf.

20

Practical Applications: Love . . . Heb 13:1–16

WHILE THERE IS A shift in authorial tone at or around Heb 13:1, there is no need to propose that this is a subsequent addition or interpolation.[1] The litmus test of faith is love. Our author may well have sat at the feet of Paul: "faith, hope and love, these three abide, and the greatest of these is love" (1 Cor 13:13). In Paul's writings, there is a recurrent demand to what I have called elsewhere the "entwinement of mutual love," or mutual, reciprocal love. "Let love be genuine," writes Paul to the Romans (Rom 12:9), for "the one who loves another has fulfilled the law" (Rom 13:8). Our author agrees: let mutual love continue (Heb 13:1). The verb *menetō*, meaning "remain" or "continue," was aired at Heb 12:27. There, it referred to that which remains after the foundations are shaken. It appears that in this aspect of the audience's interrelationships and witness there is a sign of hope (see also Heb 10:24–25). But such love, turned inwards, is no more than Paul's noisy gong or clashing cymbal (1 Cor 13:1). Given the Torah-focus of the preacher's comments, I cannot entirely concur with Robert Gordon's suggestion that "In the context, the strangers are Christian travelers,"[2] though a failure to extend love and hospitality to these strangers too is a fundamental flaw in Christian living, and that was no doubt a part of our author's message. It might be noted, as leaders of the global north's nations turn away refugees from hostile borders in the name of some chimera of "border protection," that even if this verse were obscenely limited only to compassion for fellow Christians, many of those struggling on refugee boats and in camps are dedicated followers of the Christ of the cross.[3]

---

1. For proponents of this argument, and especially for Pauline authorship of the final chapter, see Attridge, *Hebrews*, 2–3n17, 384n5–6.

2. Gordon, *Hebrews*, 186.

3. Again, it should be noted that the stark images of the body of Aylan Kurdi—images needed, it seems, to galvanize attention in a social media world—changed for a while the narrative of political discourse on refugees: "Aylan was neither the first, not will he be the last to drown in the waters of desperation. His brother Galip and

So this is not only about mutually edifying love within the new Hebrews community, though it is about that too. This is fundamentally about the notion of hospitality as love, that radical notion that drove much of the Torah delivered through Moses to the Hebrew people (Lev 19:34, Deut 10:19). In 2014, Episcopalian priest and commentator David R. Henson wrote of the refugee crisis facing the American South. He might equally have been writing about the unimaginable difficulties of the Mediterranean refugee crisis or the ghastly mismanagement by the Abbott and Turnbull Australian governments (and their predecessors of the notional Left and Right). My current country, New Zealand, almost certainly escapes notice in this context not because it is meritorious in attitude to refugees but because it is isolated and tiny, and the problem, so far, is a distant one.[4] Angered by the resistance of Americans to welcoming the children fleeing nations with the highest murder rates in the world, Henson noted caustically:

> If you take the Bible to be God's literal, inerrant truth, then you had better be on the side of these refugee children. God is unequivocally clear in Scripture that we are to welcome the alien and the refugee, not question them, detain them, and deport them.
>
> If you want to be a Christian, you have no choice but to let the little children come. You have no choice but to welcome the stranger, who just happens to be your neighbor.[5]

The author of Hebrews would and does utterly endorse Henson's assessment of Christians' responsibility to the wretched of the earth.[6] The purely sociological and economic benefits of welcoming refugees, while

---

mother Rihan and innumerable others have died, are dying, and still will die, disguised by political speech-makers as parts of a 'swarm,' 'marauders,' 'migrants' and in Australia 'queue jumpers.' But even (outside Australia) the politicians' language is changing. When Aylan died there was a groundswell of sorrow and anger, and the darkness that was most of the international community's response to an immeasurable human tragedy began to be penetrated by tiny sparks of light" (Godfrey, "Aylan Kurdi, Bryndis Bjorgvinsdottir"). Nevertheless, by the time these words were prepared for print, the groundswell was already dying.

4. "According to the UNHCR, Australia is 62nd in the world [in refugee intake]. Most Scandinavian countries host about 20 times the number of refugees per capita that New Zealand does. This makes Sweden 15th in the world and Norway 17th. And that's not to mention the countries like Jordan, Turkey and Pakistan that host millions of refugees from neighbouring countries." New Zealand's intake of less than 1000 refugees per year is, on a per-capita basis, worse than that of Australia (Stephens, "Miserly Refugee Intake"). Japan, which accepts only 0.02 percent of refugees who arrive on its shores, has arguably the worst track record among northern nations globally (BBC News, "Why Does Japan Accept").

5. Henson, "Evil at Our Borders."

6. The phrase is Frantz Fanon's. See Fanon, *Wretched of the Earth*.

clearly open to debate, are not to be ignored. In a now dated US report by The Perryman Group, the researchers observed, "the immediate effect of eliminating the undocumented workforce would include an estimated $1.757 trillion in annual lost spending, $651,511 billion in annual lost output, and 8.1 million job losses."[7] While I again do not claim to be an economist, I see no reason to doubt the economic benefits of hospitality to refugees, as flagged by The Perryman Group and others, as limited to the USA or to 2008. Ecological considerations of waves of immigration in any region must of course be managed skillfully, but a modern-day Hebrews community should, on the basis of our sermon, be at the forefront of calls to compassionate and hospitable action.[8] It is worth entering the query "famous refugees" into a search engine.

Exercising hospitality to strangers should be at the very heart of Christian witness, and there is no basis on which to doubt either on a purely humanistic level, or even a perhaps more mystical level, the benefits of entertaining angels unawares, which is probably an allusion to Gen 18:1–21. Given the harsh judgment that falls on the cities of Sodom and Gomorrah moments later in the Hebrew Scriptures, hospitality should hardly fail to be a matter of concern to those standing in the Hebrews' tradition, though the ability of religious practitioners to turn Gen 19:1–14 into a text specifically about homosexuality is legendary: "the Bible gives considerable evidence that the sin of Sodom was not specifically sexual, but a general disorder of a society organized against God."[9] It is far easier to demonize one segment of society than to take a long and critical look at the whole society's mores.

The preacher's demand to the audience that they "remember those in prison" undoubtedly, as Gordon and others argue, "included those who owed their misfortune to their fidelity to Christ."[10] However, it is worthwhile reflecting on prisoners as amongst the most hated, ostracized, and mistreated in any society. The author's thoughts may have primarily centered on those imprisoned for their faith: "remembering" implies not a momentary casting of a mind backwards but a complete identification with the thoughts and pictures "membered together once more" in the community's mind. Indeed, "remembering involves full solidarity with those imprisoned and those suffering at the hands of others."[11] It would be hard, in the light of the

7. Perryman Group, "Essential Resource," 40.

8. It is notable and encouraging that Anglican Archbishop of Adelaide Jeffrey Driver, together with other church leaders in Australia, has been outspoken in calling for hospitality to refugees.

9. Brueggemann, *Genesis*, 164.

10. Gordon, *Hebrews*, 186; Johnson, *Hebrews*, 340.

11. Craddock, "Hebrews," 163.

teachings and narrated actions of Jesus, to limit our preacher's demand that the audience remember those in prison merely to those who are Christian or those who are imprisoned for their faith.

The author's call to marital fidelity is neither more nor less than a call to integrity, perhaps in response to some whispers, though the actualities are rightly lost to us. Certainly it is the case that the Corinthian Christians addressed by Paul were engaging in some libertine sexual behavior (1 Cor 5:1–2, 7:2). I have spent sufficient words on the tragic coordinate slippage that is represented by predatory sexual behavior within the power-imbalanced structures of the church. Sorry tales of sexual exploitation have likewise been much explored above, and this catalogue of shame could be added to almost daily and seemingly endlessly. In our own society, it is probably sufficient to stress that a church body that is not implementing pastoral guidelines and protocols is a church that is by that fact alone failing in its duty of care. Marital breakdown, not always involving adultery, is a fact of life, and no one is immune. As a human journeyer who has experienced the loneliness of one broken marriage, I do not and cannot take a hard line on marital breakdown and new beginnings, but we should take a harder line on wanton sexual profligacy and sexual exploitation.[12]

Our author links marital integrity with fiscal integrity in a linkage that is perhaps rarer in today's global north than it was in the first century. Attridge notes, "The subjects of the third couplet, sex, and the fourth (Heb 13: 5), money, are commonly linked in Greco-Roman ... Jewish ... and early Christian moralists."[13] A cursory glance at the history of contemporary Christian leaders' behavior as conveyed by media reports leaves no doubt that the previously cited case of fiscal infidelity by "bishop of bling" Peter Tebartz-van Elst is not unique in Christian history, and further details of fiscal inauthenticity need not detain us. Individually and collectively, we are challenged not to remove coordinates of shame and judgment from our relationship with the God to whom we offer "acceptable worship with reverence and awe" (Heb 12:28). Our author stands firmly in the tradition of Amos and Isaiah, whose prophetic words were not and will not be limited to those prophets' centuries. It is worth citing Amos 5:18–27 expansively:

---

12. With reference to the Jesus saying at Mark 10:9, Ched Myers observes, "This teaching recognizes the fact that divorce is a profound spiritual and social tragedy. No one who has undergone the fire of 'one flesh' torn apart (as I myself have) can dispute the weight of Jesus' plea in [Mark] 10:9" (Myers, *Binding*, 266). Those of us who have experienced the tearing of divorce, particularly where children are involved, must acknowledge our complicity in a social and spiritual sin, seek forgiveness, and seek continued integrity in our subsequent lives.

13. Attridge, *Hebrews*, 387. See also Johnson, *Hebrews*, 341.

> Alas for you who desire the day of the LORD!
> Why do you want the day of the LORD?
> It is darkness, not light;
> as if someone fled from a lion,
> and was met by a bear;
> or went into the house and rested a hand against the wall,
> and was bitten by a snake.
> Is not the day of the LORD darkness, not light,
> and gloom with no brightness in it?
>
> I hate, I despise your festivals,
> and I take no delight in your solemn assemblies.
> Even though you offer me your burnt-offerings and grain-offerings,
> I will not accept them;
> and the offerings of well-being of your fatted animals
> I will not look upon.
> Take away from me the noise of your songs;
> I will not listen to the melody of your harps.
> But let justice roll down like waters,
> and righteousness like an ever-flowing stream.
>
> Did you bring to me sacrifices and offerings the forty years in the wilderness, O house of Israel? You shall take up Sakkuth your king, and Kaiwan your star-god, your images that you made for yourselves; therefore I will take you into exile beyond Damascus, says the LORD, whose name is the God of hosts.

I am frequently left to wonder if the marginalization of Western Christianity is not a contemporary leading of the Christian community by God "into exile beyond Damascus," as if we too have taken up our twenty-first-century versions of "Sakkuth your king, and Kaiwan your star-god."

The link our author makes between marital infidelity and economic greed or avarice is not altogether a surprising link, given the way the symbolic narrative of Esau and his instant gratification has been handled in the preceding chapter. Both forms of inauthenticity are far more serious and destructive than the mutual support and edification of Patrick White and Manoly Lascaris' style of monogamous homosexual love-relationship.[14] An accumulation of serial or simultaneous multiple partnerships raises more questions, though I would address them in terms of damage to the psyches of those involved and questions of justice in marital equality rather than in terms of any eternal and unbending truth. Who am I to question the morality of South African President Jacob Zuma (with regards to his

---

14. Godfrey, *Babylon's Cap*, 27.

allegedly traditional polygamy, not to other serious accusations that have been leveled against him) though in reality I have serious doubts about the effectiveness and mutual edification of either polygamous or so-called polyamorous lifestyles?

I do though have deep and abiding concerns about avarice and economic injustice. An Internet meme of the world's ten richest Christian pastors[15] makes for a sorry read, and I believe a pastor such as David Oyedepo or Creflo Dollar has much self-assessment to undertake if he or she is to maintain coordinates that recall and acknowledge the stern nature of the God of Heb 12:29. Of the ten pastors named in the meme's allegations, five minister out of Nigeria, where the chasm between rich and poor is as wide as that between Dives and Lazarus in the parable of Luke 16:19–31. To emphasize these pastors' origins is not to permit the remaining five wealthiest ministers to escape the hook of God's stern glare, for their ministries in the United States, Singapore, and the Philippines are likewise located in areas that not only experience a vast chasm between rich and poor, but also boast excruciatingly inflated resources when seen through the lens of the world's poorest economies.

There are then some clear practical indications of what constitutes "mutual love" in Heb 13:3–5. Paul's indications of the responsibilities of love are similar (Rom 15:7, Gal 6:2). But our author emphasizes that we have a Master who will help us with the complexities of love's demands: "the Lord is my helper" (Heb 13:6, citing Ps 118:6). The reference is once more to the human experiences of Jesus whose entelechy on those who stay faithful operates from the finish line.

Again echoing Paul's struggles, the preacher warns against getting bogged down with "strange teachings" (Heb 13:9); loose allusions are made perhaps to some distractions that are seducing the audience from their course, though we are given no clear indication as to what the problems are. They are similar, perhaps, to the problems Paul addresses at Gal 4:9–11. The protection against distraction is the consistency of Jesus: "the same, yesterday, today and forever" (Heb 13:8). At a slightly lesser level the audience is to remember (again: "knit together in the present the members of") those who earlier and perhaps originally proclaimed the gospel to the new Hebrews (Heb 13:7). This takes the audience's collective and individual minds back to the ecstatic first flushes of faith that have been evoked near the opening of the sermon (Heb 2:4). Members of the more staid denominations like my own could do well to re-member from time to time those enthusiasms of a youthful faith! But there is here a slightly more worrying

---

15. Ikeke, "Meet the Top 10 Richest Pastors."

tone, as "strange new teachings" (Heb 13:9) are beginning to circulate in the believers' milieu.

This is not a warning against minor new developments within the tradition of faith, liturgical changes, architectural or technological changes, even some reasoned alterations in understandings of human relationships, gender and sexuality; it is a warning about matters such as sudden new claims to "Messiahood" or to initiation or representation of the Second Coming. These are closer to the apocalyptic claims of the Joseph Smith, Jim Jones or David Koresh variety: sudden radical shifts in the way God is approached, or replacements of the Messiah Jesus with a new model. One of the reasons that, in some parts of the world, debates over the ordination of women were so vitriolic was that the proponents of change saw this as a non-doctrinal, minor change, while opponents saw it as altering the very essence of the received tradition and faith. This same anxiety is applicable to all redefinitions of marriage and sexuality, not least in my home country where there has been not only legislation passed for same-sex marriage, but recognition of a third gender (recognized in varying degrees by several countries around the world). There remains of course the question of who decides the comparative "weight" and integrity of such matters, though I tend to advise the so-called "Gamaliel principle" (Acts 5:33–40) as a reasonable litmus test.

The preacher solemnly affirms that Jesus Christ is the same, yesterday, today and forever (Heb 13:8). This serves also to reassure the faith community that, though they may experience cataclysms, may experience (as the Thessalonians did) the suffering and death of their leaders and other members, there is an unchanging "solid rock." Jesus, who was executed "outside the city" (Heb 13:12) is released from the spatial demands of the old temple cult (perhaps, like the Galatians, the Hebrews were being seduced to re-observance of Jewish Law) and his followers are no longer limited in space or time. Jesus has pioneered a journey in which we are invited likewise to engage, in which we are challenged to continue to travel. The author is wrapping up her sermon with a focus on the eschatological dimensions of faith that have been an undertone at least since the theme of judgment was highlighted in the previous chapter, but in reality throughout the address.

In *The Rock that is Higher*, Madeleine l'Engle famously muses "We are all strangers in a strange land, longing for home, but not quite knowing what or where home is. We glimpse it sometimes in our dreams, or as we turn a corner, and suddenly there is a strange, sweet familiarity that vanishes almost as soon as it comes."[16] Madeleine L'Engle captures here the ultimate sense of

---

16. L'Engle, *Rock*, 17.

eschatological coordinates that underscores the entire Hebrews sermon. The author of Hebrews never disengages the "city that is to come" (Heb 13:14) from the prism of judgment. In concluding sentences our author weaves together eschatological hope with an analysis of the audience's present concerns and challenges. At this point she addresses the temptations to stray that stem from false teachings regarding food (Heb 13:9), perseverance (Heb 13:15) and even pastoral authority (Heb 13:17). These final applied references to integrity in Christian witness may appear minor or not germane to a twenty-first century readership, but it does not take a great deal of re-interpretation or extrapolation to find considerable validity.

"Strange teachings" within the Christian community are an endless parallel of credible and authentic witness. While in our culture this description may be predicated of cults and reinventions of Christian narrative, I suspect the God of judgment has far less concern at the beliefs and practices of, for example, a well-intended devotee of a cargo cult such as New Zealand's Ratana or Ringatū, previously mentioned, or the more widespread and better known reinterpretations of Christianity represented by Mormonism or the beliefs and practices of Jehovah's Witnesses, no matter their departure from Trinitarian orthodoxy, than with cults of greed and self-interest that are practiced in the name of mainstream Christian religion. The prosperity gospel, often tendentiously based on readings of Malachi, is perhaps a teaching all the more strange because more seductive even than those of Mormons' Joseph Smith or Jehovah's Witnesses' ostensible founder Charles Taze Russell.

The suggestion that "regulations about food" are causing a distraction to the Hebrews community faithful implies that the concerns Paul addresses in his writings were not unique to Corinth (1 Cor 8:1–13), or Rome (Rom 14:1–23), but need not be taken to imply Pauline authorship of Hebrews either in its entirety or in concluding instruction any more than it should be taken as implying Markan (see Mark 7:1–8) or Lukan (see Acts 10:1–23) authorship. Paul's similar teachings about table-fellowship were more about compassion and justice and Christlike inclusion than they were about liturgical and theological nicety.[17]

There is however an equally or more important metaphorical dimension to the warnings about food. Hebrews 13:9 anchors the argument in the wellness of the heart, cardiac wellness, perhaps again showing at least a common pool of influence with Pauline thought.[18] The heart is the place

17. Collins, *First Corinthians*, 416–24.

18. See Rom 2:29, 5:5, 6:17, 10:9, 10:10; 2 Cor 1:22, 3:3, 4:6; Gal 4:6 (by implication); 1 Thess 2:4, 2:13, 3:13. Interestingly, Paul does not use cardiac references in Philippians (Phil 1:7 and 4:7 being somewhat different), that warmest and most

in which our author has seen the law of God inscribed (Heb 8:10c) and it is in this cardiac relationship that the primary ebb and flow[19] of Christian integrity dwells. It is for that reason that our author makes the link between food regulations and the altar of Christ (Heb 13:10). If we can live inside the world of the complex and implied metaphors of rivers and hearts for a moment, our author suggests that tenacious tethering to the altar of Christ insures against drifting away on eddies and flows (or perhaps systole and diastole) of new ideas and references in the estuaries of the human heart. The metaphorical world is stretched, and it is as if our preacher is in a hurry to complete her sermon, crowding and overloading her imagery: this too should not indicate subsequent interpolation but the too human skills of a narrator realizing that she may soon lose the concentration of her audience!

But it may be that the metaphorical world of our author is not completely or haphazardly overstretched. While detailed anatomical knowledge of the systolic and diastolic functions of the heart was not available in the first century CE,[20] the notion of the heart as the center of human vitality reached back at least to Aristotle, and the heart as a source of human response is a frequent image in Hebrew Scriptures. The Book of Revelation utilized the metaphor of the river of life (Rev 22:1) flowing from the throne of God, suggesting that some degree of river metaphor was available to the early Christian church, based in no small part on the imagery of Ezek 47:1-12. The linkage of river imagery, cardiac imagery tied at least to some motion of ebbing and flowing blood as a life-force, and the anchorage of credible Christian witness to the altar on which the High Priest Christ self-sacrifices, suggests that the author is drawing together metaphors of transience and flux in the attempt to call for perseverance and integrity. "Christ is the mooring where all canoes can tie up."

The imagery of Heb 13:9-13 is convoluted.[21] Again: the context that governs the passage is the demand that authentic witness be maintained, though the specifics are lost to a modern audience.[22] The guarantee of au-

---

congenial of all his letters.

19. The verb *parapherestai*, translated "carried away" in NRSV, is an estuarine verb literally referring to a river "washing away" anything in its path (Johnson, *Hebrews*, 346).

20. It emerged in the work of William Harvey (1578-1657) in the seventeenth century. The earlier theological-anatomical work of Michael Servetus (1511-1553) had been suppressed as heretical, and Servetus was executed for his troubles.

21. Perhaps the best exploration of the complexities is the excursus of Attridge, though I find the schematic presentation of Pfitzner wonderfully and refreshingly accessible! See Attridge, *Hebrews*, 394-96; and Pfitzner, *Hebrews*, 195.

22. See Ellingworth, *Commentary*, 707.

thentic witness is eschewal of the strange teachings, including teachings about food and its preparation, presumably in either a Jewish or pagan cultic routine (perhaps there is some connection to Heb 9:10). We can have no real idea where these strange teachings and practices were coming from, but the message of avoidance of aberrant doctrines and observations is clear. The author makes caustic parenthetical allusion to the failure of those who maintain culinary observances to be protected from experiencing some ill, either "spiritual" (as apostasy, perhaps), or physical: illness or physical persecution (Heb 13:9). The acidic first conclusion, that such practices "have not benefited those who observed them" is heavily sarcastic. We have noted already that sarcasm is a part of the preacher's oratorical repertoire.

Having made barbed reference to the outsiders and their strange teachings the author creates an image of the demarcation of boundary marking between outsider and insider. There has not been a great deal of boundary maintenance in this sermon, beyond the warning that the Hebrews risk slippage from "in" to "out." The peculiar reference to "those who officiate in the tent" is a scathing labeling of all and any who observe practices other than those that the preacher recognizes to be orthodox. Once more we face a situation not unlike some faced by Paul, in which practices and behaviors render the practitioners aberrant and "outsider." "Those who officiate in the tent" are any whose practice is misleading or "other." We should not in the twenty-first century accept this reference as permission to ostracize outsiders, but as with many similar Pauline references should recognize that in a context of boundary maintenance and slippage some delineations must be made. At the very least in the twenty-first century surrender of a doctrine of resurrection represents such a loss of faith coordinates that it represents an unacceptable passage from orthodoxy to heterodoxy (a "game-changer," in contemporary parlance, but one in which the game is deadly serious).

The author then elaborates the imagery of "outsideness," but in perhaps unexpected ways. These stem from her use of imagery by which those conducting the aberrant practices or "strange teachings" of Heb 13:9 are depicted as practitioners of inappropriate and life-strangling cults that are the dominant narrative in the world in which the Hebrews audience is dwelling. These practices are as ineffectual as the cults of the Hebrew forebears are considered by the author to be now that they have been rendered obsolete by the Great High Priest, Jesus. The twist in the argument is that the place of "outsideness," or in Camus' terms "outsider-ness," where animals were separated from their cleansing blood, and where their bodies were dumped and burned, is now the outsider place where Christ was slaughtered (Golgotha, Heb 13: 12), and is both the place of rejection from the mortal city and of encounter with and entrance to the eternal city (Heb 13:13). The lasting city of human experience is insignificant, to our author, when compared to the eternal city that is enacted and encountered in the authentic beliefs and practices of the Christian community. In this, incidentally, she may differ to at least one strand of Hebrew scriptural interpretation, for an analysis of the metaphorical language of Genesis can suggest that God built heavens and earth as a home for God to dwell in, deigning to share it with humankind and to dwell there in support of humankind.[23]

For a twenty-first century audience the practices that I have described as "dominant" might well be the practices that stem from the confusion of Americanization and Evangelicalization, confusion of the adoption of a "Jesus is my daddy-o" Christianity that rejoices in personal salvation and material satisfaction but ignores the plight of those left to burn outside the enclosure of evangelical (in its American sense) faith. In a brutal irony this may mean for us today that the outsider is closer to the heart of God than the complacent insider of the Christian community. Lest it be thought that I am attacking only American Evangelicalism, however, it must be emphasized that this criticism applies equally to my own highly aesthetic and cerebral Anglican cathedral tradition when it loses its coordinates of resurrection-proclamation and embracing inclusivity.

At the heart of our author's plea for propriety and integrity is the belief that the city of the populace is not where the City of God is to be found. Jesus was crucified, as the famous Good Friday hymn puts it, "without[24] a city wall." The city that is a human construct is too easily corrupted by self-absorption and material opportunism, imperial self-interest and economic exploitation. That is, if we can explain divine methodology, why the execution of Jesus must take place in the economic and political wilderness of Golgotha. The location of the place where God enters human suffering is an unwanted no-one's land, across the valley and in sight and scent of a city dump. There the outsider is called to the "insideness" of God's plan. "Jesus . . . suffered outside the city gate in order to sanctify the people by his own blood" (Heb 13:12). Members of the Hebrews audience are expected to join Jesus in that outsideness, a counter-culture "bear[ing] the abuse he endured" (Heb 13:13), not in the cozy complacency into which the Hebrews, like the church of today's global north, are slipping.

There, outside the walls of human complacency, the counterculturality of the right-minded Christ-community begins. The primary sign of our continued engagement with the counterculture of Christ will be our engagement with and in worship: "let us continually offer a sacrifice of praise to

---

23. Goldingay, *Israel's Gospel*, 83–90.

24. Semantic shift is no friend to this hymn. It is of course to say, "beyond" the wall.

God, that is the fruit of lips that acknowledge God's name" (Heb 13:15). As he concludes his prophetic *Culture and Imperialism* Edward Said turns to the twelfth-century mystic Hugo of Saint Victor:

> It is therefore, a source of great virtue for the practiced mind to learn, bit by bit, first to change about in visible and transitory things, so that afterwards it may be able to leave them behind altogether. The person who finds his homeland sweet is still a tender beginner; he to whom every soil is as his native one is already strong; but he is perfect to whom the entire world is as a foreign place. The tender soul has fixed his love on one spot in the world; the strong person has extended his love to all places; the perfect man has extinguished his.[25]

There are many echoes of Buddhist self-abnegation in this doctrine, and there is much that the Christian community may learn from Buddhism. But Edward Said is not here advocating one particular faith, but remonstrating about the confusion of faith with imperialisms and nationalisms, striking out to find a faith that "transcend[s] the restraint of imperial or national or provincial limits."[26] Imperial or national or provincial pride may have a place on the sports field, but not in faith, and the confusion of national identity as the locale of God's blessing is a serious loss of faith coordinates.

Elevation beyond the machinations of human political constructs begins, in our author's theology, in worship. To maintain our certainty that "here on earth we have no lasting city"[27] we are called to elevate our perspective with worship, and to worship through Jesus (Heb 13:15). It is no accident that formal liturgical (and perhaps all) prayer should maintain the format "through Jesus Christ our Lord." Right worship is not possible in any other way, and while a mere liturgical formula will not redeem us it may remind us of the cost and path of our access to the ear and heart of the Creator. But even appropriate liturgical observation and focus is rendered meaningless when common human decency and compassion are neglected: "do not neglect to do good and to share what you have, for such sacrifices are pleasing to God" (Heb 13:16).

---

25. Hugo of Saint Victor, cited in Said, *Culture and Imperialism*, 335.
26. Said, *Culture and Imperialism*, 335.
27. See also Ps 119:19.

21

Pray for Us: Heb 13:18–21

THE SERMON IS ADOPTING the language of a conventional first century letter. The first instruction, reverting to the "do not forget" (*mē epilanthanesthe*) construction of Heb 13:2, is about (in the NRSV) "sharing property," or more literally, "sharing the good" or even "fellowshipping goods" (Heb 13:16). The latter notion is not unlike that of Acts 4:32—5:11. Sharing in common, a radical socialism, is a commission that rapidly dropped out of the discourse of the Christian community, but was clearly a part of the countercultural witness of a community that expected the imminent *parousia*. It is doubtful it can ever be regained, for human foibles include jealousy and the proclivities to exploit others, but even in a context of a much delayed or re-interpreted *parousia* the notion of *largesse* within a faith community can be a powerful testimonial to the Christian desire not only to offer praise to God (Heb 13:15) but to demonstrate the integrity of a God-filled life through generosity of spirit. But the author's notion is not limited to material sharing. Her other reference in the sermon to a fellowship of sharing is the fellowship of suffering at Heb 10:33. It was no coincidence that a narrative of shared suffering should have implications for shared possessions and mutually edifying discourse. Perhaps the idea of "sharing the good" most clearly encapsulates the idea here, as shared discourse and shared possessions alike are in theory utilized to proclaim the countercultural hope of the Christ community. Once again though the over-riding motif is that of answerability to an unseen Other, counterculturally offering praise and appropriate lifestyle in such a way as to proclaim a hope beyond the experiences of this life.

The author moves to an instruction to obey leaders appointed "over" the Hebrews in the faith community (Heb 13:17). It is not an unusual theme in the New Testament, surfacing also at 1 Cor 16:15–18 and 1 Pet 5:1–5. A church leader today could only dream of a mandate to exercise such authority! In reality the more authoritarian leaders of some churches have not always (to say the least) exercised the mutually edifying responsibilities of leadership, and this pastor and church leader for one would be loath to attempt to demand such obedience. Nevertheless the notion remains embedded in the structures of ecclesial communities of many forms,[1] and certainly in the Anglican tradition surfaces in the oaths of canonical obedience that clergy swear (despite Matt 5:34–37 and James 5:12) on the occasions of their ordination and induction to pastoral office. To be meaningful in our own culture the mutuality of Heb 13:1 and of the Pauline writings needs re-emphasis; I suspect that we who are church leaders must rightly and continuously "earn our stripes."

The author also requests prayer for herself and for her companions (Heb 13:18). This too binds the audience to proclamatory acts of "mutual love" (Heb 13:1) and is no mere housekeeping announcement. Any person who has had responsibility for a faith community will know that there are some who rise to the challenge of love and prayer and mutual love, and some who will not. Our author longs to return and be with the people amongst whom she has loved preaching and pastoring (so too did Paul, as he notes at, for example, Phil 4:1). In mutual reciprocity our author and preacher prays blessing on the people, her audience, carefully choosing language that echoes the themes of Christ's High Priesthood and blood sacrifice, and the three great Hebrews themes of peace, covenant and God's will,[2] and crescendos in the doxology of eternity (Heb 13:20–21).

The doxology is not though quite the final word. She adds as an afterthought some final personal details. There is an appeal, perhaps unnecessary, to take seriously this (brief, remember!) sermon, or "word of exhortation" (Heb 13:22). I find it deeply moving that the fact that I am "breaking open the word" that our anonymous author wrote two thousand years ago and thousands of kilometers and cultures away, and that you are patiently engaging with that same word, now embedded in a canon of Scripture as "living word," demonstrates that her heartfelt appeal was heard. Perhaps somewhere in a heavenly city she smiles, warmly.

She sends news about Timothy (Heb 13:23), greetings from Italy[3] (Heb 13:24), and a final prayer: "Grace be with all of you" (Heb 13:25). This letter is written by a real person with real geographical location and real friendship and fellowship networks. She did not expect to be heard by you or me. Nevertheless her final words remain as meaningful today as they were when she wrote them: Grace be with all of you.

---

1. See especially Veling, *Margins*.

2. Attridge, *Hebrews*, 405.

3. The phrase is actually less specific and may mean no more than "those from Italy greet you."

22

Final Thoughts

Complex, convoluted, sometimes timeless, sometimes strangely anchored in its time. The book we know as Hebrews is a masterpiece of faith-encouragement. It speaks of the historical person Jesus Christ in terms that soar to the heavens and beyond, yet emphasizes his suffering humanity. It encourages and cajoles. It instructs and exhorts. Its author, like Paul, is desperately trying to bring a wavering audience back into the mainstream of energized faith. In that alone it would be a text for the early twenty-first century. But there are I believe "many and varied ways" (Heb 1:1) in which the Spirit of God can quicken these passionate and erudite words to the hearts of men and women, followers of Jesus Christ, "the same yesterday, today and for ever." If only for that reason I hope this journey has been of some use in a place and time so different yet not so *very* different to the place and time in which our humble, anonymous author wrote so long ago.

Ironically, if I were to summarize our author's work in a few brief words I would turn to one of her contemporaries. The author of first Peter (Peter or otherwise) writes "The end of all things is near; therefore be serious and discipline yourselves for the sake of your prayers. Above all, maintain constant love for one another, for love covers a multitude of sins. Be hospitable to one another without complaining." Our author is a little more prolix. Thank God she was, for the depths of her wisdom are untrammeled. Grace be with her, too.

Grace? I conclude by concurring with that wonderful writer on grace, Philip Yancey: "I would far rather convey grace than explain it."[1] I think our author would also concur.

Grace be with all of you. Amen.

---

1. Yancey, *What's So Amazing*, 16.

Bibliography

A New Zealand Prayer Book / He Karakia Mihinare o Aotearoa. Auckland: Church of the Province of New Zealand, 1989.

Aasgaard, R. "Brotherhood in Plutarch and Paul: Its Role and Character." In *Constructing Early Christian Families: Social Reality and Metaphor*, edited by H. Moxnes, 166–82. London: Routledge, 1997.

———. *My Beloved Brothers and Sisters: Christian Siblingship in Paul*. London: T. & T. Clark, 2004.

Achebe, Chinua. *Home and Exile*. Oxford University Press, 2000.

Adichie, Chimanda Ngozi. *Americanah*. London: Fourth Estate, 2013.

———. *Half of a Yellow Sun*. London: Harper Perennial, 2007.

Allen, John L. *The Global War on Christians: Dispatches from the Front Lines of Anti-Christian Persecution*. 2nd ed. New York: Image, 2016.

Amnesty International. "Nigeria: Abducted Women and Girls Forced to Join Boko Haram Attacks." *Amnesty International*, April 14, 2015. https://www.amnesty.org/en/latest/news/2015/04/nigeria-abducted-women-and-girls-forced-to-join-boko-haram-attacks/.

Anderson, Francis I., and David Noel Freedman. *Hosea: A New Translation with Introduction and Commentary*. Anchor Bible. Garden City, NY: Anchor, 1984.

Archer, Kenneth J. *A Pentecostal Hermeneutic for the Twenty-First Century*. Journal of Pentecostal Theology Supplement Series 28. London: T. & T. Clark, 2004.

Aristotle. *Minor Works*. Edited by W. S. Hett. Loeb Classical Library. Cambridge: Harvard University Press, 1936.

Attridge, H. W. *A Commentary on the Epistle to the Hebrews*. Hermeneia. Philadelphia: Fortress, 1989.

Augustine. *Confessions*. Translated by R. S. Pine-Coffin. Harmondsworth, UK: Penguin, 1961.

———. *Expositions on the Book of Psalms*. In vol. 8 of *The Nicene and Post-Nicene Fathers*, Series 1. Edited by Philip Schaff. 1886–1889. 14 vols. Christian Classics Ethereal Library. http://www.ccel.org/ccel/schaff/npnf108.

Barker, M. *The Great High Priest: The Temple Roots of Christian Liturgy*. London: T. & T. Clark, 2003.

———. "Our Great High Priest: The Church as the New Temple." 29th Annual Father Alexander Schmemann Memorial Lecture delivered at St. Vladimir's Orthodox Theological Seminary, Yonkers, NY, January 29, 2012. http://www.svots.edu/sites/default/files/final_barker_our_great_high_priest.pdf.

Barnes, Michael. *Christian Identity and Religious Pluralism: Religions in Conversation.* Nashville: Abingdon, 1989.

Barth, Karl. *Church Dogmatics.* Translated by G. T. Thompson et al. Edinburgh: T. & T. Clark, 1936–1977.

———. *Community, State, and Church: Three Essays with an Introduction by David Haddorff.* Reprint. Eugene, OR: Wipf & Stock, 2004.

Bayly, Paul. *David Livingstone: The Man, the Missionary and the Myth 1813–1873.* Stroud, UK: Fonthill, 2013.

BBC News. "Rezaul Karim Siddique: Murdered Bangladeshi Professor 'Not an Atheist,' Daughter Says." *BBC News*, April 24, 2016. http://www.bbc.com/news/world-asia-36125115.

———. "Why Does Japan Accept So Few Refugees?" *BBC News*, June 8, 2016. http://www.bbc.com/news/world-asia-36474444.

Beale, G. K. *The Temple and the Church's Mission: A Biblical Theology of the Dwelling Place of God.* New Studies in Biblical Theology. Downers Grove: InterVarsity, 2004.

Becker, Ernest. *The Denial of Death.* New York: Free Press, 1973.

Bellow, Saul. *The Adventures of Augie March.* Reprint. London: Penguin, 2001.

Bennett, Bill. *Gradual Praise: Ngā Waiata Whakapono.* Napier, NZ: printed by author, 2010.

Bethge, Eberhard. *Dietrich Bonhoeffer: A Biography.* Translated by Mosbacher et al. London: Collins, 1970.

Binney, Judith M. *Redemption Songs: A Life of Te Kooti Arikirangi Te Turiki.* Auckland: Auckland University Press, 1995.

Birch, Bruce C. "The First and Second Books of Samuel." *New Interpreter's Bible.* Vol. 2. Nashville: Abingdon, 1998.

Bluck, John. *Wai Karekare—Turbulent Waters: The Anglican Bi-cultural Journey 1814–2014.* Meadowbank, NZ: Anglican Church in Aotearoa, New Zealand and Polynesia, 2012.

Booth, Ken, ed. *For All the Saints: A Resource for the Commemorations of the Calendar.* Full Biography Version. Vol. 1. N.p. Anglican Church in Aotearoa, New Zealand and Polynesia, 1996.

Bos, Stefan J. "African Man Turns to Christ Moments Before Beheading." *BosNewsLife*, April 23, 2015. http://www.bosnewslife.com/35141-african-man-turns-to-christ-moments-before-beheading.

———. "21 Egypt Christians Praised Christ Before Beheadings." *BosNewsLife*, February 17, 2015. http://www.bosnewslife.com/34777-21-christians-praised-christ-before-beheading.

Bowker, John. "Kratophany." In *The Concise Oxford Dictionary of World Religions.* Oxford: Oxford University Press, 1997. http://www.encyclopedia.com/doc/1O101-Kratophany.html.

Boylan, Anthony. "Symbolism and Liturgical Formation." In volume 1 of *Symbolism and the Liturgy*, edited by Kenneth W. Stevenson, 4–16. Bramcote, UK: Grove, 1980.

Bride, Margaret. *I Wait for the Lord, My Soul Waits for Him.* Online resource book for the Martyrs of Papua New Guinea and Melanesia. Sydney: Anglican Board of Missions, 2000.

Brooks, Geraldine. *Nine Parts of Desire.* New York: Anchor, 1995.

Brown, Stuart. *Nearest in Affection: Towards a Christian Understanding of Islam.* Geneva: World Council of Churches, 1994.

Bruce, F. F. *The Epistle to the Hebrews.* 2nd ed. New International Commentary on the New Testament. Grand Rapids: Eerdmans, 1990.

Brueggemann, Walter. *Genesis.* Interpretation. Louisville: John Knox, 1982.

———. "Rethinking Church Models through Scripture." *Theology Today* 48 (1991) 128–38.

Buchanan, George Wesley. *To the Hebrews.* Anchor Bible 36. Garden City, NY: Doubleday, 1971.

Buley, E. C. *Glorious Deeds of Australasians in the Great War.* London: Melrose, 1916.

Bullard, George. "The Life Cycle and Stages of Congregational Development." *Southeastern District Evangelical Free Church of America.* August 2008. http://sed-efca.org/wp-content/uploads/2008/08/stages_of_church_life_bullard.pdf.

Cadwallader, Robyn. *The Anchoress.* Sydney: Fourth Estate, 2015.

Catherwood, Frederick, "Reform or Revolution?" In *Is Revolution Change?*, edited by Brian Griffiths, 31–45. London: InterVarsity, 1972.

Catholic Online. "Pope Francis: Time to Go to Church, You Cannot Be a Christian Without Loving the Church." *Living Faith*, February 4, 2014. http://www.catholic.org/news/hf/faith/story.php?id=54106.

Chabad-Lubavitch Media Center. "Ethics of the Fathers: Chapter Five." *Chabad.org.* Accessed September 6, 2016. http://www.chabad.org/library/article_cdo/aid/2099/jewish/Chapter-Five.htm.

Christiansen, S. J. *The Covenant in Judaism and Paul: A Study of Ritual Boundaries as Identity Markers.* Arbeiten Zur Geschichte Des Antiken Judentums Und Des Urchristen 27. Leiden: Brill, 1995.

Cicero. *On the Ideal Orator [De Oratore].* Translated and edited by James M. May and Jakob Wisse. Oxford University Press, 2001.

Clark, Paul. *'Hau Hau': The Pai Marire Search for Maori Identity.* Auckland: Auckland University Press, 1975.

Cochrane, P. *Simpson and the Donkey: The Making of a Legend.* Burwood, Australia: Melbourne University Press, 1992.

Collins, Adela Yarbro. "Persecution and Vengeance in the Book of Revelation." In *Apocaylpticism in the Mediterranean World and the Near East*, edited by David Hellhorm, 729–49. Tübingen, Germany: Mohr Siebeck, 1983.

Collins, R. F. *First Corinthians.* Sacra Pagina 7. Collegeville, PA: Liturgical, 1999.

Common Praise. Church of England hymnal. Norwich: Canterbury Press, 2000.

Cone, James H. *Black Theology and Black Power.* Maryknoll, NY: Orbis, 1977.

———. *The Cross and the Lynching Tree.* Maryknoll, NY: Orbis, 2011.

———. *The Spirituals and the Blues: An Interpretation.* Reprint. Maryknoll, NY: Orbis, 1992.

Conrad, Joseph. *Youth, Heart of Darkness, and The End of the Matter.* Reprint. London: Everyman's Library, 1974.

Cowley, Joy. *Tārore and Her Book.* Wellington: Bible Society of New Zealand, 2009.

Craddock, F. "Hebrews." *New Interpreter's Bible.* Vol. 12. Nashville: Abingdon, 1998.

Dell, Katherine J. "Covenant and Creation in Relationship." In *Covenant as Context*, edited by A. D. H. Mayes and R. B. Salter, 111–33. Oxford: Oxford University Press, 2003.

DeWitt, J. *Hope after Faith: An Ex-Pastor's Journey from Belief to Atheism*. Boston: De Capo, 2013.
Dillistone, F. W. *Christianity and Symbolism*. 2nd ed. London: SCM, 1985.
———. *The Power of Symbols in Religion and Culture*. New York: Crossroad, 1986.
Dix, Gregory. *The Shape of the Liturgy*. 2nd ed. London: A. & C. Black, 1945.
Domestic Abuse Intervention Programs. "Wheels." *TheDuluthModel.org*. Accessed November 3, 2014. http://www.theduluthmodel.org/training/wheels.html.
Dostoevsky, Fyodor. *The Brothers Karamazov*. Translated by David McDuff. Harmondsworth, UK: Penguin, 1982.
———. *Crime and Punishment*. Translated by David Magarshack. Harmondsworth, UK: Penguin, 1966.
Eckersley, R. M. "Culture, Spirituality, Religion and Health: Looking at the Big Picture." *Supplement to Medical Journal of Australia* 186 (2007) S54–S56. https://www.mja.com.au/journal/2007/186/10/culture-spirituality-religion-and-health-looking-big-picture.
Eliot, T. S. *Collected Poems 1909–1962*. London: Faber & Faber, 1963.
Ellingworth, P. *Commentary on Hebrews*. New International Greek Testament Commentary. Grand Rapids: Eerdmans, 1993.
Emmons, Robert A. "Personal Goals, Life Meaning, and Virtue: Wellsprings of a Positive Life." In *Flourishing: Positive Psychology and the Life Well-lived*, edited by Corey L. M. Keyes and Jonathan Haidt, 105–128. Washington, DC: American Psychological Association, 2003.
Fanon, Frantz. *The Wretched of the Earth*. Harmondsworth, UK: Penguin, 1967.
Farrow, Douglas. *Ascension Theology*. London: T. & T. Clark, 2011.
Fiorenza, Elisabeth Schüssler. *In Memory of Her: A Feminist Theological Reconstruction of Christian Origins*. London: SCM, 1983.
Fleer, D., and D. Bland, eds. *Preaching Hebrews*. Rochester College Lectures on Preaching. Vol. 4. Abilene: Abilene Christian University Press, 2003.
Foran, John. "The Paris Agreement: Paper Heroes Widen the Climate Justice Gap." *System Change, Not Climate Change*, December 17, 2015. http://www.parisclimatejustice.org/article/paris-agreement-paper-heroes-widen-climate-justice-gap.
Fortune, Marie. *Is Nothing Sacred? The Story of a Pastor, the Women He Sexually Abused, and the Congregation He Nearly Destroyed*. San Francisco: Harper, 1990.
Francis (pope). "General Audience of 25 June 2014." Libreria Editrice Vaticana, 2014. http://w2.vatican.va/content/francesco/en/audiences/2014/documents/papa-francesco_20140625_udienza-generale.html.
———. "*Laudato Si*: Papal Encyclical on Care for Our Common Home." *Vatican: The Holy See*, May 24, 2015. http://w2.vatican.va/content/francesco/en/encyclicals/documents/papa-francesco_20150524_enciclica-laudato-si.pdf.
Franzen, Jonathan. *How to Be Alone*. London: Fourth Estate, 2002.
Frend, W. H. C. *Martyrdom and Persecution in the Early Church: A Study of Conflict from the Maccabees to Donatus*. Reprint. Grand Rapids: Baker, 1981.
Fromm, Erich. *The Anatomy of Human Destructiveness*. London: Cape, 1973.
Gale, M. *Dhanum Djorra'wuy Dhawu: A History of Writing in Aboriginal Languages*. Underdale, Australia: Aboriginal Research Institute, 1997.

Gallacher, Lyn. "Meaning Is Such a Pissy Little Concept—Chris Mann." *And So On...* (blog), February 11, 2008. http://lyngallacher.net/2008/02/11/meaning-is-such-a-pissy-little-concept-or-chris-manns-ethics-of-language-or-the-use/.

Geering, Lloyd. *Resurrection: A Symbol of Hope*. London: Hodder & Stoughton, 1971.

Godfrey, Michael J. H. "Aylan Kurdi, Bryndis Bjorgvinsdottir, and a Garden." *Broken Moments* (blog), September 4, 2015. http://broken-moments.blogspot.co.nz/2015/09/aylan-kurdi-bryndis-bjorgvinsdottir-and.html.

———. *Babylon's Cap: Reflections on the Book of Revelation*. Eugene, OR: Wipf & Stock, 2013.

———. "Run That You May Win It." PhD diss., Australian Catholic University, 2011.

Goldingay, John. *Israel's Gospel*. Vol. 1 of *Old Testament Theology*. Downers Grove: InterVarsity, 2003.

Goleman, Daniel. *Working with Emotional Intelligence*. New York: Bantam, 1995.

Gordon, Robert P. *Hebrews*. 2nd ed. Readings: A New Biblical Commentary. Sheffield, UK: Sheffield Phoenix Press, 2008.

Gore, Charles. *Lux Mundi: A Series of Studies of the Incarnation*. London: Murray, 1890.

Green Diary. "5 Cleanest Rivers in the World." *Green Diary: Green Revolution Guide by Dr. Prem*. Accessed July 18, 2014. http://www.greendiary.com/5-cleanest-rivers-world.html.

Greene, Graham. *The Power and the Glory*. Reprint. Harmondsworth, UK: Penguin, 1978.

Gundry Volf, Judith M. *Paul and Perseverance: Staying In and Falling Away*. Louisville: Westminster John Knox, 1990.

Ham, Paul. *Hiroshima Nagasaki*. Sydney: HarperCollins, 2011.

Hamedani, Ali, and Kelvin Brown. "Gay Mullah Flees Iran Over Secret Same-Sex Weddings." *BBC News*, June 8, 2016. http://www.bbc.com/news/world-europe-36276965.

Handcock, Katherine. "Honoring Malala: Mighty Girl Books on Children's Fight for Education." *A Mighty Girl* (blog), March 9, 2014. http://www.amightygirl.com/blog?p=11621.

Handelman, Susan. *The Slayers of Moses: The Emergence of Rabbinic Interpretation in Modern Literary Theory*. Albany: State University of New York Press, 1982.

Harris, John. *One Blood*. 2nd ed. Sutherland, Australia: Albatross, 1994.

Hays, Richard B. *The Faith of Jesus Christ: The Narrative Substructure of Galatians 3:1–4:11*. 2nd ed. Grand Rapids: Eerdmans, 2002.

Head, Lyndsay. "Te Ua Haumene." In the *Dictionary of New Zealand Biography: Te Ara—the Encyclopedia of New Zealand*, October 30, 2012. http://www.TeAra.govt.nz/en/biographies/1t79/te-ua-haumene.

Henderson, J. McLeod. *Ratana: The Origins and the Story of the Movement*. Wellington: Polynesian Society, 1963.

Henson, David R. "The Evil at Our Borders: Migrants, Refugees, and the Spiritual Crisis of Immigration." *Patheos*, July 15, 2014. http://www.patheos.com/blogs/davidhenson/2014/07/the-evil-at-our-borders-migrants-refugees-and-the-spiritual-crisis-of-immigration/.

Hewitt, T. *Hebrews*. Tyndale New Testament Commentaries. Leicester, UK: InterVarsity, 1960.

Hewlett, Cecilia. *Rural Communities in Renaissance Tuscany: Religious Identities and Local Loyalties*. Turnhout, Belgium: Brepols, 2008.

Hodder, Edwin. *Heroes of Britain in Peace and War*. London: Cassell, 1898.

Hodge, Errol. *The Seed of the Church: The Story of the Anglican Martyrs of Papua New Guinea*. Sydney: Australian Board of Missions, 1992.

Holden, Stephen. "Paul Simon Brings Home the Music of Black South Africa." *New York Times*, August 24, 1986. http://www.nytimes.com/1986/08/24/arts/paul-simon-brings-home-the-music-of-black-south-africa.html.

Hollingworth, Peter, and Lyn Comben. *Memories of Bush Ministry and the Challenge of the Future*. Brisbane, Australia: Anglican Diocese of Brisbane, 1999.

Hollows, Fred, and Peter Corris. *Fred Hollows: An Autobiography*. 3rd ed. N.p.: Kerr, 1992.

Horne, Charles F., et al. "The Bereshith or Genesis Rabba." In Medieval Hebrew, translated by W. Wynn Westcott et al., 42. The Sacred Books and Early Literature of the East 4. New York: Parke, Austin, and Lipscomb, 1917. Scanned and redacted by J. B. Hare, December 2002. http://sacred-texts.com/jud/mhl/mhl05.htm.

Hughes, G. *Hebrews and Hermeneutics*. Society for New Testament Studies Monograph Series 36. Cambridge University Press, 1979.

Hustad, Donald. "The Historical Roots of Music in the Pentecostal and Neo-Pentecostal Movements." In *The Hymn: A Journal of Congregational Song*. Vol. 38. January 1987.

Ikeke, Nkem. "Meet the Top 10 Richest Pastors in the World." *NAIJ*, 2015. https://www.naij.com/302279-meet-the-top-10-richest-pastors-in-the-world.html.

Irwin, Alexander C. *Eros toward the World: Paul Tillich and the Theology of the Erotic*. Minneapolis: Fortress, 1991.

Jay, Nancy. "Sacrifice as a Remedy for Having Been Born a Woman." In *Women, Gender, Religion: A Reader*, edited by Elizabeth Castelli, 174–94. New York: Paladin, 2001.

John of the Cross. *John of the Cross: The Living Flame of Love by St. John of the Cross with His Letters, Poems and Writings*. Translated by David Lewis. New York: Cosimo, 2007.

John Paul II (pope). "*Et Unum Sint*: Encyclical on Ecumenism." *Vatican: The Holy See*. May 25, 1995. http://w2.vatican.va/content/john-paul-ii/en/encyclicals/documents/hf_jp-ii_enc_25051995_ut-unum-sint.html.

Johnson, L. T. *The First and Second Letters to Timothy*. Anchor Bible 35A. New York: Doubleday, 2001.

———. "Hebrews' Challenge to Christians." In *Preaching Hebrews*, edited by David Fleer and Dave Bland, 11–28. Abilene: Abilene Christian University, 2003.

———. *Hebrews: A Commentary*. New Testament Library. Louisville: Westminster John Knox, 2006.

Josipovici, Gabriel. *The Book of God: A Response to the Bible*. Reprint. New Haven: Yale University Press, 1990.

Käsemann, E. *The Wandering People of God: An Investigation of the Letter to the Hebrews*. Translated by R. A. Harrisville and I. L. Sandberg. Minneapolis: Augsburg, 1984.

Kazantzakis, Nikos. *Christ Recrucified: A Novel*. Translated by Jonathan Griffin. Oxford: Cassirer, 1954.

Keown, John. *Euthanasia Examined: Ethical, Clinical and Legal Perspectives*. Cambridge: Cambridge University Press, 1995.

Kierkegaard, Søren. *Fear and Trembling and The Sickness unto Death*. Translated by Walter Lowrie. Princeton: Princeton University Press, 1954.

King, Martin Luther, Jr. "Letter from a Birmingham Jail." *University of Pennsylvania African Studies Center*, April 16, 1963. http://www.africa.upenn.edu/Articles_Gen/Letter_Birmingham.html.

Kirby, Peter. "Philo of Alexandria." *Early Jewish Writings*. 2013. http://www.earlyjewishwritings.com/text/philo.

Klostermaier, Klaus. *Hindu and Christian in Vrindaban*. Translated by Antonia Fonseca, London: SCM Press, 1969.

Knust, Jennifer Wright. *Unprotected Texts: The Bible's Surprising Contradictions about Sex and Desire*. New York: HarperOne, 2011.

Koester, C. R. *Hebrews*. Anchor Bible 36. New York: Doubleday, 2001.

Köhler, Ludwig. *Old Testament Theology*. Translated by A. S. Todd. London: Lutterworth, 1957.

Krailsheimer, A. J. *Conversion*. London: SCM, 1980.

Kraus, Hans-Joachim. *Psalms 1–59*. Translated by Hilton C. Oswald. Continental Commentary. Minneapolis: Fortress, 1993.

———. *Psalms 60–150*. Translated by Hilton C. Oswald. Continental Commentary. Minneapolis: Fortress, 1993.

———. *Theology of the Psalms*. Translated by Keith Crimm. Continental Commentary. Minneapolis: Fortress, 1992.

Kreider, Alan. *The Change of Conversion and the Origin of Christendom*. Christian Mission and Modern Culture. Harrisburg: Trinity Press International, 1999. Reprint. Eugene, OR: Wipf & Stock, 2007.

Kreider, Hannah. "Openly Gay Imams Serve as an Affirming Gleam of Hope in Muslim LGBT Community." *GLADD*, June 21, 2013. http://www.glaad.org/blog/openly-gay-imams-serve-affirming-gleam-hope-muslim-lgbt-community.

Küng, Hans. *Why Priests?* Translated by John Cumming. London: Collins Fount, 1972.

Kuruvilla, Carol. "Snake Handler's Son Picks up the Same Rattler That Killed His Dad." *New York Daily News*, February 25, 2014. http://www.nydailynews.com/news/national/snake-handler-son-takes-rattler-killed-dad-article-1.1701252.

Le Roy Ladurie, Emmanuel. *Montaillou*. Translated by Barbara Bray. Harmonsdsworth, UK: Penguin, 1980.

Land, Steven Jack. *Pentecostal Spirituality: A Passion for the Kingdom*. Cleveland: Centre for Pentecostal Theology, 2010.

Lane, Robert. *Reading the Bible: Intention, Text, Interpretation*. Lincoln, NE: Authors Choice, 1994.

Lane, William L. *Hebrews 1–8*. Word Biblical Commentary 47a. Dallas, Word, 1991.

———. *Hebrews 9–13*. Word Biblical Commentary 47b. Dallas, Word, 1991.

Lawrence, D. H. *The Letters of D. H. Lawrence*. Vol. 1. Edited by James T. Boulton. Cambridge University Press, 1979.

Lawson, S. D. "The State in the Theology of Karl Barth." Presented at the American Academy of Religion Southeastern Regional Meeting in Greenville, SC, March 16, 2013. www.academia.edu/2607651/The_State_in_the_Theology_of_Karl_Barth.

Leavis, F. R. *The Great Tradition*. Harmondswoth, UK: Penguin, 1962.

Lebacqz, Karen, and Ronald G. Barton. *Sex in the Parish*. Louisville: John Knox, 1991.

L'Engle, Madeleine. *The Rock That Is Higher*. 2nd ed. Colorado Springs: Crosswicks, 2002.

Leo XIII (pope). "*Apostolicae Curae*: On the Nullity of Anglican Orders." *Vatican: The Holy See*, September 18, 1896. http://www.papalencyclicals.net/Leo13/l13curae.htm.

Lewis, C. S. *The Lion, the Witch and the Wardrobe*. Chronicles of Narnia 1. London: Puffin, 1970.

―――. *Surprised by Joy: The Shape of My Early Life*. Reprint. London: Fount, 1983.

Long, Tom. Foreword to *Preaching Hebrews*, edited by David Fleer and Dave Bland, xi–xiv. Abilene: Abilene Christian University Press, 2003.

Lucas, Julianna. "Meet America's First Gay Black Imam." *The Voice*. December 24, 2013. http://www.voice-online.co.uk/article/meet-america%E2%80%99s-first-gay-black-imam.

Mail Foreign Service. "Hospitalised for Her Own Safety: California 'Cult' Leader Kept under 72-Hour Supervision after Sparking Mass Suicide Fears." *Daily Mail*, September 20, 2010. http://www.dailymail.co.uk/news/article-1313461/California-cult-Reyna-Chicas-mass-suicide-fears.html.

Marsden, George M. *Understanding Fundamentalism and Evangelicalism*. Grand Rapids: Eerdmans, 1991.

Marshall, I. Howard. *1 Peter*. InterVarsity New Testament Commentary. Leicester, UK: InterVarsity, 1991.

McGowan, Andrew B. *Ancient Christian Worship: Early Church Practices in Social, Historical and Theological Perspective*. Grand Rapids: Baker, 2014.

McKay, Jim. *No Pain, No Gain: Sport and Australian Culture*. Sydney: Prentice Hall, 1991.

McKenna, Megan. *Angels Unawares*. 2nd ed. New York: Paulist, 2015.

Meehan, Karen. "Rare Books Offer a Rare Treat." *Monash Magazine*, Autumn 1999. http://www.monash.edu.au/pubs/monmag/issue3-99/item-13.html.

Metzger, Bruce M. *The Canon of the New Testament: Its Origin, Development, and Significance*. Oxford: Clarendon, 1987.

Milgrom, Jacob. *Leviticus*. Continental Commentary. Minneapolis: Augsburg, 2004.

Moltmann, Jürgen. *The Crucified God: The Cross of Christ as the Foundation and Criticism of Christian Theology*. Translated by R. A. Wilson and John Bowden. London: SCM, 1974.

―――. *God in Creation: An Ecological Doctrine of Creation*. Translated by Margaret Kohl. London: SCM, 1985.

Monmonier, Mark. *Rhumb Lines and Map Wars*. Chicago: University of Chicago Press, 2004.

Montefiore, H. W. *The Epistle to the Hebrews*. Black's New Testament Commentaries. London: Black, 1964.

Mooney, Tom. *All the Bishop's Men: Clerical Abuse in an Irish Diocese*. Doughcloyne, Ireland: Collins, 2011.

Moses, John. "Bonhoeffer's Fiction from Tegel Prison, 1943–1945: His Reflections on the Dark Side of Cultural Protestantism in Nazi Germany." In *The Dark Side: : Proceedings of the Seventh Australian and International Religion, Literature and the Arts Conference, 2002*, edited by Christopher Hartney and Andrew McGarrity, 89–98. Sydney: RLA Press, 2004.

Moxon, David. "Tarore and the Spread of the Gospel." *New Zealand Church Missionary Society*, January 16, 2014. http://www.nzcms.org.nz/200-years/wp-content/uploads/Tarore.pdf.

Myers, Ched. *Binding the Strong Man*. Maryknoll, NY: Orbis, 1988.

Nagel, Thomas. *Mind and Cosmos: Why the Materialist Neo-Darwinian Conception of Nature Is Almost Certainly False*. Oxford: Oxford University Press, 2012.

Newman, Keith. *Bible and Treaty: Missionaries among the Māori—A New Perspective*. Rosedale, NY: Penguin, 2010.

———. *Ratana Revisited: An Unfinished Legacy*. Auckland: Reed, 2005.

Ngũgĩ wa Thiong'o. *A Grain of Wheat*. London: Heinemann, 1967.

Nicholls, David. *Deity and Domination: Images of God and the State in the Nineteenth and Twentieth Centuries*. Hulsean Lectures. London: Routlege, 1989.

Nock, A. D. *Conversion: The Old and the New in Religion from Alexander the Great to Augustine of Hippo*. Oxford Paperbacks 30. Oxford: Oxford University Press, 1961.

Nuechterlein, Paul. "Girardian Reflections: Proper 8 (June 26–July 2) — Year A/ Ordinary Time 13." *Girardian Lectionary*. June 26, 2014. http://girardianlectionary.net/year_a/proper_8a.htm.

Obama, Barack. "Transcript: Illinois Senate Candidate Barack Obama." *Washington Post*, July 27, 2004. http://www.washingtonpost.com/wp-dyn/articles/A19751-2004Jul27.html.

O'Brien, Peter T. *Commentary on Philippians*. New International Greek Testament Commentary 11. Grand Rapids: Eerdmans, 1991.

O'Connor, Lydia. "Malala Doesn't Want Us to Forget about Nigeria's Abducted Schoolgirls." *The Huffington Post: World Post*, April 14, 2016. http://www.huffingtonpost.com/entry/malala-letter-nigeria-schoolgirls_us_570e97fbe4b03d8b7b9f3df7.

Ormerod, Neil, and Thea Ormerod. *When Ministers Sin: Sexual Abuse in the Churches*. Alexandria, Australia: Millennium, 1995.

Orwell, George. *A Collection of Essays*. 1st Harvest ed. Reprint. San Diego: Harcourt, 1981.

Owen, Wilfred. *The Collected Poems of Wilfred Owen*. Edited by C. Day Lewis. Reprint. London: Chatto & Windus, 1972.

Pais, Janet. *Suffer the Children: A Theology of Liberation by a Victim of Child Abuse*. Mahwah, NJ: Paulist, 1991.

Paul VI (pope). "*Presbyterorum Ordinis*: Decree on the Ministry and Life of Priests." Vatican: *The Holy See*, December 7, 1965. http://www.vatican.va/archive/hist_councils/ii_vatican_council/documents/vat-ii_decree_19651207_presbyterorum-ordinis_en.html.

Perryman Group. "An Essential Resource: An Analysis of the Economic Impact of Undocumented Workers on Business Activity in the US with Estimated Effects by State and by Industry." *Special Report*, April 2008. https://www.perrymangroup.com/wp-content/uploads/Impact_of_the_Undocumented_Workforce.pdf.

Pfitzner, V. C. *Hebrews*. Abingdon New Testament Commentaries. Nashville: Abingdon, 1997.

Phillips, L. Edward. *The Ritual Kiss in Early Christian Worship*. Joint Liturgical Studies. Bramcote, UK: Grove, 1996.

Platten, Stephen. "The Bible, Symbolism and Liturgy." In vol. 2 of *Symbolism and the Liturgy*, edited by Kenneth W. Stevenson, 4–16. Grove Liturgical Study 26. Bramcote, UK: Grove, 1981.

Powers, Ann. "Nevermore: The Death of an Anti-Hero." In *Cobain*, edited by Holly George-Warren et al., 100–107. San Francisco: Rolling Stone Press and Little, Brown, 1994.

Profitt, Fiona. "How Clean Are Our Waterways?" *NIWA*, July 22, 2010. https://www.niwa.co.nz/publications/wa/water-atmosphere-1-july-2010/how-clean-are-our-rivers.

Race, Alan. *Christians and Religious Pluralism: Patterns in the Christian Theology of Religions*. London: SCM, 1993.

Radcliffe, Timothy. *Why Go to Church? The Drama of the Eucharist*. London: Continuum, 2008.

Rahner, Hugo. *Greek Myths and Christian Mystery*. Translated by Brian Battershaw. London: Burns and Oates, 1963.

Rahner, Karl. "Christianity and the Non-Christian Religions." In *Later Writings*, vol. 5 of *Theological Investigations*, translated by Karl H. Kruger and Boniface Kruger, 115–34. London: Darton, Longman & Todd, 1966.

Rambo, L. R. *Understanding Religious Conversion*. New Haven: Yale University Press, 1993.

Randerson, Richard. *Slipping the Moorings*. Hataitai, New Zealand: Matai House, 2015.

Riss, Richard M. "Singing in the Spirit in the Holiness, Pentecostal, Latter Rain and Charismatic Movements." Presented at the Orlando '95 North American Congress on the Holy Spirit and World Evangelization sponsored by the North American Renewal Service Committee, Orlando, FL, July 28, 1995. http://www.pctii.org/arc/riss.html.

Rosenfeld, J. V. "The Effects of 'Nature and Nurture' on Leadership: What Can We Learn from the Life of General Sir John Monash?" Swinburne Leadership Dialogues presentation delivered at the Swinburne University of Technology Swinburne Leadership Institute, Hawthorn, Australia, May 24, 2013. https://commons.swinburne.edu.au/file/3e56b37c-c35f-486e-8e8f-00c63d811faf/1/leadership_dialgoues-effects_of_nature_and_nurture-notes.pdf.

Ross, Will. "Chibok Girls: Kidnapped Schoolgirl Found in Nigeria." *BBC News*, May 18, 2016. http://www.bbc.com/news/world-africa-36321249.

Ruether, Rosemary Radford. *Sexism and God-talk: Towards a Feminist Theology*. London: SCM, 1983.

Russell, Jeffrey Barton. *The Devil: Perceptions of Evil from Antiquity to Primitive Christianity*. Ithaca: Cornell University Press, 1977.

———. *Satan: The Early Christian Tradition*. Ithaca: Cornell University Press, 1981.

Russell, Jesse, and Ronald Cohn, eds. *Together in Song: Australian Hymn Book II*. Second edition. Sydney: HarperCollins Religious, 2005.

Sacks, Jonathan. *To Heal a Fractured World: The Ethics of Responsibility*. New York: Schocken, 2005.

Said, Edward W. *Culture and Imperialism*. New York: Vintage, 1994.

San Martin, Inés. "Pope Francis Apologizes for Exploitation of Native Peoples, Calls for Economic Justice." *Crux*, July 9, 2015. http://www.cruxnow.com/church/2015/07/09/pope-francis-apologizes-for-exploitation-of-native-peoples-calls-for-economic-justice/.

Sartre, Jean Paul. *Nausea*. Translated by Robert Baldick. Harmondsworth, UK: Penguin, 1970.

Schmemann, Alexander. *Great Lent: Journey to Pascha*. Crestwood, NY: Saint Vladimir's Seminary, 1969.

———. *The World as Sacrament*. 2nd ed. London: Darton, Longman & Todd, 1966.

Schmiechen, Peter. *Saving Power: Theories of Atonement and Forms of the Church.* Grand Rapids: Eerdmans, 2005.
Sentilles, S. *Breaking Up with God: A Love Story.* New York: HarperCollins, 2011.
Serle, G. *John Monash: A Biography.* Melbourne: Melbourne University Press, 1982.
Sewllall, Harry. "Writing from the Periphery: The Case of Ngugi and Conrad." *English in Africa* 30 (2003) 55–69. http://www.jstor.org/stable/40238974.
Sherwood, Harriet. "Church of England Bishop George Bell Abused Young Child." *The Guardian*, October 23, 2015. http://www.theguardian.com/world/2015/oct/22/church-of-england-bishop-george-bell-abused-young-child.
Sinclair, Rob. *All God's Children: A Story of Physical and Sexual Abuse.* New Westminster, Canada: Sinclair International, 1993.
Slack, Kenneth. *George Bell.* London: SCM, 1971.
Southwell, Robert. *The Complete Poems of Robert Southwell.* Westport, CT: Greenwood, 1970.
Sparks, Allister, and Mpho A. Tutu. *Tutu: The Authorised Portrait.* Sydney: Hachette, 2011.
Speiser, E. A. *Genesis.* 3rd ed. Anchor Bible. New York: Doubleday, 1981.
Spong, John Shelby. *Eternal Life: A New Vision.* New York: HarperOne, 2009.
———. *Resurrection: Myth or Reality?* San Francisco: HarperSanFrancisco: 1994.
Stedman, R. C. *Hebrews.* InterVarsity New Testament Commentaries. Leicester, UK: InterVarsity, 1992.
Stephens, Murdoch. "Miserly Refugee Intake Shows New Zealand Has to Do More." *The Dominion Post*, September 5, 2014. http://www.stuff.co.nz/dominion-post/comment/10026355/Miserly-refugee-intake-shows-New-Zealand-has-to-do-more.
Strong, Philip. *The Good Shepherd: Bishop Strong and the New Guinea Martyrs.* Melbourne: Saint Peter's Bookroom, 1983.
Tankard Reist, Melinda, ed. *Big Porn Inc.: Exposing the Harms of the Global Pornography Industry.* North Melbourne, Australia. Spinifex, 2011.
———. *Getting Real! Challenging the Sexualisation of Girls.* North Melbourne, Australia: Spinifex, 2009.
———. *Giving Sorrow Words: Women's Stories of Grief After Abortion.* Sydney: Duffy & Snellgrove, 2000.
Thomas, Dylan. *Collected Poems 1934–1952.* London: Dent & Sons, 1952.
Thomas, M. Lucie. "Enmegahbowh: A Life of Faithful Witness." *Soundings* 24 (2002) 11–12. http://archive.episcopalchurch.org/documents/NAM_Enmegahbowh.pdf.
Thomas, R. S. *Frequencies.* London: Macmillan, 1978.
———. *H'm.* London: Macmillan, 1972.
———. *Later Poems: 1972–1982.* London: Macmillan, 1983.
Tillard, Jean M. R. *What Priesthood Has the Ministry?* Grove Booklet on Ministry and Worship 13. Bramcote, UK: Grove, 1973.
Tillich, Paul. *Dynamics of Faith.* New York: Harper & Row, 1957.
Tippet, Krista. "Luke Timothy Johnson and Bernadette Brooten—Deciphering *The Da Vinci Code*." *On Being*, podcast audio transcript, June 1, 2006. Transcript online at http://www.onbeing.org/program/deciphering-da-vinci-code/transcript/821.
Treece, Patricia. *A Man for Others: Maximilian Kolbe, Saint of Auschwitz, in the Words of Those Who Knew Him.* New York: Harper & Row, 1982.

Trible, Phylis. *Texts of Terror: Literary-Feminist Readings of Biblical Narratives*. Minneapolis: Fortress, 1984.
Tutu, Desmond. "Exhibitions." *Desmond Tutu Peace Foundation*. Accessed September 17, 2016. http://www.tutufoundation-usa.org/exhibitions.html.
Ullmann, Walter. *The Individual and Society in the Middle Ages*. Baltimore: Johns Hopkins, 1966.
van der Loeff, A. Rutgers. *Children on the Oregon Trail*. Translated by Roy Edwards. Harmondsworth, UK: Puffin, 1975.
van Gend, Anne. "Speaking of Mysteries: Atonement in Teenage Fantasy Books." PhD diss., Victoria University of Wellington, 2015.
Veling, Terry. *Living in the Margins: Intentional Communities and the Art of Interpretation*. New York: Crossroad Herder, 1996.
Volf, Miroslav. *Exclusion and Embrace: A Theological Exploration of Identity, Otherness, and Reconciliation*. Nashville: Abingdon, 1996.
Vonnegut, Kurt. *Cat's Cradle*. Penguin Science Fiction. Harmondsworth, UK: Penguin, 1965.
von Campenhausen, Hans. *The Formation of the Christian Bible*. Translated by John Austin Baker. Beiträge zur historischen Theologie 27. London: Black, 1972.
von Rad, Gerhard. *The Theology of Israel's Historical Traditions*. Vol. 1 of *Old Testament Theology*. Translated by D. M. G. Stalker. 2nd ed. London: SCM, 1975.
———. *The Theology of Israel's Prophetic Traditions*. Vol. 2 of *Old Testament Theology*. Translated by D. M. G. Stalker. 2nd ed. London: SCM, 1975.
Wainwright, Geoffrey. *Doxology: The Praise of God in Worship, Doctrine and Life*. London: Epworth, 1980.
Waite, Terry. *Taken on Trust*. London: Hodder & Stoughton, 1993.
Wayne, Melanie Klink. *Whose House We Are*. Bloomington, IN: WestBow, 2014.
Webb, R. A. F. *Brothers in the Sun: A History of the Bush Brotherhood Movement in the Outback of Australia*. Adelaide, Australia: Rigby, 1978.
Welby, Justin. "Archbishop of Canterbury on Religious Freedom." Accessed July 17, 2015. http://www.archbishopofcanterbury.org/articles.php/5591/archbishop-of-canterbury-on-religious-freedom.
Westermann, Claus. *Genesis 1–11*. Translated by John J. Scullion. Continental Commentary. London: SPCK, 1984.
———. *Genesis 12–36*. Translated by John J. Scullion. Continental Commentary. London: SPCK, 1985.
———. *Genesis 37–50*. Translated by John J. Scullion. Continental Commentary. London: SPCK, 1986.
Westminster Seminary California. "*Canons of Dort*: A Brief Introduction on the Nature of History of the Canons of Dort." With an introduction by Daniel R. Hyde. Accessed September 26, 2016. https://www.wscal.edu/about-wsc/welcome-to-wsc/doctrinal-standards/canons-of-dort.
Wildberger, Hans. *Isaiah 1–12*. Translated by Thomas H. Trapp. Continental Commentary. Minneapolis: Fortress, 1991.
———. *Isaiah 13–27*. Translated by Thomas H. Trapp. Continental Commentary. Minneapolis: Fortress, 1997.
———. *Isaiah 28–39*. Translated by Thomas H. Trapp. Continental Commentary. Minneapolis: Fortress, 2002.

Williams, Rowan. *Eucharistic Sacrifice—The Roots of a Metaphor*. Bramcote, UK: Grove, 1982.

———. "Your Calling Is You." *Trinity Wall Street*, March 16, 2005. https://www.trinitywallstreet.org/blogs/news/rowan-williams-your-calling-you.

Wiser, Carl, et al. "Homeless by Paul Simon." Songfacts. Accessed September 6, 2016. http://www.songfacts.com/detail.php?id=2377.

Wolff, Hans Walter. *Hosea: A Commentary on the Book of the Prophet Hosea*. Translated by Gary Stansell. Hermeneia. Philadelphia: Fortress, 1974.

Wordsworth, William. *Selected Poetry*. Edited by Mark van Doren. New York: Random House, 1950.

Wynne, Catherine. "The Teenager Who Saved a Man with an SS Tattoo." *BBC News Magazine*, October 29, 2013. http://www.bbc.com/news/magazine-24653643.

Yancey, Philip. *What's So Amazing about Grace?* Australian ed. Sydney: Strand, 2000.

Yousafzai, Malala, and Christina Lamb. *I Am Malala: The Girl Who Stood up for Education and Was Shot by the Taliban*. London: Weidenfeld & Nicholson, 2013.

Subject Index

"27 Club", 162

Aaron, 133, 142
Abel, 17, 159, 171, 182, 185, 208
Abraham, 10, 41, 123–26, 133, 159, 169, 172–73, 182, 187–97
Abrahamic faiths/religions, 54–55, 57, 74
Absolution, 26, 29–31, 47, 150
Acton, Lord (John Emerich Edward Dalberg-Acton), 38–39, 58, 88
Adam, 81, 172, 208
All Blacks, 50, 199–200
Alzheimer's.
  See Dementia.
Anamnesis, 49–50, 149
ANC (African National Congress), 164–65
Angels, angelology, 12, 16, 20–24, 28, 29, 32, 41–42, 54, 63, 110, 123, 208, 215
Angst, 6, 162–64, 171
ANZAC, 49, 108, 185
Apokatastasis, 205
Apollos, 9, 14
Apostasy, 44, 64, 119, 147, 205
Arianism, 100
Armistice Day, 49
Ash Wednesday, (see also Lent), xii
Atonement, 41, 43–53, 54, 191–92
  Day of, 110
Auschwitz, 161–62, 167, 170
Australia
  Refugee policies of, 12

Beatles, The, 108

Barak, 182
Barnabas, 2
Berlin Conference, 96
Bhopal, 106
Blood, sacrificial, 46, 51–52
Boko Haram, 45, 148
Bolshevik Revolution, 96
Book of Common Prayer, 142
Border protection, 213

Cain, 17, 171, 208
Canons of Dort, 206
Cessasionism, 7
Charismatic movement(s), 32
Christology, 1, 9, 19, 46, 100
Chronicles of Narnia, 17
Church, institutional, x
  abuse in, x, 78, 90, 192, 194, 203, 209, 216
  as community, 63
  as prophetic community, 186, 192, 215n8
  architecture in, 148, 150
  burnout in, 6–7
  cerebralism in, 8
  corruption in/of, 39, 88, 168, 181–82
  ecstasy in, 168
  formalism in, 5
  life cycles of, 7, 9
  rationalism in, 23
  rites of, 6, 43, 48–49, 62, 201
  ministry selection procedures, 88, 134–35, 226
  sensationalism/emotionalism in, 5–7

Communion / fellowship with God, 12, 55, 89
Communion, Holy
    See Eucharist.
Confession, (general and auricular) 26, 46–47, 154, 177
Conscience, 90–91, 152
Constantine, conversion of, 6, 84n53, 119
Conversion, 6, 40, 86–87, 115, 205
Corinthian Christians, 4, 31, 84n53, 216
Counterculture, Christian community as, 12, 223, 225
Covenant, (generic) 9, 17, 34, 50–51, 67, 136, 139, 226
    Abrahamic, 140n11, 195–96
    broken, 50–51, 140, 141n11
    Davidic, 50
    eschatological, 50
    Mosaic, 50
    New, 137–44, 208
    Noahic, 50, 190n55
Creeds, 40, 93

Daesh, 25n11, 103, 104n16, 124, 148, 202, 205
David, (King), 22, 50, 70 109, 134, 182, 190, 211n2
Death, and dying, 35–37, 41, 67, 105, 108–9, 119, 147, 148, 190, 198, 204
Death, of Jesus (see also atonement), 4, 9, 41, 43, 50, 54, 88–89, 101, 102, 104, 106, 108, 133–34, 168, 201
Dementia, 33, 122n28
Devil.
    See Satan.
Dies Irae
    See Judgment.
Diocletian persecution, 205
Dispensationalism, 7
Divinization, 40
Doxa (glory – of God), 17, 21, 34, 48

Ecstasy, religious, 6, 25–27, 121, 168, 212

EFM (Education for Ministry Program), 14
Endurance, 26, 28, 122, 123, 146, 147–48, 152, 153–57, 199–200
Ennui, 6, 69–70, 80, 119, 171, 188–90, 201, 202, 212
Enoch, 159, 171, 182, 185–86
Entelechy, 69, 199, 201, 208–9, 218
Episcopate, 138n4, 142, 180
Esau, 197, 202–6, 209, 217
Eucharist, 17, 18, 20–21, 33, 46–49, 87, 142, 148, 149–50
Evil, 37, 39, 46, 58, 65–66, 87, 90n13, 94, 95, 107, 108, 119, 167, 191–92, 214n5
Exclusivism, 58–59, 66
Exodus (*Haggadah*), 48, 50, 51, 168, 176, 197, 212
Expiation,
    See blood.

Fundamentalism, 5, 39, 46n12, 66, 75n22, 116, 127, 129, 194, 196

Galatian Christians, 219
Gallipoli.
    See Anzac Day.
Genocide, 30, 148
Gideon, 182
Global warming / climate change, 190, 209n11
Gutenberg Bible, 15

Hagar, 188n53
Haggadah.
    See Exodus.
Hamartiology.
    See sin.
Hannah, 188
Hau Hau (Pai Marire), 177–78
Hebrew Scriptures, ix, 10–11, 15, 22, 28, 60, 67, 85, 125, 187, 207–8, 215, 221
Hiroshima, 74–76, 160–62
Holocaust (*Shoa*), 11, 17, 48, 68, 119, 162
Hospitality, 12, 52n31, 213–15

Imago Dei, 144
Immaculate Conception, 109n28
Inclusivism, 58–59
Independence Day, 49
Individualism, 45–46, 52–53, 56, 63–64, 108, 194
Interfaith dialogue, 55–59
Ishmael, 188n53
ISIL/ISIS.
   See Daesh.
Isaac, 123–26, 169, 182, 191–97
Islam, 21, 44–45, 54–55, 57, 58,74, 103n10, 124, 135, 189n53

Jacob, 169, 182, 197
Jehovah's Witnesses, 143, 220
Jews.
   See Judaism.
Jepthah, 182
Jochebed, 182
Jonestown, 79
Joshua, 122, 169
Jubilee, 69
Judaism, x, 11, 17, 21–22, 32, 48, 50–52, 56–57, 68, 74, 111, 121, 138–40, 143–44, 163, 189n53
Judgment, doctrine of, 61, 65–66, 71, 79, 116, 118, 119, 147–48, 153–54, 184, 208, 211–12, 216, 220

Ku Klux Klan, 76, 168
Kuruman, 181

Ladysmith Black Mambazo, 166
Latter Day Saints, 135
Lent (see also Ash Wednesday), 199
Lincoln, Abraham, 4
Liturgy, liturgical renewal, 2, 3, 14, 16, 26, 33, 48, 50, 52, 61, 63–64, 77, 81, 140, 145, 148–51, 156–57, 201, 224
Liturgical music, 162
Lord (Christological title), 1, 20–21, 25, 28–29, 31–32, 40, 111, 133–34, 154, 189,
Lynching, lynch mobs, 105–6, 119, 125, 148

Male privilege, 14n31
Mango Groove, 164–67
Manus Island.
   See Papua New Guinea.
Marks of Mission, 68–69, 82
Martyrs, martyrdom, 25, 71–76, 103–4, 130–32
   of Aotearoa, 71–74
   of Egypt (Coptic) in Libya, 130, 212
   of Japan, 74–76
   of Papua New Guinea, 130–32
   of Melanesia in the Solomons, 132
Mau Mau (Kenya Land and Freedom Army), 96, 178
Mauvaise foi, 36
Melchizedek, 109–112, 114, 117, 127–29, 133–36, 159
Mercator projection, 103
Mohammed, 54, 143
Montaillou, 77–79, 87
Mormons, 220
Moses, 10, 54–56, 58, 64–65, 122, 128, 169, 176–77, 182, 207–8, 212, 214
Muslim.
   See Islam.

Nagasaki, 74–76, 87
Nauru, 12
Nero, 205
New Zealand Prayer Book / He Karakia Mihinare o Aotearoa, 1, 20, 21, 27, 47n13, 178
Ngāpuhi, (iwi), 73n15
Ngāti Hauaā, (iwi), 72–73
Noah, 50n21, 159, 171–72, 182, 186, 190n55

Papua, 12, 45, 130–32, 148
Passover.
   See Exodus.
Paul,
   and perseverance, 27, 206
   and signs, 4, 5
   and Scripture, 10
   and Timothy, 27

general references, xii, 4, 9, 30, 33, 35, 48, 56, 58, 68, 90–91, 175, 198, 222, 226, 227
Christology of, 9, 102
Paul (*continued*),
chronology of, 9
contrast with Hebrews, 43, 147, 220
hamartiology of, 45, 77
influence of, 1, 46, 61n25, 115, 123, 188, 195, 200, 213n1, 218
life of, 1
oratory/rhetoric of, 3, 115, 122n27
soteriology of, 30, 52, 108, 184
world-view of, 17, 83
writings of, *in toto*, 1, 3, 9, 11, 16, 60, 71, 120, 121, 123, 205, 213, 218
Romans, 10, 107, 213, 213
Corinthians, 10, 31, 216
Galatians, 10, 145
Philippians, 1, 99
Thessalonians, 27
Peace / *Pax*, liturgical, 201
Pearl Harbor, 49n18
Perichoresis, 63
Perryman Group, 215
Perseverance, 17–18, 24, 26–31, 57, 60, 67, 113–22, 205
Petrine writings, 3, 47–48, 141
Pharisees, 135
Pluralism, 58–59
Power,
divine, 5, 30, 31, 65, 110, 125, 207–8
human, 33, 38–39, 41, 43, 58, 78–79, 84, 88, 90, 96, 149, 193n67
of evil, 37, 39, 52–53, 142, 171
of ritual and symbol, 49, 51n29, 148, 176
Powerlessness,
of God, 43, 89, 90
of humans, 90, 97, 167
Presbyterate/*presbyteros*, 47, 134, 135, 138n4, 142, 148
Priesthood,
Aaronic, 134, 137
hiereus, 47, 137, 139, 141–42
of believers, 47–48

of Christ, 41–42, 46, 51n29, 54–66, 99, 100–112, 115, 136, 137–44, 147, 154, 170, 193, 194, 221, 222
Levitical, 134
sacramental/liturgical, 46–48, 110, 117, 139
Priscilla, 13
Psychological/emotional abuse (in the church), x, 29, 30, 33, 78, 90–91, 105, 124, 192

Qur'an, 54–55

Rachel, 188
Rahab, 182
Rastafari, 135
Ratana, 135, 220
Rebekah, 187, 197
Redemption (see also Absolution), 29, 31, 41, 45, 65n39, 108–9, 179
Refugees, 12, 161, 213–15
Reign of God / eschatological reign, 63, 71, 79–83, 87, 157
Religious Studies, 58
Resurrection, xi, 4, 50, 85, 104–6, 116, 129–30, 132, 147, 153, 182, 190–91, 196, 222, 223
Revelation, Book of, 3, 9, 190
Ringatū, 220
Rohingya Muslims, 161

Sabbath, 69–70
Sacrifice,
blood/cultic (Jewish and other), 17, 43, 65, 100, 138, 154, 185, 217
child, 193–94
in faith martyrdom, 104, 170, 212
in war, 65, 108–9
of Christ (see also Atonement), 149–50, 195, 221, 226
of Isaac, 123–24, 191, 192, 193
of praise, 223
re-sacrifice, 48, 149
Sadducees, 135
Sampson, 182
Sanctification, 40, 223
Sarah, 187–90
Satan, 35, 37–41

Scandal of particularity, 16n32
Sclerosis of the heart, 61, 66, 68, 69, 81, 83, 107, 161
Sexual abuse/exploitation (in the church), x–xi, 29, 30, 77, 78–79, 83, 84, 88, 90, 124, 186, 192, 194, 203, 209, 216
Signs and wonders, 4–7, 18, 27, 32–33, 115, 138, 152
Sin, xii, 21, 30, 38, 43–47, 52–53, 64, 67, 77–79, 83, 93, 99, 100, 107–8, 126, 147, 152, 154, 202, 209, 215, 216,
Snake-handling, 5, 8
Sodom and Gomorrah, 215
Sorry Day, 49
Staines family, 103–4
Suffering,
　human, 1, 9, 10, 17, 25, 27, 29, 30, 33–34, 45, 54, 76, 92, 96, 102, 104, 107, 126, 130n13, 136, 147, 148, 153, 157, 194, 196, 198, 199, 215, 219, 223, 225
　of Christ (specifically), 39, 41, 42, 50, 54, 88, 99, 101–2, 106, 113, 167–68, 193, 198, 201, 223, 227
　of God, 34, 39, 106, 195
Suicide, 193–94
Suneideisis.
　See Conscience.
Supercessionism, 48
Symbolism, symbolic narrative/action, 14n31, 40, 41, 51n24, 58, 95, 96, 109–111, 124, 129, 139, 142, 146, 148–51, 183, 185–86, 193, 194, 201, 211n2, 217,
Syncretism, 59, 74–75, 83–84
Syria (modern), 14n31, 161

Taliban, 124
Temple,
　Christ as, 46, 48, 49, 52
　destruction of, 9, 51–52, 138, 139
　rites and significance of, 8, 50–53, 81–82, 145–47, 219
　first Jerusalem, 110–11, 137, 139, 150
　second Jerusalem, 8–9, 111, 138–39, 148
Temptation(s), 3, 40, 75, 93–94, 139, 188, 220
Temptation narratives, 40, 92–93, 107
Terrorism, 105, 114n4, 124
Thessalonian Christians, 27, 219
Third Reich, 57
Time, concepts of, 23, 48, 49, 51, 61, 81, 103, 111, 123, 128, 138, 149, 155, 157, 159–60, 170–71, 181, 197, 219, 227
Torah, 81, 127–28, 135, 154, 213–14, 219
Toronto Blessing, 5–6
Trinity (bomb), 160
Trinity, doctrine of, 18, 25, 26, 60, 63, 85, 102, 143, 179, 220
Nicholas, Tsar II, 96–97

Ubuntu / abuntu, 52, 201–2

Vineyard Fellowship, 4–5
Virgin Birth, 109

Waco, TX, 79
Waitangi Day, 49
Westboro Baptists, 143, 153
Westminster Confession, 40–41
West Papua
　See Papua.
Word of God, 85
Wycliffe Translation, 15

Xenophobia, 45, 66

Yezidis, Syrian, 161
Yom Kippur, 44

Name Index

Aasgaard, R., 43n1
Abbott, Tony, 186, 214
Abdullah, Daayiee, 180n26
Achebe, Chinua, 97-98
Acton, Lord John, 38-39, 58
Adichie, Chimamanda Ngozi, 98-99, 164, 165, 178-17
Aesop, 196
Al-Asad, Khalad, 104n16
Allen, John L., 103n14
Anderson, Francis L., 50n23
Anselm, 45, 125
Archer, Kenneth J., 5
Aristotle, 34, 221
Attridge, Harold, xi, 21n6, 115n9, 129, 140, 203, 208n5, 213n1, 216n13, 221n21, 226n2
Augustine, 87, 149n13, 155

Bakker, Jim, 38, 40, 88
Barker, Margaret, 51, 81, 100n1, 110-12, 139, 142, 148, 150
Barnes, Michael, 59
Barth, Karl, 17n35, 30-31, 76, 85, 117
Barton, Ronald, 90n13
Bayly, Paul, 118n19, 166n21
Beale, G. K., 82n49
Becker, Ernest, 35
Bell, George, 186
Bethge, Eberhard, 39nn38, 39, 72n11, 88n10
Bellow, Saul, 38
Bennett, Bill, 156
Bernstein, Leonard, 162
Bieber, Justin, 211

Binney, Judith, 135n31
Birch, Bruce c., 50n22
Björgvinsdóttir, Bryndís, 161
Black, Richard, 25
Bluck, John, 178n22
Bode, John Ernest, 1n1
Bolt, Usain, 40
Bonhoeffer, Dietrich, 37, 38-39, 71-72, 88, 130
Bonhoeffer, Klaus, 39n39, 212
Booth, Ken, 176n16
Botha, P. W., 167
Bourjedi, Manteghi, 124
Bowker, John, 207n3
Boylan, Anthony, 148
Breivik, Anders Behring, 65n39
Britten, Benjamin, 89
Brooks, Geraldine, 103n8
Brother Lawrence, 69n5
Brown, Dan, xi n3
Brown, Stuart, 55n1
Bruce, F.F., 10n20, 10n21, 51n29, 56n10, 148-49
Brueggemann, Walter, 139, 187, 215n9
Buchanan, George Wesley, 183
Buley, E. C., 186n44
Bullard, George, 7
Bush, George W., 108, 114
Byron, Lord George, 35-36

Cadwallader, Robyn, 161
Catherwood, Frederick, 167
Chicas, Reyna Marisol, 79-80
Christiansen, S. J., 138n4
Churchill, Winston, 3-4

NAME INDEX

Cicero, 19n1
Clapton, Eric, 165n15
Clark, Paul, 178n20
Cobain, Kurt, 162, 164
Coleridge, Samuel Taylor, 122n28
Collins, Adela Yarbro, 65
Collins, R. F., 220n17
Cone, James, 106, 119n23, 124–25, 147, 164, 165n17, 167n22, 168
Conrad, Joseph, 94–96
Coots, Jamie, 5
Copernicus, 163
Cowley, Joy, 74n17
Craddock, Fred, xi, 114, 116, 117, 129n11, 182n33, 215n11
Crosby, Fanny J., 141
Cullmann, Oscar, 134
Cyrus, Miley, 211

Danby, Francis, 172
Dawkins, Richard, 118n20, 204–5
Dawson, Katrina, 124
de Klerk, F. W., 167
Dell, Katherine, 50n21
DeWitt, J., 119n20
Dillistone, F. W., 14n31
Dix, Gregory, 52n32, 141
Dix, William Chatterton, 17
Dobson, Dobby, 25
Dollar, Creflo, 218
Dostoevsky, Fyodor, 87, 185n43
Driver, Jeffrey, 215n8

Eckersley, R. M., 194n68
Eliot, T. S., 53, 94n8, 161–62
Ellingworth, Paul, xi, 8–9, 11, 13n28, 56n12, 67n1, 92n2, 106n22, 114n2, 115, 141n12, 145, 196n78, 203, 221n22
Emerson, Ralph Waldo, 184
Emmons, Robert A., 204
Enmegahbowh, John Johnson, 179–80
Epictetus, 122n27

Fonda, Jane, 101, 200n4
Fanon, Frantz, 98, 214n6
Farrow, Douglas, 141n13
Fayman, Werner, 161

Fiorenza, Elisabeth Schüssler, 14, 182n31
Foley, James Wright, 103, 104
Foran, John, 209n11
Fortune, Marie, 90n13
Franzen, Jonathan, 97, 103
Freedman, David N., 50n229
Frend, W. H. C., 205n27
Fromm, Erich, 191–92, 193, 194–95
Fugelsang, John, 138n5

Gale, M., 173n10
Gajowniczek, Franciszek, 170, 185
Gallacher, Lyn, 159–60, 163
Geering, Lloyd, 71, 191
Godfrey, Michael J. H., 3n6, 9, 41n45, 59n20, 65n39, 69n4, 73n15, 86, 119n21. 199n1, 205, 207n2, 217n14
Goldingay, John, 17, 51n24, 57, 109n29, 128n6 n7, 188n52, 190n55, 223n23
Goldtooth, Tom, 209n11
Goleman, Daniel, 202
Gooder, Paula, 99n28
Gordon, Robert, xi, 12n26, 12n27, 30n20, 116, 213, 215
Górecki, Henryk Mikolaj, 161
Greene, Graham, 170
Gregory of Nyssa, 63
Gundry Volf, Judith, 206

Haines, David, 103n11
Hall, Ronald, 180
Ham, Paul, 74–76, 87n9,
Handelman, Susan, 127–28
Harding, James, xiii, 118n18
Harris, Barbara, 180
Harris, John, 174
Harvey, Wil;liam, 221n20
Haumene, Te Ua, 177–78, 179
Haussleiter, Johannes, 184n39
Hays, Richard, 184n39
Heber, Reginald, 95n11
Hemming, Alan, 103n11
Henderson, J. McLeod, 135n30
Henderson, Richard Alexander, 185
Hendricks, Muhsin, 180n26

NAME INDEX

Henry, Graham, 2
Henson, David R., 214
Hewlett, Cecilia, x, 79
Hick, John, 58
Hippolytus, 63n30
Hitler, Adolf, 167
Hodder, Edwin, 180n28
Holden, Stephen, 166n18
Hollows, Fred, 183–84
Hooker, Richard, 135n28
Hugo of St Victor, 224
Hustad, Donald, 157

Ibrahim, Meriam Yehya, 44–45

Jamieson, Penny, 180
Jay, Nancy, 193
John Chrysostom, 63
John of the Cross, 153
Johnson, Claire, 167
Johnson, Luke Timothy, xi, 2, 8, 18n36,
    32, 51n28, 55n7, 56, 57n13, 64,
    70n6, 92n1, 93n7, 100n3, 101–2,
    104–5, 106, 113n1, 114–115n6,
    120n25, 120n26, 137, 143–44,
    146, 182n32, 183, 185, 186,
    197n79, 199, 200n3, 201n8, 202,
    207n1, 211n1, 216n13
Johnson, Tori, 124n4
Jones, Dean, 200n4
Jones, Jim, 219

Käsemann, Ernst, 68n2
Katzantzakis, Nikos, 119
Keble, John, 53n38
Keke, Harold, 132
Kendrick, Graham, 107
Kennedy, John F., 22n7, 162
Kierkegaard, Søren, 124, 195
King, Martin Luther Jr., 37, 47, 49, 201
Kipling, Rudyard, 97n23
Klostermaier, Klaus, 66n40
Knitter, Paul, 58
Knust, Jennifer Wright, 193
Koester, Helmut, xi
Köhler, Ludwig, 69n4
Kolbe, Maximillian, 130, 170, 171, 172,
    185

Koresh, David, 219
Krailsheimer, A.J., 6n10
Kreider, Alan, 6
Kraus, Hans-Joachim, 61, 109
Küng, Hans, 135n28, 137n3
Kurdi, Aylan, 161, 213n3
Kurdi, Galip, 213n3
Kurdi, Rihan, 214n3

Ladurie, Emmanuel Le Roy, x, 77–78
La Haye, Timothy, 70
Land, Steven Jack, 211n2
Lane, Robert, 195–96
Lane, William L., 116
Langdon, Stephen, 15–16
Lawrence, D. H., 65
Lebacqz, Karen, 90n13
Leavis, F. R., 95
l'Engle, Madeleine, 219–20
Lennon, John, 58
Lewis, C. S., 17, 86, 154
Lincoln, Abraham, 4
Lindsay, Hal, 70
Livingstone, David, 118n19, 166n21,
    181
Long, Tom, xi, 24, 120

Man Haron Monis.
    See Bourjedi, Manteghi.
Mandela, Nelson, 37, 167
Mann, Chris, 159–60, 163, 164
Manson, Charles, 65n39
Marsden, George M., 46n12
Marshall, I. Howard, 47n17
Marx, Karl, 71
Mascalis, Manoly, 217
McCaw, Richie, 200
McKay, Jim, 200n4
McLachlan, Sarah, 166n19
McDowell, Josh, 126
McGowan, Andrew, 2, 14n31, 85
McKenna, Megan, 24n9, 32
Merkel, Angela, 161
Metzger, Bruce M., 85n2
Milgrom, Jacob, 43–45, 50n20, 52
Moffat, Mary, 180–81
Moffat, Robert, 180–81
Mohamed-Zahed, Ludovic, 180n26

NAME INDEX

Moltmann, Jürgen, 34n25, 47–48, 63, 69, 88–89, 102, 147, 162
Monash, General Sir John, 92–93
Monmonier, Mark, 103n9
Mooney, Tom, 90n13
Morris, Gerald, xiii, 29n17, 49n18
Moses, John, 38–39
Moxon, David, 74n17
Mueller, Kayla, 25n11, 59n19
Muldoon, Sir Robert, 22
Myers, Ched, 25, 45–46, 58n16, 216n12

Nagai, Takashi, 75n21
Nagel, Thomas, 117–18
Napoleon, 167
Newman, Keith, 135n30, 174, 175n14
Ngākuku, 72–73
Ngũgĩ wa Thiong'o, 97–98, 178
Nicholls, David, 181n29
Nixon, Richard, 22n7
Nock, A. D, 6n10
Noel, Caroline Maria, 29n18
Nuechterlein, Paul, 196n75

Obama, Barrack, 165n16
O'Brien, Peter T., 30n19
Ormerod, Neil and Thea, 78, 90–91, 192–93, 203
Orwell, George, 97n23
Otto, Rudolf, 159
Owen, Wilfred, 108
Oyedepo, David, 218

Pais, Janet, 90n13
Panikkar-Alemany, Raimon, 58
Penderecki, Krzysztof, 160, 162, 164
Pfitzner, Vic, xi, 221n21
Phillips, L. Edwards, 201n7
Philo, 56, 186
Picasso, Pablo, 160, 162, 164
Platten, Stephen, 151n19
Plato, 34, 137
Pope Benedict XII, 77
Pope John Paul II, 104, 209
Pope Francis, 62, 88, 209
Pope Leo Xiii, 135n29
Pope Paul VI, 62, 135n29
Profitt, Fiona, 80

Quayle, Dan, 3

Race, Alan, 58n15
Radcliffe, Timothy, 153n2
Rahner, Hugo, 63n32
Rahner, Karl, 110, 184
Rambo, L. R., 6, 86
Randerson, Richard, 76–77
Ratana, Tahupōtiki Wiremu, 135
Reagan, Ronald, 22n7
Revere, Paul, 186
Ripahau, 73
Romero, Oscar, 170–71, 172
Rosenfield, J. V., 93n6
Ruether, Rosemary Radford, 14
Runcie, Robert, 186
Russell, Charles Taze, 220
Russell, Jeffrey Barton, 37, 39
Rutter, Peter, 90n13

Sacks, Jonathan, 52n31, 82, 91, 144n19, 171, 172
Said, Edward W., 95, 96, 224
Sartre, Jean-Paul, 36, 37–38
Selwyn, George, 175–76
Shabalala, Joseph, 166
Schmemann, Alexander, 35–36, 83
Schmiechen, Peter, 40n43
Schwartz, Stephen, 162
Seneca, 122n7
Sentilles, S., 119n20
Serle, G., 93
Servetus, Michael, 221n20
Sewall, Harry, 97n22
Shelley, Percy Bysshe, 159
Siddique, Rezaul Karim, 103, 104, 110
Simon, Paul, 162, 165–66
Simpson, John Kirkpatrick, 185
Sinclair, Rob, 90n13, 192, 203
Slack, Kenneth, 186n46
Smith, Joseph, 143, 219, 220
Smith, Linda Tuhiwai, 98
Sotloff, Steven, 103n11
Southwell, Robert, 89
Soyinka, Wole, 98
Speiser, E. A., 196
Spong, John Selby, 71–72, 129–30, 132, 191

NAME INDEX

Springsteen, Bruce, 208
Stalin, Josef, 94
Stimson, Henry, 75–76
Strong, Philip, 130–31

Tankard Reist, Melinda, 186
Taplin, George, 174
Taplin, Martha, 174n11
Tārore, 71–74, 174
Tebartz-van Elst, Franz-Peter, 88, 216
Teilhard de Chardin, Pierre, 117–18
Tennyson, Lord Alfred, x
Te Kooti, Arikirangi Te Turuki, 135
Te Rauparaha, Tamihana (Katu), 73–74
Thatcher, Margaret, 22n7, 52, 186
Thomas, Dylan, 35
Thomas, Keisha, 76
Thomas, M. Lucie, 180n25
Thomas, R. S., 164
Tillard, Jen M. R., 134n27, 144
Tillich, Paul, 167, 204, 212
Tim-Oi, Li, 180
Tippet, Krista, xi n3
Trible, Phylis, 177
Trump, Donald, 75n22, 186
Turnbull, Malcolm, 214
Tutu, Desmond Mpilo, xi, 37, 52n33, 167, 173, 201

Uita, 73–74
Ullmann, Walter, 194n69
Unaipon, David, 173, 180
Unaipon, James, 173, 174, 180

van der Loeff, A. Rutgers, 191n56

van Gend, Anne, xii, 50
Veling, Terry, 226
Volf, Miroslav, 12n25, 65
Von Harnack, Adolf, 13–14
Vonnegut, Kurt, 53
Von Campenhausen, Hans, 85n2
Von Rad, Gerhard, 51n30

Wainwright, Geoffrey, 149n13
Waite, Terry, 62–63, 72, 153
Waitoa, Rota, 175–76, 177, 179, 180
Warhol, Andy, 204
Wayne, Melanie, 157n8
Welby, Justin, 181
Wesley, Charles, 40–41, 156
Wesley, John, 40–41
Westermann, Claus, 109, 123, 171n4, 187, 193
White, Bronwyn Angela, 26n16, 29
White, Patrick, 217
Whitlam, Gough, 22n7
Wildberger, Hans, 51n26
Wilde, Oscar, 44
Williams, Rowan, 149, 173n8
Wimber, John, 4–5, 33
Winkett, Lucy, 157
Wolff, Hans Walter, 51n25
Wordsworth, William, 35

Yancey, Philip, 227
Yekya, Qassem Abdullah, 104n16
Yousafzai, Malala, 45n7

Zuma, Jacob, 168, 217–18

Ancient Document Index

Hebrew Bible

Genesis

1–2	16	22:1–19	191
1	69, 82, 127–28	22:8	196
1:3	188	22:10	193
1:31	15	22:15–18	123
2:4	15	25:21	188
2:15	81	25:32	202
2:18	63	27:40a	197
4	171	27:40b	197
4:4b	17	29:31	188
5:22	171	47:31	197
6:5	186	48:14–22	197
6:9	186	50:25	197
6:18	50		
9:9–17	50		
9:21	186		
11:31–13:18	190		

Exodus

12	188
14:17–24	109
14:18	109
15:5	123
15:7–11	140n11
15:9	140n11
15:17	140n11
17:19	196
18	188
18:1–21	215
18:12	188
18:14	188
19:1–4	215
21:12	193
22	193

2:1–2	182
6:20	182n31
7:3	32n24
13:8	48–49
15:21	176
19:9–25	207
20:19	207, 212
24:7	50
30:12–13	43
31:17	56
33:18	56
33:20	17

Leviticus

4:1–5:13	46
4:2	43
4:3–12	44
4:13–21	44
4:13	46
9:8	100
10:10	203
16:16	100
16:20–28	146
16:20–22	44
19:34	214

Numbers

12:7	56
14:29	64
18:21–32	133
24:6	114n5
35:33–34	51

Deuteronomy

1:27	64
4:11	207
4:32	128n7
4:34	32n24
5:22	207
5:25	207
6:22	32n24
9:19	207, 208n5
9:27	64
9:29	65
10:19	214
17:2	154
26:8	32n24
29	50
29:1–30:20	50
29:3	32n24
29:17	202
30:19	50
32:43	22
32:51	55

Joshua

6:14–26	169
24:32	197

Judges

20–21	177
20:35–36	177

1 Samuel

1:2	188

2 Samuel

6:5	190
6:20–23	190
7	50
7:14	21, 22
18	176

Job

7:17	30

1 Chronicles

17:11–14	50

2 Chronicles

6:16	50

Nehemiah

9:10	32n24

Esther

10:9	33n24

Psalms

2:4	21
2:7	22
8	29–29, 31
8:4–6	28
8:4	30
22:22	34
32:1	43
45:2	22
85:2	43
95	61–62, 69–70
95:6	61
95:7–8	64
95:7b-8a	70
95:7–11	60
95:11	62
97:7	22
104:4	22
102:25–27	26
106:20	48
110	111, 133
110.1	26, 111, 133
110:4	109, 111, 133, 135
118:6	218
119:19	224n27
135:9	33n24
144:3	30

Proverbs

3:11–12	200
18:24b	v

Isaiah

2:4	58
24:5	51, 52
40:26	123
43:10	144
54:1	186
65:21–25	69
66:1	139
67:7	43

Jeremiah

17:12	100n1
18	30, 31
18:5	117
18:6	117
22:5	125
24:4–13	51
31:31–34	151
31:31	140
31:32b	141
34:18	141n11

Ezekiel

4:14	203
9:4	150
47:1–12	221

Hosea

1:3	50
2:18	50
8:1	50

Joel

3:3	4

Amos

5:18–27	216–17

Apocrypha

Wisdom

2:24	37
4:10	186
6:16	208n4

Sirach

2:10b, 12–14	113
34:5	208
44:16	186

New Testament

Matthew

4:8–10	107
5:34–37	125, 226
6:7	151
12:38–39	4
16:1–4	4
18:6	203
19:21	87
20:15	117
26:11	88

Mark

7:1–8	220
8:11–12	4
10:9	216n12
16:8	170
16:17	5

Luke

4:5–8	
6:39	54
9:62	118
11:16	4
11:24–26	167
11:29–32	4
12:4	43
13	113
13:13b	113
16:19–21	218
17:2	203
17:10b	15

John

1:1–18	20, 99, 158
1:1	22, 138, 188
1:19–12:50	4
5:17	70
6	4
8:29	100n3
15:13–14	43
15:13	108
19:4	100n3
19:30	141
19:35	9, 138

Acts

2:19	4
2:22	4
2:43	4
2:44–45	120
2:44	154
4:16	4
4:32–5:11	225
4:32–35	11
4:32	120
5:33–40	219
8:1	15
10:1–23	220
10:14	203n15
11:26	60, 111n41
20:9	113
28:1–6	5

Romans

1:18–32	52
1:23	48
1:24	107
2:13–16	90
2:29	220n18
3:23	46, 52
4:13–25	123, 188
5:5	220n18
5:7	108
5:8b	33
6:17	220n18
7:14–20	52
9:18	61n25
9:20	117
9:21	30
10:9	220n18
10:10	220n18
10:15	68
11:17	48
11:25	61n25
12	121
12:8	121
12:9	11
13:1–7	182
13:13–14	18, 87
14:1–23	220
15:7	218
15:19	4
16:20	26

1 Corinthians

1:1	60
1:22	4
1:23	35
1:26	58, 60
1:30	33
3:2	115
5:1–2	216
5:6	202
6:19	56
7:2	216
8:1–13	220
9:24–26	122n27, 200
10:7	115
11:23–26	49
12:3	57
12:12	56
13	11, 121, 158
13:1	213
13:11	27
13:12	17
13:13	213
14:1	11
14:34	85
16:15–18	225

2 Corinthians

1:3	2
1:5	33
1:22	220n18
3:3	220n18
4:6	220n18
5:2	100n3
12:11	115
12:12	4

Galatians

1:6	27
2:2	122n27
2:22	200
3:6–29	123
3:13	33, 198
3:28	85
4:9–11	
5:5	122n27
5:7	200
5:9	202
6:2	121, 218

Ephesians

1:19	33
2:19	56n11
5:2	33
5:5	203n13

Philippians

2:1–5	99n28
2:5–11	22
2:6–11	9
2:6–7	99
2:12	30n19
2:16	122n27
4:1	226
4:19	25
5:16	200

Colossians

1:15–20	48

1 Thessalonians

1:1	10
1:7	220n18
3:1–3a	27
4:7	220n18
4:11–12	120
5:10	33

1 Timothy

1:10	203n13
2:1–4	182
3:16	116
4:13	2

2 Timothy

2:5	122n27
3:16	10, 28, 60
4:7	122n27

Titus

2:14	33

Hebrews

1:1–14	16
1:1–4	9, 13, 21, 54
1:1–3	106
1:1–2	129
1:1	21, 24, 48, 227
1:2	16, 24, 104, 134
1:2a	10
1:3	16, 17, 20, 22, 41n46, 54, 56, 67, 138, 151
1:4	20, 28, 42
1:4b	134
1:5–13	23, 54
1:5	22
1:6	22
1:10	26
1:13	26
1:14	23, 24, 28, 145
2	29
2:1–4	8, 13, 18
2:1	4, 9, 10, 13, 16, 17, 23, 24, 32, 55, 70
2:1a	23
2:1b	24
2:2	13, 32
2:3–4	13, 115
2:3	20, 24, 32, 145
2:4	4, 27, 32, 152, 218
2:5–9	31
2:5	13, 28
2:6–8	10
2:6b	31
2:7a	29
2:8	7, 31
2:9	22, 31, 198, 199
2:9a	32
2:9b	32
2:9c	34
2:9d	34
2:10	16, 34, 133, 198
2:11–13	34
2:14–15	17
2:14	13, 35, 37, 146
2:15	37, 67

2:16	41, 123, 122	4:13b	90
2:17-18	43-53, 92, 126	4:14-16	92-99, 112
2:17	41, 43, 52, 107, 151	4:14	92, 151
2:18	122, 199	4:15	40, 107, 153
3	122	4:16	13
3:1-19	54-66, 67	5:1-10	100-112
3:1	1, 10, 13, 43, 86, 151	5:1-7	100
3:2	8, 55, 56	5:1-5	8
3:3	56	5:1-4	101
3:4	56	5:1	8, 100
3:5	56	5:2	100, 106
3:6	10, 13, 56, 59, 60, 183	5:3	100, 201n6
3:6b	56	5:5	151
3:7-19	67	5:7-10	122, 201n6
3:7	13, 60	5:7-8	101
3:7b-8	70	5:7	17, 101, 102, 106, 109, 201
3:11	62, 101	5:8-10	115
3:12-19	66	5:8-9	106
3:12-18	101	5:8	101
3:12	10, 16, 17, 62, 63-64, 211	5:9	107, 109, 134
3:13	64	5:10	151
3:14	60, 64, 71, 92, 152	5:11-6:8	113-22
3:15	35, 64	5:11-14	3, 27, 115, 120
3:16-19	64	5:11	13, 114
3:16-18	13	5:12-14	115
3:17	10	5:12	113, 114
4:1-11	17, 67-84	5:14	120
4:1-2	15	5:18	128
4:1	67, 68	6:1-3	10
4:2	16, 20, 67, 68, 188	6:1	114, 116-18, 134
4:3	80	6:3	117
4:4-5	70	6:4-8	118, 154
4:6	16, 67, 70, 90	6:4-6	17, 24
4:7	13, 70	6:5	13
4:8-9	13	6:6	16, 154
4:8	122	6:7-8	13
4:11	16, 80, 121	6:9-12	122, 145
4:12-14	13	6:9	13, 115, 118, 152n20
4:12-13	13, 79, 85-91	6:10	120
4:12	85, 87	6:11	121, 183
4:13	13	6:12	10, 120
4:13a	90	6:13-20	123-26
		6:13-18	13
		6:14	147
		6:15	123, 133

Hebrews (continued)

6:16	13
6:17	133
6:18	125
6:19	34, 125
6:20	16, 115, 151
7	127–29, 133–36
7:1–3	13
7:4–10	13
7:3	136
7:4	133
7:5	8
7:7	133
7:10	133
7:11–12	13
7:11	133, 134, 151
7:12	13, 134
7:14–15	134
7:14	133
7:15	135
7:16	133
7:17	133
7:18–19	136
7:18	134
7:19	133, 151
7:22	133, 136
7:23–25	136
7:26–28	151
7:28	136, 151
8	137–44
8:1	137
8:3	8
8:4–6	145–46
8:4	138
8:6–7	139
8:6	139
8:7	139
8:8	140
8:10	141
8:10c	221
8:11	141
9:1–10:18	145–52
9:3	34
9:5	13
9:6	8
9:10	222
9:13	142, 146
9:15	147
9:16–22	13
9:16	147
9:20	147
9:22	147
9:23	17
9:24–25	148
9:24	17, 147
9:25	147
9:27	147
9:28	147
10:1	151
10:2	13
10:7	31
10:9	120
10:12	149
10:13	151
10:14	149
10:15	60
10:18	152
10:19–25	13
10:19	152–53
10:20	34, 149
10:22	16
10:22b	152
10:23	153, 183
10:24–25	213
10:24	141, 146, 153
10:25	16, 149, 153–54
10:26–27a	154
10:28	154
10:29	17, 154
10:30	208
10:31	154
10:32–39	26, 154
10:32–35	17
10:32–33	11
10:32–34	10
10:32	154
10:33	26, 28, 154, 225
10:34	11, 13
10:34a	154
10:34b	154
10:35	155
10:36	145, 155, 163
10:37	8
10:39	4, 11, 116
11:1–13:8	158
11	17, 158–68, 182, 198
11:1	13, 152

11:2	183	12:18–21	207
11:4	159	12:18	13, 207
11:5–6	159	12:19	13, 212
11:7	159	12:20	14
11:8–12	169	12:21	207
11:13–16	169	12:22–24	13, 207
11:13	123, 159	12:22	208, 210
11:16	164, 169, 191, 208	12:24	209
		12:25–13:25	211–12
11:17–19	169	12:25	211, 212
11:17–22	169	12:26–29	212
11:17	13	12:28	216
11:19	196	12:29	211, 218
11:20	169, 202	13:1–16	213–24
11:21b	197	13:1	11, 213, 226
11:22–24	207	13:2	8, 225
11:22	197	13:3–15	218
11:23–28	169	13:4	208
11:23	17	13:5	216
11:25	153	13:6	218
11:27	17	13:7	8, 218, 225
11:29–31	169	13:8	16, 23, 61, 218, 219
11:29	169, 170		
11:32–38	169	13:9–13	221
11:32	12, 13	13:9	16, 218, 219, 220, 222
11:37	8		
11:39	170	13:10	221
12:1–17	198–206	13:12–13	1
12:1–2	204	13:12	199, 219, 222, 223
12:1	16, 17, 122, 199		
12:2	16, 133, 182, 198, 199	13:13–14	18
		13:13	16, 222, 223
12:3–4	198	13:14	18, 220
12:4–11	106	13:15	18, 220, 224, 225
12:4	11, 201	13:16	11, 224, 225
12:5–13	199	13:17	220
12:5–6	200	13:18–21	225–26
12:8	199	13:18	226
12:10–11	199	13:19	20
12:11	13	13:20–21	18, 226
12:12–13	11, 199	13:22	2, 18, 113, 226
12:12	199	13:23	226
12:13	18, 200	13:23b	20
12:14	201, 202	13:24	226
12:16–17	197	13:25	226
12:16	202		
12:17	204		
12:18–24	13, 207–210		

James

2:18	145
5:12	125

1 Peter

1:18	100n3
2:5	141
2:9	48
2:22	100n3
5:1–5	225
5:12	2, 226

2 Peter

2:17–22	3
3:16	113

1 John

3:5	100n3
4:7	121

3 John

6	121

Revelation

8:1	86
21:8	203n13
22:1	221
22:15	203n13

Dead Sea Scrolls

1QS

8:10	138n4

Rabbinic Writings

Mishnah
Pirkei Avot

5:21	101, 200n4

Horayoth

12a	150

Babylonian Talmud
Erubin/Eruvin

13a	127

Jerusalem Talmud
Chagigah

2:1	128n7

Greco-Roman Writings

Aristotle
De Mirabilibus Auscultationibus

108   208

Cicero
De Oratore

1:18   19

Epictetus
Dissertations

4.4.11–13   122n27

Philo
Life of Moses/De Vita Mosis

1.60.364   55

Seneca
De Otio

6.2, 94–95   122n27

Early Christian Writings

1 Clement

36:1–5   8

Augustine
Confessions

8:12   87

Contra Pelagius (fragment)

1:3   149

Expositions on the Psalms

98   155

Cyprian
Epistles

6:4   201n7

Hippolytus
De Pascha Homilia

6   63

www.ingramcontent.com/pod-product-compliance
Lightning Source LLC
Chambersburg PA
CBHW071245230426
43668CB00011B/1596